Microfinance, Debt and Over-Indebtedness

Although microcredit programmes have long been considered efficient development tools, many forms of debt-induced distress have emerged in their wake. This has brought to light the problem of over-indebtedness, a topic that has been previously underexplored in the literature.

This new book, from a group of leading scholars, explores the manifestations, scale, and economic and social implications of household over-indebtedness in areas conventionally considered as financially excluded. The book approaches debt not only as a financial transaction, but also as a form of social bond, and offers a socioeconomic analysis of over-indebtedness.

The volume puts forward a broad definition of over-indebtedness, highlighting its situational and semantic complexity and diversity. It provides a close analysis of local conceptions of debt and over-indebtedness, highlighting frameworks of calculation and the constant renegotiation of their boundaries. On top of this, it looks far beyond microcredit to examine all the financial practices that individuals juggle. The volume argues that over-indebtedness has more to do with social inequalities than financial illiteracy, and should therefore be understood in the light of global trends of financialization. It also reveals the ambiguity of "financial inclusion" policies, and in many respects questions the actions of new credit providers.

This book will be valuable reading for students, researchers and policy makers interested in microfinance and development issues.

Isabelle Guérin is Senior Research Fellow at the Institute of Research Development/Paris I Sorbonne University (Research Unit "Development and Societies"), Paris, and a Research Associate at the French Institute of Pondicherry and CERMi.

Solène Morvant-Roux is Assistant Professor at the Department of Political Economy, University of Fribourg, Switzerland, and Associate Researcher to the Centre for European Research in Microfinance (CERMi).

Magdalena Villarreal is Senior Researcher and Professor at the Centre for Advanced Research and Postgraduate Studies in Social Anthropology, Mexico.

Routledge studies in development economics

Microfinance, Debt and Over-Indebtedness

Juggling with money

**Edited by Isabelle Guérin,
Solène Morvant-Roux and
Magdalena Villarreal**

Routledge
Taylor & Francis Group

LONDON AND NEW YORK

First published 2014
by Routledge
2 Park Square, Milton Park, Abingdon, Oxon OX14 4RN

and by Routledge
711 Third Avenue, New York, NY 10017

Routledge is an imprint of the Taylor & Francis Group, an informa business

British Library Cataloguing in Publication Data
A catalogue record for this book is available from the British Library

Library of Congress Cataloging in Publication Data
Microfinance, debt and over-indebtedness: juggling with money/edited by Isabelle Guérin, Solène Morvant-Roux and Magdalena Villarreal.
  pages cm
  Includes bibliographical references and index.
  1. Microfinance. 2. Debt. 3. Poor–Social conditions. I. Guérin, Isabelle.
  HG178.3.M536 2013
  332–dc23

2013012890

ISBN: 978-0-415-83525-1 (hbk)
ISBN: 978-0-203-50881-7 (ebk)

Typeset in Times New Roman
by Wearset Ltd, Boldon, Tyne and Wear

Printed and bound in the United States of America by Publishers Graphics, LLC on sustainably sourced paper.

Contents

Illustrations

Figure

Tables

Boxes

Contributors

Lourdes Angulo Salazar is a teacher and researcher at the Universidad Pedagógica Nacional, Guadalajara, México. She holds a PhD in Social Anthropology from CIESAS (Center of Research and Advanced Studies in Social Anthropology, 2009). In 2009 she was a post-doctoral fellow in the Rural Microfinance and Employment Project (RUME). She co-edited the book *Las Microfinanzas en los intersticios del desarrollo: cálculos, normatividades y malabarismo*, in 2012. Her main areas of interest include microfinance, gender, social policies and rural women.

Emmanuelle Bouquet, PhD, is a rural development and rural finance specialist. She currently holds a research position at the French Agricultural Research Center for International Development (CIRAD) in Montpellier, France, where she conducts research and consultancy projects on rural finance. She co-leads the EU-funded impact study of Cecam, a major rural finance network in Madagascar (2005–2008) and has been a member of the ANR funded research project "Rural microfinance and employment" (RUME, 2008–2011), conducting field research in Mexico and Madagascar. Her research interests include household economics and institutional analysis of rural markets, with a strong focus on both quantitative and qualitative empirical analysis.

Hélène Ducourant is lecturer in sociology at the University of Marne-La-Vallée (France). Her PhD thesis deals with the development of consumer credits in France and her research shows how payment facilities provided by retailers to their trustworthy clients has turned into a market with credit firms, banks and credit scoring models to select potential debtors. She has published several articles in French peer reviewed journals on the success of revolving credit in France, the evolution of credit advertisements and the new practices of door-step credit sellers.

Isabelle Guérin is senior research fellow at the Institute of Research Development/Paris I Sorbonne University (Research Unit "Development and Societies"), and a research associate at the French Institute of Pondicherry and CERMi. Her academic interest spans from the political and moral economy of money, debt and labour to the social economy, NGO interventions, empowerment programmes and linkages with public policies. She coordinates the research programme "Labour, finance and social dynamics" at the French Institute of Pondicherry. She is also leading the RUME project (rural employment and microfinance, www.rume-rural-microfinance.org) and the Microfinance in Crisis project (www.microfinance-in-crisis.org).

Barbara Harriss-White joined Oxford University in 1987 after seven years at the London School of Hygiene and Tropical Medicine. Her research interests are in Indian political economy: agriculture, energy and food; aspects of deprivation; informal capitalism; rural development; and low carbon transition – all through primary field research. (Co)author of 40 books/major reports and over 200 journal papers and chapters, she has directed Oxford University's Department for International Development, Queen Elizabeth House, and also the Contemporary South Asian Studies Programme in Area Studies. She helped found Oxford's MPhil in Development Studies and the MSc in Contemporary India. She is now Emeritus Professor of Development Studies.

Agatha Hummel is a PhD candidate at the Institute of Ethnology and Cultural Anthropology at the University of Poznań, Poland, and a graduate of doctoral studies at the Graduate School for Social Research at the Polish Academy of Sciences.

Susan Johnson is a senior lecturer in International Development at the University of Bath. She has a background in economics and agricultural economics and worked in development organizations before joining academia. In the field of microfinance she has used the institutional analysis of local financial markets to examine their social embeddedness. She has undertaken extensive research into financial inclusion, particularly focused on its gender dimensions, the role of informal financial services and the impact of microfinance interventions on poverty. She was also a researcher with the Wellbeing in Developing Countries Research Group based at Bath.

Nithya Joseph gathered the narrative accounts presented in this volume towards a dissertation for the MSc in Contemporary India programme at the School of Interdisciplinary Area Studies, University of Oxford. She is now beginning a study of the politics of production and reproduction across the Karnataka silk industry, as part of two larger projects – one on debt bondage and another on financial inclusion in crisis – at the French Institute of Pondicherry.

K. S. Santhosh Kumar is a research associate in the field of sociology. He has worked with many different researchers over the past 18 years, with a specific focus on women's empowerment in the field of health and economic development. He currently works on the topic of women's empowerment through microfinance with the RUME project and the "Labour, Finance and Social Dynamics" project of the French Institute of Pondicherry. He is also collaborating on an international research programme on debt bondage. His special areas of interest are the role of credit and debt in women's daily life and decision-making.

Solène Morvant-Roux is an assistant professor at the department of political economy, University of Fribourg, Switzerland. She is also associate researcher of the Centre for European Research in Microfinance (CERMI). Her research interests span from financial inclusion in rural areas, debt and social institutions, to agricultural daily labourers and migration dynamics in Mexico and Morocco where she has been leading several intensive field works. She is currently involved in a research project funded by the European Investment Bank on the crisis of the microfinance sector (www.microfinance-in-crisis.org).

David Picherit holds a PhD in social anthropology from the University of Paris 10 Ouest Nanterre La Defense (France). His thesis concerns the circulation of manual labourers and the changing rural economies and politics in Telangana, Andhra Pradesh, India. He was a member of the RUME project and is now Research Associate at the Department of Anthropology of the University College of London, UK. His current research deals with everyday forms of politics in Rayalaseema, Andhra Pradesh.

Eliane Ralison holds a Masters degree in economics from the University of Antananarivo, Madagascar. She holds a research position in the national centre for agricultural research FOFIFA. She has conducted several major surveys in rural Madagascar, in collaboration with international organizations, and has been involved in a number of international publications. Her research interests include rural household economics and the impact of financial services.

Marc Roesch holds a PhD in agro-economics from Montpellier University. After 20 years of field work in Africa, especially in agronomic research, he moved on to micro-economic research at CIRAD, mostly on aspects related to microfinance and the rural economy at the household level. Since 1999 he has been working on microfinance in Africa, Madagascar, Morocco and India. He has spent three years in South India (2005–2008). His most recent research has focused on the evolution of informal finance, indebtedness and poverty. He retired in 2013 but remains a member of the RUME research team (rural microfinance and employment, www.rume-rural-microfinance.org) and Microfinance in Crisis (www.microfinance-in-crisis.org).

Hadrien Saiag studied economics, socioeconomics and development studies at the University Paris-Dauphine and the Ecole des Hautes Etudes en Sciences Sociales (EHESS). He is currently a post-doctoral fellow at the University of Pretoria (Human Economy program). He is the author of "Les pratiques financières des milieux populaires de Rosario (Argentine) à l'aune du démantèlement du rapport salarial fordiste" (*Revue Française de Socio-Economie*, n°8), and a PhD dissertation (*Le* trueque *argentin au prisme de la dette: une socioéconomie des pratiques monétaires et financières* – defense 12/02/2011). His current research is on the financial practices of low-income households in Argentina and Cuba.

Jean-Michel Servet, Professor Emeritus of Lyon University, is currently a professor at the Graduate Institute of International and Development Studies in Geneva and research associate at the Institut de Recherche pour le Développement (Paris), the French Institute of Pondicherry (India) and the CERMI (ULB). He teaches at graduate level in Geneva and in Lima (Peru) in the areas of development studies and finance. His research focuses on social finance, local exchanging trading systems, financial globalization, the history of economic thought, and interdisciplinary methods. He is a member of the French Red Cross Committee for Social Credit.

G. Venkatasubramanian, is a research engineer at the Department of Social Sciences at the French Institute of Pondicherry, India. He has been working on socio-geographical questions for the past 15 years. His area of interests include migration, labour standards, livelihood and rural–urban linkages. At present he is associated with two international research programmes dealing with debt bondage and rural–urban linkages.

Magdalena Villarreal is senior researcher and professor at the Mexican Center for Advanced Research and Postgraduate Studies in Social Anthropology (CIESAS Occidente) and member of the National Research System and the National Academy of Science. Her PhD is from Wageningen University in the Netherlands.

Betty Wampfler is Professor of Agricultural and Development Economics and directs the Masters programme in Agricultural Development at Montpellier SupAgro, France (an international centre for higher education in agricultural sciences). Her research focuses on rural and agricultural finance, analysed as constitutive of broader agrarian change. She mainly works on West African countries and Madagascar. She is a founding member and current president of CERISE, a French network for microfinance development and research.

Francesco Zanotelli, PhD in social anthropology at the University of Turin, is currently an associate researcher and lecturer in anthropology at the Department of Human and Social Sciences of the University of Messina. He has published extensively on debt networks and the ritual economy in Mexico and on kinship, work, migration and social welfare in Italy. He is the author of the monograph *Santo Dinero* (last edition 2012), and co-editor with Simonetta Grilli of *Scelte di famiglia. Tendenze della parentela nella società contemporanea* (2010). He is the co-author in English with Pier Paolo Viazzo of the essay "Welfare as a Moral Obligation: Changing Patterns of Support in Italy and the Mediterranean" (2010).

Acknowledgments

We would like to thank a lot of people for the assistance and encouragement that have made this volume possible. The initial idea for this volume came about in early 2009 in the context of the ANR-funded (Agence Nationale de la Recherche) research project "Rural microfinance and employment" (RUME). This work focused on South India, Mexico and Madagascar, which is why these countries are so well represented in this book. We encountered the problem of household over-indebtedness (which we had not anticipated at the outset) to varying degrees across these countries, and decided to organize a seminar on the subject, which extended to other countries and colleagues. We held the seminar in December 2009 at the Development and Societies research centre (Paris I Sorbonne University/Institute of Research for Development), with the financial support of both institutions. We sincerely thank André Guichaoua, Pascale Phélinas and Monique Selim for their support and encouragement. This volume is the outcome of this seminar. Unfortunately the contributions of Laurence Fontaine, Marek Hudon, Wendy Olson and Daniel Neff could not be published, but they greatly enriched discussions during the seminar. Comments and suggestions by Eveline Baumann, Cyril Fouillet and Blandine Destremau were also very useful. For the editing process, we received financial support from the Political Economics Department of the University of Fribourg, and we are grateful to Jean-Jacques Friboulet.

The insights in this volume also reflect informal conversations with Florent Bédécarrats, François Doligez, Deborah James, Marc Labie, Jean-Yves Moisseron, Jonathan Morduch, Susana Narotzky, Pascale Phelinas, Monique Selim, Ariane Szafarz and Bruno Théret. We had the opportunity to share some of the results of this work at several seminars and conferences organized by the Cermi (Center for European Research in Microfinance). We thank the directors of Cermi (Marek Hudon, Marc Labie and Ariane Szafarz) for giving us this platform for exchange and sharing. We would also like to express our sincere appreciation fro the valuable comments received from four anonymous reviewers. Barbara Harriss-White, beyond her own chapter, has offered invaluable support throughout the preparation of this book, and has reviewed and commented in detail on certain chapters. We are also extremely indebted to the contributors to this volume, who patiently dealt with revisions of their individual chapters at different stages of preparing the manuscript. Jane Weston has been in charge of proofreading the text, and has been consistently available and responsive. Finally, we are also grateful to the many practitioners in the field in the various countries on which this research is based, for their open-mindedness and their capacity to engage with us in critical discussions about microfinance and financial inclusion policies. By suggesting fresh ways of analyzing finance for the low income sectors of the world's population, we hope that this volume will be of use to them, and all those who consider themselves as politically engaged scholars and practitioners concerned with financial inclusion policies, and with development and social change in general.

Introduction

Isabelle Guérin, Solène Morvant-Roux and Magdalena Villarreal

Debt is difficult to escape or ignore. It has always been central to the circulation of capital and the reproduction of capitalism and the financial system, taking up a more distinctive and expansive space over time. Private companies increasingly depend on financial markets, putting them at the mercy of shareholder demands and speculation. The same goes for governments, which have no choice but to accept the diktat of private finance when faced with the blackmail of sovereign debt bankruptcy. While in the past debt mainly crushed the so-called Southern countries with obligations to adopt structural adjustment programmess, today no one is spared. The fear of public over-indebtedness not only legitimises drastic austerity plans and deficit-cutting policies, sweeping away welfare states, but, furthermore, threatens democracy. Debt also affects households, which are often forced into vicious debt cycles to compensate for the weakness of labour income and protective mechanisms.

Meanwhile in Southern countries 'financial inclusion' policies and microcredit programmes, long considered as efficient development tools, now face an unprecedented crisis. Although investors are increasingly enthusiastic about this new market niche, many forms of debt-induced distress (such as suicide) have emerged in its wake, highlighting the seriousness of over-indebtedness as an issue. This raises the question as to whether microcredit policies are part of the solution, or in fact part of the problem.

Going beyond stereotypes that tend to typecast over-indebted households as heroes, villains or victims, how do the poor really live and experience household over-indebtedness? What are its underlying processes, meanings and consequences? In this book, we discuss the manifestations, scale and economic and social implications of household over-indebtedness in areas conventionally considered as financially excluded. We also scrutinise evolving thresholds for over-indebtedness, examining the boundaries of debt in different contexts and their effects on the workings of poverty-stricken financial systems. We look far beyond microcredit to examine all the financial practices individuals juggle. While microcredit is often considered as the only alternative to financial 'exclusion', in fact it is only a small part of the debt that binds most poor people. So-called 'informal finance' (i.e. unregulated financial transactions) has kept pace with the monetarisation and financialisation of contemporary societies

(Collins *et al.* 2009; Servet 2006), and remains vigorous and extraordinarily diverse. Informal finance, regardless of whether it is a source of exploitation and pauperisation (Breman 2007), solidarity and social cohesion (Shipton 2007) or a high-risk enrichment strategy for the poor (James 2012), is closely linked to formal finance, and is an integral part of the poor's daily social and financial life.

This volume addresses processes of over-indebtedness and their economic, financial, social and cultural implications. Its chapters are unique in various ways, drawing on interdisciplinary approaches and comparative geographical locations. It is primarily concerned with understanding household debt in the broader context of social, economic and political change. It combines micro and macro analysis with the idea that the way in which ordinary people perceive and experience debt and finance is as fundamental to understanding macro trends as vice versa. Empirically, this book examines economic relations and financial practices with a particular focus on debt and over-indebtedness across a variety of regions from around the globe including India, Mexico, Madagascar, Kenya, Bangladesh, France and the United States. Its comparative perspective helps to highlight both disparities and strong similarities across cases. It addresses the diversity of debt circles, the ongoing tension between market and non-market debts, the embeddedness of finance in social, cultural and political settings, and the way debt and over-indebtedness are inseparable from social inequalities. Power relations, knowledge processes, human wellbeing, frameworks of calculation and social differentiation are key to discussing debt and financial practices throughout the chapters.

The diversity of contexts which the collection covers, offers some unique major conclusions; our key arguments include:

1   Over-indebtedness has surged during the current financial crisis. While debt is not new in poor areas, increasing financialisation and global recession bring new dangers. We argue that over-indebtedness is shaped by and constitutive of the contradictions currently faced in the regions studied, albeit to varying degrees. On the one hand, aspirations for integration and individuation are increasing, resulting most notably in rising consumption and the willingness to enter into contractual debt relationships. On the other hand, real incomes are stagnant or declining, and social protection is inadequate or entirely absent. Microcredit crises not only show up the limits of a development model, emphasising individual responsibility and market forces, but, much more broadly, highlight the contradictions of the present system of accumulation and redistribution. As a number of authors in this volume suggest, a systematic analysis of household over-indebtedness must be grounded in an analysis of how it frames, and is framed by, accumulation regimes and the legitimisation crisis of capital.

2   We argue that over-indebtedness – defined here as impoverishment from debt – can take many different shapes, ranging from material loss to feelings of downward social mobility, extreme dependency, shame and humiliation, leading to a variety of manifestations and perceptions of over-indebtedness.

Rather than restricting over-indebtedness to financial and accounting matters, it should be approached as a social process involving power relationships as well as issues of wellbeing, status and dignity.

3 Financial illiteracy is a common misconception in terms of the causes of over-indebtedness. This stereotype reflects a profound ignorance of the complexity of local financial reasoning and calculation frameworks. Our case studies highlight the subtleties of budget management and debt behaviour. We argue that over-indebtedness is not caused by financial illiteracy but that it is shaped by, and reinforces, pre-existing inequalities in categories such as gender, caste, ethnicity and religion. Power and social differentiation shape debt processes, reproducing dependence and resistance.

4 These considerations have many implications for current micro-financial practices, which have become a necessary component of the economy of the poor. On the one hand, we note the poor's considerable capacity to appropriate finance and microfinance in a variety of sometimes surprising ways. Clients do not passively consume microcredit services, but translate and interpret them according to their own frames of reference, adjusting and adapting them, and often bypassing the rules to do so. Conversely, microfinance institutions adapt their own policies to local frames of reference. We equally examine how microfinance is part of the broader financialisation process of exchange practices and how it reflects structural inequalities. While microfinance may improve households' cash flow and management, it can also lead to financial vulnerability, credit addiction and debt traps. These policies can do more harm than good, not only because of commercial aggressiveness and competition, but also because microfinance promoters lack a proper vision of local socioeconomic dynamics and financial needs.

Microfinance crises: the tip of the iceberg?

Over the last thirty years or so, microfinance and more recently 'financial inclusion' have emerged as some of the highest-profile policies for tackling poverty and under-development in Southern countries. While microfinance was almost unknown to the public twenty years ago, it has developed considerably over the past decades, both in scale and institutional diversity (Armendáriz and Labie 2011). It has been characterised by innovation, dynamism and continuous growth. It has benefited from widespread international recognition from a wide variety of both public and private stakeholders. In late 2011 it was estimated that over 200 million 'poor' people had benefited from microfinance services (Reed 2013). In Washington in 1997, the first Microcredit Summit was held to mediatise the success of this development tool against poverty. Some people spoke of a 'revolution in finance' and even a historical turning point in the history of development (Fernando 2006). The United Nations declared 2005 as the 'International Year of Microcredit'. The following year, the Nobel Peace Prize was awarded to the founder of the

Grameen Bank, Muhammad Yunus, for the fight against poverty, for women's empowerment and the democratisation of local societies.

While microfinance as a development tool is supported by many actors, including policymakers, activists, philanthropists and development scholars, it is also highly – and increasingly – controversial. Is microfinance really a step towards economic growth and development, or is it a short-term palliative, keeping poor people poor (Dichter and Harper 2007)? The available literature gives contrasting opinions, reflecting the differing ideologies behind development policies. In brief, market and individual responsibility versus redistribution policies. Microfinance advocates including the Nobel Prize winner Muhammed Yunus, view microfinance as having the potential to create a 'world without poverty' by pioneering a model for what is now called 'social business', a new, more humane form of capitalism (Yunus 2007). The idea of consumer credit for the poor is now also increasingly accepted. Having long been considered taboo owing to the premise that the poor only need so-called 'productive' credit to create income-generating activities, consumer microcredit for the poor is now not only accepted, but is celebrated as an idea (Collins *et al.* 2009; Karnani 2009).

Today however, microfinance faces growing criticism and its heyday looks to be over. Some impact studies showing microcredit to be highly beneficial in reducing poverty, and which had been instrumental in building its reputation, have been seriously challenged over their methodologies (Roodman and Morduch 2009). Randomised trials, currently considered by many actors as the only possible evidence of impact, seriously challenge microfinance's impact in poverty reduction, without however questioning its *raison d'être* (Banerjee and Duflo 2011). Others take their criticisms much further, arguing that microfinance is nothing more than an efficient vehicle for neo-liberal economic ideology worldwide (Fernando 2006; Servet 2006) and that it is in fact a major barrier to sustainable economic and social development, and therefore to sustainable poverty reduction. For example, Bateman argues in his recent work *Why Doesn't Microfinance Work?* (Bateman 2010) that microfinance is nothing but a 'poverty trap and an anti-development policy' (ibid.: 5).

Microfinance is an extremely diverse sector in terms of approach, methodology, history and ideology, so the question of whether microfinance is 'good' or 'bad' has not been very helpful. Its outcomes depend on how it is implemented, to which audience, in what contexts and under what conditions. There has, however, undeniably been an excessive focus on the supposed advantages of microfinance, which has too often been presented as a powerful tool for job creation, the eradication of poverty, the empowerment of women and the promotion of democracy.

The rise of the business paradigm within microfinance is also undeniable. Historical analysis of what has now become an 'industry' shows that the original alternative, reformist movement has gradually transformed into a standardised, highly commercial platform, at least for the largest institutions (Bédécarrats 2013; Roy 2010). Though many microfinance institutions do not acknowledge this shift themselves, the microfinance industry's strong growth over recent years is connected to the increasing involvement of private capital in search of profit.

Meanwhile various parts of the world are facing unprecedented credit delinquency crises. While, until recently, mass defaults used to be isolated and solvable phenomena, they are on the rise and unpreventable for some countries. Crises first emerged in the late 1990s in Bolivia, in Bangladesh in 1999 (Rhyne 2001), in Kenya in 2003 (Johnson *et al.* 2003) and in Zambia in 2008 and 2009 (Dixon *et al.* 2007). These were limited in time and scope, but some areas of the world today are experiencing chronic crises, including in Nicaragua, Bosnia Herzegovina, northern Pakistan and Morocco since 2007 (Chen *et al.* 2010), as well as in southern India. In 2009 in Karnataka, there were mass defaults in four towns. The Andhra Pradesh crisis has undoubtedly been on one of the greatest and most tragic of scales. Clients were recorded as committing suicide after facing poor return to production and over-indebtedness as early as 2006, but this first crisis was temporarily resolved. Since October 2010 however, the Andhra Pradesh State has failed to emerge from a deep crisis characterised by contagion and systemic risk. In September 2011 repayment rates fell to 10 per cent. In March 2013, while we were finalising this manuscript, micro-lending activities were almost stopped. In Cameroon, Benin and Niger, several microfinance institutions (MFIs) were put under state supervision. Last but not least, there are many latent crises. Some regions are close to saturation (the Philippines, Cambodia, Ghana and Mongolia to name but a few). In some places, practices of debt rescheduling conceal major repayment difficulties, including in some parts of India, Bangladesh and Morocco.

These crises are all the more worrying considering that some of the countries experiencing difficulties were taken as 'models' for their region, such as Benin in West Africa, Morocco in the Arab world, and Andhra Pradesh in India. These cases reveal that microfinance clients are facing over-indebtedness and/or that there is loss of legitimacy and trust in microfinance institutions. They widely confirm that mission drift has indeed taken place, as has been denounced for several years,[1] but ignored by many practitioners and policymakers and often reinterpreted in a dominant vision.

There have been various analyses of the microcredit delinquency crises, which have, however, mostly been limited to industry insiders and the media. These have mainly served to point out governance and regulation defaults. A CGAP[2] study, for instance, claims uncontrolled growth to be the main explanatory factor for crises in Nicaragua, Bosnia Herzegovina, northern Pakistan and Morocco. Three main problems are highlighted: concentrated market competition and cross borrowing, overstretched MFI systems and controls, and erosion of MFI lending discipline (Chen *et al.* 2010). For Andhra Pradesh, mainstream analyses primarily report a lack of regulation, aggressive marketing and the cost of loans.

There is no doubt that microcredit delinquency crises vividly highlight how portfolio growth has been prioritised over social proximity and the quality of financial services provided. In certain parts of the world, social models are now in the minority compared to for-profit business models, whose primary objectives are to attain financial self-sustainability and profitability as quickly as possible.[3] The true origin of these crises seems to lie somewhere deeper, however. We believe that they are only the tip of the iceberg. How can we explain the mass adhesion of the poor to a tool that is unable to keep its promises? Whether in terms of job creation or women's empowerment, the effects of microcredit are not what was expected, as evidenced by many studies available today.[4] But demand for microcredit remains very strong. As shown by various chapters in this volume, microcredit responds to the need and desire to increase debt ties, whether to make ends meet, to climb social ladders or to become free from oppressive debt bonds. Such aspirations, of course, far exceed clients' capacities and creditworthiness. Cross-debt, debt rescheduling, juggling with informal debt and migration may maintain an illusion of creditworthiness for some time. But sooner or later, the illusion is shattered.

In other words, while some microfinance institutions take some active responsibility, the case studies in this volume show that household over-indebtedness stems not only from aggressive microfinance policies, but also from the broader context of the evolution of modern societies and economies. The volume's authors present in-depth descriptions of microfinance as a social process embedded in savings and multiple debt relationships. They also analyse the social and institutional processes through which microfinance intersects with a local cultural context of neo-liberal political economics. A main thesis of this book, developed in more detail by Servet and Saiag (Chapter 1),[5] is that present-day societies are facing a widening gap between needs and cash incomes, due to increasing informal labour, growing urbanisation and rising envy and consumer needs, including among the poor. This widening gap leads to an increase in household debt and new forms of exploitation. These are not necessarily based in face-to-face relations as typical capital/labour relationships are, but on a global scale, with the financial sector extracting added-value from the labour sector. Microcredit practices both reflect and reinforce these conflicts. The macro-picture that Servet and Saiag paint translates into various forms and shapes, as is illustrated by the volume's various micro-studies.

Crossing the line into over-indebtedness

Over-indebtedness has been at the heart of recent microcredit crises, but its conceptual definition is very vague and frequently confusing. Current debates refer to over-indebtedness in an overly narrow way, focusing on economics and the individual, while ignoring the scale and dynamics of informal finance, and taking little account of a phenomenon that should primarily be understood and analysed as an indicator of wider socioeconomic and political trends.

Intuitively, everyone agrees that over-indebtedness occurs once there is 'too much' debt. But what does 'too much' mean and where is its threshold? Who defines the meaning and signification of over-indebtedness, and on whose behalf? Which indicators matter, and why? What should be the unit of measurement?

What constitutes 'bad' and 'good' debt? When must a debt be paid off and what is that debt? This volume does not seek to quantify over-indebtedness, but rather to analyse its underlying processes.

There are a wide variety of definitions and indicators of over-indebtedness, each reflecting specific objectives and disciplines (Schicks forthcoming) while sharing a common concern for quantification. The most commonly used indicators include default rates, cross-debt and ratios to compare debt and income. Recently, sophisticated indexes have also been elaborated, aiming at capturing the various facets of the phenomenon[6] or borrowers' subjectivity.[7]

Measurement and quantification are, of course, a major policy preoccupation for policymakers, reflecting a justifiable concern with the cost/benefit analysis of competing claims for scarce resources. The concrete, practical world of development policy needs clear definitions based on solid and objectively verifiable grounds. Definitional choices, however, are anything but neutral and necessarily embedded within wider theoretical frameworks. Measuring reality is an attempt to objectivise and categorise it. This raises the fundamental question of the nature of the reality to be measured, the scientific value of this measure and the gap between the measure and the reality.

While the state of knowledge of over-indebtedness is still in its infancy, it seems useful, even indispensable, to consider the local meanings of over-indebtedness. One of this volume's goals is to examine the management and significance of debt, the boundaries between healthy debt and over-indebtedness and how these are themselves subject to negotiated redefinition. How are contradictory meanings circulated, manipulated and enacted? Our purpose is not to offer ready-made formulas for policymakers, but to study the complexity and depth of social reality.

Given that the indicators of debt (e.g. delayed payments, income–debt ratios, number of loans contracted) are all open to a variety of interpretations, we shall define over-indebtedness *as the processes of social and economic impoverishment that can develop in mutual contradiction*. The fact that debt is perceived in a variety of ways is central to this analysis. Our theoretical constant is to approach debt as a financial transaction and a form of social bond. Over the past two decades, our understanding of the social significance of debt has empirically and theoretically advanced to a considerable extent. A number of areas have been examined, including the diversity of framework of references, the multiplicity of debt relationships and their embeddedness in social ties, the role of monetary exchanges and debt in shaping and reshaping identities, individual agency and social reproduction.[8] We work from the hypothesis that an understanding of over-indebtedness cannot ignore its social dimensions and implications, applying this body of knowledge for socioeconomic analysis. We consider debt first and foremost as a relationship between individuals as debtors and creditors with unequal resources, rather than in terms of the atomised, anonymous and short-term transactions examined by standard economists.

The variable significations of debt are key when assessing over-indebtedness. Various chapters here demonstrate that in cases where there is 'too much' debt, this does not necessarily stem from financial criteria. A financially expensive debt may be considered less dangerous than a dishonourable or a degrading one. While bankers, development scholars and activists might define over-indebtedness from a financial perspective, our close analyses of field realities show that individuals also have their own categories. In many cases wellbeing, honour, reputation, independence and dignity matter much more than figures and numbers. It is therefore clear that debt and over-indebtedness have different dimensions of meaning for different people.

The local meanings of over-indebtedness reveal the extent to which account-ing definitions can be far from the realities they seek to measure. Default rates, for instance, are often taken as directly tied to over-indebtedness, and used as a key indicator of the financial performance of the microfinance industry (Chapter 3). But timely repayment does not necessarily mean that borrowers are satisfied with their loans. It is now widely acknowledged that excellent repayment rates may as much reflect a high degree of pressure placed on borrowers than satisfac-tion or wellbeing.[9] Conversely, late payment is not necessarily a sign of over-indebtedness. It may reflect local frameworks in which the debt is conceived as something that can be repaid in multiple ways over extended timeframes (Chapter 3). It can also be indicative of a reduced incentive to repay and bor-rower 'resistance'. This may have various causes, such as exit opportunities due to competition, user dissatisfaction, and willingness to take revenge on lenders who are seen as unfair (Chapter 13).[10]

Informal loan arrears are not just difficult to assess, but usually reflect greater scope for negotiation than trouble in repaying. As various chapters in this volume discuss in echo of observations elsewhere (Collins *et al.* 2009; Guérin *et al.* 2011; Johnson 2004; Rutherford 2001), debt modalities are frequently highly flexible and 'negotiability' is the rule rather than the exception. Repayment deadlines are not necessarily fixed in advance. Negotiability is not financially and socially cost-free, but the fact remains that there are often no strict repay-ment deadlines. Cross-debt may also be used as an indicator of over-indebtedness (Chen *et al.* 2010). It is true that in Northern countries, where mono-banking is more the rule than the exception, households having several creditors may be considered as indicative of financial fragility (Gloukoviezoff 2010). But cross-debt can simply mean that credit providers are offering insufficient loan amounts. Moreover, in the contexts studied here, cross-debt is an integral part of house-holds' cash flow management strategies. We shall return to this in the following section in terms of the concept of 'juggling'.

Other common indicators have used fixed thresholds for debt service to income ratio. Static analyses using ratios at a particular point in time can offer indications, but also mislead, as they say little about households' vulnerability and the nature of their relationship with creditors. In cases where debt is prim-arily a matter of networking, interpersonal skills, trust and reputation, a high out-standing debt can be indicative of a large social network and the ability to mobilise and activate it. Debt service indicators may also be misleading, as they hide what is owed to the borrowers (See Chapter 8). In most of the case studies in this volume, even the poorest borrowers are also lenders (see also Collins *et al.* 2009; James 2012; Morvant-Roux 2009).

While households are often our primary unit of analysis, debt and over-indebtedness are clearly not gender neutral. Several chapters highlight the paradoxes women face. Many are not just fully responsible for managing their household budget (Chapters 9, 11 and 12) but have no control over their income. As they are forced into financial dependency while having to make ends meet, they have no choice but to deploy a variety of strategies for saving, borrowing, lending and creating their own financial networks (Chapter 9; see also Bruce and Dwyer 1988; Guérin 2011). Women must also choose their creditors carefully to avoid any suspicion over their 'morality'. The social control of women's debt is closely linked to the control of their bodies and sexuality (Chapter 6).

The fallacy of financial education: calculation frameworks and juggling practices

The poor are often denounced for lacking any financial literacy. Notwithstanding lender greediness as a contributing factor, over-indebtedness is thought to result from poor people's inability to plan, calculate, anticipate and save. In the micro-finance industry – whether regulators, donors, practitioners or apex organisations – and more broadly in the development field, financial literacy programmes for improving 'financial capabilities' are increasingly thought to be a way to prevent over-indebtedness and to guarantee responsible financial practices (Guérin 2012). This volume does not directly address the issue of financial education, but does question its underlying assumptions.

Financial education is not a new idea. Charitable projects have always looked to help the poor to manage their budgets better. But over the past decade, financial education has become a rallying cry in both developed and developing countries. An OECD (Organization for Economic Cooperation and Development) report considered as a reference document states that in an increasingly financialised world where individuals have to use increasingly complex financial tools, financial education is thought to help individuals to take advantage of the best market opportunities (OECD 2005). Financial education is a matter of information and skills, such as understanding interest rates, learning to plan a budget and to compare loan offers. It is also a question of appropriate behaviour, such as prudence, planning and taking on just moderate debt.

Wide-ranging financial literacy programmes first emerged in the late 1990s in the most financialised rich countries such as the US, UK and Australia, and then spread throughout most northern countries (Erturk *et al.* 2007). Financial education fever now seems to have spread across the globe. According to an OECD review (early in 2000) seventy-five countries were presently involved in public and private financial education programmes (OECD 2005) and their number is probably much higher today. BRICS (Brazil, Russia, China and South Africa) and emerging countries faced with rising household debt and the rapid development of financial markets have particularly favoured such programmes.

In countries with low levels of so-called 'formal' financial inclusion but where microfinance is expanding, microfinance stakeholders often create financial education programmes. In the wake of the recent microcredit delinquency crises, the incorporation of financial education into financial services is expected to protect consumers and mitigate default risks for MFIs (CGAP 2011). NGOs (non-governemntal organisations) and bilateral and multilateral aid organisations are all instrumental here.[11]

The idea of helping the poor to take advantage of the financial services offered to them is certainly laudable. There are, however, a number of risks. Besides, while financial education has attracted some enthusiasm, there has also been a good deal of criticism. First, this relates to regulatory issues, because financial education is frequently considered as a partial substitute for market regulation (Dickerson 1999; Erturk *et al.* 2007), as many of its promoters openly state.[12] As argued by Erturk *et al.* (2007), the conventional wisdom is that financial inclusion can deliver private and social benefits, as long as citizens can acquire increased financial literacy. A further criticism has been that structural factors of over-indebtedness are ignored, which again shifts responsibility from institutions onto individuals. Many financial education promoters implicitly assume that most debtors are irresponsible or credit-ignorant.[13] But when people fall into debt and over-indebtedness because they are chronically unable to make ends meet, or because of an unexpected catastrophic event, they need far more than literacy classes or credit counselling. In many cases, it is insufficient and irregular income rather than financial mismanagement that is the key barrier to long-term financial health (Porter and Thorne 2006). In these contexts, formal or informal credit and savings services substitute for missing social protection systems. It would thus be unrealistic for the only solution to come from improved financial literacy.

A third problem, which is developed in greater detail in this volume, is ignorance of local frameworks of calculation and management. This volume's authors strongly believe that the concept of 'financial illiteracy' – a prerequisite for financial education – is based on false premises (Chapter 10; see also Guérin 2012). Most writings on financial illiteracy assume that individuals often make financial management 'mistakes' while adopting 'sub-optimal' behaviours. Most financial education programmes probably try to foster a supportive and accepting environment, for instance by emphasising the need for courses that take local specificities into account. But the language of textbooks reflects a profound ignorance of the ways people perceive and use finance. A further widespread mistaken assumption is that marginalised groups such as women, ethnic minorities, immigrants and poorly educated people are often the most financially illiterate groups (Martin 2007). Frequent 'mistakes' and 'sub-optimal' behaviours quoted in the literature and in teaching modules include a lack of savings, planning and budgeting, excessive use of debt, and ignorance of basic financial concepts such as interest rates and the workings of interest compounding, the difference between nominal and real values and the basics of risk diversification.

This idea of financial illiteracy goes completely against the teachings of economic anthropology, however. Collins *et al.* (2009) recently comprehensively challenged the concept in *Portfolios of the Poor*. The authors undertake a painstaking analysis of how the poor manage their cash flow to demonstrate that the poor have extremely complex and sophisticated skills and know-how, and do in fact plan, calculate, anticipate and save. These strategies and motivations are sometimes surprising, but have a clear rationale. A shortcoming of *Portfolios of the Poor*, however, is to restrict money and finance to their technical and instrumental functions. Money, finance and calculations are stripped of their moral and social value. Issues of identity and power, which are central to debt, are shrugged off.

An economic anthropology of debt, such as the one defended here, allows us to grasp the substance and depth of debt, and the subtlety and complexity of debt calculations.[14] Calculativeness is often thought of as the preserve of the economic sphere and economic theory. Calculation is thought to look only to satisfy personal interest on the basis of quantifiable indicators and units of measure. History and ethnography shows that calculation goes far beyond economic acts, however. Its reasoning and rationale are complex and embedded within social settings (Weber 2001). The poor are not just hungry stomachs desperate to make ends meet. They seek to advance or hold on to particular individual and group identities. They are part of a variety of entitlement and obligation networks that they may seek to reinforce, appease or flee. Calculations serve multiple – and often conflicting – purposes. These may be making ends meet, respecting social structures, positioning oneself in local social networks and hierarchies, or asserting or attempting to assert one's individuality.

Financial ties are central to these processes because of their social meaning. As pointed out above, debts first and foremost constitute social ties between individuals, transmitting feelings and emotions such as dignity, prestige, respectability or, conversely, shame or humiliation. They are embedded into broader entrustments and obligations (Shipton 2007).

We argue that borrowers and lenders resort to specific calculation frameworks, defined here as the sets of thinking tools that are available and mobilised by individuals in specific situations to appreciate risk, take financial decisions and arbitrate between various financial tools. Calculation frameworks have socio-cultural, legal and normative components. Calculation tools are not necessarily sophisticated or formal, but have multiple cognitive, routine and social-based dimensions (Coquery *et al.* 2006). They stem from social interactions and are thus embedded in individuals' social positions, particularly in terms of class, caste, gender and ethnicity (Chapters 2, 3 and 10; see also Villarreal 2009).

The chapters all highlight the specific frameworks of calculation that people resort to when dealing with money and debt and the prevalence and sophistication of 'juggling' practices. Juggling literally involves throwing, catching, and keeping several things in the air at once, demanding speed and dexterity, but also risk-taking. These three facets are excellent in evoking the nature of financial practices: people combine multiple financial tools in the context of ongoing borrowing, repayment and reborrowing practices (one borrows from one place to repay elsewhere). Individuals swap roles between debtor and creditor, and even the poorest people are also likely to be creditors.

There is no doubt that juggling debt is a form of financial calculation that attempts to substitute cheap debts for expensive ones. Juggling with debt is also a matter of temporalities, as lenders impose different time scales. But social motivations also count. Juggling practices often reflect deliberate choices, strategies or tactics aimed at multiplying and diversifying social relationships, and strengthening or weakening the burden of dependency ties. As several ethnographies on money and debt usage in daily life have noted, monetary exchanges and debt ties are a driving force in social life and social structures.[15] Permanent tension between the individual and the group, and between personal aspirations and collective responsibilities is inherent to debt and its modalities. This volume's various case studies highlight the multiple meanings of lending and borrowing, which are constantly manipulated and negotiated to serve individual purposes, while remaining inseparable from local culture and structural constraints. The multiple logics of debt are under constant tension, with subtle, complex reasoning and trade-offs. This leads to a plethora of complementary and often incommensurable, non-substitutable financial practices.[16] No pure market price can reflect relative demand and supply, or different types of financing. Financial practices are instead regulated through a web of social institutions. The terms and conditions of debt reflect micro-politics and the history of relative statuses. Debt practices are fragmented and hierarchical, as is illustrated in this book by the case of Dalits and lower castes in India (Chapters 5, 6 and 7), indigenous communities in Mexico (Chapters 8, 9 and 11), Hispanic migrants in the United States (Chapter 2), lower classes in Madagascar (Chapter 10) and in France (Chapter 4), and for women (Chapters 6, 9, 11 and 12).

A specific economic amount of debt can thus widely vary in its social meaning. Notwithstanding opportunity costs and interest rates, the social distance between the lender and the borrower is highly valued in debt decisions. Kinship, marital or neighbourhood-based debt ties may be favoured, or at times criticised and fled from. Debt relationships are clearly ambiguous within close kinships, households or neighbourhood groups and 'formal' debt does nothing to change this, as our French case study clearly demonstrates (see Chapter 4). While the French credit market is fully 'formal' in the sense that it is regulated by banking laws, it is both shaped by and constitutive of class relationships. Not only do the poor and lowest classes pay more, but they also suffer from the moral judgments and contempt of bankers. When given a choice, they prefer the anonymity of financial companies that are extremely costly financially speaking, but less humiliating, as transactions are carried out over the telephone or the Internet.

Lending and borrowing presupposes that the two parties already share a relationship of trust, but it also serves to maintain, reinforce and renew such relationships. In many cases, financial practices reflect deliberate choices and strategies geared to multiply and reinforce social relationships to maintain a certain balance, considering the inherent ambiguity of all debt relations.[17] This ambiguity lies in the fact that while debt can provide protection and solidarity, and a means of expressing reciprocal trust and respect, when it is not honoured or is too imbalanced, it can be a source of humiliation, shame, exploitation and servitude. It is both 'a net that sustains and imprisons us', a 'lifeline and a death knot' as Malamoud (1980) wrote on debt in Vedic India. These are the reasons for the subtle game of regularly reducing one's debt while taking on debt elsewhere. Criteria for assessing 'bad' and 'good' debts might therefore significantly differ from financial education 'good practices'. According to the Global Financial Education programme for instance:

> simply put, borrowing is good when it helps you gain financially and bad when it becomes a financial burden [...] and still owed after the item is consumed or the income earned from the asset is less than the cost of the loan.
> (Global Financial Education, nd: 5)

The addition of social and moral values into the picture further complicates things. The same amount of debt with the same cost can have a variety of meanings and very diverse consequences, depending on the nature of the social relationship between the lender and the borrower. Some debts are primarily of monetary value, while others reflect social value. Some debts are supposed to be repaid, whilst others are not, or delays in repayment are habitually anticipated. Some debts are viewed as a right, others as a due, privilege or punishment.

Low monetary savings are often taken as the first indicator of financial illiteracy. While the modality of savings varies from one context to another, monetary hoarding is a rarity. But it is often much more rational for the poor not to save in cash. This is as much a question of safety as it is an effort to resist the temptation to spend and to ward off requests from one's entourage. Furthermore, immobilised money – at home or in a bank account – serves no purpose. Money must circulate: it is both a necessity and a 'social game' (Fontaine 2008). In this volume, Morvant-Roux discusses an 'institution of debt' that establishes a form of 'collective management' of individual surpluses: all forms of wealth (not only coins and notes but also bricks, food products or cattle) can be loaned if the owner does not have an immediate need for them. The slightest riches, whether in cash or in kind, are loaned to conceal ownership and cement social bonds. This allows both to avoid spending and to sustain solidarity links with close circles. Preconceptions about financial illiteracy seem to ignore the existence of these financial circuits, which are also forms of savings – and are often considered as such – as any loan is meant to be reciprocated (Chapter 3).[18]

Preconceptions about financial illiteracy ignore the fact that in-kind saving practices are highly widespread and often extremely rational. All things being equal, it is often much more beneficial for the poor to save in kind, for example using cattle, jewels, beads or clothing. Goods used as savings fulfil a number of economic and social functions. Choices are based on sophisticated calculations, including price volatility (for instance for gold or livestock) (Guérin *et al.* 2011;

Shipton 1995). Reasons for saving are also diverse and sometimes contradictory, given ongoing tension between social obligations and individual desires. The result is a plethora of complementary and at times impossible to substitute saving practices. Hence efforts to collect cash savings and instil 'saving discipline' may not bring the anticipated results.

Microcredit and over-indebtedness

We shall return now to financial inclusion policies and microcredit. This volume's first original contribution is to situate microcredit within the totality of financial practices into which borrowers are embedded. Taking this into account improves understanding of how microfinance services are used, abused and (mis) appropriated – or at least used in a way that was unintended by its providers. Analysis of local pre-existing financial arrangements reveals how people appropriate financial services offered by outsiders – i.e. not just how they use them, but how they assimilate them in a way that reflects their own frame of social and cultural references (Guérin *et al.* 2011; Morvant-Roux 2009; Morvant-Roux *et al.* forthcoming; Shipton 2010).

The implementation of microfinance services is too often considered a technical and linear process conforming to guidelines that credit officers merely apply, and clients passively consume. Microfinance organisations are mostly analysed through the narrow prism of their official mission – here financial services – and within a defined space-time setting, without paying any attention to their 'social life' (Long 2001). Microfinance, however, is not a monolithic project. Its initiatives are contextually specific and nuanced processes. They are part of a social, economic, political and cultural environment that is a source of opportunities as well as constraints. Local environments shape both how microfinance services are implemented and the nature of credit demand, in terms of whether microcredit customers are indeed potential entrepreneurs as microfinance supporters claim, or instead poor people desperately in need of cash. As with any development project, microfinance should be considered as a process of continuous compromise and negotiation between the many stakeholders directly or indirectly engaged in the project. These individuals' goals, well before the launch of the project, have been to build or maintain an image, identity, or status; to create or to sustain power, relationships or access to resources (Mosse 2005). The chapters in the final part of this volume offer a nuanced vision of microfinance's effects on over-indebtedness, precisely because they approach microfinance in terms of existing social and political institutional arrangements.

Examining the social life of microfinance highlights the complexity and diversity of these appropriation processes. Diverting loans for so-called 'social purposes' (i.e. that do not generate income), which has been banned by most MFIs, is the rule rather than the exception, as is recycling microloans into informal loans. This either takes the form of on-lending microcredit to others, or borrowing informal loans to repay microcredits. These chapters point out divergent and conflicting interpretations and meanings, whether in terms of so-called 'solidarity groups' or the concept of default. Clients often decry solidarity groups, although they are officially praised for their effectiveness in enforcing repayments and social cohesion (Chapter 11; see also Jauzelon 2007; Molyneux 2001; Rankin 2002). In some cases moreover, they tend to replicate rather than abolish social divisions, and to reinforce pre-existing social hierarchies.

Not only borrowers, but staff also misappropriate and manipulate microcredit funds. Several of the volume's chapters show that when repayments flag in highly competitive environments, MFI staff use increasingly aggressive technologies and methods, both to locate customers and to enforce repayments (Chapters 11, 12 and 13). Several chapters meanwhile describe the intricate spirals of debt into which borrowers, who are mostly women, can become sucked. They then have no choice but to reborrow, even if they no longer want microcredit, as this is the only way to preserve their creditworthiness. While the social costs of over-indebtedness, such as humiliation, isolation or exclusion cannot be ignored (Chapters 11 and 12), borrower resistance is also important to note (Chapters 3 and 13). In Karnataka for instance, local leaders have not only instigated defaults, but some clients have also decided to defy the MFI's established lending rules, encouraging local borrowers, leaders, and government to support their stand (Chapter 13).

As already pointed out, microfinance alone is rarely the sole cause of household over-indebtedness, which equally involves unexpected crises and/or structural constraints. Microcredit catalyses pre-existing imbalances and accelerates declines. Conversely, when supply matches the diversity of local needs in contexts with economic activity development potential, microcredit can play a positive role, as the Malagasy case study illustrates (Chapter 10). Opening the black box of microfinance practices to understand their implications in social, economic and political change processes also allows for an innovative analysis of repayment crises. Here, we focus on the Karnataka crisis. Described as a "Muslim revolt", it should be situated within a context of daily production, distribution and reproduction relations, which were influenced by how the microfinance sector's interests interacted with and challenged local interests and power relations (Chapter 13).

All of the chapters in the volume highlight the tension at the core of the paradoxes and ambiguities of microcredit. Microcredit is a desirable form of credit for borrowers because it appears to be a way out of oppressive debt traps. It is a promise of an egalitarian relationship contracted outside local circles of social hierarchies, between individuals considered as equals. Unfortunately this hope for freedom often proves illusory for several reasons. Given that formal social protection is often non-existent or ineffective, people desperately need protective debt, as oppressive as it might be. The terms and conditions themselves are relatively impoverishing and any substantive equality would require extricating a household from its subordinate status in a number of cross-cutting exchange relations. Such radical changes in social relations, coming from outside as well as inside the economy, are beyond individual households' control.

Structure of the volume

The first chapter, by Servet and Saiag, tackles the issue of over-indebtedness from a macro perspective. Incomes are evolving in a way that is incompatible with rising cash needs, which are increasing as home consumption decreases due to urbanisation. The widespread desire to imitate others' consumption patterns is motivated by the potential for equality between individuals with the rise of informality and irregular income flows. It is argued that household over-indebtedness stems from this contradiction.

Chapters 2 and 3 argue that meanings and framing processes are instrumental in the social, cultural and political fabric of over-indebtedness and its lived experience, whether by borrowers or lenders. Both chapters use Callon's notion of framework of calculation while drawing on specific examples – over-indebtedness of Mexican migrants in the United States (Villarreal) and non-repayment of microcredit clients in Kenya and Bangladesh (Johnson).

The following six chapters use case studies to examine the daily manifestations of debt and over-indebtedness. In contrast to any evolutionary perspective, Ducourant shows that the French consumer credit market, although 'formalized' and regulated, does not escape the contradictions that have been highlighted in this introduction. The three following chapters deal with southern India, examining different facets and manifestations of over-indebtedness. Harriss-White looks at how, in commodity systems involving multiple transactions, unsynchronised and asymmetrical payments shape patterns of accumulation and pauperisation of small and medium entrepreneurs. Guérin *et al.* discuss the multiple debt ties rural households juggle with, the incommensurability of these multiple debts and the contradictions between their financial costs and their social and moral meaning. Drawing on the ethnography of labour migrants, Picherit argues that in the context studied, over-indebtedness emerges when the moral, violent and physical obligation to repay a debt meets a lack of durable social and political protection-dependence and a decline in social and economic positions. The next two chapters take us to Mexico. Morvant-Roux analyses the links between indebtedness, over-indebtedness and migration, observing that migration is a specific household strategy that is deployed when indebtedness levels are such that neither households' usual revenue nor their social networks suffice to help them to clear their debts. Zanotelli focuses on the specific case of women, arguing that women's debt is shaped by and constitutive of intra-household and gender relationships. He finds that the diversification of women's debt ties serves material purposes while attenuating the sources of social and moral dependence that they experience at home. His analysis suggests that the difference between juggling with debt and over-indebtedness is a matter of degree of *dependency*.

The four final chapters deal more explicitly with microfinance. Wampfler *et al.* draw on fieldwork conducted in Madagascar to examine the multiple forms of interaction and juggling between microfinance and informal finance, not just in terms of financial transactions, but of knowledge and relationships. They show that juggling may involve vulnerability and over-indebtedness in some specific situations, but that it can also be an elaborate and successful form of money management, allowing households to overcome the inadequacies of single formal and informal financial products. Drawing on two Mexican case studies, Angulo Salazar and Hummel's respective chapters focus on microcredit clients' over-indebtedness. Both authors highlight the social costs of over-indebtedness for the clients and the responsibility of microfinance organisations in this process. They describe the high hidden costs of microcredits, the aggressivity of marketing and enforcement techniques by credit officers and the intense competition between microfinance organisations. But both authors also emphasise the role of local factors in over-indebtedness processes, including the emergence of consumerism and the growing social aspirations of households. The last chapter, by Joseph, deals with the political economy of the microcredit crisis in Karnataka (southern India). Here too, we see that the mission drift of microfinance organisations is certainly a key factor in households' vulnerability (injection of massive flows of liquidity, aggressivity of loan officers). But we also see that microfinance activities are embedded into local structures of accumulation and power, which are instrumental in shaping microfinance practices. The conclusion discusses a number of suggestions, recommendations and policy implications that emerge out of this collection of chapters. These concern the microfinance industry but also the development sector as a whole.

The book thus looks to analyse the multiple facets of over-indebtedness, focusing on the practices, processes and meanings underpinning it. This includes analysis of financial exclusion, ownership and control of time, and the social and economic relations of credit, debt and indebtedness.

It explores the ways in which monetary and non-monetary flows of resources are saved, invested, spent or utilised in households to make ends meet, focusing on the management and significance of debt, and the boundaries of over-indebtedness. The relevance of boundaries and meanings and how they are negotiated also runs through the chapters. Frameworks of calculation come into play in reckonings of value, which often involve hierarchies, caste, ethnic and class categories. Such frameworks are also important in estimates of risk and notions of default. The boundaries between healthy debt and over-indebtedness are themselves subject to negotiated redefinition. On the other hand, individuals are often both debtors and creditors, or move from one category to the other.

In short, this book addresses a potentially critical issue for the impoverished in the world. It carefully covers new ground in the interdisciplinary analysis of debt and over-indebtedness, suggesting fresh ways of analysing finance for the low-income sectors of the world's population, and offering novel contributions to current debates on policies for financial inclusion.

Notes

1 See for instance Fouillet (2006), Roesch (2006), Rozas (2009).
2 Consultative Group to Assist the Poor.

3 For an overview of the risks and challenges of mission drift, see Morduch (2000), Armendariz and Szafarz (2011), Cull *et al.* (2011). For India, see for instance, Nair (2011).

4 For an overview, see Armendariz and Morduch (2010). Regarding gender, see for instance Kabeer (2001); Kabeer (2001); Garikipati (2008); Johnson (2005); Agier and Szafarz (2013); Guérin *et al.* (2013); Mayoux (2000).

5 See also Servet (2010).

6 For instance a Consumer Financial Vulnerability Index has been drawn up in South Africa, drawing on European initiatives (Finmark Trust and Unisa 2009). It includes four sub-indicators: income vulnerability (which includes job security, income growth, social grants and transfers from family and friends), saving vulnerability, expenditure vulnerability (which includes various factors such as whether a consumer is able to cope with the rising costs of food and transport) and debt service vulnerability (which is driven by the level of debt and the cost of servicing debt).

7 Schicks (forthcoming), for instance, considers that an individual/household is over-indebted when she/he is 'continuously struggling to meet repayment deadlines and repeatedly has to make unduly high sacrifices to meet his loans obligations'. Borrowers may be able to repay but only at the cost of 'unacceptable' sacrifices.

8 See for instance Aglietta and Orléans (1998); Akin and Robbins (1999); Baumann *et al.* (2008); Bloch and Parry (1989); Graeber (2011); Guyer (1995); Maurer (2006); Peebles (2010); Servet (1984, 1995); Shipton (2007); Thérêt (2009); Villarreal (2004); Weber (2000); Zelizer (1994).

9 In the case of Ghana studied by Schicks for example, borrowers repay very well while one third are over-indebted (as defined by the author, that is to say that repayments require 'sacrifices' from the borrowers) (Schicks 2012).

10 Similar observations have been made in rural Morocco, where mass default in certain areas is mainly due to microcredit providers' lack of legitimacy. They are placed in the same category as the *Maghzen* – the central authority – or as foreign aid. People simply do not want to repay (Morvant-Roux *et al.* forthcoming).

11 For more details, see Guérin (2012).

12 For more details, see Guérin (2012).

13 On the International Gateway for Financial Education's website for instance, it is argued that the concern for financial education stems from the observation that individuals take on more financial risks while their financial knowledge is extremely low. This results in 'passive resilient behaviour' which in turns translates into numerous problems, starting with 'excessive household debt'. The subprime crisis is quoted in brackets (see www.financial-education.org/pages/0,3417,en_39665975_39667032_1_1_1_1_1,00.html).

14 See also the work of the Institute for Money, Technology and Financial Inclusion at the University of California, Irvine, which develops and supports ethnographic research on the everyday use of money and finance, including microfinance, and their social and cultural meaning (see www.imtfi.uci.edu/). For an overview, see Schwittay (2011).

15 See for instance Akin and Robbins (1999); Baumann *et al.* (2008); Bloch and Parry (1989); Guyer (1995); Maurer (2006); Thérêt (2009); Villarreal (2004). For a review see Peebles (2010).

16 See for instance Aglietta and Orléans (1998); Servet (1984, 1995); Shipton (2007); Zelizer (1994).

17 This has also been developed in Guérin *et al.* (2011).

18 The blurring of savings and loans is found throughout the world (Guérin *et al.* 2011; Guyer 1995; Lont and Hospes 2004). In fact, borrowing is simply a means to force oneself to save in the future (Rutherford 2001), just as lending is a form of saving that presupposes the right to borrow later.

References

Agier, I. and Szafarz, A. (2013) 'Microfinance and gender: is there a glass ceiling on loan size?', *World Development*, 42: 165–182.

Aglietta, M. and Orléans, A. (1998) (eds) *La monnaie souveraine*, Paris: Editions Odile Jacob.

Akin, D. and Robbins, J. (1999) *Money and Modernity. State and Local Currencies in Melanesia*, Pittsburgh: University of Pittsburgh Press.

Armendáriz, B. and Labie, M. (eds) (2011) *Handbook of Microfinance*, London and Singapore: World Scientific Publishing.

Armendáriz, B. and Morduch, J. (2010) *The Economics of Microfinance*, 2nd edition, Cambridge: MIT Press.

Armendáriz, B. and Szafarz, A. (2011) 'On mission drift in microfinance institutions', in Armendáriz, B. and Labie, M. (eds) *Handbook of Microfinance*, London and Singapore: World Scientific Publishing, pp. 341–367.

Banerjee, A. and Duflo, E. (2011) *Poor Economics: a Radical Rethinking of the Way to Fight Against Poverty*, New York: Publicaffairs.

Bateman, M. (2010) *Why Doesn't Microfinance Work? The Destructive Rise of Local Neoliberalism*, London: Zed Books.

Baumann, E., Bazin, L., Ould-Ahmed, P., Phelinas, P., Selim, M. and Sobel, R. (eds) (2008) *L'argent des anthropologues, la monnaie des économistes*, Paris: l'Harmattan.

Bédécarrats, F. (2013) *La microfinance entre utilité sociale et performances financières*, Paris: l'Harmattan (Collection Critique Internationale).

Bloch, M. and Parry, J. (eds) (1989) *Money and the Morality of Exchange*, Cambridge: Cambridge University Press.

Breman, J. (2007) *Labour Bondage in West India: From Past To Present*, Oxford: Oxford University Press.

Breman, J., Guérin, Isabelle and Prakash, Aseem (eds) (2009) *India's Unfree Workforce of Bondage Old and New*, New Delhi: Oxford University Press.

Bruce, J. and Dwyer, D. H. (1988) (eds) *A Home Divided: Women and Income in the Third World*, Standford: Standford University Press.

Collins, D., Morduch, J., Rutherford, S. and Ruthven, O. (2009) *Portfolios of the Poor: How the World's Poor Live on $2 a Day*, Princeton: Princeton University Press.

CGAP (2011) 'Credit reporting at the base of the pyramid. key issues and success factors', Access to Finance Forum, n°1, available online at: www.cgap.org/gm/document-1.9.55445/FORUM_1.pdf (last accessed 25 March 2012).

Chen, G., Rasmussen, S. and Reille, X. (2010) 'Growth and vulnerabilities in microfinance, *Focus Note*, 61, *CGAP*.

Coquery, N., Weber, F. and Menant, F. (eds) (2006) *Écrire, compter, mesurer. Vers une histoire des rationalités pratiques*, Paris: Éditions rue d'Ulm.

Cull, R., Dermirgüç-Kunt, A. and Morduch, J. (2011) 'Microfinance trade-offs: regulation, competition and financing', in Armendáriz, B. and Labie, M. (eds) *Handbook of Microfinance*, London and Singapore: World Scientific Publishing, pp. 141–159.

Deaton, A. (2010) 'Instruments, randomization, and learning about development', *Journal of Economic Literature*, 48: 424–455.

De Soto, F. (2000) *The Mystery of Capital: Why Capitalism Triumphs in the West and Fails Everywhere Else*, New York: Basic Books.

Dichter, Th. and Harper, M. (2007) *What's Wrong with Microfinance?* London: Practical Action.

Dickerson, M. (1999) 'Can shame, guilt, or stigma be taught? Why credit-focused debtor education may not work', *Loyola of Los Angeles Law Review*, 32(4): 945–964.

Dixon, R., Ritchie, J. and Siwale, J. (2007) 'Loan officers and loan "delinquency" in microfinance: A Zambian case', *Accounting Forum*, 31(1): 47–71.

Erturk, I., Froud, J., Johal S., Leaver, A. and Williams, K. (2007) 'The democratisation of finance? Promises, outcomes, conditions', *Review of International Political Economy*, 14(4): 553–575.

Fernando, J. (2006) *Microfinance: Perils and Prospects*, Routledge: London.

Finmark Trust and Unisa (2009) *A Consumer Financial Vulnerability Index for South Africa*, Pretoria: Finmark Trust and Unisa, available online at: www.finmarktrust.org. za/search/search.aspx?SearchTerm=financial vulnerability index (last accessed 23 November 2011).

Fontaine, L. (2008) *L'Economie morale. Pauvreté, crédit et confiance dans l'Europe préindustrielle*, Paris: Gallimard.

Fouillet, C. (2006) 'La microfinance serait elle devenue folle? Crise en Andhra Pradesh, *Espace Finance*', Gret-Cirad, 25 avril.

Garikipati, S. (2008) 'The impact of lending to women on household vulnerability and women's empowerment: evidence from India', *World Development*, 36(12): 2620–2642.

Global Financial Education (n.d.) 'Debt management: handle with care', content note, available online at: www.globalfinancialed.org/documents/CN_DebtMgmt.pdf (last accessed 23 November 2011).

Gloukoviezoff, G. (2010) *L'exclusion bancaire. Le lien social à l'épreuve de la rentabilité*, Paris: Presses Universitaires de France.

Graeber, D. (2011) *Debt: The First 5,000 Years*, New York: Melville House Publishing.

Guérin, I. (2006) 'Women and money: multiple, complex and evolving practices', *Development and Change*, 37(3): 549–570.

Guérin, I. (2011) '*Do* women need specific microfinance services?', in Armendariz B. and Labie M. (eds) *Handbook of Microfinance*, London and Singapore: World Scientific Publishing, pp. 563–589.

Guérin, I. (2012) 'The fallacy of financial education: insights from economic anthropology', *Microfinance in Crisis Working Papers Series*, 1, Paris, Paris I Sorbonne University/IRD, available online at: www.microfinance-in-crisis.org/wp-content/uploads/ WP1.pdf, (last accessed 12 January 2013).

Guérin, I., Agier, I. and Kumar, S. (2013) (forthcoming) 'Women's empowerment: power to act or power over other women? Lessons from Indian microfinance', *Oxford Development Studies*.

Guérin, I., Morvant, S. and Servet, J.-M. (2011) 'Understanding the diversity and complexity of demand for microfinance services: lessons from informal finance', in Armendariz, B. and Labie, M. (eds) *Handbook of Microfinance*, London and Singapore: World Scientific Publishing, pp. 101–122.

Guyer, J. (1995) (ed.) *Money Matters: Instability, Values and Social Payments in the Modern History of West African Communities*, London and Portsmouth (NH): Currey/ Heinemann.

James, D. (2012) 'Money-go-round: personal economies of wealth, aspiration and indebtedness', *Africa* 82(1), pp. 20–40.

Jauzelon, C. (2007) 'Microfinance et pratiques sociales des femmes paraiyars en Inde du sud: solidarité "organise" ou solidarité "héritée"?', *Revue Tiers Monde*, 2(190): 275–289.

Johnson, S. (2004) 'Gender norms and financial markets: evidence from Kenya', *World Development*, 32(8): 1355–1374.

Johnson, S. (2005) 'Gender relations, empowerment and microcredit: moving from a lost decade', *The European Journal of Development Research*, 17(2): 224–248.

Johnson, S., Mule, N., Hickson, R. and Mwangi, W. (2003) 'The managed ASCA model innovation in Kenya's microfinance industry', in Harper, M. (ed.) *Microfinance: Evolution, Achievements and Challenges*, London: ITDG Publishing, pp. 159–171.

Kabeer, N. (2001) 'Conflicts over credit: re-evaluating the empowerment potential of loans to women in rural Bangladesh', *World Development* 29(1): 63–84.

Karim, L. (2011) *Microfinance and its Discontents: Women and Debt in Bangladesh*, Minneapolis: University of Minnesota.

Karnani, J. A. (2009) 'Romanticising the poor harms the poor', *Journal of International Development*, 21(1): 76–86.

Long, N. (2001) *Development Sociology: Actor Perspectives*, London and New York: Routledge.

Lont, H. and Hospes, O. (eds) (2004) *Livelihood and Microfinance: Anthropological and Sociological Perspectives on Savings and Debt*, Delft: Eburon Academic Publishers.

Malamoud, C. (ed.) (1988) *La dette*, Paris: Éditions de l'École des hautes études en sciences sociales (coll. *Purushartha*, vol. 4).

Martin, M. (2007) 'A literature review on the effectiveness of financial education', Federal Reserve Bank of Richmond Working Paper Series, WP07–3, available online at: www.richmondfed.org/publications/economic_research/working_papers/index.cfm, (last accessed 8 August 2011).

Mayoux, L. (2000) 'Microfinance and the empowerment of women: a review of the key issues', Social Finance Unit Working Paper, 23, Geneva: ILO.

Maurer, B. (2006) 'The anthropology of money', *Annual Review of Anthropology*, 35:15–36.

Molyneux, M. (2002) 'Gender and the silences of social capital', *Development and Change*, 33(2): 167–188.

Morduch, J. (2000) 'The microfinance schism', *World Development*, 28(4): 617–629.

Morvant-Roux, S. (2009) 'L'anthropo-économie: un détour indispensable pour comprendre l'appropriation de la microfinance', *Revue Tiers-Monde*, 197, pp. 109–130.

Morvant-Roux, S., Guérin, I., Roesch, M. and Moisseron, J.-Y. (forthcoming) 'Adding value to randomization with qualitative analysis: the case of microcredit in rural Morocco', *World Development*.

Mosse, D. (2005) *Cultivating Development: An Ethnography of Aid Policy and Practice*, London: Pluto Books.

Nair, T. (2011) 'Microfinance: lessons from a crisis', *Economic and Political Weekly*, 46(6): 23–26.

OECD (2005) *Improving Financial Literacy: Analysis of Issues and Policies*, Paris: OECD.

OECD/World Bank/DFID/CGAP (2009) *The Case for Financial Literacy in Developing Countries Promoting Access to Finance by Empowering Consumers*, Washington: OECD/World Bank/DFID/CGAP.

Peebles, G. (2010) 'The anthropology of credit and debt', *Annual Review of Anthropology*, 39: 225–240.

Porter, K. M. and Thorne, D. (2006) 'The failure of bankruptcy's fresh start', *Cornell Law Review*, 92: 67–128.

Prahakad, C. K. (2004) *The Fortune at the Bottom of the Pyramid: Eradicating Poverty Through Profits*, Wharton School Publishing.

Rankin, K. N. (2002) 'Social capital, microfinance and the politics of development', *Feminist Economics*, 8(1):1–24.

Reed, L. R. (2013) *Vulnerability: The State of the Microcredit Summit Campaign Report, 2013*, Washington: Microcredit Summit Campaign.

Rhyne, E. (2001) *Mainstreaming microfinance, How Lending to the Poor Began, Grew and Came of Age in Bolivia?* Bloomfield, Conn: Kumarian Press.

Roesch, M. (2006) 'Des dettes jusqu'à ne plus en vivre', *Espace Finance*, Gret-Cirad, 11 avril.

Roodman, D. and Morduch, J. (2009) 'The Impact of Microcredit on the Poor in Bangladesh: Revisiting the Evidence', CGD Working Paper 174.

Roy, A. (2010) *Poverty Capital: Microfinance and the Making of Development*, New York and London: Routledge.

Rozas, D. (2009) 'Is there a microfinance bubble in south-India?', *Microfinance focus*, number17, available online at: www.danielrozas.com/2009/11/17/is-there-a-microfinance-bubble-in-south-india/, (last accessed 22 March 2012).

Rutherford, S. (2001) *The Poor and Their Money*, Oxford: Oxford University Press.

Schicks, J. (forthcoming) 'Microfinance over-indebtedness: understanding its drivers and challenging 5 common myths', *Oxford Development Studies*.

Schicks, J. (2012) 'The over-indebtedness of microfinance customers – an analysis from the customer protection perspective', PhD Dissertation, Centre for European Research in Microfinance (CERMi), Solvay Brussels School of Economics and Management/ Centre Emile Bernheim/Université Libre de Bruxelles.

Schwittay, A. F. (2011) 'The financial inclusion assemblage: subjects, technics, rationalities', *Critique of Anthropology*, 31(4): 381–401.

Servet, J.-M. (1984) *Nomismata. Etat et origines de la monnaie*, Lyon: Presses Universitaires de Lyon.

Servet, J.-M. (ed.) (1995) *Épargne et liens sociaux. Études comparées d'informalités financières*, Paris: AEF/AUPELF-UREF.

Servet, J.-M. (2006) *Banquiers aux pieds nus*, Paris: Odile Jacob

Servet, J.-M. (2010) *Le grand renversement. De la crise au renouveau solidaire*, Paris: Desclée de Brower.

Shipton, P. (1995) 'How Gambians save: culture and economic strategy at an ethnic crossroad' in Guyer, J. (ed.) *Money Matters: Instability, Values and Social Payments in the Modern History of West-African communities*, London andPortsmouth (NH): Currey/Heinemann, pp. 245–277.

Shipton, P. (2007) *The Nature of Entrustment; Intimacy, Exchange and the Sacred in Africa*, New-Haven, CT: Yale University Press.

Shipton, P. (2010) *Credit Between Cultures: Farmers, Financiers And Misunderstandings in Africa*, New Haven and London: Yale University Press.

Thérêt, B. (2009) 'Monnaie et dettes de vie', *L'Homme*, 190: 153–179.

Villarreal, M. (2004) 'Striving to make capital do "economic things" for the impoverished: on the issue of capitalization in rural microenterprises, in Kontinen, T. (ed.) *Development Intervention: Actor and Activity Perspectives*, Helsinki: Center for Activity Theory and Developmental Work Research (CATDWR), Institute for Development Studies (IDS) and University of Helsinki, pp. 67–81.

Villarreal, M. (2009) *Mujeres, finanzas sociales y violencia economica en zonas marginadas de Guadalajara*, Guadalajara: IMMG/IJM.

Weber, F. (2000) 'Transactions marchandes, échanges rituels, relations personnelles. Une ethnographie économique après le Grand Partage', *Genèses*, 41: 85–107.

Weber, F. (2001) 'Settings, interactions and things: a plea for multi-integrative ethnography', *Ethnography*, 2(4): 475–499.

Yunus, M. (2007) *Creating a World Without Poverty: Social Business and the Future of Capitalism*, Pretoria: New Africa Press.

Zelizer, V. (1994) *The Social Meaning of Money*, New York: Basic Books.

1   Household over-indebtedness in northern and southern countries

A macro-perspective

Jean-Michel Servet and Hadrien Saiag

Introduction

Neo-liberal policies have shaped modes of production, trade and financing for the last thirty years and the crisis of 2007–2008 revealed the untenable nature of household indebtedness in the United States. Apologists of neo-liberalism are convinced that such policies enabled two decades of prosperity, following the 1973–1974 crisis. The approach has become hegemonic, explicitly opposing interventionist Neo-Keynesian policies under which public and private debt drive demand for investment and consumer goods, through deficit spending and money creation. This makes it possible to anticipate demand and make it 'effective', because it is solvent. By contrast, neo-liberals believe deficits should be banned; for them, a balanced budget is a precondition of equitable distribution. To the extent that deficits are considered the culprits of rising prices, they favour debtors at the expense of creditors. Although neo-liberal morality (if we can call it that) opposes this type of imbalance, growing levels of household indebtedness reveal that such opposition is naive. China and India notwithstanding,[1] overall growth rates were on average two times higher during the so-called 'Keynesian' period (the post-Second World War boom from the 1950s to early 1970s) than they were during the neo-liberal years that followed[2] and precarious working conditions have greatly increased. Since the 1980s, the 'fruits of economic growth' have been distributed in an increasingly unequal manner. While this period has been the 'golden age' for financial markets,[3] it could also be called the 'calamitous years'. Unemployment rates, in particular, were much higher from 1980–2000 than 1950–1960.

The purpose of this chapter is to show that the rise of household debt is not unique to 'developed' countries. In the North, indebtedness is a well-documented fact; it has been quantified and its contribution to macroeconomic relationships has been studied. However, little data is available from the South. This could lead one to think that rising household debt is not an issue. Yet, the contributions in this volume indicate the opposite. In fact, the South is also affected by over-indebtedness. There is a growing mismatch between monetary income and cash needs, the source of debt.

Our argument draws on two kinds of sources. Concerning the North, we rely primarily on the work of the French School of Regulation. In the South, rising household debt has not, to our knowledge, been the object of thorough macro-economic analysis. Nor is it measured by statistics, due to the extent of informal financial practices. In this chapter, we aim to shed light on the gap created by the slow growth of most households' cash incomes and their growing financial needs. Therefore, we rely on official reports (mainly from the International Labour Organization, concerning remuneration and employment trends) and statistics (from World Bank, concerning the growth of cash needs).

This chapter is organized into three parts. The first part addresses the growing role of household indebtedness in so-called 'developed' countries. Around the world, debt has bolstered consumer spending, which has been affected by slow income growth and a rise in social inequality. The hegemonic role of the United States at the heart of global finance has allowed it to drain considerable resources. As a result, household debt has become linked to inflation in real estate and capital markets, leading to an ephemeral accumulation regime 'driven by finance' (Boyer 2000). The second part examines the rise of indebtedness in the South. To grasp its magnitude, we revisit the process of financialization. It is based on a growing monetization of social relationships. As in the North, the slowdown of growth in workers' earnings has been accompanied by a sharp rise in social inequality. Incomes are evolving in a way that is incompatible with cash needs, which are growing as home consumption decreases due to urbanization; the widespread desire to imitate the consumption patterns of others due to the potential equality between individuals (see Dumont 1976); and the rise of informality and irregular income flows. Household over-indebtedness stems from this contradiction. Finally, the third part discusses a key element of over-indebtedness: inflation. If social relations would allow it, modest inflation would be a relatively peaceful way to solve the problem of growing private and public debt in a way that favours lenders.

Household debt in the North: the heart of an ephemeral accumulation regime

To understand the rise of household indebtedness in the North, we must first reconstruct debt's role in macroeconomic dynamics. The latter have been studied in depth by the Regulation School. Between 1950–1970, according to this school of mainly French economists, Northern countries experienced different forms of a single accumulation regime called 'Fordism'.[4] It was characterized by a conflictual, albeit stable compromise between capital and labour concerning the distribution of productivity gains (the Fordist wage–labour nexus) resulting from the 'rationalization' of production. As economies were rarely open to international trade at the time, wage gains engendered an increase in effective demand. Moreover, government intervention helped support economic activity (through budget deficits and advances to the Treasury) and a relatively equitable distribution of wealth. Added to this was constant inflation, whose negative real interest rates were advantageous to borrowers.

The crisis that hit in the 1970s fundamentally threatened the institutions underpinning these macroeconomic relationships: the rise of real wages collided with an opening of economies (Boyer 2004). The institutional forms[5] that provided the scaffolding of the accumulation regime were overturned. Thus, since the 1980s, governments have scaled back direct intervention in the economy: they now create institutions designed to 'deregulate' modes of production, trade and financing. They have provided the impetus to significantly develop financial markets (particularly those dealing with public debt) and dismantle the Fordist wage-labour nexus. In the North, the result has been the development of new forms of work on the margins of wage labour[6] (short-term, part-time, student jobs, sub-contracting, etc.). These new forms of employment have driven down the salaries of unskilled workers and increased insecurity (due to poor benefits packages). Consequently, social inequality has skyrocketed (Feller and Stone 2009; Picketty and Saez 2003).[7]

Despite the escalation of social inequality caused by these changes, this new institutional arrangement has sometimes given way to macroeconomic coherence, as in the case of the United States and, to a lesser extent, the United Kingdom. This appears paradoxical, since the dismantling of the Fordist wage system and the increasingly inequitable distribution of wealth has depressed effective demand. As a result, households are heavily indebted, through various forms of consumer credit (particularly credit cards). But the novelty of this finance-led accumulation regime[8] does not lie herein. Rather, it is the way it disconnects consumer spending and income generation. Indeed, the advent of loan securitization (especially mortgages) has fostered a new form of household debt: the main limitation is no longer anticipated household income, but the valuation of the securities that serve as collateral. In other words, the only limit to household indebtedness is the valuation of real estate and financial securities. As the values and volume of these securities increase, so does debt. As a result, massive household indebtedness now underpins the American economy, household debt at one point reaching 96 per cent of GDP (gross domestic product) in 2009. In 1954, total domestic debt in the United States was only US$500 billion. In the first half of 2009 alone it exceeded US$50,000 billion.[9]

The United States' unique position in the global financial system has made this situation possible. At a global level, this headlong rush was facilitated by trade surpluses from countries like China and oil exporting countries with small populations. Their investments appeared safe, because they were made in one of the world's most developed countries, and because the dollar became the financial world's reserve currency following the SecondWorld War. Thus, a considerable amount of money flowed into the United States.

This accumulation regime is based on a reversal of roles whereby the productive sector must now answer to the financial sector. According to Robert Boyer (2000), the break with Fordism is obvious. In Fordism, the wage labour relationship prevailed, insofar as it allowed the synchronization of mass production and consumption by institutionalizing a distribution of productivity gains from the 'productive' sphere. In the finance-led accumulation regime, there is a reversal of the hierarchical relationship between institutional forms – finance and the wage relation – that is advantageous to the financial sector, which now controls the economy. Indeed, stock prices simultaneously determine investments decisions, household debt and consumption choices, fiscal policy (the tax burden has been shifted to employees to enable the development of capital markets) and finally, monetary policy (aimed at financial stability). Finance no longer relies on production and trade; it has reversed the relationship at a scale never before seen. While financiers claim to serve society and create prosperity, finance has become increasingly predatory (Servet 2012), destroying wealth through the constant processes of valuation/devaluation that ensure its development and result in precarious living conditions for the immense majority of the population.

This accumulation regime has really only flourished in the United States and the United Kingdom. The supposed virtuous circle of debt, financial markets and household consumption has not been observed elsewhere. In other words, the modes of regulation in Northern countries are very diverse. Michel Aglietta (1998)[10] has argued that the equity-based ('patrimonial') growth regime would become a permanent fixture in continental Europe. The argument is consistent with the increasingly widespread use of household debt to offset loss of income. But we cannot conclude from this alone that worldwide economic growth is characterized by a finance-led accumulation regime. Indeed, according to the typology created by one regulationist theorist (Boyer 2004), an accumulation regime must be capable of reproducing institutional forms consistently over a relatively long period. Currently, debt allows households to significantly boost their consumption by increasing the value of their assets in order to compensate the loss of wage income. This implies that household wealth is increasingly based on asset-backed securities. Robert Boyer (2000) has showed that this only holds true in the United States and possibly the United Kingdom.[11] Elsewhere, the model has not taken hold. Thus, although the financial sector now has considerable influence over economic developments in continental Europe,[12] we have not yet seen an accumulation regime that is capable of generating steady growth since Fordism.

Despite the different trajectories of 'developed' countries, debt expansion has been the common vector, draining resources to the benefit of the financial sector. Hence, tremendous financial growth (such as the sextupling of stock market capitalization between 1990–2007 and the boom in securitized financial products) frequently goes hand in hand with outflows from the 'productive' sphere (just look at the financial sector's profits and extraordinary salaries).[13] Here too, the United States stands apart:

> The enormous financial growth that has accompanied market deregulation and globalization suggests that the process could not go on forever. In 1980, the profits generated by the American financial sector represented 10 per cent of total private sector profits; in 2007, it was 40 per cent. The same year, the financial sector employed only 5 per cent of the salaried workforce of the private sector, and contributed only 15 per cent of value added. The financial sector has thus sucked out the value created by the economy; the value has disappeared in exorbitant salaries for traders, extravagant

commissions for capital restructuring operations, securitization and asset management. Market capitalization of the financial sector collapsed in 2008 because it had inflated without restraint, increasing six fold; the financial sector's share grew from 6 per cent in 1980 to 19 per cent in 2007.

(Aglietta and Rigot 2009: 19)

In other words, the United States and perhaps the United Kingdom notwithstanding, growing household debt has not been able to stave off the decline in effective demand. There are several reasons for this. The dismantling of the Fordist wage regime may be justifiable from a microeconomic perspective, but it reveals pressure to drive down global demand on a macroeconomic scale, all things being equal. The surge in income inequalities has stripped wealth of its reproductive capacity, because households' marginal propensity to consume is decreasing in relation to the level of income: wealthy people's financial investments do not create effective demand because they do not stimulate production. In addition, increased international competition for domestically produced goods has reduced fiscal pressure on the private sector in the name of competitiveness. Customs duties collected by the governments have decreased considerably. And since public expenditures have not been cut, these tax revenues have been recovered through taxes on salaries, and very occasionally and to a much lesser extent, on real estate, assets, and luxury goods. These direct and indirect taxes have pushed down incomes of the majority at the same time as social benefits have come under threat; health care and education costs are eating up increasingly large portions of family budgets, leading to an overall pressure to reduce other expenses.

Thus, the current crisis is very much endogenous to modes of production, trade and financing based on growing household debt. It reveals the contradictions inherent to the current phase of capitalism. The finance-driven accumulation regime can no longer reproduce itself. It has effectively shot itself in the foot: over-indebted households can no longer honor their debts. The financial sector has sucked its victims dry. The corollary of diminished income is increased debt, which augments outflows from the productive sector to the financial sector, thereby increasing inequality, which depresses demand and income, which in turn tends to increase indebtedness. In the medium term, this translates into healthy financial institutions on the one hand, depressed incomes for the majority with rising unemployment on the other (a 'stagboom') (Servet, 2010a). But ultimately, these outflows end up 'suffocating' those they 'feed'. The crisis of 2008 erupted because the amounts drained by the financial sector surpassed the surplus actually generated. The race for debt has produced unsustainable disequilibrium. It has undermined the balanced reproduction of modes of production, trade and financing. Extend the analogy of David Ricardo's position on the limits of the capitalist system of production in terms of increased rents, and Karl Marx's regarding falling rates of profit, and it would appear that the limit of the neo-liberal accumulation regime is the extent to which the financial sector drains value from all other productive activities (capitalist or otherwise), public resources and salaried income.

Southern countries and financialization: exacerbating the gap between needs and income

According to statistics from international organizations, household debt does not appear to be a problem in the South. True, the portion of private sector macro-economic debt from financial institutions compared to GDP has grown significantly between 1980 and 2007 (see Table 1.1), doubling in Africa and the Middle East, and increasing by almost 150 per cent throughout the Asia and Pacific. Only Latin America and the Caribbean seem to be an exception, with a mere 29 per cent increase during the period. This increase is partly due to consumer credit, which has grown considerably in the South in recent years.[14] Nevertheless, the private sector debt-to-GDP ratio remains much lower in the South than in the North: in Latin America and the Caribbean, this ratio for accounts 26 per cent of that of developed countries, 52 per cent for Asia and the Pacific, 34 per cent for the Middle East and 39 per cent for Africa. Adults in developed countries are four times more likely to have a loan from a bank than in developing countries. Banks in developing countries mainly lend to the rich, who supposedly offer better guarantees: in the North, the average loan to a household represents 53 per cent of national income. In developing countries, the rate is 128 per cent.[15] These figures might suggest that debt problems are relatively foreign to southern countries...

However, such data tend to underestimate household debt. It is difficult to quantify precisely: statistic bureaus only take into account indebtedness to financial institutions when in fact, a large part of household debt in the South comes from 'informal' practices,[16] with large national and regional differences regarding the weight and the forms. As this book demonstrates, informal financial practices are as diverse as the contexts in which they evolve. Besides rotating savings and credit associations where debt and credit balance out over time, there exist many other forms of associations and community organizations

Table 1.1 Domestic credit to private sector, as a percentage of GDP, 1980–2007

Regions	1980	1994	2007	Variation 1980–2007 (%)
Africa	31.96	54.71	65.55	(+) 105.13
Asia and the Pacific	34.88	69.68	86.44	(+) 147.79
Latin America and the Caribbean	34.25	46.34	44.09	(+) 28.71
Middle East	28.61	43.48	56.23	(+) 96.56
Developed economies and European Union	86.25	127.83	166.72	(+) 93.30

Source: World Bank national accounts data, OECD National Accounts data files (GDP), IMF and World Bank (credit); authors' calculations.

Note

Domestic credit to private sector refers to financial resources provided to the private sector, such as loans, purchases of non-equity securities, and trade credits and other accounts receivable, that establish a claim for repayment. For some countries these claims include credit to public enterprises. Geographical pooling has been made following ILO (2008: 93–106).

(Servet 1996). They cover funeral expenses, local celebrations, community works and infrastructure development. There are also a multitude of private intermediaries. These include formal or informal specialized financial providers that may or may not lend against collateral: shopkeepers who offer cash advances; traders who extend credit based on standing crops; employers or inter-mediaries who offer salary advances; merchants selling goods on credit that they immediately buy back at lower prices; in-kind advances by suppliers to small shopkeepers, artisans and itinerant traders; loans from a former employer for apprentices who want to start their own business, etc. Savings collectors still exist: shopkeepers and acquaintances who allow the unbanked to save in a safe place rather than hoard at home. These 'moneykeepers' often lend, as well. The repayment schedule varies according to the collector's own collection schedule –weekly, monthly, harvest time. In some cases, the creditor may only demand interest payment and not the principle, much as a landlord who collects rent does not try to sell the property to the tenant.

To understand the rise of debt in the South, let us clarify what we mean by financialization. Financialization cannot be reduced to the expansion of financial markets (as is often the case). We distinguish three levels (Servet 2006: 35–60, 2010a). At the base is monetization of the economy. Monetization is due to the increased commodification of the everyday conditions of domestic reproduction. It is the result of a diminution of economic organization based on the household and public institutions. This has led to a decrease in home consumption and increased monetization of family budgets. For the first time, money is needed to meet the most basic needs: it is no longer reserved for special occasions (Coppet 1998). Next, comes financial intermediation, as it becomes increasingly neces-sary to use an intermediary to access loans, payments, transfers, insurance and savings;[17] the intermediary, however, is not necessarily a financial institution. At the highest level are financial speculative markets. The summit (speculation) cannot exist without the base (monetization). But at the heart of the current financialization, the former dominates the latter through a process of exploita-tion. As in any exploitative relationship, the 'superior' feeds off the 'inferior'. Speculative markets are thought to be indispensable to the very existence of monetization, especially since high finance has become absolutely necessary for people to 'make ends meet' and acquire the production means for the majority. Thus, although it is impossible to accurately quantify the second level of finan-cialization in the South (which includes household debt), it is possible to identify its source of growth: the growing gap between needs and cash incomes.

Income transfer programmes implemented in so-called 'developing' countries are really part of the process of financialization. These programmes aim mainly to cover the health care and education costs of low-income families. They are particu-larly common in Latin America. The best documented example is probably that of Mexico – the *Progresa Programme*, now known as *Oportunidades* – but such pro-grammes can also be found in other Latin-American countries, Africa and Asia (Handa and Davis 2006). These programmes encourage the monetization of expen-ditures, as opposed to transactions in kind. Such monetization may also encourage debt, by increasing financial flows at the local level to the benefit of microfinance institutions and local moneylenders. In Mexico, for example, these subsidies are very popular with small businesses, as they enable clients to reimburse purchases made on credit (*fiado*) (Morvant-Roux 2006: 225).

Various factors underscore the growing gap between incomes and needs. First of all, as in the North, the slow progression of incomes in the South has been accompanied by inequitable income distribution, in a context marked by sluggish and more volatile economic growth (ILO 2008: 3). On average, wages grew more slowly between 2001 and 2007 than between 1995 and 2000. Between 2001 and 2007, they increased an average of only 0.3 per cent per year in Latin America and the Caribbean and 1.8 per cent in Asia. In addition, there appears to be a levelling-off effect during economic crises, particularly in Latin America: wages are hit hard during declining growth in this region, and they rarely recover their pre-crisis level (ILO 2008: 3–12). Between 1990 and 2006, wages grew less quickly than productivity, resulting in a shift in the distribution of value added to the benefit of capital (ILO and IILS 2008: 7). Inequalities in income distribution have thus increased: the gap between the incomes of the poorest 10 per cent of the population compared to the richest 10 per cent has widened from 1995–2000 and from 2001–2006 in most Southern countries where data are available (ILO 2008: 24). Similarly, the Gini coefficient (which measures inequalities in income distribution) has increased in most countries of Asia and the Pacific, Latin America and the Caribbean, and Central and Eastern Europe. Africa seems to be an exception: the Gini coefficient has declined in most countries where statistics are available (ILO and IILS 2008: 11–12).

These income inequalities are part of a broader context characterized by persistent exclusion, marginalization and discrimination of social groups. In this sense, inequality is not, fundamentally, a consequence of poverty due to inadequate resources. Conversely, poverty should be seen as the result of inequality, particularly structural inequalities and discrimination, that causes exclusion and marginalization of ethnic, linguistic, caste and some immigrant groups (Diop 2007). The probability of being poor varies significantly and it is difficult to attribute it to a particular social class. It is probably no coincidence that nearly 44 per cent of the world's 'poor' is concentrated in South Asia: 80 per cent of humanity considered to be living 'in absolute poverty' is in India, Bangladesh, Pakistan, Sri Lanka, Bhutan, Nepal and the Maldives, although the Gini coefficient in these countries is not higher compared with other regions of the world. In analysing the caste system in India as a social structure of accumulation, Barbara Harriss-White (2003: 176–199) highlights its key role in perpetuating inequalities, particularly by fragmenting the labour market. Countries like the Indian Union, Pakistan, Bangladesh and Nepal have much higher poverty rates than most other countries because of the persistence in these societies of untouchability – one of the most abject forms of inequality – and the high incidence of debt bondage (Breman *et al.* 2009). More generally, William Easterly (2001) has shown a close correlation between high poverty rates and strong social fractures. According to Easterly, this is because the dominant groups do not seek to build the capacity of excluded groups, who may challenge and weaken their power. Thus, there is greater consensus around sharing resource in countries where social divisions are less.

Parallel to the slowdown in income growth in most households, there has been an exacerbation of cash needs. This is partly due to the decline in consumption of food and clothing from one's own production. There is little data available on this subject; we have identified only two recent household budget surveys[18] that allow us to quantify changes in home consumption: one conducted in Mexico in 2008 (Dirección de Análisis Económico y Social 2008) and in Tanzania in 2001 (National Bureau of Statistics Tanzania 2001). In the first, non-cash income in 2008 accounted for 19.9 per cent of all household income, whereas this proportion was 21.4 per cent eight years earlier. Similarly, in Tanzania, subsistence agriculture covered 28.6 per cent of total food expenditures in 2000–1,[19] compared to 35.5 per cent ten years earlier (p. 70). Most importantly, this survey shows that home consumption is much higher in rural than in urban areas.[20] Thus, the decline in home consumption is related to growing urbanization rates. As Table 1.2 shows, growth rates throughout the South increased considerably and steadily from 1960 to 2008. Consequently, monetary needs have increased substantially, in order to access food.[21]

The growth of urbanization rates has also increased cash needs in other ways. When slum dwellers are expelled from their homes, for example, they are often forced to move to farther away from the urban areas that provide them with jobs and cash income, thereby decreasing their monetary resources. Urban sprawl in some cities in the South has also made it particularly difficult for small farmers to maintain their activities: streams used for irrigation are diverted, water increasingly polluted, and distances to walk made even longer due to new fences set up around housing estates. The capitalist regime, under the pretext of spreading prosperity, relies on the development of private property rights (de Soto 1989), in other words, exclusive access to previously public goods. The poor were once thought of as a kind of 'industrial reserve army', driving salaries downward and, in periods of expansion, providing a labour pool to meet needs.

Table 1.2 Urbanization rates, 1960–2008

Regions	1960	2008	Variation (%)
Africa	18.51	38.87	(+) 109.98
Asia and the Pacific	17.11	38.46	(+) 124.70
Central and South-Eastern Europe and CIS	45.90	64.41	(+) 40.31
Latin America and the Caribbean	48.32	78.23	(+) 61.91
Middle East	33.51	65.59	(+) 95.75

Source: World Development indicators; authors' calculations.

Note
Urbanization refers to the ratio of the number of people living in urban areas (as defined by national statistical offices) to the number of residents in each country.

This downward pressure has not disappeared in all countries, but contemporary forms of economic development tend to make the poor redundant.

Globalization has also led to an explosion of needs; and, in absence of a sharp rise in disposable income or a new ascetic morality, the inevitable consequence is significant subjective impoverishment. In some ways, the wealth of some creates the poverty of others, not necessarily because the poor are pillaged, in a quasi-mercantilist sense, but because poverty is exacerbated by the desire to imitate the consumption patterns of others. In ancient hierarchical societies, where social status determined consumption capacity and ostentation, the desire to imitate was limited, as the social order was consensual. The destruction of these hierarchies led to a widespread desire to access the same goods and services (see Ortega y Gasset, 1994 [1930]). The potential equality between individuals created by the 'flattening' of the values of hierarchical societies has been accompanied by a rise of a society of envy in which needs are exacerbated. One cannot need something that one does not know exists, or considers to be part of a world that is not one's own. Most economists have long thought scarcity to be the cause, the motive, the underlying assumption of rational economic behavior to meet universally felt needs (Rist 2011); all one needs to do is adjust one's scarce means to meet their desires. However, scarcity is not a cause. Rather, it is a consequence of economic behavior (Salhins 1972). Yet, the needs that have emerged with the flattening of hierarchies are not mere 'whims': they are a way for people to integrate into society. Indeed, the observations of Maurice Halbwachs (1933: 106) in his study *L'évolution des besoins dans les classes ouvrières* on the nature of social needs are still relevant: through consumption, the working class participates in a civilization that is beyond themselves.

For this reason, we have recently seen a boom in consumer goods in the South. Subscriptions to telephone lines (mobile and landlines) skyrocketed between 1990 and 2008 (Table 1.3), growing by over 4,000 per cent in Asia and the Pacific, nearly 3,000 per cent in Africa and about 700 per cent in the Middle East. Similar growth can be observed in Internet access and computer ownership. Consumption of other goods has also risen sharply, although the proportions are not as impressive. For example, between 2002–2007, the number of households owning a car doubled in Asia and the Pacific, and shot up elsewhere

Table 1.3 Subscription of mobile and landlines (as a percentage of population, 1990–2008)

Regions	1990	2008	Variation (%)
Africa	1.40	42.52	(+) 2,930.43
Asia and the Pacific	1.30	58.91	(+) 4,442.34
Central and South-Eastern Europe and CIS	12.31	132.99	(+) 980.04
Latin America and the Caribbean	5.30	83.92	(+) 1,484.29
Middle east	15.30	121.74	(+) 695.77

Source: International Communication Union and United Nation Populations Division – World Development Indicators; authors' calculations.

(57 per cent, 56 per cent and 35 per cent respectively for the Middle East, Africa and Latin America – Table 1.4). The social nature of these goods is ambivalent: their need is exacerbated by a desire to imitate (Guérin and Selim 2012), but at the same time they are essential to a growing number of income-generating activities, including in rural areas.

Finally, the last thirty years have seen a rise in so-called 'informal' jobs.[22] In the late 1980s, studies on informality showed it was not in regression; it was more than a remnant destined to disappear with economic growth. Rather, it was a structural element at the heart of accumulation strategies in developing countries (Portes *et al.* 1989; Bernard 1991 on the Maghreb; on India, see Srivastavan 2012; and Harriss-White and Sinha 2007). The phenomenon is difficult to quantify, given the many possible indicators and definitions of 'informal' jobs. Jacques Charmes (2009) nevertheless makes an attempt: he quantifies the growth of informal employment in all non-agricultural employment between 1997 and 2007 in forty-seven countries. He defines informal employment by the absence of a written contract and social protection. This amounts to the inclusion of informal self-employment, domestic labour and paid jobs without social protection, whether the company is declared or not. In North Africa and Sub-Saharan Africa, informal employment as a portion of total employment outside agriculture has grown gradually. It even started accelerating in the 1990s.[23] South Asia and Southeast Asia saw a similar trend for the years 1985–1989[24] (no data available before this period). Finally, in Latin America, the growth of informal employment has been constant since the 1990s[25] (again, no data is available prior to this period).

The rise of 'informal' employment supports our argument in two respects. First, let us underline the singular relationship of 'informality' to time.[26] Income from the so-called 'informal' economy is generally more volatile than income from 'formal' jobs: job changes are more frequent (Arias *et al.* 2008) and many of these jobs are outside the wage system. This last point is particularly important, because the growth of 'informal' jobs has gone hand in hand with a

Table 1.4 Number of households possessing at least one passenger car

Regions	2002	2007	Variation (%)
Africa	9,297,703,971	14,523,157,030	(+) 56.20
Asia and the Pacific	22,864,456,152	45,529,094,925	(+) 99.13
Central and south-eastern Europe and CIS	38,491,499,429	50,059,394,164	(+) 30.05
Latin America and the Caribbean	18,547,572,289	24,974,251,553	(+) 34.65
Middle East	7,849,753,158	1,233,140,122	(+) 57.09

Source: International Road Federation and United Nation Populations Division; World Development Indicators; authors' calculations.

Note
Passenger cars refer to road motor vehicles, other than two-wheelers, intended for the carriage of passengers and designed to seat no more than nine people (including the driver).

rise in independent workers in all regions of the South between 1996 and 2006, except in Africa (ILO 2008: 10). The temporal nature of productive activities outside of wage employment differs greatly from those specific to wage employment. For example, a significant portion of revenues for informal activities comes from expenses incurred by salaried employees. These expenses are not spread evenly throughout the year: there are strong seasonal fluctuations. Therefore, summer months are often synonymous with school holidays and reduced activity, as are some religious festivals. Moreover, expenditures are not distributed evenly over the month: when incomes are limited, the bulk of spending takes place once or twice a month. Indeed, low-income wage earners incur a significant portion of their expenses a few days after being paid.[27] In other words, a significant portion of income earned in jobs that fall outside of wage employment depends on the expenditures of the owners of capitalist production means (wages), which control the creation of money based on their anticipation of future revenue.[28] The temporality of the 'informal economy' is not monthly: supplier relations, 'informal' finance, investment needs, etc. arise on a weekly basis at best. The poor manage their household budgets on a day-to-day basis, incurring substantial indebtedness primarily due to cash flow difficulties.

The rise of informal employment in Latin America has been accompanied by a decline in social protection systems since the 1990s.[29] Indeed, in most countries across the region, social coverage depends on contributions made during one's working life. And yet, one of the characteristics of 'informal' employment is the absence or very low level of income (Saavedra-Chanduvi 2007; Rofman and Lucchetti 2006; Apella and Casanova 2008). In most countries in the region, there was a sharp decline between 1990 and 2000 in the share of the workforce contributing to the pension system.[30] Those individuals contributing to the system also became more unequal: during the same period, contributions to pension schemes from the first four quintiles of the population declined sharply as the inputs of the fifth quintile grew or remained relatively stable.[31] It is true that type of employment is less an element of hierarchization in social protection systems than in the past, thanks to assistance programmes for the poor and non-job-related social protection programmes set up since the 2000s in the region. However, these changes have occurred with the deregulation of the labour market and overall weakening of social protection systems since the 1980s, resulting in less social protection for the whole population (Barrientos 2009). In Africa, the situation is different. There is a decline in family solidarity because of the increasing individualization of society. This decline is not being offset by the institutionalization of social protection. These developments have led to new cash needs (and expenditures) for the affected populations: to protect themselves against precarious and unstable employment (and unemployment) and health care issues (or the death of a relative), it is necessary to mobilize savings or use debt. These 'unexpected' events can have a significant impact on income-generating activities and plunge the vulnerable into debt.

These developments lead us to refine our notion of savings, even for China. Presently a land of savers, China's savings fund Western countries. This is true from a macroeconomic standpoint. But refine the analysis by social groups, and it becomes clear that it would be wrong to think in terms of averages and imagine that every Chinese family has the ability to save. Even with an annual growth rate of 8–9 per cent that allows formal businesses to absorb twelve million additional workers, an equivalent number of people appear to be supernumerary (Monteil 2010: 11). To survive, they engage in small informal activities. This category (known as *ruoshi qunti* in official Chinese terminology) appears unable to save. As elsewhere, they face the hard knocks of life through debt.[32] It is estimated that the country has 130 million urban informal workers (Monteil 2010: 12), plus another 150 million rural supernumeraries. In the survey conducted for her thesis (ibid.), Amandine Monteil reveals that 43 per cent of respondents in six districts of the cities of Chengdu and Leshan claim they are unable to save (ibid.: 66, 83; this percentage is even higher among urban residents over thirty years of age). While official propaganda stresses autonomy and the virtue of not going into debt (ibid.: 365), three-quarters of those interviewed said they had already borrowed: 49 per cent to cover medical expenses (this rate is higher among migrants at 52 per cent (ibid.: 39–40, 61)), 39 per cent for children's education, 23 per cent to cover daily needs and 27 per cent for business purposes; 7 per cent indicated having done so often. To borrow, they resort to family (54 per cent), friends (44 per cent) and neighbours (19 per cent), while only 11 per cent use financial institutions. Amandine Monteil also reports (ibid.: 78) on the practice of gambling (*mahjong*, a high-stakes card game), which illustrates, as revealed in the case of Haiti and *borlette* (Servet 2010b), another expedient way to make ends meet. These urban poor are the outright opposite of China's economic and financial miracle. Moreover, the weak social protection in China, which explains the population's high saving rate, reveals a universal consequence for the most vulnerable: debt (albeit at much lower rates than what is observed in many other parts of the world). There is probably a relationship between this indebtedness among a fraction of China's population and the rise of pawnbrokers, astutely analysed by Thierry Pairault (2002, 2003), and the low growth of microfinance (Pairault 2009).

As in North, the rise of household debt in the South implies that households are increasingly subject to outflows of income. Contrary to popular belief, these practices do not always involve so-called 'usury' interest rates. However, shops that keep customers loyal by selling on credit generally have higher prices than businesses that do not. Similarly, merchants who advance credit during the lean season, or for the purchase of inputs in exchange for unharvested crops, get produce at a better price than if they had to purchase it at harvest time. Consequently, the disposable income of the most vulnerable households is whittled away by the seller's profit margin, which is in fact a hidden interest rate. When the cost of credit exceeds the surplus created by the activities financed, the borrower is ultimately impoverished, which explains some cases of over-indebtedness.

It is against this backdrop that an increasing number of microcredit institutions have entered crises: in 2008–2009 Nicaragua, Morocco, Bosnia-Herzegovina and

Pakistan, and, at the end of 2010, the Indian states of Karnataka and Andhra Pradesh (Servet 2011). It is tempting to attribute the rise in arrears not to the global crisis itself but to the poor management of microfinance institutions and uncoordinated competition.[33] Of course, if we consider these crises as the results of the financial crisis created by developed countries (and primarily the United States), which has led to an almost universal crisis in production and trade, then the microfinance institutions are not to blame. This said, the direct or indirect impact on the decline in migrant remittances has affected some institutions (Servet 2010a) and the decline in resources from tourism and multinationals with subsidiaries in the South has caused a drop in the volume of activities of microenterprises and workers' wages, thereby decreasing the volume of loans granted by microfinance institutions that serve these clients. But what is really at issue here is the rush to extend larger loans to more people, without ensuring microcredit's effective contribution to income-generating activities.[34] Of course, if only the managers of these microfinance institutions had been more vigilant, if only they had more effective information systems, they would have better anticipated portfolio risk, having identified clients with multiple loans from different organizations. In Nicaragua, 40 per cent of borrowers had loans from more than one institution in 2009. In Morocco, the portion was 40 per cent in 2007, 39 per cent in 2008 and 29 per cent in 2009. In Bosnia-Herzegovina, it was 40 per cent in 2009. In Pakistan, 21 per cent nationally and 30 per cent of the regions were affected by a default movement (Chen *et al.* 2010). Although Peru is not yet in this situation, it is not far away. The same is true for some parts of India.

The analysis put forth in this chapter suggests a different interpretation than that of poor governance of microfinance institutions. It explains why the default movement in Nicaragua, Andhra Pradesh and Pakistan has been organized by lobby groups – political in the first two cases and Islamist in the third. Of course clients took advantage of the microfinance institutions' inability to limit their loans and to assess their own institutional weaknesses. But if these customers sought out credit (not just with microfinance institutions but also with so-called 'usury' lenders), it was because they had to, in order to live and make payments on previous loans. The managers of microfinance institutions have often assumed that clients return for larger loans because they are satisfied with the services offered. They did not consider that repeated borrowing could be the sign of a growing addiction to credit, which would eventually lead to over-indebtedness.

Overcoming over-indebtedness with inflation

At the first level of financialization (Servet 2010a) where the crisis has erupted, there is an economy of debt (Graeber 2011). It has different terms and conditions depending on the country, but everywhere, indebtedness has appeared to compensate for the relative impoverishment caused by slower growth in countries with neo-liberal economic policies and unequal income distribution. As Warren E. Buffett said, 'There's class warfare, all right, but it's my class, the rich class, that's making war, and we're winning.'[35] It is common to understand unequal distribution of income and the exploitation associated with it from a perspective of wage relations or subordination in the workplace.

But reducing exploitation to the direct exploitation of labour is limited, because the dependencies and transfers from one sector to another and between social groups can also be achieved through forms of debt. These debts, like any subordinate relationships in the productive sector, allow capital to exploit labour, thanks to transfers that occur via usurers. The draining of financial resources through various forms of debt can be interpreted as a particular form of the capital–labour relationship. The way this relates to exploitation is not through the face-to-face relationship of an employee paid by the hour or on a piece basis (and then selling products that appear to be handicrafts).[36] But generally speaking, paying interest to develop productive or trading activities is the equivalent of paying a levy on the income from this activity. There is no capital–labour relationship at an interpersonal level but on a global scale, we can identify transfers from one sector to another. By decreasing the income earned through interest and repayment on the principal, inflation can contribute to reducing exploitation.

When debt becomes so unbearable that it endangers the harmonious interactions between social groups and the reproduction of society itself, the economic system can create an escape valve through reforms or debt reduction thanks to price increases. Since the 1970s, there have been four types of policy to deal with public debt. In 1998, Russia declared default and its public debt was rescheduled through re-negotiation. A similar situation has been observed in many developing countries over the past two decades. Public spending in the United Kingdom in the early 1980s and in Sweden in the 1990s was reduced by deep economic reforms. In the 1970s Japan and the United States turned to innovation and growth by stimulating investment. Finally, Western Europe and Argentina used monetary weapons – devaluation and inflation – to reduce their debts, somewhat moderately in Europe in the 1970s and more radically in Argentina in 2002. History is full of examples, dating back to antiquity, that show how price increases have been a way of reducing debt in a way that allows society to 'settle its accounts' more or less peacefully, provided social and political relations allow for it. Many ancient cities even practiced debt forgiveness (under popular pressure), to the detriment of creditors, who were forced by the political establishment to accept the terms. A moderate price increase of 4–5 per cent per year would, over the course of one decade, depreciate borrowed capital by half. If the nominal interest rate is fixed, and is less than 2 per cent, the real interest rate appears negative. Naturally, reversing the trend in terms of the distribution of income from capital and income from labour implies a simultaneous adjustment to real wage and quasi-wage income and the income of small producers, so that they do not see their purchasing power drastically reduced. But, regardless, the actual amount of repayment of interest and principal will be reduced by inflation anyway.

Inflation can also alleviate the debt burden borne by households through the management of public debt. Over the last thirty years, public debt in many countries has increased inequalities in terms of income redistribution (both the cause and consequence of household over-indebtedness). It is paradoxical, since unlike private debt, public debt can have an equalization effect: its cost can be borne by the affluent even while public expenditures benefit everyone, especially the poorest (Barba and Pivetti 2009). But this implies a political will to raise taxes. This has not been the case for nearly thirty years. In fact, the term 'paradox' is too weak, as we are at complete odds with the situation described by Aldo Barba and Massimo Pivetti: public debt has benefited the richest, because it represents a portion of tax they did not have to pay, even though they benefited from the remuneration of public debt, while the poorest are the first to suffer from the reduction of public expenditure.[37] In other words, for more than a quarter of a century, the part of the budget that the richest have not wanted to tax becomes a collective debt that benefits the most affluent and tends to decrease the well-being of the poorest, and even the majority of the population. Perhaps because of the political causes of this debt, we will one day speak of it as a 'debilitating debt', which would justify a collective movement to default on it.

It is difficult to compare debt reduction during growth years (even low ones) and the period post-2008, because economic stimulus policies appear less effective and credible while policies to reduce public spending play a deflationary role for all production and trade activities. Since declaring default ultimately leads back to debt, due to the high level of growth that potential creditors will require later, a solution that calls for the return of inflation appears the most likely scenario, even most desirable in the medium term, to overcome massive public and private debt. Admittedly, at a time (September 2010) when large firms are borrowing long term (forty to fifty years) at near-zero rates,[38] proposing to return to price increases may seem preposterous. But, given the experience of the last 100 years, is it not the same thing as making an investment at a very low interest rate, which would suppose a stability of the prices for several decades?

Maybe this is how we should interpret the increase in fuel and food prices in 2007. Although price increases were influenced by the shift in the object of speculation following the collapse of the derivatives market based on American subprime mortgages, they acted as a kind of systemic reality check, by depreciating real estate and financial assets compared to real goods. Similarly, in late 2010, there were once again new price hikes for some commodities, not to mention a rise in the price of gold, especially sought after by the Chinese. From this standpoint, the turnaround in food and fuel prices in 2008 can be seen as the effect of deflationary pressures related to the beginning of the crisis and its subsequent development as a 'stagboom'. But, the dominant monetary ideology among financial authorities and interest groups that adhere to it to advance neoliberal policies have prevented and continue to prevent the system from purging itself through price increases.[39]

As economies are currently dealing with the consequences of monumental debt, it is surprising to hear so many experts propose to revive production and trade by … private debt from financial markets. Among the many statements along these lines is included this quote from Marek Belka, Executive Director of the IMF's European Department:

I think what is most important for the pace of economic recovery in the euro zone is how decisive policies are toward revitalizing the banking sector [...]. So much depends on the health of the banks [...]. The more that is done to clean the banks, to enable them to perform their functions best the more robust the recovery will be. [40]

However, if the dominant forms of private credit are at the root of the crisis, it is hard to imagine that they will be able to solve it. It is as if a therapist who, after forcing a patient to become an alcoholic to attain illusory happiness, proposes a treatment that involves drinking more wine.

Notes

1 Massive government intervention in these countries has fuelled growth; their governments do not comply with neo-liberal dogma.
2 Pollin (2003: 131) shows that the overall growth rates of low-income and middle-income countries (excluding China) were 5.5 per cent between 1961–1980, and only 2.6 per cent during the neo-liberal era (1981–1999). Growth rates per capita fell from 3.2 per cent to 0.7 per cent during the same period.
3 Term used by the Observatoire de la Finance in Geneva.
4 In the terminology of regulation theory, accumulation regimes are the result of interactions between key institutions that underpin the economic process. They last several decades, the time it takes to generate a surplus without being interrupted by a crisis that calls into question its main characteristics.
5 The term 'institutional form' refers to the social relations key to the regulation of economies. Regulation theory identifies five main forms: the monetary regime, the wage-labour nexus, forms of competition, state intervention and the international regime (Boyer 2004: 39–41).
6 Vatin (ed.) 2007. See also ILO and IILS (2008: 119). ILO (2009) discusses the rise of temporary work in the North.
7 For updated data from Piketty and Saez (2003), see http://emlab.berkeley.edu/~saez/index.html.
8 Robert Boyer's expression (2000).
9 This was possible because China, Japan, Hong Kong and Taiwan accumulated $1.65 trillion in US Treasury bonds.
10 Clévenot (2008) discusses this article and internal controversies among regulation theorists over the nature of this new economic structure in the United States.
11 For more on the unequal distribution of financial assets in France, see Le Duigou (2000).
12 See Coriat (2008) concerning France.
13 There is a point of consensus among economists who study this issue. For a detailed calculation, see publications of the Political Economy Research Institute (PERI) of the University of Massachusetts Amherst (see www.peri.umass.edu/). For a sociological analysis of the rise in household debt in France, and its draining effect, see the review *Sociétés contemporaines*, no. 46 (2009), particularly articles by Hélène Ducourant and Ana Perrin Heredia. For Germany, see Haas (2006).
14 For data on Argentina, see de Nigris (2008). For Peru, see ASPEC (2009).
15 For a detailed look at access to banking services for different countries see data from Kendall *et al.* (2009).
16 For example in Andhra Pradesh (India) the majority of debt of rural households comes from practices related to the informal sector. According to Johnson and Meka (2010)

93 per cent of households in the state are in debt; 57 per cent of these households have borrowed with interest from "friends" while 17 per cent used an informal lender.

17 See for example the boom in mobile payments in the South.

18 The authors would like to acknowledge Nicolas Brice of CIRAD for informing us of these studies.

19 Waters (2007 p. 155) provides a different estimate, without specifying his methodology. He argues that in 2000, 70 to 85 per cent of food production came from subsistence farming in rural areas, compared to the 57 per cent reported in the National Bureau of Statistics survey. Regardless of the exactitude of this figure, it is clear that self-subsistence agriculture has dropped over time.

20 These data converge with those of the household budget survey carried out in Uganda in 2005–2006 (Uganda Bureau of Statistics 2006: 74).

21 The current situation differs from the little-monetized African economies of the late 1960s, described by Hallu (1970) and Servet (1976).

22 We would like to underscore the importance of these inverted commas: this is not our category. We have used it here to support our argument, but it is not within the scope of this article to conduct a critical analysis. For an analysis of the multiple relationships between formal and informal, and a study of informal organizational arrangements, see Lautier (2004).

23 This growth is noticeable in countries where we have enough data over time. This includes Algeria, Morocco, Tunisia, Mauritania, Mali, Kenya, Guinea and Chad. Egypt has taken a slightly different path: the share of informal employment declined sharply between 1975–1989 and 1985–1989, before starting to grow.

24 Thailand is an exception.

25 Chile and Mexico notwithstanding.

26 Space does not permit us to expand on this argument. For more details, see Saiag (2011: 25–7).

27 In Argentina, relatively poor households often make their food purchases once every two weeks (when the head of family receives his pay). This practice helps limit spending so as not to go into debt in order to access food.

28 According to the terms of creation and destruction of payment means as they apply to 'modern' credit currencies. We acknowledge Benetti and Cartelier (1980) for proposing a distinction between workers and capitalists based on the conditions that govern access to means of payment.

29 Brazil is exceptional in this respect.

30 Argentina, Brazil, Uruguay, Chile, Costa Rica, Venezuela, Colombia, Paraguay and Bolivia. In Mexico, the rate remains stable. It has increased slightly in Nicaragua and Guatemala, and more significantly in El Salvador and Peru.

31 The only exceptions were Peru, Guatemala, El Salvador and Mexico.

32 Amandine Monteil (2010) clarifies that the sums are small and quickly reimbursed, but it is still debt.

33 See comparative analysis done by Chen *et al.* (2010), and studies specific to each of these countries referenced in the bibliography of this article.

34 See the critical analysis conducted by Jude (2006), Servet (2006, 2010c) and Bateman (2010).

35 Warren E. Buffett, quoted by Richard H. Thaler, 'What the Rich Don't Need', *New York Times*, 25 September 2010.

36 Ancient societies have many examples like this, where exploitation does not occur via direct employment of labour. This applies, for example, to domestic work that confers upon the worker the status of craftsman; it is the case for all rents based on advancing seed or lending land.

37 In this case, income redistribution is more unequal after taxes than before. The example of the United States is striking (Aglietta and Berrebi 2007: 139–43).

38 On 14 September 2010, EDF borrowed £1 billion over forty years; GDF Suez borrowed £700 million for fifty years, while their German rival RWE simultaneously launched a 'perpetual' bond issue for €1.75 billion. UK pension funds appear to be the buyers of these securities. Microsoft's loan of $4.75 billion is practically ephemeral (three years), but the rate is well below the increase in prices: 0.875 per cent per annum.

39 Robert Boyer (2009: 33) posits a deflationary depression scenario (the excess of debt leads to a cumulative fall in prices) by looking at the hypothesis of Irving Fisher (1933). Similarly Paul Krugman, in an article in the *New York Times*, says that the risk of deflation is much greater than that of inflation, despite strong growth in government deficits. He draws on the example of Japan between 1997 and 2003, when the Bank of Japan bought huge amounts of bank debt, while consumer prices continued to fall (Paul Krugman 'The Big Inflation Scare' *New York Times*, 28 May 2009).

40 Marek Belka, quoted in the *Wall Street Journal* by Ilona Billington and Terence Roth, 'IMF urges EU to sustain fiscal stimulus,' 31 July–2 August 2009.

References

Published work

Aglietta, M. (1998) 'Le capitalisme de demain', *Notes de la fondation Saint-Simon*, (101):1–52.

Aglietta, M. and Berrebi, L. (2007) *Désordre dans le capitalisme mondial*, Paris: Odile Jacob.

Aglietta, M. and Rigot, S. (2009) *Crise et rénovation de la finance*, Paris: Odile Jacob.

Apella, I. and Casanova, L. (2008) 'Los trabajadores independientes y el sistema de seguridad social. El caso del Gran Buenos Aires', in *Aportes a una nueva visión de la informalidad laboral en la Argentina* (ed.) World Bank, Buenos Aires: World Bank and Ministerio de Empleo, Trabajo y Seguridad Social (Argentina).

Arias, O., Demonbynes, G., Moreno, J. M. and Rofman, F. (2008) 'Informalidad, protección social y mercado de trabajo en la Argentina', in *Aportes a una nueva vision de la informalidad laboral en la Argentina* (ed.) World Bank, Buenos Aires: World Bank and Ministerio de Empleo, Trabajo y Seguridad Social (Argentina).

ASPEC (2009) 'Crédito y sobreendeudamiento de los consumidores en el Peru', Lima: Sociocan/European Commission.

Barba, A. and Massimo, P. (2009) 'Rising household debt: its causes and macroeconomic implications – a long-period analysis', *Cambridge Journal of Economics* 33(1): 113–37.

Barrientos, A. (2009) 'Labour markets and the (hyphenated) welfare regime in Latin America', *Economy and Society* 38(1): 87–108.

Bateman, M. (2010) W*hy Doesn't Microfinance Work? The Destructive Rise of Local Neoliberalism*, London and New York: Zed Books.

Benetti, C. and Cartelier, J. (1980) *Marchands, salariat et capitalistes*, Paris: Maspero.

Bernard, C. (ed.) (1991) *Nouvelles logiques marchandes au Maghreb: l'informel dans les années 80*, Paris: Editions du Centre National de la Recherche Scientifique.

Boyer, R. (2000) 'Is a finance-led growth regime a viable alternative to Fordism? A preliminary analysis', *Economy and Society* 29(1): 111–45.

Boyer, R. (2004) *Théorie de la regulation*, Paris: La Découverte.

Boyer, R. (2009) 'Feu le régime d'accumulation tiré par la finance', *Revue de la régulation* (5): 35.

Breman, J., Guérin, I. and Prakash, A. (eds) (2009) *India's Unfree Workforce: of Bondage Old and New*, New Dheli: Oxford University Press.

Charmes, J. (2009) 'Concepts, measurement and trends', in J. Jütting and J. de Laiglesia (eds) *Is informal normal? Towards more and better jobs in developing countries.* Paris: OECD, pp. 27–62.

Chen, G., Rasmussen, S. and Reille, X. (2010) Growth and vulnerabilities in microfinance', *Focus Note CGAP* (61): 1–16.

Clévenot, M. (2008) 'Les difficultés à nommer le nouveau régime de croissance', *Revue de la régulation* (3/4): 1–18.

Coppet, D. de. (1998) 'Une monnaie pour une communauté mélanésienne comparée à la nôtre pour l'individu des sociétés européennes', in M. Aglietta and A. Orléan (eds) *La monnaie souveraine*, Paris: Odile Jacob.

Coriat, B. (2008). 'L'installation de la finance en France: genèse, formes spécifiques et impacts sur l'industrie'. *Revue de la régulation*, vol.3/4, 34. Available at http://regulation.revues.org/6743

Diop, A., Hillenkamp, I. and Servet, J.-M. (2007) 'Poverty vs. Inequality', in B. Balkenhol (ed.) *Microfinance and Public Policy: Outreach, Performance and Efficiency*, London: Palgrave Macmillan/ILO, pp. 27–44.

Dumont, L. (1976) *Homo aequalis – Tome 1: Genèse et épanouissement de l'idéologie économique*, Paris: Gallimard.

Easterly, W. (2001) 'The middle class consensus and economic development', *Journal of Economic Growth* 6(4): 317–35.

Feller, Avi and Stone, Chad (2009) 'Top 1 percent of Americans reaped two-thirds of income gains in last economic expansion: income concentration in 2007 was at highest level since 1928, new analysis shows', Washington: Center on budget and policy priorities, 9 September (available online at: www.cbpp.org/cms/index.cfm?fa=view&id=2908).

Fisher, I. (1933) 'The Debt-Deflation Theory of Great Depressions', *Econometrica* 1(4): 337–57.

Graeber, D. (2011) *Debt: The First Five Thousand Years*, Brooklyn, New York; Melville House.

Guérin, I. and Selim, M. (eds) (2012) *À quoi et comment dépenser son argent. Hommes et Femmes face aux mutations globales de la consommation en Afrique, Asie, Amérique latine et Europe*, Paris: L'Harmattan.

Haas, O. (2006) 'Overindebtedness in Germany', ILO Working Paper (Social Finance Programme), 46, p. 30.

Halbwachs, M. (1933) *L'évolution des besoins dans les classes ouvrières*, Paris: Nouvelle bibliothèque économique.

Hallu, R. (1970) 'Réalités africaines et enquêtes budget-consommation', *Economie et statistique* (11): 21–32.

Handa, S. and Davis, B. (2006) 'The experience of conditional cash transfers in Latin America and the Caribbean', *Development Policy Review* 24(5): 513–36.

Harriss-White, B. (2003) *India Working: Essays on Society and Economy*, Cambridge: Cambridge University Press.

Harriss-White, B. and Sinha, A. (eds) (2007) *Trade Liberalization and India's Informal Economy*, New York and New Delhi: Oxford Univesity Press.

Johnson, D. and Meka, S. (2010) 'Access to finance in Andrha Pradesh', Institute for Financial Management and Research, Tamil Nadu: Centre for Micro Finance, Tamil Nadu.

Jude, F. (ed.) (2006) *Microfinance: Perils and prospects*, London and New York: Routledge.

Kendall, J., Mylenko, N. and Ponce, A. (2009) 'Measuring access to financial services around the World', Policy Research Working Paper (5253), Washington: World Bank/ CGAP.

Lautier, B. (2004). *L'économie informelle dans le tiers monde*. Paris: La découverte.

Le Duigou, J.-C. (2000) 'Faut-il patrimonialiser les droits sociaux?' in H. Jacot and J.-C. Le Digou (eds) *Capitalisme patrimonial ou nouveau statut salarial*, Paris: L'Harmattan.

Monteil, A. (2010) 'Emploi informel et gestion des inégalités en Chine urbaine. Les politiques de promotion de "l'emploi communautaire" parmi les "groupes vulnérables" à Chengdu (2006–2009)', Unpublished thesis, Paris: EHESS.

Morvant-Roux, S. (2006) 'Processus d'appropriation des dispositifs de microfinance: un exemple en milieu rural mexicain', Unpublished thesis, Lyon: Université Lumière – Lyon II.

Nigris, A de (2008) 'La bancarización en Argentina', in Working paper – Serie Financiamiento del desarrollo (204), Buenos Aires: CEPAL.

Ortega y Gasset, J. (1994 [1930]) *The Revolt of the Masses* [original: *La rebelión de las masas*], London: W.W. Norton & Company.

Pairault, T. (2002) 'Les habits neufs des maisons de prêt sur gage chinoises', *Mondes en développement* 30(118): 21–37.

Pairault, T. (2003) 'Maisons de prêt sur gage en Chine: une visite de Chongqing', *Anthropologica (Review of the Canadian Society of Anthropology)* 45(2). 283–91.

Pairault, T. (2009) *Pratiques populaires et microfinancières chinoises*, Paris: Edition des Archives Contemporaines.

Piketty, T. and Saez, E. (2003) 'Income inequality in the United States, 1913–1998', *Quaterly Journal of Economics* 113(1): 1–39.

Pollin, R. (2003) *Contours of Descent: U.S. Economic Fractures and the Landscape of Global Austerity*, London and New York: Verso.

Portes, A., Castells, M. and Benton, L. (eds) (1989) *The Informal Economy: Studies in Advanced and Less Developed Countries*, London: The Johns Hopkins University Press.

Rist, G. (2011) *The Delusions of Economics, The Misguided Certainties of a Hazardous Science*, London: Zed Books.

Rofman, R. and Lucchetti, L. (2006) 'Pension systems in lain America: concepts and measurements of coverage social protection discussion', in Social Protection Discussion Paper (601), Washington DC: World Bank.

Saavedra-Chanduvi, J. (2007) 'Informality, social protection and antipoverty policies', in G. Parry (ed.) *Informality: Exit and Exclusion*, Washington: World Bank/International Bank for Reconstruction and Development.

Sahlins, M. (1972) *Stone Age Economics*, Chicago: Aldine-Atherton.

Saiag, H. (2011) 'Les pratiques financières des milieux populaires de Rosario (Argentine) au à l'aune du démantèlement du rapport salarial fordiste', *Revue Française de Socio-économie* 2011/2(8): 9–30.

Servet, J.-M, (1976) 'Des ethnies aux paysanneries noires (insertion de l'agriculture africaine sub-saharienne dans le marché mondial et genèse des paysanneries noires', *Cahier AEH* (9):141–99.

Servet, J.-M. (1996) 'Community relations, individual, social and economic constraints in the saving and loans associations', in M Cangiani (ed.) *The Milano Paper*, Montréal and London: Black Rose Books.

Servet, J.-M. (2006) *Banquiers aux pieds nus: la microfinance*, Paris: Odile Jacob.

Servet, J.-M. (2010a) *Le grand renversement: De la crise au renouveau solidaire*, Paris: Desclée de Brouwer.

Servet, J.-M. (2010b) 'Inadequate growth, exclusion and indebtedness', *New Orleans*, American Anthropologist Association Meeting, Session Flows of Money and Freedom, 17 November.

Servet, J.-M. (2010c) 'Microcredit' in K. Hart, J.-L. Laville and A. D. Cattani (eds) *The Human Economy*, Boston, Cambridge and Oxford: Polity Press, pp. 130–41.

Servet, J.-M, (2011) 'La crise du microcrédit en Andhra Pradesh', *Revue Tiers Monde* 2011/3(207): 43–59.

Servet, J.-M. (2012) 'Genève dans l'empire de la liquidité', in L. Abdelmalki, J. P. Allegret, F. Puech, M. Sadui Jallab and A. Silem (eds) *Développements récents en économie et finances internationals: Mélanges en l'honneur de René Sandretto*, Paris: Armand Colin.

Sociétés contemporaines (2009) 'Vivre et faire vivre à crédit', special issue (76).

Soto, H. de (1989) *The Other Path: The Invisible Revolution in the Third World*, New York: Harper & Row.

Srivastava, R. (2012) 'Changing employment conditions of the Indian workforce and implications for decent work', *Global Labour Journal* 3(1): 63–90.

Vatin, F. (ed.) (2007) *Le salariat: théorie, histoire et forme*, Paris: La Dispute.

Waters, T. (2007) *Life Beneath the Level of the Marketplace*, Plymouth: Lexington books.

Official reports

Dirección de Análisis económico y social, México (2008) 'Resultados de la encuesta de ingresos y gastos de hogares (ENIGH) y estimaciones de pobreza, 2008', in *Nota de analisis: Direccion general adjunta de inteligencia sectorial*.

ILO (2008) 'Global wage report 2008/09', Geneva: International Labour Organization. (available online at: www.ilo.org/wcmsp5/groups/public/--dgreports/--dcomm/documents/publication/wcms_100786.pdf).

ILO (2009) 'Private employment agencies, temporary agencies workers, and their contribution to the labour market', Geneva: International Labour Organization. (available online at: www.ilo.org/wcmsp5/groups/public/--ed_dialogue/--sector/documents/meetingdocument/wcms_162740.pdf).

ILO and IILS (2008) 'World of work report 2008: income inequalities at the age of financial globalization', Geneva: Internatinoal Labour Office and International Institute for Labor Studies (available online at: www.ilo.org/wcmsp5/groups/public/@dgreports/@dcomm/@publ/documents/publication/wcms_100354.pdf).

National Bureau of Statistics, Tanzania (2001) 'Household budget survey: final report', Dar Es Salaam: Natoinal Bureau of Statistics, Tanzania (available online at: www.tanzania.go.tz/hbs/HomePage_HBS.html).

Uganda Bureau of Statistics (2006) 'Uganda national household survey: report on the socio-economic module', Kampala: Uganda Bureau of Statistics.

Newspaper articles

Billington, I. and Roth, T. (2009) 'IMF urges EU to sustain fiscal stimulus,' *Wall Street Journal* 31 July–2 August 2009.

Krugman, P. (2009) 'The big inflation scare' *New York Times* 28 May 2009.

Thaler, R, (2010) 'What the rich don't need' *New York Times* 25 September 2010.

2 Indebted Mexicans in the Californian mortgage crisis

Magdalena Villarreal

Introduction

In July 2007 the unfolding of massive losses in world stock markets was disclosed by the media. Disaster sparked after the revelation of what many knew but preferred to ignore: that certain financial instruments, whose success in markets had been very significant, were based on mortgage loans that would never be paid back. Such instruments, designed by Wall Street finance engineers to satisfy the appetite for risk of millions of investors, had produced juicy profits for many, but were now discovered to be largely backed by thin air. In California, one of the most critical North American states involved in the mortgage crisis, a number of the non-payable loans had been ascribed to African-Americans and immigrant Mexicans.

The mayhem that has followed reveals a great deal concerning the workings of today's financial systems, particularly with regards social and cultural processes involved in calculations. The relevance of non-commoditized transactions in financial spheres and the differential value attributed to goods, property and money show how social, cultural, domestic, ethnic and power relations are part of the economy's constituent elements. These relations may act to mediate and structure financial practices.

The measurement of capital, on the other hand, which most of us take to be a straightforward calculation, is itself fraught with ambiguities and grey areas. For one, the promise of future value is often included as capital. This is considered normal in economic life. As pointed out by Steve Keen (2001, 141–145), the value of a machine – typically regarded as a form of capital – is measured according to price, where future gains to be made with it are included in the calculation. Monetary value, then, is partly based on what the machine is expected to produce. In a similar vein, inasmuch as immigrants in California were expected to earn dollars that would spill over to their kin in their place of origin, their migration enterprise had increased their "worth." And as we already knew, but were made acutely aware of with the mortgage crisis, the value of a house includes reckonings as to whether its price will augment in the future. Expectations regarding increase in value can – according to prevailing circuits of valuation – be counted in as "capital."

Using such reckonings as "equity" to obtain loans – even in cases where there was an initial mortgage on the house that had not been paid off – was not considered too problematic. Calculations were carried out in accordance with market value. The assumption was that once the house was sold, the whole amount could be recovered. But in some instances, this rationality was deemed to be taken too far: such was the case of Enron,[1] for example, where promises of profit appeared in accountancy books as actual profits. This enterprise was chastised, but it appears that these kinds of procedures are not too uncommon. Many such estimates were prevalent in the housing bubble. Borrowing was encouraged under a calculation of profit: the more you lend, the more proceeds you obtain. In simplified terms, one can say that the same arithmetic guided stock market partakers. Promises of profit from debt were sold and re-sold, often in packages, which, as I will explain below, might only include derivatives of the transactions. Such promises were assessed within circuits werein their value was acknowledged as legitimate.

In what follows, I analyze the case of a composite household conformed by Mexican immigrants. The case highlights the dynamic flows of money and social relations that circulate among these immigrants, facilitating but also constraining their everyday economic endeavors. It is important to keep these monetary and social flows and the circuits they inhabit in mind when trying to understand the social and cultural nature of their financial transactions, particularly those related to debt. Despite their similar backgrounds and circumstances, the members of this social group engaged in different financial practices and faced dissimilar conditions in their incursion into the housing market. Only one of the three members who bought houses lost his investment, and one defaulted in some payments but was able to restructure her debt on several occasions, however, all three resorted to "reverse remittances" – money coming from Mexico[2] – in order to meet their payments. This is the focus of the first part of the chapter. The second addresses the build up towards a crisis and its implications. The different circuits of valuation that operate simultaneously in these scenarios become evident. These inform the calculations that serve to evaluate and tackle everyday life predicaments.

Circuits of valuation entail webs of interaction wherein assessments, judgments and expectations concerning the value attributed to goods, property and transactions are formulated and reproduced. All of those involved in such circuits, directly or indirectly, participate in making, repeating or reinterpreting attributed value. This refers us to what Callon (1998) identifies as framing. The market is performed, he says, by calculating agents – including financial experts, brokers, buyers and sellers and economists themselves – who are involved in drawing boundaries between the relations that will be taken into account and which will serve in their calculations and those which will be thrown out of the calculation as such. Economists use the term externalities for those relations that remain outside the frame. Certain ties must be cut in order to disentangle an object or a relation, to "purify" products that are marketed and adjust the relation to a measurable, mathematical equation that can be subject to prediction.

In this case we are speaking of different frameworks of calculation that co-exist and interrelate in the definition of value equivalences. Although such equivalences tend to be represented in monetary terms, money itself does not necessarily function as a standard measure of value. What money does do is "delimit the circle of actions between which equivalences can be formulated" (Callon 1998: 21). But by providing the facade of a universal yardstick, we can brush off a number of social and economic relations (generally considered erratic, volatile or subjective) as externalities. However, the relevance of "intangibles" such as knowledge, clientele, image and prestige have come to occupy many pages in management books and are the topic of conferences for entrepreneurs. And as we will see in the case discussed below, issues such as ethnicity, gender and race constitute critical categories involved in the process of framing.

That I am here focusing on calculations is not to imply in any way that people always calculate their options explicitly in order to reach a better decision as would be suggested by rational choice theory. Calculations, as dealt with here, are often an a posteriori exercise in evaluation, and most frequently taken for granted assumptions, such as suggested by Bourdieu's notion of "*doxa.*"

One of the issues I want to highlight is that the identification of what can become a valuable asset, precisions regarding how valuable it is, and explanations concerning how today's value is related to what is expected for tomorrow are not easily addressed with numbers. Frameworks of calculation entail certain notions of promise, reliability, hazard and risk. These acquire particular relevance in volatile markets, often sought after by investors because variations provide the opportunity for good profits. While transactions take place under the understanding that certain financial institutions and market regulators can be trusted, there is an acute awareness that a not-so-calculable amount of risk is entailed. Fear is thus an important component of financial transactions, and parameters are established to curtail hazards. These parameters incorporate classifications as to risk prone categories of people and perilous behaviours. Such classifications necessarily involve social and cultural criteria.

It is in this context that Mexicans and African-Americans (among other categories of people) in the United States were considered "unsafe" clients, and hence not eligible for standard loans. Rather, most of them received "sub-prime" loans, which, according to some sources, could cost five times as much as some of the other "prime" loans. The banks thus "secured" themselves against the risk of default, which, paradoxically, was an important factor in *bringing about* default. Much can be questioned concerning the accounting taking place in the loan defaults, such as why the money banks received as initial payments is left out of calculations, as is that coming from sales of debt packages. But this is not our focus for the moment: enough pages have been written and political discourses made concerning the greed and immoral behavior of many bankers.

As is to be expected, the conclusion that has been arrived at is that order should be enforced: the financial system must be better regulated and seriously monitored. This is all very reasonable, but what interests us for the purpose of the present discussion – and this is the second issue I want to highlight – is that such order is conceived according to understandings and interpretations prevailing within particular circuits of valuation, comprised by a predominant – yet not always explicit – set of unquestioned conventions and assessments that provide some kind of form and format to financial transactions. This is manifest in the way of platforms from which to speak truths, the angle from which the economy and those participating in it are to be judged and analyzed. Circuits of valuation are articulated and framed in people's everyday financial practices.

What is to be perceived as risky, what is promising, what can be appraised as reliable, are assessed – often following elaborate studies – according to specific formulas that, however technical, cannot avoid reliance on social and cultural criteria wherein certain beliefs, assumptions, classifications and regulations make sense.[3] Here certain hierarchies are acknowledged, portraying sequences of priorities: what is most relevant and is to be taken into consideration in a calculation and what is "coincidental noise" and is to be excluded. Unquestioned conventions – here including, for example, the mechanisms by which certain social groups are judged untrustworthy – are often borrowed from, and yet influence, other arenas of social life. In the process, scope for calculation is formatted.

I speak of circuits of calculation to stress the fluid nature of such criteria of valuation. Assessments vary in tune with circumstances and events, often following interaction with other circuits of valuation within particular domains. Certain codes and interpretations acquire significance in such interaction. Here it is important to underline the relevance of what have been identified as dominant discourses. Values portrayed within such discourses tend to be considered set, immovable. Inasmuch as such values are replicated without questioning, their permanence and stability are largely assured. But it is also important to acknowledge that dominant discourses are pushed forward and sustained in a constant struggle to maintain legitimacy. Processes of valuation, then, are fed, nourished and recreated within these circuits.

It is thus quite impossible to pin down and spell out precise boundaries and frameworks of calculation. The structure is forever experiencing shifts. Its boundaries are porous and fluctuating. What we can more clearly observe are processes of *framing* and *structuring*. We see social actors busy building frames, defining boundaries and negotiating definitions to conform to such frames. Actors are not free to impose or change frames, being as they are produced in social interaction. They can, however, rework meanings and interpretations to a degree, in such a way as to influence the process of framing. Thus, what is of interest to us is not so much to list or classify the boundaries and the frames, but to come to an understanding of the processes by which they are assigned and operated. The notion of circuits of valuation is useful as a heuristic device to name the dynamic flows wherein processes of plotting meanings to frames and structures takes place.

For example, depending on our angle of observation, the financial system can be perceived as conforming to one fixed structure framed by capitalistic money making goals. Yet, as we will see below, while making money is a clear aim of most of the actors participating, the frameworks of calculation are differentially mapped, in such a way that priorities, hierarchies and meanings are diverse, as are norms (particularly of the non-explicit kind). Agricultural producers, politicians, investors and farm labourers participating in financial markets will probably weigh and calculate transactions according to different sets of values and interpretations, even when following the same sets of rules and procedures. But one and the same actor might resort to different circuits of valuation within diverse scenarios, thus articulating variegated frames to make sense of the processes at play.

Circuits of valuation interacting in financial markets entail distinct processes of negotiation of identities and boundaries. Social positioning –including gender, race, generation and national considerations – differentially affects people's scope for calculation. Here we resort to the notion of calculability introduced by Callon (1998). The notion of calculability allows us to take into account the margins within which people are able to conceive and concoct calculations, to look into the socially constructed boundaries within which they construe significations and the tools they are able to draw upon in so doing. Many of the relations entailed – which might not be strictly defined as capitalist – mediate and structure monetary processes.

In this light, the very definition and classification of debt can vary within and between these different circuits of valuation and frameworks of calculation. Debt can, in some scenarios, be calculated as a liability, and in others, as an asset.[4] This is the focus of this chapter. Through the case of Mexicans caught up in the mortgage crisis, my aim is to examine the workings of frameworks wherein people – and institutions – articulate social, cultural and political factors to signify and weigh their financial options and those of others. Circuits of valuation feeding such frameworks can, as we shall see, reach out to international dimensions and do not necessarily entail direct interaction.

Eva and her "composite family": intertwined economies

In their everyday lives, Mexican women that have migrated to the United States juggle with multiple economies that cross different kinds of boundaries, including national ones. Such is the case of Eva, a woman who struggles to organize her life in California, but whose livelihood is still very much tied to Mexico. Unlike many other Mexicans, Eva was not under a great deal of economic strain when she crossed the Mexico–US border. She did, however, hold great expectations of finding new opportunities to make money.

In the early eighties her father owned a small bookshop in Mexico City and he financed her trip to Tijuana, in northern Mexico, where she was to live with her godmother. Eva worked for two years as receptionist in her godmother's hotel, which, located very close to the international border, served as point of encounter between migrants and *coyotes*.[5] It was here that Eva met her now husband, who was from the state of Jalisco, in Western Mexico, but had lived in the United States for ten years.

In the mid eighties she crossed the border to California with her husband. Here their economy was closely tied to family and regional ties in Mexico. Eva speaks of two phases of her life: when she was a "princess" (*sic*) in Mexico, and her married life in the United States. The latter she subdivides in two: when she did not have a house and worked in the fields and now that she has one and lives in fear of losing it.

After they married, Eva and her husband came to form part of what I am labeling a "composite household," very common among Mexican immigrants to the United States, who crowd together in a single house in order to share expenses – particularly rent – and save money. This "household" was composed of:

- Eva and her husband
- Eva's husband's sister, Violeta
- Violeta's ex-husband's sister, Enriqueta
- Enriqueta's family, comprising:

  - her husband René
  - her three children and
  - her niece, daughter of a sister who had died
  - Enriqueta's brother Julián

- In addition, there was Ernesto, a friend from Violeta's community of origin.

In total there were two couples, four children, a woman who had left her daughter and son with her mother-in-law in Mexico, a single man and another man who had left his wife and children in Mexico.

The group changed residence and composition on several occasions, following work. At times they all lived in a two-bedroom house, at other times they separated, some living in labor camps and others sleeping in their cars. On occasions someone else joined them – Rene's mother and brother, Ernesto's wife, Violeta's nephew, etc. – and at times some of them joined other groups.

They first lived in Santa Maria, a town located north of Los Angeles that hosted a number of large producers, as well as worker families from four Mexican states: Michoacán, Guerrero, Jalisco and Guanajuato. Santa Maria had grown demographically due to the arrival of workers – mostly Mexican – who came to the United States in search of work, although, unlike other rural towns in Central California, Santa Maria still hosted an important percentage of the Anglo population. The largest producers in the area came from this sector. Initially Eva and her husband found accommodation in certain segregated sections of the small city. But later they came to dwell close to the centre.[6]

They worked in the agricultural fields: first, picking strawberries in central California's coast, and when the season was over, they would move north to pick apples in Oregon. It goes without saying that in this type of work, they had no contract and no benefits. They were remunerated on the basis of daily work. They shared a house, bought groceries together and solved the issue of transportation as a group. Here René, who had lived longest in the United States and had bought a car, obtained extra income, charging the rest for the rides to work. Although it was not cheap, they did not complain. It was an expense that they had to cover, be it paying him or someone else.

In this context, the members of the group were faced with the need to juggle different financial scenarios, each of which had its own rules, meanings and values following non-explicit economic criteria that had everything to do with social life. On the one hand, the stated purpose of their hard work and sacrifices was to earn money for their families in Mexico. Except for Eva, all of the adult members sent money home at one point or another, but obligations were as much social as they were monetary. They had to show that they cared for their kin in the community of origin. Family back home required following certain rules and complying with gender roles. This included the responsibility of looking after the family, especially if they were doing well financially. Since in local codes it would be considered disgraceful to show themselves as poor – it was as if they had failed in their big migration enterprise – they were obliged to send money for the family. The latter were classified as "poor" and "needy" even though this was sometimes far from the case. The amounts of money sent, the periodicity and the ways in which they were remitted were estimated within these frameworks. Only Ernesto sent money home systematically, but never enough to cover his family's expenses. His wife worked in the agricultural fields in Mexico to make sure their two children were fed.

But all of them complied with specific requirements from family back home: money to take grandma to the doctor, to buy shoes for the kids, to pay community fees and ensure land ownership, etc. They were also expected to follow social and cultural norms, such as proper behavior as a wife, mother, brother or sister, both to relatives in the United States and in Mexico. Even though Violeta had separated from her husband – Enriqueta's brother – her relation to men was closely observed, not only by her ex-sister-in-law, but by her own family and friends, whose gossip could quickly travel. And if Enriqueta spent too much money on clothes, or her husband bought a car, it would be known back home, where they were expecting her to contribute more towards her mother's health bills, and if possible, help her sister, whose husband had suffered an accident. Such gender and other norms thus imposed certain restrictions as to the use of time and the kinds of spending that would be considered adequate.

On the other hand, the group dynamics had to be tended to. Some, like Ernesto, the most recent member of the group, found it difficult to share in on the costs. He was desperate to earn as much money as he could before returning to Mexico. This created certain tensions within the group, where, in addition to groceries, soap and the like, he was sometimes expected to share (and once in a while pay for) a beer or some other small "luxury" with the rest.

Enriqueta and her husband provided critical information as to work opportunities and contacts. It was in this scenario that the group formulated (or reformulated) frameworks of calculation and norms of exchange. Through such networks Mexicans learn the ropes of social and financial life in the US.

And Eva's husband was the only member of the group who had his documents in order, having been awarded the status of "resident" (although this category does not entail the same rights as citizenship, it does signify that he is legally in the country). Enriqueta's boys had been born in the US, but her niece was still "illegal," as were most of the household members. Thus, Eva helped her husband open a bank account. She could not open one in her own name but she was quick to learn the procedures and quite skillful at filling in paperwork. The account was useful for all to cash checks, which, for most immigrants, was a very difficult task. They were often forced to go to local shops or small supermarkets to cash their checks for a fee.[7]

Juggling with diverse economic scenarios is part of everyday life. But actors are differentially positioned within such scenarios, and the positioning affects their scope for calculation. For example, their positioning as illegal immigrants restricted some of the composite family members' calculation of risk, to the degree that certain enterprises that could have been viable were not even considered.

Paradoxically, in the agricultural fields – where most of the adult members of the family worked during their first years in the United States – it was frequently Mexicans who took on the riskier stages of agricultural production. Hazards such as climate and market prices make agricultural production a dicey enterprise, and companies were careful to circumvent the most risk prone segments of the farming enterprise, often by resorting to different forms of sharecropping with Mexicans seeking to have a go at the American dream. In addition to profits from cooling, packing and marketing, investors could benefit from tax write-offs awarded to agriculture.

Buying a house: the American dream and the debt economy

For the vast majority of Mexicans in California, buying a house was not initially on the agenda. The aim was to work hard, earn money and return home. This has been very much in line with agricultural employer's interests, who tended to want a constant renewal of strong, young labor. However, prime quality agricultural products cultivated in California require a great deal of skill as well. With new technology, lands yield three crops a year. Good workers are hired year round by the same company, thus encouraging a more permanent settlement of migrants.[8] On the other hand, from the point of view of the immigrants, the expected "fortune" that they will bring home is hard to get. And it is quite humiliating to return as they say, "with empty hands." Hence, years go by with the expectation that it will get better. With time, children grow into the American way of life, and it becomes more cumbersome to leave.

It is thus difficult to establish with precision when the decision to buy a house is taken, but the first step appears to be acquiring a small trailer, which they park in friends' or relative's gardens. This is what Eva and her husband did. When Eva discovered she was pregnant, she insisted they move out of the composite household. They bought a small trailer, which was placed in the garden of the house they were living in. In this way they had some independence, but still had the support of the household members. The trailer was bought with a loan that Eva obtained from her godmother in Mexico. Such loans were often, as Eva smilingly labeled them, "government loans," meaning that she might or might not pay them back. She said that her godmother never charged interest and almost always told her to keep the money. Her godmother also lent them money so that Eva's husband could buy tools and work as a builder, making repairs and additions to houses. The problem was that, although her husband was good in this job, and was also "legal" in the United States, he could not register himself as a builder because he had only studied up to third grade in Mexico. One of the requirements for registration was training, and for that he needed some background education and English. And it was difficult to work without being registered. He feared that if he were to be caught without a registration, his immigration documents could also be taken away from him. Hence, although he worked all day fixing houses and was able to buy a truck to transport construction material, he worked "on the black" and he had to charge much below market standards.

In the early nineties Enriqueta and her husband were offered the possibility of buying a house. Because their level of income did not allow them to qualify for a loan, they bought the house together with her brother (Julián), and her brother-in-law. Co-ownership was, at the time, very common amongst Mexican immigrants. Joining their names meant adding their income, so they were able to meet the criteria to qualify for a loan. Although at the time real estate agents and bank officers were not nearly as aggressive in offering loans as they would become a decade later, immigrants were encouraged to bypass certain restrictions, as long as they had enough money for the down payment.

In this case, a *compadre* (fictive kin) from Mexico lent them money to cover this. Although this would not, strictly speaking, qualify as reverse remittance, it is important to note that they did not pay interest rates on this. Like in many such transnational transactions, the expectation was that the relationship would be kept strong. This did not only call for simple reciprocity – that included, of course, the *compadre's* family – but also required the upkeep of networks, and, as mentioned above, the need to follow certain social norms and behavior. Such norms and behavior were quite different to those expected of them within a banking scenario. Whilst trust and loyalty were expected in both cases, the meanings and values underlying such notions varied. The interpretations under which such transactions were formulated, were quite different.

At the beginning Enriqueta, her husband, her sons and niece, Violeta, Julián, René's brother and his mother all lived in this house. They helped with the payments, Violeta in the form of rent. With much sacrifice – tying their tripe, as they say, but also doubling work time – Enriqueta and René were able to save enough money to pay out the other two co-owners and continue making the monthly payments themselves. But more than 15 years later, they continue renting out part of the house to cover these expenses. In their calculations, however, this is still much better than having to pay rent. This house – and the one they managed to build in Mexico (which is uninhabited other than the short weeks they visit every two years) – is the only inheritance they will leave their offspring.

Julián, on the other hand, landed himself a very good job in a broccoli farm. His responsibility was to manage the farm, including taking charge of machinery, organizing production and overseeing labor. He married and was soon able to buy a house on his own. His steady job and relatively good income allowed him to qualify for a loan. In 2004, he was still paying for his house, which had increased significantly in value, when a consultant, who often came to the farm and had become his friend, advised him to use the equity of the house to acquire a loan. Having wanted to start a business of his own for some time, he obtained a loan to buy two lorries. This was not difficult, since offers had been practically thrust in his face for some time now. But, although considering his credit history and his income he would have qualified for a standard loan, he received a sub-prime loan. Julián believes it was due to his nationality, but he also explains that he was not very familiar with financial institutions and was not able to formulate many questions.

Four years later his business had not picked up and the value of the house had plummeted. He was forced to sell his deceased father's land in Mexico. This created problems with his siblings, who were deeply disappointed to see their family patrimony change hands. Their father had struggled for many years for that land, and he would have liked to see it continue producing. Although being the youngest, Julián could legally dispose of the land, they objected to his cold calculations and lack of consideration for their mother, who was still alive and could benefit from renting out the land. At least, they said, she could eat a papaya or two from it. To make matters worse, the money Julián obtained from the land was not enough. He sold the house and relocated to Arizona, where he and his family moved in with his brother, and are still struggling to pay the debts. His brother later transferred to Cancun, Mexico, and sometimes sends money to help out with the payments. Here again, we find reverse remittances and different financial formulations at play.

Eva, on the other hand, had always dreamed of a new house. She believed passionately in the American dream and considered their difficulties to be transitory. In 2003, she came across a friend who was a real estate agent and who convinced her that she could buy a house. Her friend did not take her to low-income housing, but instead they visited a middle-range but quite elegant-looking residence in San Isidro, close to the Mexican border. Eva says she immediately fell in love with the house, but she hesitated, thinking it would be way beyond her means. The real estate agent, a Mexican American herself who had struggled to acquire training in this profession, convinced her that only by taking risks would she be able to achieve the American dream.

Eva decided that she would buy the house. The next step was to convince her husband. Knowing that he would disapprove, she carried out all the paperwork herself, and only informed him once the documents were ready. She narrates how she took him to the house, where the real estate agent was already waiting, and said: "this is ours, the documents are ready, you have no option but to sign." And he did. Eva proudly insists that they finally have the house they deserve: a house worthy of a princess.

At the time she did not know it, but the loan she obtained was more expensive than normal loans. As in the case of Julián, it was a sub-prime loan, given out to people that are not considered fully trustworthy, such as Latinos and African-Americans. For the first two years, the interest rates were quite low. This, of course, was the case with most of the sub-prime loans. In this initial period, they were not paying towards "the principal."

In order to meet payments, Eva rented out two rooms. Violeta, her sister-in-law, lived in the garage and another couple occupied one of the bedrooms. The value of the house increased, and with the equity, Eva managed to obtain another loan to buy a vehicle.

But her boarders left following work. Eva and her family stayed behind, even though their sources of income were still unstable. But now they could not migrate north to follow work. Like many other Mexican families in their situation, they were tied to the new house. To make matters more difficult, Eva's daughter got pregnant at 17 and her boyfriend moved in. The couple now have two children, Eva's daughter works in Walmart and her partner sometimes finds jobs as a gardener. Eva has struggled enormously to make payments, which sometimes amount to more than their volatile income. They have restructured their debt on two occasions and she has once again taken loans from her god-mother in Mexico. Even Violeta has pitched in to help her brother and sister-in-law meet payments.

The mortgage bubble and the crisis

The mortgage bubble encouraged construction companies to build numerous new houses, particularly in small cities where they could obtain land at reasonable prices. There was an abundance of Mexican labor and there were roads to allow commuters easy access to big cities. The increase in the supply of housing led to the opening of the market to sectors of the population that had previously been excluded because they were considered risky, including, as I mentioned above, the African-American and Latino population.

At the beginning, it was a win–win situation for all: real estate agents, banks, construction companies and Mexican migrants contracted as masons or to install roofing. Remittances to Mexico were also high at this time. Amongst Mexicans, the American dream was advocated by realtors and banks who offered low interest rates in the first two years, but were unclear about the fact that after that, the amounts to be paid would increase. They did not inform their clients of commissions that would appear on their bills. They convinced their clients that the American dream could only be obtained by taking risks.

The juiciest businesses were not the lenders, construction companies and real estate agents, but the chain of investors involved in the debt swaps. Mortgage debts, as we know, do not remain in the bank that provides the loan. They are transferred to third parties, who are willing to take on the risk, betting on the possibility of obtaining larger gain. They buy debt in packages, among which – they may or may not be aware – there will be some un-payable debts. But that is not too important, since they will resell them or use them as collateral to finance other businesses. Those acquiring the packages often obtained exponential monetary gains. To complicate the scenario even more, some enterprises created innovative financial products called Collateralized Debt Obligations (CDO), within which only portions of diverse mortgage instruments are combined, recurring to new techniques in the calculation of risk. In 2006, the market was flooded with such instruments, which comprised almost $500,000 million.

It is hard to believe that thousands of millions of dollars were generated on the basis of debt. This is because, in everyday life, we tend to think of debt as a deficit. But debt also entails hope and expectations of (generally increased) payment. This is why debt (mortgage loans) was used as collateral to obtain loans (stock exchange instruments based on mortgages). The chain was sustained by an expectation of gain, as well as by a belief that the chain of payments was secure, that it would not break, being, as it was, in the hands of "trustworthy" institutions. And it would not break while enough investors with appetite for risk would continue betting on its strength.

But investors also knew that participants in the stock market could enter into panic, and it was important to be the first to run as soon as there was any indication of fluster. By then, job cuts in a great number of North American industries were taking place – in part due to the increases in the price of petroleum, Asian competition and the lower cost of labor in Third World countries, as well as losses in the agricultural sector due to climate change – producing greater instability in sources of employment. With this, the number of defaulting loan bearers was on the increase. It was then that many Mexicans found out that their adjustable-rate mortgages had been augmented, and that, in addition to payment of the loan and interests, they owed banks another series of charges, including exaggerated bills for consultations with "experts," legal assistance, and even sending a document via fax. The cases of bankruptcy were increasing, and with them, the number of people that were losing their homes.

Many, particularly Latinos and African-Americans, found themselves in a situation where it was impossible to continue meeting their payments. In this process, racial differentiation played an important role. This is because loans to Mexican population (or, for this case Latinos and African-Americans) were considered to be high risk. Hence they were mostly endowed sub-prime loans, which at times were five times more expensive than normal loans. The mortgage rates were adjustable, established to increase in the second or third year. To enroll them in a credit scheme, they were promised low rates for the first years, without informing them that these would increase later.

In California, the prices of houses increased by 51 percent between the end of 2003 and mid 2006. The increase in value created an equity buffer that loan beneficiaries could use to refinance their mortgages when the shock of payment exceeded their possibilities of pay. A study carried out by the Consumers

Federation in America, in January 2008, reports that more than a third of those that obtained loans to buy a house in California also used a second loan based on the first mortgage.[9]

Another study from the *Wall Street Journal* (2007) found that, at the national level, 61 percent of borrowers that obtained sub-prime loans would actually have been entitled to normal loans if their credit history had been taken into account.[10] And both the analysis of the Federal Reserve and a study of the Center for Responsible Lending claim that the high costs charged on such loans were not justifiable.[11] They suggest that, in many cases, such high costs were ascribed out of racial discrimination. Higher interest sub-prime loans were attributed to Latinos, African-Americans, and, in some regions, Asians when compared to Anglo-American loan recipients. ACORN reports that, in California, 55.3 percent of African-American borrowers and 46.6 percent of Hispanics received sub-prime loans vis-à-vis 20.4 percent of "white" borrowers. Twice as many Hispanics resorted to refinance sub-prime loans than did North American "whites".

Between November 2006 and the same month in 2007, the prices of houses in California fell between 12 and 20 percent, according to the zone and the type of house. With the "cooling of the market," borrowers that had resorted to second loans based on the equity of their homes found themselves with debts larger than the value of their properties. Few could sell or refinance their homes. Later efforts from the mortgage industry to modify the loans were clearly insufficient.

As the situation began to be made public, panic took over Wall Street, with, as we know, the consequent bankruptcy of a number of large and many small enterprises. Thousands of millions of dollars evaporated in a few weeks, not only those belonging to large investors, but those of innumerable small debtors, among them a significant number of Mexicans.

At least in the initial stages, government efforts to steady the economy were oriented, not so much to mend errors as to recover the trust of investors and increase money in circulation to encourage consumption.

Juggling over-indebtedness

The financial crisis discloses a series of mechanisms through which value is attributed and equivalences established in financial markets. A virtual economy is revealed, where wealth appears and disappears as if by magic. We are experiencing an economy that is constructed on quicksands, wherein social relations and trust play a fundamental role.

For Mexicans that have migrated to California, however, it does not feel so virtual. Construction workers are forced to find jobs elsewhere. Some are employed as car mechanics, waiters or gardeners, but many return to agricultural labor, where climate change is also affecting their work options. Freezes, flooding and fires have affected this sector, which was already receiving a significant amount of migrants. Jobs have not been easy to find.

A relatively small percentage of Mexicans got involved in real estate, but many acquired goods on credit in furniture shops and local businesses, and a significant number of them now work with credit and debit cards, although this is difficult for the undocumented. But all interact everyday with the direct and indirect effects of these bizarre financial systems, which neatly dovetail with the kinds of structuration they encounter – and contribute to reproduce – in the agricultural fields where they work, with the forms of consumption, payment and tributary systems. It also dovetails with other economies, which one can label Third World or backward, but which also sustain the trans-local financial scaffolding within which they operate.

On the other hand, exponential increase of remittances to Mexico, seen in previous years, has suffered sharp decrease. Part of this can be explained by the expectations surrounding political discussions on the possibility of a new amnesty for illegal immigrants. Mexicans in California began to save to pay intermediaries offering to help them get the coveted documents that would make them legal. This entailed a reduction in the amount of remittances sent home. Moreover, a large percentage of Mexican immigrants worked in the construction sector, which was badly affected by the crisis. Mexicans who lost their houses and the money invested in them also were curtailed in their possibilities of continuing to remit, although it should be said that, in many cases, the reduction in remittances began the moment they started using their savings to pay their loans.

Enriqueta's mother died in 2004, so she no longer sends money, but she has also stopped sending funds to the upkeep of her house in the small Mexican village where she used to live. Violeta has not found it easy to land a job, but does not want to return to Mexico, where she finds it very difficult to maintain her customary level of expenditure.

For the lay reader, all of those who lost their houses in the mortgage crisis were over-indebted. And those, like Eva and Enriqueta, who spend more than 30 percent of their income to pay debts, would perhaps also be in that category.

However, Enriqueta has not for a moment doubted that the efforts they have made towards paying their home are very much worth it. Although, in the village in Mexico, she could have obtained a larger house with a garden, she has established her life in the United States. Like others who would probably not meet the official criteria to qualify for loans, she takes money from here and there, works extra hours, makes tamales to sell to friends and has moved to one bedroom with her husband (now that her children have married out) renting the other rooms to different Mexicans that come to California seeking work. She feels supported by her network in the Evangelical Church, to which she has become a devotee. She talks about the difficulties entailed in paying, but does not feel over-indebted.

While Eva does know that she owes beyond her means, she also does not regret having acquired a loan, and does not feel the door has closed on her. She will keep struggling. She cannot at this moment rent out rooms, because she only has one available since her daughter is living in one room with her husband and child, and another is used by her son. She prefers to leave the empty one for when her godmother comes to visit from Mexico, since she constantly resorts to her for loans. She has also had to ask for loans from her father and has twice restructured her debt. Her conviction of deserving a better life for herself and her family gives her energy to keep going. Fortunately she also found a job in Walmart, and her husband has managed to get small contracts here and there because people need to repair their houses and cannot afford established constructors. But reflecting on her situation, Eva comments that, although the aim of women who migrate is not to become millionaires, they did seek to leave poverty behind. They thought that by migrating "north" they would find progress, but here they face many difficulties. However, she has great faith in the possibilities of making a better life in the US.

Ironically, Julián – the only member of the group that really met the criteria to qualify for a loan (except perhaps that of his national identity) – was the one who defaulted. The entrepreneurial "rationality" he had learned in his work in the broccoli farm, and the advice of a professional, led him to take on a large business risk. But like the rest, he was forced to resort to his networks in Mexico and he sold his family's land to try and overcome the situation.

Both Eva and Violeta have resorted to networks to keep their homes, particularly in the way of "reverse remittances" from Mexico. They have taken on loans from friends and family, most of which they have not repaid and some of which they might not be able to repay. Violeta, Enriqueta, Julián and Enrique have also received "subsidies" in the way of un-remunerated care for their close relatives, i.e., children, wife and mother. This shows the pluri-dimensionality of flows that are not only directed from the US to Mexico but also from Mexico to the US. With these, there also flow constraints that are activated in the different grammars of transnational economic interaction. Such is, as we have detailed above, the case of gender.

Networks that cross national boundaries also constitute spaces wherein migrants learn to manage socially and financially in North American society. Social, cultural and moral parameters reproduced within such networks give form and content to monetary transactions. Hence, gender roles are woven into the tapestry of everyday economy, both in Mexico and the United States. They contribute to processes wherein transactions are signified and weighed, and social relations evaluated. Women are faced with the need to juggle between economies and between cultural calculations that infuse value into financial scenarios in the interaction and interplay of geographies.

However, flows of information are limited within such networks. This is an important factor in forging margins of calculability. Many Mexicans could not negotiate standard loans because they did not have information concerning financial management, and they "fell" into the avaricious games of bankers and intermediaries. Here, predominant cultural calculations in North American society were instrumental. As we have seen, the identity of Latino or African-American entails (the latter might have changed a bit in these last years due to the election of an African-American president) labeling as "not trustworthy" or "risky", which implied elevated costs for borrowers. This shows how, in financial transactions, monetary and non-monetary values and transactions are intertwined. Social fabric comes to form part of the transaction, while at the same time being reconstructed within it. Mexicans' economy in the United States is woven into this in many ways, but is also embedded in other economies, both local and transnational.

And in an economy marked by uncertainty and fear, it is important to take into account the tools people are able to draw upon in making their calculations, and the mechanisms by which information is formatted within certain frameworks to include, exclude, transform, deny or curtail interpretations and understandings.

Notes

1 A Texas based corporation focused on energy that employed 21,000 people before declaring bankruptcy in 2001. Through a series of fraudulent accounting techniques, the enterprise had been ranked as one of the most promising in the United States.
2 I will discuss "reverse remittances" more below. At this stage it is important to mention that these have seldom been taken into consideration in migration studies. An interesting study carried out by the BBVA bank, for example, calculated Mexican expenses in migrants' education before they left the country. They found that, in the period from 1994 to 2008, Mexico transferred, on average, US$6 million per year to the United States, equivalent to half a percentage point of its GIP (BBVA Bancomer (2010)).
3 Financial systems are to a degree constrained by such rules and regulations, but not necessarily determined by them, or at least, not only by them.
4 For example, within a typically capitalist evaluation, it is considered "sound" for enterprises to work with a degree of debt: those who have never worked with loans might be classified as too conservative, not forward looking, and even inefficient. And at the individual level, when soliciting a loan, consumers with good credit history have advantages over consumers who have never engaged in debt.
5 Coyotes help immigrants cross illegally to "the other side" (the US), and can charge as much as US$400 for doing so.
6 As Palerm (2007:10) rightly points out:

> ...today's (migrant) workers do not live in colonies, neighborhoods and yesterday's labor camps. They occupy the nucleus of communities, towns and agricultural cities of California, where they are constituted as the overarching majority of local population. It is as if yesterday's colonies had been recuperated and swallowed whole American villages and cities that previously hosted them as marginalized appendices.

7 It is interesting to note that some shop owners even act as "lenders" to producers, who ask them to please pay check holders, but withhold from cashing the checks themselves until they have enough funds in the account to cover them. Other producers do not pay with checks, which means that this money does not go into their formal accounting system and therefore is not included for taxes and benefits. But undocumented immigrants prefer to get paid in cash, since they will not be able to receive the benefits anyway and they can save on the fee that bank account holders might charge.
8 Palerm (2007); Hernández (2010) pp. 70–83.
9 Black *et al.* (2001).
10 Brooks *et al.* (2007).
11 Bernanke (2006); Gruenstein *et al.* (2006).

References

Arce, Alberto (2003) "Value Contestations in Development Interventions: Community Development and Sustainable Livelihoods Approaches," in *Community Development Journal* 38(3): 199–212.

BBVA Bancomer (2010) *México: Situación Migración,* BBVA Research, November 2010.

Black, Harold, Boehm, Thomas P. and DeGennaro, Ramon P. (2001) "Is There Discrimination in Mortgage Pricing? The Case of Overages," Atlanta: Federal Reserve Bank of Atlanta Working Paper 2001–2004a.

Brooks, Rick and Ruth, Simon (2007) "Subprime Debacle Traps Even Very Credit-Worthy," *Wall Street Journal,* December 3.

Bernanke, B. S. (2006) "Community Development Financial Institutions: Promoting Economic Growth and Opportunity," Remarks to the Opportunity Finance Network's Annual Conference, Washington, DC, November 1.

Bourdieu, Pierre (1994) *Language and Symbolic Power,* Cambridge: Polity Press (first published 1991).

Callon, Michel (ed.) (1998) *The Laws of the Markets,* Oxford: Blackwell Publishers.

De Soto, Hernando (2000) *The Mystery of Capital: Why Capitalism Triumphs in the West and Fails Everywhere Else,* New York: Basic Books.

Folbre, N. (1993) *Who Pays for the Kids? Gender and the Structures of Constraint,* New York and London: Routledge.

Forrester, Viviane (2000) *El Horror Económico,* México: Fondo de Cultura Económica.

Fraad, H., Resnick, S. and Wolff, R. (1994) *Bringing it all Back Home: Class, Gender and Power in the Modern Household,* London: Pluto Press.

Gibson-Graham, J. K. (1996) *The End of Capitalism (As We Knew It) A Feminist Critique of Political Economy,* USA: Blackwell.

Gruenstein, D. B., Ernst, K. S. and Wei Li (2006) "Unfair Lending: The Effect of Race and Ethnicity on the Price of Subprime Mortgages," Center for Responsible Lending, May 31.

Hart, Keith (2001) *Money in an Unequal World,* New York and London: Texere.

Hernández, Romero and Manuel, Adrián (2010) *Estabilización de Trabajadores Agrícolas Migrantes: ¿Base para su plena proletarización?* Mexico: Tesis Doctoral, CIESAS.

Hudson, Mike and Reckard, E. Scott (2005) "More Homeowners with Good Credit Getting Stuck with Higher-Rate Loans," *Los Angeles Times,* October 24.

Keen, Steve (2001) *Debunking Economics: The Naked Emperor of the Social Sciences* Australia: Pluto Press.

Long, Norman (ed.) (1984) *Family and Work in Rural Societies: Perspectives on Non-wage Labour,* London: Tavistock.

Long, Norman and Villarreal, Magdalena (1998) "Small Product, Big Issues: Value Contestations and Cultural Identities in Cross-Border Commodity Networks," *Development and Change* 29(4): 725–750.

Long, Norman and Villarreal, Magdalena (2004) "Redes de deudas y Compromisos: La Trascendencia del Dinero y las Divisas Sociales en las Cadenas Mercantiles," en Villarreal, Magdalena (ed.) *Antropología de la Deuda: Crédito, Ahorro, Fiado y Prestado en las Finanzas Cotidianas,* México, D.F.: Ciesas, Porrúa y La Cámara de Diputados, pp. 27–56.

Palerm, Juan Vicente (2007) "De Colonias a Comunidades. La evolución de los asentamientos mexicanos en California Rural," Ponencia presentada en el Coloquio sobre migración y movilidad laboral, celebrado el 14 y 15 de junio en UNAM, México DF.

Polanyi, Karl (2001) [1944] *The Great Transformation: The Political and Economic Origins of Our Time,* Boston: Beacon Press.

Reich, Robert (1993) *L'èconomie Mondialisèe,* Paris: Dunod.

Sen, Amartya (1981) *Poverty and Famines: An Essay on Entitlement and Deprivation*, Clarendon Press: Oxford.

Sen, Amartya (1984) *Resources, Values and Development*, Basil Blackwell: Oxford.

Soros, George (1999) *La Crisis del Capitalismo Global: La Sociedad Abierta en Peligro*, México: Plaza y Janés.

Sraffa, P. (1960) *Production of Commodities by Means of Commodities: Prelude to a Critique of Political Economy*, Cambridge: Cambridge University Press.

Tinker, Irene (1995) "The Human Economy of Microentrepreneurs," in Dignard, Louise and Havet, Jose: *Women in Micro- and Small-Scale Enterprise Development*, London: Westview.

Touraine, Alain (1984) *El Regreso del Actor*, Buenos Aires: Eudeba.

Valencia Lomelí, Enrique and Aguirre, R. R. (1998) "Discursos, Acciones y Controversias de la Política Gubernamental Frente a la Pobreza," en *Los Rostros de la Pobreza: El Debate*, ITESO y la Universidad Iberoamericana, México DF: Tomo I.

Villarreal, Magdalena (1994) *Wielding and Yielding: Power, Subordination and Gender Identity in the Context of a Mexican Development Project*, The Netherlands: Wageningen Agricultural University.

Villarreal, Magdalena (2000) "La Reinvención de las Mujeres y el Poder en los Procesos de Desarrollo Rural Planeado," en *Revista de Estudios de Género La Ventana*, Numero 11, Universidad de Guadalajara.

Villarreal, Magdalena (2004a) *Antropología de la Deuda: Crédito, Ahorro, Fiado y Prestado en las Finanzas Cotidianas.* México, DF: Ciesas, Porrúa y Cámara de Diputados.

Villarreal, Magdalena (2004b) "Striving to Make Capital do Economic Things for the Impoverished: On the issue of Capitalization in Rural Microenterprises," in Kontinen, Tiina (ed.) *Development Intervention: Actor and Activity Perspectives*, Finland: University of Helsinki.

Viola, A. (1999) *Antropología del Desarrollo. Teorías y Estudios Etnográficos en América Latina*, Barcelona: Paidós.

Wallman, S., Buchanan, I. M., Dhooge, Y., Gershuny, J. I., Kosmin, B. A. and Wann, M. (1982) *Living in South London: Perspectives on Battersea 1871–1981*, Aldershot: Grower, for the London School of Economics and Political Science.

Weatherford, Jack (1997) *The History of Money*, New York: Three Rivers Press.

Wilson, Ara (2004) *The Intimate Economies of Bangkok*, Berkeley and Los Angeles: University of California Press.

Wood, G. (1985) *Labelling in Development Policy: Essays in Honour of Bernard Schaffer*, London: Sage Publications.

Zelizer, Viviana (1997) *The Social Meaning of Money*, New Jersey: Princeton.

3 Debt, over-indebtedness and wellbeing

An exploration

Susan Johnson

Introduction

As financial markets develop, so new forms of debt relations emerge. These have a huge range of consequences: from the ability to accumulate resources and improve wellbeing to impoverishment and the associated stress and anxiety, which can lead to the tragedy of suicide. That debt can have such drastic consequences, signals that its dimensions go beyond the financial (or material) and provokes a need to examine it using a broad conception of wellbeing.

Debt relations are multi-dimensional. The material transfers of resources they represent operate within social relationships and have subjective meaning for those involved. Hence, who they are with, what actors and institutions they connect people to (and how they operate within those relationships) alongside how they are perceived: whether they are seen as fair and how they are viewed by others, all matter for whether engagement with them promotes wellbeing or its antithesis – illbeing. These dimensions are critical to understanding when debt becomes 'over'-indebtedness because it is not only the process of material impoverishment that matters but how this interacts with how people experience and perceive their ability to be in the world.

Over the past 20 years, the microfinance sector has institutionalised debt relations in particular ways. In order to become commercially viable, one of its central requirements has been the need to achieve on-time repayment.[1] The means of doing this have involved the social technology of joint liability lending and the need to shift the culture of credit giving NGOs from assisting beneficiaries to becoming MFIs with 'clients'. This evolution has not been unproblematic, and offers an opportunity to examine how different dimensions of wellbeing are affected by these changing debt relations and how the microfinance sector has, in turn, been influenced by these.

In order to do this, the chapter first conceptualises and examines the interaction between the construction of debt relations and people's wellbeing. It approaches this task by drawing together two areas of theory. First, within a Polanyian perspective that markets have to be instituted using specific strategies, it draws on Callon's notion (1998a) of the need for transactions to be 'framed' and adequately 'disentangled' from the complexity of their context in order for them to take place and for market transactions to emerge. As a result, such framing inevitably produces 'overflowing' into other parts of social life because in order to disentangle and create a transaction not all of its dimensions can be managed. Callon suggests that the process of instituting markets therefore involves socio-technical devices through which this is carried out.

Second, I draw on a three-dimensional conceptualisation of wellbeing. This goes beyond the material dimensions of income, assets, shelter and so on, to recognise two further dimensions. First, the role that people's relationships play in their construction of their wellbeing and, analytically, these range from those that are personal to those created by social structures and the power relations these give rise to. Second, people's wellbeing is also created through subjective dimensions of meaning, that is, not just what they can do and be, but also what they think about this. Analytically, this also operates at multiple levels of specific needs, intermediate norms and wider normative contexts of morality and its consequences. It is important to point out that the term 'wellbeing' is not therefore being used here in a normative way and does not imply a positive assessment of debt relations. Rather it points to the dimensions that are important to people in constructing their wellbeing and therefore allows us to analyse where and how these can be under stress or fail to be achieved and result in its converse – illbeing. This approach also helps us to recognise that 'local' understandings of wellbeing interact in different ways with 'universal' understandings, which can create conflict and tensions as processes of development play out.

Using these two theoretical frameworks, I then discuss how the process of instituting debt relations is illuminated by recognising the ways in which these are framed; the consequences of these framings for different dimensions of debt relations; and, given this, the scope for differential consequences and interpretations across contexts. In turn, these interpretations will produce dynamics in which these relationships are constructed and re-constructed in the context of the power relations involved. I then use the theoretical insights this synthesis offers to explore the way in which the microfinance sector has constructed and re-constructed debt relations. Drawing on research primarily in Kenya, but also in Bangladesh, I illustrate how the subjective and relational dimensions of wellbeing have operated in debt relations to influence the way in which the microfinance sector has evolved.

Conceptualising transactions for market development

Institutionalist approaches to markets see them as 'a set of social institutions in which a large number of commodity exchanges of a specific type regularly take place and to some extent are facilitated and structured by those institutions' (Hodgson 1988: 176). Underpinned by the work of Polanyi and his concepts of embeddedness and institutedness, 'man's economy, as a rule, is submerged in his social relationships' (Polanyi 2001: 48). He argues that the formal idea of the market of liberal theory, by contrast, is one that is disembedded in that these social relations are expected to have no influence on economic activity.

Economic sociologists have taken up the theory of embeddedness and re-worked it from what has been criticised as Polanyi's strongly substantivist and hence 'over-socialised' account. Granovetter's notion of embeddedness is one that allows for the interaction of agency and structure and is 'less sweeping than either alternative argument, since networks of social relations penetrate irregularly and in differing degrees in different sectors of economic life, thus allowing for what we already know: distrust, opportunism, and disorder are by no means absent' (Granovetter 1992: 62). But, while Granovetter argues that anthropologists' views of economic action are over-socialised and economists views are under-socialised, part of the question is how they are in fact related (Gudeman 2001).

One approach to conceptualising this interaction is offered by the French economic sociologist Michel Callon. He suggests the need to understand what he calls 'framing' in the construction of market transactions, that is, what is taken into account in the calculation and what is ignored. He accepts the idea of the market as a space of calculation, but not the idea that agents are able to undertake the calculations through which they can optimise. So he is interested in the 'practical arrangements' through which actors calculate (Slater and Tonkiss 2001: 111):

> If calculations are to be performed and completed, the agents and goods involved in these calculations must be disentangled and framed. In short a clear and precise boundary must be drawn between the relations which the agents will take into account and which will serve in their calculations and those which will be thrown out of the calculations as such ... how is the delimiting or framing of relationships at a point in the network achieved?
>
> (Callon 1998b: 16)

Callon demonstrates this issue particularly cogently through a discussion of externalities. For economists, externalities are precisely those aspects of market exchange, connections and relations that agents do not take into account in their calculations. Not only does this notion allow the limitations of the 'market' to be understood but constructing a market therefore involves 'framing' and 'over-flowing' (ibid.: 17). When externalities are internalised they are reframed, but other externalities still exist and it is impossible to bring everything into the calculation – there is always "overflowing". This helps us to see the "investments that have to be made in order to make relations visible and calculable in the network" (ibid.: 17). It requires that agents and goods are framed and that there are operations through which this is in fact achieved, which themselves require investments. It is through these processes that a market is actually constructed although complete framing is never possible. Callon therefore concludes that, in order to:

> construct a market transaction, that is to say, to transform something into a commodity, and two agents into a seller and a consumer, it is necessary to

cut the ties between the thing and the other object or human beings one by one. It must be decontextualised, dissociated and detached.... If the thing remains entangled, the one who receives it is never quit and cannot escape from the web of relations. The framing is never over. The debt (*sic*) cannot be settled.

(Ibid.: 19)

The work of economic sociologists and anthropologists is useful in understanding these 'entanglements' and how processes of framing and overflowing operate, in that as soon as something is framed and enters into some kind of calculative sphere, it produces different ways in which it overflows in relation to other things. Callon's notion of framing suggests, then, a dynamic process through which market transactions may be constructed. But he argues that for markets to exist on a wide scale requires that we move beyond looking at over-isolated individuals and look to the environment. He argues that the uncertainties that surround exchanges in the market are dealt with through an underlying 'primitive' reality:

... if agents can calculate their decisions, irrespective of the degree of uncertainty regarding the future it is because they are entangled in a web of relation and connections; they do not have to open up to the world because they contain their world.

(Ibid.: 7–8)

This moves us to the view that markets 'must be articulated through definite social institutions and legal and political strategies' (Slater and Tonkiss 2001: 104). It is therefore through the development of specific and wider sets of institutions – both formal and informal – that transactions are structured.

However, it is necessary to be careful here. While some have suggested that Polanyi saw the development of the market between pre-capitalist societies and advanced economies as an historical process of disembedding markets (Block 2001), this is not the case. Rather, Polanyi took the view that the formal view of a disembedded economy was in fact impossible because it would in turn provoke resistance – what he calls the 'double movement' – in which those whose welfare was threatened by these processes would resist it. This is important because we should not interpret either Polanyi or Callon as suggesting that embeddedness can be fully removed – and that an economy that is disconnected and disentangled from social relations is ultimately achievable. Callon suggests that disembedding requires the 'institution of various practices, knowledges and spaces' (Slater and Tonkiss 2001: 112). These construct transactions that in turn produce overflowing and reframing in other areas, which in turn signal their ongoing embeddedness in social relationships.

Callon develops his concept of 'performativity' out of this perspective to suggest a process of markets being instituted that emphasises the role of the tools of accounting, marketing and economics as in themselves instrumental in the process of framing what is calculated, and hence in instituting the economy more broadly. For him, assumptions regarding the ability of individuals to perform calculations are too strong – he suggests rather that these abilities are part of a collective ability and practice of performing calculations. But collective ability to achieve this does not infer individual mental competence. He argues that some analysts have examined the ways in which different cultural contexts influence this practice of calculation emphasising the social and cultural aspects of it. The idea that different abilities are influenced by culture is strong and used both to explain the emergence of market relations in some contexts, and its non-emergence in others, as due to embeddedness in societies and cultures that do not lend themselves to it. Moreover, he asks, when calculativeness does emerge from what were non-calculative societies, how then can it be explained? How does the 'equipment' for this calculative agency develop? He argues that once something becomes measured (for example, a particular aspect of profit) this in itself changes the behaviour of managers, who will adjust their own modes of calculativeness to attend to the performance of this measure. This he refers to as the way in which these tools actually 'perform the economy' (ibid.: 27). As a result 'there is no need to involve agents who defy the implacable logic of institutional devices and arrangements. Tools are at the heart of this dynamic and are responsible for formatting the calculating agencies' (ibid.: 26). In turn, these tools become linked to the very justification for how action comes about and the discourse around our account of our actions – the manager will explain his actions in relation to the measures of profit and performance.[2]

Callon sees such devices as socio-technical but it is clearly necessary to place them within the wider framework of the political economy of institutional change, as they necessarily involve struggles over power and meaning. The means through which particular devices are institutionalised will be affected by the political and economic power that those utilising them have. Hence, while Callon's 'technology economy' has been critiqued for its lack of political economy (Fine 2003), my focus here is on the idea that transactions require framing rather than necessarily adopting a position on the nature of the economy as solely a problem of asymmetric information (Fine 2003).

This perspective offers an approach to recognising that as markets expand and penetrate into new areas of social life, they involve ongoing processes of framing in order to produce a degree of disentanglement of the exchange from its social context. At the same time, this produces a specific entanglement in the debt relation, and an overflowing of the consequences into other spheres. Callon's argument is that individuals do not have to deal with managing these disentanglements themselves but that tools are produced, which are collective devices that enable certain approaches to disentanglement to be institutionalised.

Wellbeing: an overview

The intellectual endeavour to conceptualise and operationalise notions of wellbeing has a long and erudite lineage reaching back to ancient philosophers, such as Aristotle, and their attempts to define what it means to live well. It has recently become central to policy debates in a number of contexts – in both developed countries such as the UK (Layard 2005) and developing countries such as Bhutan and Thailand. These recent developments have focussed primarily on notions of subjective wellbeing, most frequently defined by indicators of happiness, but more broadly based in positive psychology. The approach on which this paper draws has been influenced by these developments but is broader based in a concern for an interdisciplinary analysis of poverty, inequality and the quality of life in developing countries, which would integrate an understanding of the subjective dimensions of quality of life with existing and broader based approaches to the analysis of poverty and inequality. The approach used here therefore recognises three dimensions which are mutually constituted: material, relational and subjective, and places these within a structuration dynamic highlighting both processes of activity as well as outcomes.

The definition of wellbeing that has been developed by the WED Research Group at Bath is as 'a state of being with others, where human needs are met, where one can act meaningfully to pursue one's goals, and where one enjoys a satisfactory quality of life' (Wellbeing in Developing Countries Research Group 2007). White (2010) presents this at a more intuitive level as 'Doing Well, Feeling Good' and 'Doing Good, Feeling Well'. 'Doing well' conveys the material dimension, while 'feeling good' recognises that perceptions and satisfaction with this is also necessary and it is these dimensions that have been the main focus of many policy definitions to date. The 'doing good' and 'feeling well' dimension, on the other hand, encapsulates the essence of findings from the WED research programme. It recognises the importance of the moral dimension of people's lives in which 'living a good life' was important – a level at which the collective understanding of how the world is, and should be, is recognised and finds its way into individual perceptions. The 'feeling well' aspect both emphasises the aspect of individual health but at the same time 'goes beyond this to a moral sense about feeling at ease with one's place in the world – which is critically associated with how one is in relationship to others' (ibid.: 4).

As a result, this formulation sees wellbeing as the analytical integration of three critical dimensions: the subjective, material and relational – which interact with one another as people pursue their wellbeing (White 2010).[3] In this formulation the traditionally 'objective' aspects of material wellbeing disappear because what is objective differs depending on your point of view – i.e. is socially and culturally constructed. White's view hence emphasises the interconnectedness of material with social and cultural needs rather than seeing the achievement of the material dimension as delinked and independent in meeting 'objective' needs for practical welfare. The subjective dimension focuses on what 'people value and hold to be good' (p. 9) and this can – following Appadurai (2004) – then recognise three levels. First, a 'visible inventory of wants' (White 2010: 6), which represents those that are most usually clearly articulated as specific needs or goals; second, a level of 'intermediate norms', which may not be articulated but may influence and structure the articulated needs because they capture norms and ideas about how these should operate. Finally, a 'higher order normative context', which relates to people's views of how the world should be – the cosmic order regarding life and death, peace and conflict, material and social wellbeing. This allows the subjective dimension to be seen as something more than simply a set of individual idiosyncratic concerns but recognises that these are structured by systems of meaning, which affect the relational and material dimensions themselves. Finally, the relational is vital at both the individual and social structural levels. WED's empirical research confirmed the recurring emphasis of wellbeing as concerned with relationships of family, friends and community (see, e.g. Devine (2007). It also recognises the role of social structure in the way these relationships operate and the outcomes they deliver for particular individuals at particular points in space and time. The critical issue here is the way in which social structure interacts with power relations. This can be understood using Lukes' (2005) three level approach of decision making, agenda setting and preference shaping, to recognise the way particular social differences, such as class, caste, age, gender, ethnicity, religion and so on, affect political processes.

Further, the WED approach situates the way in which wellbeing is constructed as operating in space and time. It works with a Gidden's structuration perspective (McGregor and Kebede 2003) and so understands the construction of wellbeing as a dynamic of both processes and the outcomes that are inseparable and iterate through time (McGregor 2007; White 2010). Material wellbeing as outcomes in terms of income, assets, employment and so on has long been understood to have social status and symbolic dimensions, but this approach also emphasises these dimensions to the process through which economic activity takes place. It also works with a human ontology (Bevan 2007; McGregor 2007) and puts a 'social human being' at its centre; and these human beings relate to others both in the pursuit of their own goals and in society in the pursuit of human goals more generally. Recognising wellbeing as a process rather than an end state emphasises the politics of its negotiation and that this is always done in community in relation to others, which also moves us away from an individualistic interpretation and from methodological individualism.

This Wellbeing framework offers an analytical lens on the interaction of the material, relational and subjective dimensions, which ensures they are treated together. In contrast much discipline-based academic study has the scope to separate out economic, socio-political and cultural elements in studying processes of change. With this background, we now turn to how this multi-dimensional approach to wellbeing, and Callon's ideas of framing, can be brought together to understand the implications of debt relations for wellbeing.

Debt and wellbeing – framing and overflowing

First, Callon's approach suggests that the exchange of money as debt in market relationships requires 'framing'. In order for funds to be received – and then repaid – the transaction has to be understood in a way that enables each party to 'disentangle' the funds and the nature of the transaction sufficiently from the context in which it is happening. The complexities of borrowing and repaying between friends or family members well illustrate the multi-dimensional character of debt relations and how the material is bound up with social relations and meaning, such that these are completely entangled. Funds may be given as a loan but the repayment date is flexible and it is very hard to demand repayment if the borrower's circumstances are difficult. The borrower may feel obliged in other ways to the lender and the loan changes the dynamics of the relationship, creating obligations in their social interactions that were not felt before. This helps to see how it is possible for market transactions to occur that centre on the financial dimension. Such entanglements need to be limited and managed.

Second, the wellbeing approach allows us to see that the dimensions of entanglement, that have to be framed for each party to have a similar understanding of it, are in multiple dimensions and multiple levels. They concern both the material implications of the exchange and the elements of subjective meaning that these entail, alongside how these interact with the relationship with the person lending or borrowing the funds. As indicated in the discussion of wellbeing above, this leads us to examine the consequences not only for material outcomes (i.e. whether someone is able to repay) but how the debt relates to the three levels of meaning: visible wants; intermediate norms; and 'cosmic consequences' at a higher normative level. Further, how it has an impact on relationships, whether those of family, friends and community, or at the level of social structure and power relations, as all of these can have consequences for the parties involved.

Third, and as a result, it is necessary that the 'framing' of the exchange is understood similarly by each party. The elements of this 'framing' must be able to deal effectively with the entanglements each party may face (with others as well as each other). In particular, if these parties are not operating within the same social and cultural context, there is scope for different understandings to exist of how the relationship is being framed. This would seem to be particularly pertinent in the context where new forms of financial service provider enter an area, for example, microfinance institutions or even banks. Their approaches to the framing of a debt relationship derive from perspectives and cultural contexts that may not be interpreted similarly by local people.

As markets develop and financial service providers extend their services into new areas, this suggests that processes of debt creation will involve encounters between different frames of meaning and different relationships involved in social structure and power relations, which will have consequences for wellbeing. These financial service providers may bring their understandings of the nature of debt relations embedded in the devices of profit and loss and portfolio at risk. These can be understood as the 'universal' concepts around which the financial service sector is structured. They are concepts that, in turn, 'perform' the financial services sector as the mechanisms through which the performance of lenders is measured. The concepts that come with them, such as compound interest and default, may then come into tension and conflict with 'local' understandings of debt relations.

'Over'-indebtedness is not then simply about an inability to pay, but concerns the tension caused by the encounter of these different framings of how debt operates and what it represents. Indeed, the idea of 'default', for example, may be entirely new. The invoking of a specific point of time as a point at which the funds have to be repaid and which triggers particular punitive actions in the relationship, may be at odds with local framings in which the debt is conceived as something that can be repaid in multiple ways over extended timeframes. Indebtedness results in suicide when the consequences of the material demand for repayment on social relationships and meaning dimensions can no longer be adequately contained – often through the pain of seeing other family members suffer through the situation and the feelings of shame and loss of social status. Hence it signals a moment when the structure of debt relations has completely overwhelmed and undermined a person's wellbeing. This is, of course, an extreme instance, but it helps to highlight not only the interaction of the dimensions of wellbeing, but the need for them to be appropriately framed and their overflowing contained.

This perspective implies that constructing debt relations requires means to be found to frame the transactions for all parties. But this process bears the potential for disjuncture in the way this evolves and is enacted because it cuts across material, relational and subjective dimensions, all of which have implications for how people experience their wellbeing. The next section therefore examines evidence that demonstrates what is needed to construct debt relations in microfinance and the ways people have responded to this.

The microfinance industry and the re-construction of debt relations

A commercially viable microfinance industry is now emerging out of two decades of experimentation and development with lending to poor and low-income people. In this section, I illustrate how the construction of debt relations has had an impact on and responded to relational and subjective dimensions of wellbeing in the ways they have been framed, reframed and negotiated from the perspective of both MFIs and their borrowers. This draws primarily from in-depth research in Kenya, but also draws on material from Bangladesh.

Group-based finance: 'local' framings

The primary challenge of institutional lending, whether in microfinance or other financial institutions, is ensuring repayment. Earlier banking experience of lending to poor people, in which repayment was often as low as 30 per cent, appeared to have been overcome by the late 1990s when mainstream microfinance institutions were achieving on-time repayment rates of 95 per cent. The technology that was thought to have achieved this was, first and foremost, the use of so-called 'solidarity' or group-based lending. This involved bringing borrowers together in groups, not only to achieve economies of scale in the provision of very small loans, but additionally through the use of joint liability, which made other member's responsible for repayment of an individual's loan. Analytically, economists pointed out that this resulted in a range of beneficial impacts for repayment. First, members would screen out those they knew were poor in repayment when forming the group (Besley *et al.* 1993; Ghatak 2000). Second, the members could monitor each other's performance with the loan as they were able to see what was going on locally, and the consequences for regular, usually weekly, repayments. Third, peers would enforce repayment on their colleagues by following up and using local sanctioning methods as their own interests in securing further loans depended on it (Aghion and Morduch 2005).

The process of reframing debt relations that the implementation of this methodology requires can be illustrated through a case study of a programme where repayment is poor. An in-depth qualitative study of an NGO's savings and credit groups in Kenya (Johnson and Sharma 2007) where, overall, some 50 per cent of loans were overdue, investigated group dynamics. This NGO had not followed repayment very closely, as it took the view that this was a community-based programme and that the groups would be able to manage the recovery process themselves once the group had been given a collective loan for on-lending to members.

Cases of 'default' were identified, and the majority of these were among men rather than women. The group referred to these as cases of 'delay' in payment. Members mainly relied on 'insisting' that their colleagues repaid. While they were aware of options to seize assets, or take their colleagues to the chief, they had not done this, largely because they felt this would mean that the group as a whole was seen as a 'bad' group locally. Moreover, the commonly held view that sanctions might be applied in other parts of local social life, such as exclusion from community activities, was found to be used only weakly and the only clear use of them was when the member had himself signalled his non-cooperation with the group, at which point it would appear that they would be unlikely to have much sanctioning effect. Further, four cases of misappropriation were also identified, which members referred to as cases where 'the records were not kept properly'. All of these cases of misappropriation involved office holders – two men and two women. When it came to enforcing sanctions to try to recover either misappropriated or loan funds, the male office holders were left in place and members explained that they wanted them to repay before they were demoted, while two women office holders were demoted and continued repaying.

This evidence illustrates three points. First, the difference between delay and default highlights the interaction of relational and material dimensions of debt and the different ways they are understood by members and MFIs. Second, it highlights that the strategy of ensuring repayment through creating consequences for others needed to be specifically instituted to create 'overflowing' of the material dimensions into domains of social relationships and meaning. Third, within these dynamics, social structures underpin the role different actors can play. These points are now explored in more depth.

First, those members whose loans were overdue were not regarded as being in default by the group or the NGO if they did not pay the loan by the due date – although this would be the classification that an MFI would now use. As long as a member continued to pay – even a small amount – this was seen locally as 'delay' rather than default. Default is only understood to have occurred when the individual clearly signals that they are unwilling to pay by a clear and outright refusal to honour the debt, rather than a situation in which they are *willing but unable* to pay. That is, the relationship between the finance as a material dimension operates within the relational dimension and, for members, default does not occur because the relationship has not ended. The term 'default' was not therefore locally understood as about on-time repayment, but about willingness to pay. For members, 'default' refers to a situation in which the relationship has broken down. By contrast, outside lenders are unable to distinguish between willingness and unwillingness in this way and instead use a point in time to change their relationship with the borrower to one that assumes unwillingness to pay and initiates particular actions to recover funds.

This issue of the understanding of what default is, is also evident in the literature on rotating savings and credit associations (ROSCAs), which were revealed to be particularly effective indigenous mechanisms for financial intermediation by anthropologists. The literature has been fascinated by their apparent ubiquity, diversity and adaptability (Ardener 1964; Ardener and Burman 1995; Geertz 1962). In these, it was frequently reported that default was very low or non-existent (specifically for example see (Nelson 1995)) but it appears that anthropologists took such claims of 'no default' at face value when in fact they masked a range of scenarios of non-payment (Bouman 1995).

Second, and following on from this, the only action members would take against their colleagues was to 'insist' that they paid. Taking action that might involve people outside the group such as the local chief – who plays a key role in dispute resolution – was feared to create a reputation as a 'bad' group. This further shows that it is not only the issue of the relationships among members that matter, but also the intermediate norms about how a group is expected to interact with its members such that action evident to outside parties would disrupt these with negative consequences for members' perceptions of their own relationships. Hence their failure to do this can be understood as acting to limit the 'overflowing' of the mechanism of group liability into other parts of their social lives, the externalities of which were clearly more significant to them than the non-payment of a loan from an outside NGO.

This point highlights the fact that peer group, or joint liability, lending, was not supported by underlying social relationships that made it spontaneous in this context. It is a specific strategy in which the lender creates externalities and consequently it must find ways to make them occur. Indeed, in other research in Kenya where MFIs operate, it is this process that is particularly disliked. Microcredit lenders require that groups sign to acknowledge each other's loans. The loan officer then works with the group to involve the local chief and support them to seize a member's assets rather than doing it himself/herself. Nevertheless, the seizing of assets – especially iron sheets from the roof – is widely condemned, especially when this affects vulnerable family members such as children. So it is the institution rather than the group members that gains a bad reputation as it signals what is locally seen as an entirely unacceptable overflowing of the material consequences of non-payment and disrupts both social relationships and the normative order.

That debt relations involve complex interconnections of the material, social and cultural, has long been the study of economic anthropology. For example, in his critique of the narrow view taken by development financiers in Kenya, Shipton argues the need for wider frameworks for understanding 'fiduciary culture' in the context of the Luo, which considers concepts of entrustment and obligation in a much broader way, rather than one that focuses on monetary credit and debt. He argues that such an approach captures much more effectively the ways in which 'land, money, animals, labour and even humans themselves are all transferred and returned later' (Shipton 2007: 11). Entrustment, he argues, does not necessarily produce an obligation to repay in the same form, rather 'whether an entrustment or transfer is returnable in kind or in radically different form – be it economic, political, symbolic, or some mixture of these – is a matter of cultural context and strategy' (ibid.: 11) and may also be discharged by passing a benefit onto another rather than returning it directly. Such research demonstrates well the challenges of framing and creation of acceptable entanglements for MFIs seeking to institutionalise repayment mechanisms.

The third point from the case study above is that of the way social structure, in particular gender relations, underpins debt relations within the groups. There were more cases of non-payment by men than women as members; and when it came to 'recording errors', men could not be sanctioned by demotion from their positions before they had repaid, although women could. This raises the issue of how the power dynamics endemic in social structures impede the 'institutionalising [of] suspicion' (Johnson and Sharma 2007).

The way in which traditional solidaristic social ties and social relations make internal enforcement difficult is again evident when the literature on indigenous groups is reviewed in depth (Johnson *et al.* 2010). In contrast to the again somewhat idealistic view of these mechanisms that the anthropological literature has produced, and which the 1990s promotion of the concept of social capital assisted in obscuring, there is also a literature on ROSCAs and ASCAs (accumulating savings and credit associations), that discusses the 'pathology' of power relations that operate within them (Johnson *et al.* 2009: 7) and shows how village headship, gender, kinship, and age operate within groups to mediate the ways in which norms of debt repayment are instituted, invariably favouring those with greater social status.

Geertz, in his classic 1962 article on ROSCAs, suggested that they were a 'middle rung' in economic development because they helped accomplish the task of helping to create disentangled relationships. He argued that they were a means through which peasants:

learn to be traders, not merely in the narrow occupational sense but in the broad cultural sense; an institution which acts to change their whole value framework from one emphasizing particularistic, diffuse, affective and ascriptive ties between individuals to one emphasizing-within economic contexts – universalistic, affectively neutral and achieved ties between them.

(Geertz 1962)

However, the evidence suggests that in and of themselves, ROSCAs do not shift frameworks of relationships and meaning in this way. Rather the social relations and context in which they are being implemented plays a critical role.

Research in central Kenya found a range of approaches to ROSCAs, which ranged from 'kurekera' or 'patient' ROSCAs to those which were much more strict (Johnson 2003: 149). A particularly strict ROSCA was found among business people and dealt in relatively large contributions. However, it was as strict in instituting processes of welfare support among members in the case of shocks and emergencies as it was in the savings and loan process, so enabling it to balance the material needs of members with the relational dimensions. Indeed, it is the 'negotiability' (Johnson 2003) of social relationships in these indigenous savings and credit groups that is the key to both their popularity and also their success and failure. They create a set of relationships around the material need for finance that enable members to have various avenues of access to funds – whether through the group directly as loans or welfare support, through side lending or gifted support – which enables them to sustain livelihoods that are vulnerable to uncertainty and shocks.

Indeed, in reviewing the failure of development interventions to effectively operate with such groups on their own terms, Bouman (1995: 382) concludes that '[a]fter 40 years of development aid, we must finally accept that indigenous self-help societies have their own ways of helping themselves and their own ideas of what Utopia looks like and at what tempo to get there'. Such a conclusion eloquently captures the challenge that reframing debt relations has to overcome, in order to build a microfinance industry.

Creating a microfinance sector

The above case study reflects what many in the field of microfinance would regard as a poorly managed 'old' and failed model of NGO credit in which repayment was insufficiently well enforced and which was seen as too deferential to the community basis of the intervention. This perspective in itself indicates how far MFIs have gone in revising the approach.

One of the first steps that NGOs had to undertake was to reframe their own expectations of repayment and institute their own discipline to achieve this. Previously, both NGOs and their beneficiaries had a perspective and understanding of their relationship as being one in which funds were grants and need not be repaid if 'beneficiaries' were unable to. Loan recipients also knew that NGOs were there to help them so would not press them for repayment. This is not to say that recipients did not understand that loans from other sources – for example the local money-lender or even the bank – would need to be repaid. The point is that the receipt of a loan from a particular source is necessarily 'framed' through past experience in the relationship and within the meaning that is invoked about it – in this case that NGOs should be lenient and contribute to local people's wellbeing.

As indicated above, the recipe for the success of the microfinance model, as a financially sustainable industry as understood by a swathe of the literature and strongly informed by the analysis of new institutional economics, has been the ability to re-design incentives and contracts to ensure repayment using solidarity or joint liability lending. However, in practice, this analysis of its success is not the whole story. Jain (1996) analyses the Grameen Bank in Bangladesh, showing the organisational characteristics required and highlighting that it is the effectiveness of MFI managers in creating strong organisational systems and cultures of monitoring and supervision that mean that credit officers are strong in enforcing repayment and ensuring they do not leave customers without it. He reports that the group guarantee was not functioning in Grameen groups he visited, as money to cover missing repayments was not raised from other group members. Nevertheless the loan officer did not leave the group until the payment was received from the member in question. The emphasis in the literature on strong management for MFIs and, for example, the design of staff incentive systems, demonstrates that organisational effectiveness and not solely contract design have been clearly recognised as critical (Ledgerwood and White 2006). More significantly however, Jain, analyses how the processes of loan officer training and management and supervision systems across the levels of bank operation fostered the creation of cultural habits among both staff and members, which enabled them to follow the norms of the bank in terms of acceptable behaviour and obligations for repayment.

Devices for institutionalising on-time repayment have been developed at the sector level also. One key development in the industry was in 1995, when the SEEP Network in Washington published its guide to financial ratio analysis for assessing the financial sustainability and performance of MFIs (SEEP Network 1995), which introduced portfolio at risk indicators for 30 days, 60 days and 90 days, and which was eventually institutionalised in industry consensus guidelines by CGAP in 2006 (CGAP 2006). Previously, NGOs had often operated on the basis of a cumulative repayment indicator which was insensitive to time.[4] This, along with the wider range of financial indicators introduced (e.g. operational self-sufficiency; return on assets, etc.), has operated as a performative device for MFIs and their widespread adoption has instituted the discipline of financial performance in order for them to become commercially viable entities. This has led, for example, to a portfolio at risk figure of less than 5 per cent being seen as a benchmark of good performance and has itself challenged the quality of bank lending portfolios.

This socio-technical device has emerged in microfinance within a broader context of economic restructuring and neo-liberal reforms, which means that the material, relational and subjective dimensions of poor people's wellbeing that are found in their financial arrangements have been the subject of restructuring through global policy processes. The theoretical economic critique of financial sector intervention policy dates back to the 1970s and this contributed to the cocktail of Washington Consensus neo-liberal reform policy that was implemented globally in the 1980s. Critiques of interventionist policy in the financial sector – especially of subsidised interest rates – were seen as having suppressed market incentives to mobilise and allocate funds efficiently and led to the rise of the financial systems approach (World Bank 1989). The rise of group lending methodologies discussed above converged with these developments in theory and policy to create a powerful demonstration of neo-liberal reform policy in practice in which it appeared that poor people could pay their loans, could do so on time and at interest rates that would cover the costs of provision, so allowing for mutually reinforcing and sustainable financial sector development. Critics, however, observed that microfinance served an instrumental role in providing a crisis management safety-net for poor people in the wake of reform policies which further legitimated them (Weber 2002).

Microfinance groups as opportunities for containing and facilitating entanglements

Understanding the appeal of the microfinance sector to borrowers in the financial market in Kenya is also illuminated by seeing the ways it contains or facilitates entanglements between different dimensions of wellbeing in relation to financial arrangements.

One of the reasons microfinance groups have appeal is because they do not use land as collateral, as has historically been the case for formal financial institutions. In Kenya, land is hugely important not only for sustaining material livelihoods but because of its subjective and relational dimensions, such that the fear of losing it is something to be avoided at any cost. Land is significant not only for sustaining material livelihoods, but because its loss will also be felt by future generations – especially sons – who expect to inherit it and to establish their own rural homes on it. This connection with the land is core to ideologies of origin and, hence, identity and belonging. Its ownership and maintenance within families and lineages has 'cosmic consequences'. For example, for the Luo of Western Kenya, the importance of burial in the homestead is hugely meaningful (Cohen and Odhiambo 1992). Since a baby's afterbirth is traditionally buried at the threshold to the house where it is born, to return the body to burial at the homestead is to reunite these two parts and hence complete the physical person in death. Such powerful meanings have led the use of land as collateral to be referred to as 'mortgaging the ancestors' (Shipton 2009).

Because land is so important, the actual process of repossession and sale of rural land is very difficult for financial institutions to complete. Relatives find ways to prevent land being auctioned and others locally will therefore be deterred from buying it, while those from the outside the area would also find it difficult to overcome the social consequences of buying such a piece of land and living among hostile neighbours. As a result, repossession is rarely successful and banks actually prefer not to take it as collateral; although, in one bank it was (and still is)[5] seen as enough to simply hold the title deed for relatively small but substantial loans without actually legally charging it, since the psychological consequences for the borrower were regarded as sufficiently strong. However, this is an irregular process, which is not sanctioned by banking regulations. The overall result of this is that engaging with financial mechanisms that do not involve land as collateral, such as co-operatives and ROSCAs, and more recently group-based microfinance, is much more acceptable (Johnson 2004).

Moreover, and as already indicated, groups create the means through which social support can be accessed and hence offer scope for 'overflowing', which relationships with banks do not allow. Saving with others in the group is a process that creates social as well as material obligations. As one woman commented about the importance of ROSCAs: 'If I take my money to the bank, then when I have a problem who will help me?' (Johnson 2004: 267). She was acutely aware that saving with a bank does not lead to an entanglement that has social dimensions therefore it does not allow her to call on it in ways that fit her perspective on debts and obligations.

However, it was also pointed out above that the way entanglements play out is influenced by social structures, which confer power in relationships of seniority, gender, age, kinship and so on, and which can have negative material consequences for some since they are likely to lose out in getting loans or fail to recover their savings. For these people, an MFI operates as an external actor with sanctioning power that it is willing to, and does, employ. In this way, the repayment of the debt is taken out of other group members' hands by the MFI – a potentially welcome shift for those who are put into vulnerable positions by intra-group power relations. On the other hand, the power vested in the hands of credit officers can be used in ways that result in it overflowing into dimensions of relationships and meaning that result in efforts to disentangle oneself from these relationships, instances that other authors in this volume find evidence of in South Asia and Mexican contexts (see Guerin and Hummel, this volume).

In Kenya, therefore, the resistance to the use of rural land as collateral can be seen as a means of containing the consequences of institutional debt relations on the subjective and relational dimensions of wellbeing. This has altered the trajectory of financial sector development and made group-based financial arrangements more acceptable (Johnson 2004). At the same time, group-based arrangements can facilitate forms of overflowing which support people's sense of social connections and access to social support. On the other hand, intra-group dynamics, which disadvantage some members, can benefit from the 'disentangling' role that an MFI brings into the picture.

Re-negotiating the framing and overflowing of microfinance

These processes of framing and overflowing of different dimensions of wellbeing operate differently as microfinance is implemented in different social, economic and cultural contexts. An interesting contrast to Kenya is that of Bangladesh, where the context of interlocked transactions between credit and land and labour markets is particularly strong, and where wider social and political factors contributing to structures of patron–client relations are also at work. As Wood points out, power relations of patron–clientelism in Bangladesh underpin poor people's wellbeing in a 'Faustian bargain'. This is where poor people are unable to plan to meet future needs because of their current state of dependent security, since shifting these relationships involves 'chronic aspects of risk induced by inequality, class relations, exploitation, concentrations of unaccountable power and social exclusion' (Wood 2003: 457). Hence, this state of dependent security means that the costs of exit from the patronage relationships in which they are locked may be unacceptably high (Devine 2002) (see also Picherit, this volume).

Investigation of the way in which microcredit interventions in Bangladesh relate to wider power structures has shown that they similarly become part of these clientelistic relations (McGregor 1994). Devine reports that local elites were key to the rapid establishment of microcredit groups by NGOs, as this was a shortcut for field workers to operating within existing frameworks of loyalty and solidarity. Drawing on Fernando (1997), he argues that there had been a dramatic role reversal. While in the past NGO's were seen as standing by the poor in times of need, the new discipline in loan repayment meant that traditional moneylenders were now seen as the more flexible option for negotiating terms and conditions of loans that were responsive to poor people's requirements. Devine reports an incident where attempts at strict repayment enforcement provoked the ransacking of a local NGO's offices, explaining this in terms of the fact that this was a conflict over the 'perceived moral content of the NGO-member relationship' in which the 'social and moral contents of the same relationship have been squeezed out' (Devine 2003: 239). This then, is an example of a struggle over the NGO's attempt to reframe the debt relationship to exclude these elements, which were regarded as important to their wellbeing and which, in this case, 'overflowed' directly into violence.

Moreover, Matin (1997) also analyses repayment strikes by Grameen Bank borrowers in 1995. These were due to their dislike of the way funds contributed and managed at the group level were used to ensure repayment of other members, along with various irregularities in the way they were managed. Matin calls this the 'unzipping' of joint liability as non-payment escalated, and the strikes eventually led to the re-designing of the rules, which involved a greater individualisation in ownership of the group fund. This was a means of preventing individuals from being liable for others' debts and hence can again be understood as the re-negotiation of an externality and 'overflowing' of a material dimension of the programme's design due to its relational consequences.

In this context, it is interesting to reflect on Grameen's re-design of its programme in 2001. As Collins et al. (2010) explain, Grameen II is a much more flexible set of loan products and includes a flexible savings account. They explain the origins of the Grameen re-design as arising from the poor repayment performance[6] resulting from the 1998 floods, which compounded existing problems with the rigidity of the system. While the original core loan product was a 50-week loan, the re-designed loan products involved variable loan terms from three months to three years, with the possibility of topping up the loan, and of rescheduling it by extending the term in the case of repayment difficulties. The requirements for group solidarity were also relaxed and hence borrowers were no longer responsible for paying each other's loans. At the same time, a flexible and voluntary savings product was introduced, through which Grameen also sought to mobilise capital for its lending operations.

Collins *et al.* (2010) interpret these developments as a better matching of savings and loan products to the needs of members for better flexibility to manage their small, irregular and unpredictable cash flows. This explanation restricts the interpretation to one that is about the relationship between products and clients in relation to their material welfare. It does not consider the broader patronage function that has been evident in the studies of Bangladeshi micro-finance discussed above. When considered in this way, it can be suggested that the Grameen Bank was not adequately performing its function as a flexible patron through its rigid system, which gave poor people few opportunities to re-negotiate repayment with the organisation at times of difficulty, or obtain addi-tional loans as their needs changed. One study explains that it was moneylenders who stepped in to fill this gap, giving loans to bridge the gap between one Grameen loan and the next, and that moneylender operations were found to increase as a result of microfinance lending (Sinha and Matin 1998).

To be an organisation that is successfully contributing to its members' well-being in the Bangladeshi context means that it must behave as a patron[7] that offers its clients material support, which has acceptable entanglements in social relations and moral meaning. The increased flexibility of the relationship and the removal of joint liability therefore directly responded to the concerns of clients, which arose over time and through various avenues.[8] This analysis allows us to see clients as having negotiated away the 'overflowing' that joint liability pro-duces for borrowers on their local social relationships and which has material consequences for them. This alternative perspective suggests that the re-design involved important moves to restructure the debt model to one that was more in line with members' own visions of how and what degrees and types of entangle-ments contribute to their wellbeing.

Conclusion

This paper has proposed that Callon's view that the framing and disentanglement of transactions is necessary in order for markets to be instituted, is helpful in understanding the ways in which debt relations develop. In particular, it high-lights the fact that transactions are necessarily multi-dimensional and have implications for other aspects of social and moral interaction. A multi-dimensional view of wellbeing, which identifies the relational and subjective alongside the material, offers an approach that allows for conceptual integration of these dimensions and offers specific dimensions against which this framing and overflowing can be examined. Bringing these two approaches together allows us to argue that as new debt relationships emerge in changing financial markets, these involve encounters between different frames of meaning and different relationships involved in social structure and power relations, which will have consequences for whether or not people experience them as contributing to their wellbeing. From this perspective 'over'-indebtedness is not simply about an inability to pay, but concerns the nature of the framing and disentanglements involved and how these overflow and create tensions. It is a social and moral state and not only a financial one.

Financial service providers have developed their own 'universal' understandings of the terms and conditions for debt relations. The institutionalisation of on-time repayment by the microfinance sector through group-based lending and changing the culture of NGOs to become MFIs, is also embedded in the devices of measuring portfolio at risk and indicators of profitability and returns that assist industry 'performance'. In order to institute on-time repayment, NGOs had to disentangle themselves from being seen as supporting poor people in times of need. The use of joint liability lending was used to reframe this relationship with borrowers into one that prioritised repayment and disentangled NGOs from the consequences of non-payment. In doing this, it deliberately created new entanglements among group members and the overflowing of the transaction into other aspects of social life. The empirical evidence illustrates that this creates tensions with how debt relationships are experienced and perceived. In Kenya, understandings of 'delay' in repayment rather than 'default' indicate the importance of the ongoing social relationship relative to the material consequences of non-payment and how the complexities of meaning and relationships in indigenous groups have made it hard for MFIs to work with them directly. The framing of MFI debt therefore requires investments to create overflowing into other areas of social life, which may be regarded as detrimental to relationships and, therefore, resisted. On the other hand, in contrast to the mortgaging of land in formal financial institutions, group-based lending contains the potential overflowing of non-payment into highly sensitive consequences for the normative order as well as social relationships. Moreover, it fits with the experience of group finance mechanisms that facilitate overflowing through developing social connections between members, which allow the negotiability of financial transactions among members. The evidence from Bangladesh on the other hand, shows how efforts to institutionalise on-time repayment have provoked overt reaction to the reframing of debt relationships towards strict repayment terms. Over time, these have led to the re-negotiation of the terms and conditions of debt contracts, which have, in turn, transformed the Grameen Bank into a more flexible patron and removed the 'overflowing' involved in joint liability.

These examples have therefore illustrated how different dimensions of wellbeing, ranging from social relations at structural and personal levels, to aspects of meaning, have influenced the development of microfinance interventions. As users encounter these services they interpret and operate within their own frames of reference in terms of subjective, relational and material dimensions. These affect whether they are willing to engage with the intervention at all, and when they do so, how they experience them and whether, in consequence, they may act in order to re-negotiate the terms of engagement in ways that better support their wellbeing.

It is therefore necessary to understand 'over'-indebtedness not only as a process of material impoverishment, but one that violates dimensions of meaning and breaks up social relationships when there is insufficient scope for re-negotiation.

Notes

1 Another has been the need to charge interest rates that cover costs and produce profits for their owners – depending on the nature of the investors involved.
2 We can clearly see this in many areas of development and we understand that what is measured and how it matters in terms of its impact on action. Hence in microfinance the explicit framing of a set of social performance questions for MFI managers and boards as well as suggestions about the methodologies and indicators that can be used to answer them intends to hold MFIs to account over their social performance (see www.imp-act. org). This is indeed intended to 'reframe' the calculativeness of MFI managers and internalise some of the 'overflowing' which, up to this point, an emphasis on financial tools had 'externalised' in the decision making of MFI boards and managers.
3 As pointed out above, this is an analytical approach and does not imply a normatively positive assessment. As the approach is applied in practice where people assess their achieved wellbeing as low, they may term this illbeing.
4 The indicator would simply report the total amount repaid as a proportion of the total amount ever lent, regardless of the time periods of the loans involved.
5 This was reported to me in 1999 and again in 2010.
6 Morduch – an analyst in this field, see, e.g. Morduch (1999), had long suspected that Grameen Bank's repayment performance was not as good as publicity indicated, it had never published full financial information (personal communication).
7 It is worth recalling that in 2007, Mohammad Yunus – chair of the Grameen Bank – formed a political party with the intention of running for the premiership, though he did not follow through in this attempt. He was, however, seen as an ongoing political threat by the government, which used age limit legislation to remove him from the chairmanship of the bank in 2011.
8 Joint liability has now been removed, or its consequences reduced, in many MFIs across the world.

References

Aghion, B. A. D. and Morduch, J. (2005) *The Economics of Microfinance*, Cambridge, Mass.: MIT Press.

Appadurai, A. (2004) 'The capacity to aspire: culture and the terms of recognition', in V. Rao and M. Walton (eds) *Culture and Public Action*, Stanford: Stanford University Press.

Ardener, S. (1964) 'The comparative study of Rotating Credit Associations', *Journal of the Royal Anthropological Institute* 94(1): 201–229.

Ardener, S. and Burman, S. (eds) (1995) *Money-Go-Rounds: The Importance of Rotating Savings and Credit Associations for Women*, Oxford/Washington DC: Berg.

Besley, T., Coate, S. and Loury, G. (1993) 'The Economics of Rotating Savings and Credit Associations', *American Economic Review* 83(4): 792–810.

Bevan, P. (2007) 'Researching wellbeing across the disciplines: some key intellectual problems and ways forward', in I. Gough and A. McGregor (eds) *Wellbeing in Developing Countries: From Theory to Research*, Cambridge: Cambridge University Press.

Block, F. (2001) *Introduction to Karl Polanyi's The Great Transformation*, Boston: Beacon Press.

Bouman, F. J. A. (1995) 'Rotating and Accumulating Savings and Credit Associations: A development perspective', *World Development* 23(3).

Callon, M. (1998a) 'An essay on framing and overflowing: economic externalities revisited by sociology', in M. Callon (ed.) *The Laws of the Markets*, Oxford: Blackwells.

Callon, M. (1998b) 'Introduction: the embeddedness of economic markets in economics', in M. Callon (ed.) *The Laws of the Markets*, Oxford: Blackwells.

CGAP (2006) 'Good practice guidelines for funders of microfinance: microfinance consensus guidelines ', Washington, DC: CGAP.

Cohen, D. W. and Odhiambo, E. S. A. (1992) *Burying SM: The Politics of Knowledge and the Sociology of Power in Africa*, London and Portsmouth, NH: James Curry and Heinemann.

Collins, D., Morduch, J., Rutherford, S. and Ruthven, O. (2009) *Portfolios of the Poor: How the World's Poor Live on $2 a Day*, Princeton and Oxford: Princeton University Press.

Devine, J. (2002) 'Ethnography of a policy process: a case study of land redistribution in Bangladesh', *Public Administration and Development* 22: 403–414.

Devine, J. (2003) 'The paradox of sustainability: reflections on NGOs in Bangladesh', *Annals of the American Academy Of Political And Social Science* 590: 227–242.

Devine, J. (2007) 'Country report – Bangladesh', University of Bath, UK: Wellbeing in Developing Countries Research Group.

Fernando, J. L. (1997) 'Nongovernmental organizations, micro-credit and empowerment of women', *Annals of the American Academy of Political and Social Sciences* (554): 150–177.

Fine, B. (2003) 'Callonistics: a disentanglement', *Economy and Society* 32(3): 478–484.

Geertz, C. (1962) 'Rotating Savings and Credit Associations: the middle rung in economic development', *Economic Development and Cultural Change* 10(3): 241–263.

Ghatak, M. (2000) 'Screening by the company you keep: joint liability lending and the peer selection effect', *Economic Journal* 110: 601–631.

Granovetter, M. (1992) 'Economic action and social structure: the problem of embeddedness', in M. Granovetter and R. Swedberg (eds) *The Sociology of Economic Life*, Boulder: Westview Press.

Gudeman, S. (2001) *The Anthropology of Economy: Community, Market and Culture*, Oxford and Malden: Blackwell.

Hodgson, G. M. (1988) *Economics and Institutions: A Manifesto for a Modern Institutional Economics*, Cambridge: Polity Press.

Jain, P. (1996) 'Managing credit for the rural poor: lessons from the Grameen Bank', *World Development* 24(1): 11–21.

Johnson, S. (2003) '"Moving Mountains": an institutional analysis of financial markets using evidence from Kenya', Department of Economics and International Development, University of Bath.

Johnson, S. (2004) '"Milking the elephant": financial markets as real markets in Kenya', *Development and Change* 35(2): 249–275.

Johnson, S. (2010) 'The role of informal groups in financial markets: evidence from Kenya', available online at: www.bath.ac.uk/cds/bpd/index.html:, Centre for Development Studies, University of Bath.

Johnson, S. and Sharma, N. (2007) '"Institutionalizing suspicion": the management and governance challenge in user-owned microfinance groups', in T. Dichter and M. Harper (eds) *What's Wrong with Microfinance*, Rugby: Intermediate Technology Publications Ltd.

Johnson, S., Malkamaki, M. and Nino-Zarazua, M. (2009) 'The role of informal groups in the financial market: evidence from Kenya', Paper presented at CERMI conference, June 2009.

Layard, R. (2005) *Happiness: Lessons from a New Science*, London: Allen Lane/Penguin.

Ledgerwood, J. and White, V. (2006) *Transforming Microfinance Institutions: Providing Full Financial Services to the Poor*, Washington, DC: International Bank for Reconstruction and Development/World Bank.

Lukes, S. (2005) *Power: A Radical View*, Basingstoke: Palgrave Macmillan.

McGregor, A. (2007) 'Researching wellbeing: from concepts to methodology', in I. Gough and A. McGregor (eds) *Wellbeing in Developing Countries: From Theory to Research*, Cambridge: Cambridge University Press.

McGregor, A. and Kebede, B. (2003) 'resource profiles and the social and cultural construction of wellbeing', Paper to the Inaugural Workshop of the ESRC Research Group on Wellbeing in Developing Countries, January 2003: mimeo.

McGregor, J. A. M. (1994) 'Village credit and the reproduction of poverty in contemporary rural Bangladesh', in J. M. Acheson (ed.) *Anthropology and Institutional Economics*, Lanham, Maryland: University Press of America.

Matin, I. (1997) 'Repayment performance of Grameen Bank borrowers: the 'unzipped' state', *Savings and Development* XXII(4): 451–472.

Morduch, J. (1999) 'The role of subsidies in microfinance: evidence from the Grameen Bank', *Journal of Development Economics* 60: 229–248.

Nelson, N. (1995) 'The Kiambu Group: a successful women's ROSCA in Mathare Valley, Nairobi (1971 to 1990)', in S. Ardener and S. Burman (eds) *Money-Go-Rounds: The importance of Rotating Savings and Credit Associations for Women*, Oxford/Washington, DC: Berg.

Polanyi, K. (2001) *The Great Transformation: The Political and Economic Origins of Our Time*, Boston: Beacon Press.

SEEP Network (1995) *Financial Ratio Analysis of Microfinance Institutions*, New York: Pact Publications and Calmeadow.

Shipton, P. (2007) *The Nature of Entrustment: Intimacy, Exchange and the Sacred in Africa*, New Haven and London: Yale University Press.

Shipton, P. (2009) *Mortgaging the Ancestors: Ideologes of Attachment in Africa*, New Haven and London: Yale University Press.

Sinha, S. and Matin, I. (1998) 'Informal credit transactions of micro-credit borrowers in rural Bangladesh', *IDS Bulletin* 29(4): 66–80.

Slater, D. and Tonkiss, F. (2001) *Market Society: Markets and Modern Social Theory*, Oxford: Polity Press.

Weber, H. (2002) 'The imposition of a global development architecture: the example of microcredit', *Review of International Studies* 28(3): 537–556.

Wellbeing in Developing Countries Research Group (2007) 'Wellbeing and international development: research statement', University of Bath, available online at: www.welldev.org.uk: WED Research Group.

White, S. C. (2010) 'Analyzing wellbeing? A framework for development practice', *Development in Practice* 20(2): 158–172.

Wood, G. (2003) 'Staying secure, staying poor: the "Faustian bargain"', *World Development* 31(3): 455–471.

World Bank (1989) *World Development Report: Financial Systems and Development*, Washington, DC: World Bank.

4 Why do the poor pay more for their credit?

A French case study

Hélène Ducourant

Why do low-income households pay more for consumer credit debt than other households? The question may sound trivial to bankers or scholars, who might argue that as these individuals' payment defaults are statistically higher, their credit rates must be higher (Eber, 2000). The question may also sound trivial to some sociologists: a large body of research has shown that there is unequal access to markets (Caplovitz, 1963). It has, for instance, been argued that "ungifted" individuals are obliged to embed their buying practice routines into social relations (frequenting community shops where their mother tongue is spoken, dealing with the same cashier who knows the difficulties faced by an innumerate client), even if this proves costly (Lazarus, 2007). Nevertheless, the question is relevant in order to analyse the French consumer credit market, and raises two major issues in economic sociology.

The first is to understand how different suppliers offering differing products at variable prices match up with potential clients with specific payment default risks. The second is to explain why in this market, in contrast to many others, low-income individuals try not to embed their economic transactions into social relations. Indeed, they usually become indebted to consumer credit companies (who do not know them)[1] rather than to their own bank, where they are personally known.

Economic sociology research (Bourdieu, 1997; Garcia-Parpet, 2007; White, 1981) has demonstrated that the construction of supply (technical features of products, targeted client profiles, prices levels, etc.) can be explained as a consequence of the differentiation strategies of each "producer" within a market. In contrast to microeconomic theory, suppliers are not considered rational strategic actors who create strategies consciously based on profit opportunities and anticipated consumer demand. They are seen as actors with little leeway when it comes to establishing their position in the market. This paper therefore focuses on the socio-historical genesis of differentiation within the French consumer market, and its consequences on low-income individuals' borrowing conditions.

In undertaking such a project, this paper does not directly focus on over-indebtedness. However, over 90 per cent of French households considered 'over-indebted' have consumer credit debts (in comparison, only 31.5 per cent of French households have consumer loans).[2] It is therefore important to examine the borrowing conditions offered to low-income populations.

Box 4.1 Over-indebtedness in France

In France, a growing number of households unable to pay off debt led to the cre-ation of legislation for protecting both lenders and borrowers. While various meas-ures were created to tackle the problem from the end of the 1970s, it was in 1989 that an overarching means of tackling over-indebtedness was created in France through a specific law. There have since been other laws, which have all been aimed at establishing pre-trial agreements for repaying debts without discouraging credit market growth. The main solution favoured is to reach agreement on rescheduling debt repayments.

According to De Montlibert (De Montlibert, 2006), growing rates of over-indebtedness in northern countries such as France can be explained through two joint causes, which are unexpected life events – which nonetheless imply social causes – and the effects of economic policies. Indeed, over-indebtedness is linked to neoliberal economic policies. Increased rates of unemployment and precarious forms of employment, limited growth in household purchasing power, disinflation, public incentives to establish a home ownership market, and the weakening of social policies at a time when family structures have become destabilised, have all heavily contributed to this phenomenon's growth.

In June 2010, in France, 778,500 households[1] had "dis-indebtedness", namely an over-indebtedness plan to improve their financial situation. The average debt levels of newly over-indebted households in that year amounted to €44,700. The sociologist Montlibert has highlighted that the unemployed, employees, workers, people living alone and in single parent families, unskilled individuals, lodgers, and more generally, people accumulating "domination effects", are over-represented among the over-indebtedness population.

Note:
1   According to the Barometer of over-indebtedness of juin 2010, Banque de France.

In order to explain market structuring processes and the differences in how clients are treated, we apply different types of data: historical archives from the leading consumer credit firm in France, interviews with credit companies' top executives (n=31) and a national statistical survey on household indebtedness practices and costs (Patrimony Survey, 1998).

In the first part of this paper, we offer an overview of the creation and historical development of the market, principally with reference to the history of the leading consumer credit company Cetelem. We show how companies needed to target their products according to two axes, which tend to structure the market: the means of contacting potential clients (axis 1) and the type of consumer credits (personal loans, instalment loans, revolving accounts) they focus on (axis 2). Second, we present the viewpoints of consumer credit firm executives as regards their activity, market competition, and clients, offering insights on why the positions companies adopt (around axis 2) fit specific types of clients. In the final part of the paper, we consider the consequences of this kind of market matching process for the borrow-ing conditions offered to clients according to their socioeconomic status.

Box 4.2 The three most popular types of consumer credit in France

Personal loans are consumer loans granted for personal, family or household use. They are unsecured by the asset purchased in France, and advanced on the basis of the estimate of the borrower's credit ability to repay the loan from personal income. Repayment is carried out via monthly payments over a fixed term.

Instalment credit is a consumer loan for financing capital goods, where the principal and interest are repaid in equal instalments at fixed intervals. These loans are secured by the item the borrower purchases.

Revolving credit[1] is a credit sum that does not have to be repaid in full (reduced to a zero balance) before obtaining goods or services against the available credit limit.

Note:

1 Revolving credit should not be confused with revolving funds, a common practice in developing countries for the poor. A revolving fund is a common fund established to finance a cycle of operations to which repayments and collections are returned for reuse in order to maintain the principal of the fund.

The development of the French consumer credit market

To understand credit suppliers' borrowing conditions, we must first examine the context in which consumer credit activity has developed. The recent history we present here does not tackle the social obligations or political power of debt (see Fontaine, 2008), but pursues a more modest objective. It aims at illustrating how businessmen seeking to develop an economic activity established common economic interests and tried to obtain reciprocal benefits. They acted at a time when state regulation was evolving to control this growing activity and, later, to organise competition between firms. Ultimately, as for many others' businesses, the final product was not first and foremost a response to "demand", but the outcome of the genesis of the economic activity's creation (Garcia Parpet, 1986).

Retailers as key partners (1950–1975)

According to Laferté (Laferté *et al.*, 2010), 1964 was a turning point in French consumer credit regulation. Up until then, major regulatory initiatives had sought to discourage the growth of consumer credit and credit firms. But from 1964 onwards, regulation began to establish the terms of its development. Indeed, the idea was that "grey" credit was de facto on offer in many shops, considered as an over-expensive service that retailers granted to low-income groups. Various measures were taken to legalise such credits, which in turn allowed their improved regulation. For instance, the cost of credit was separated from the price of the product to be financed, and the cost of credit had to be converted into an annual credit rate in order for clients to compare the attractiveness of credit offers. Nevertheless, far from supporting consumer credit development in France, state regulation still kept control over its outstanding growth up until 1986 (Bezbakh, 2006). In this regulatory context, consumer credit "industries" emerged.

The company Cetelem was created in 1953 and was the first French credit company that aimed to offer high levels of household credit not to finance real estate or cars, but household goods. In order to attract clients, be viewed as legitimate, and lower default risks, the company planned for retailers and consumer goods' industry lobbies to cooperate. The commitment of the capital goods industries was indeed intended to legitimise credit activity for retailers selling appliances. Retailers were requested to sell credits to their clients in order to enhance their sales. In return, they were to take responsibility for the default payment risk. Meanwhile the mechanisation of debt collection and the delegation of credit decisions to retailers through standardised scoring criteria paved the way for a new consumer credit industry business model.

In this model, furniture and appliance retailers, and the first retail shops, became essential partners in the development of consumer credit activity.[3] A newly created consumer credit companies lobby was named *Groupe des établissements de financement des ventes* ("Retail Sales Financer Group"). This reflected the fact that these professionals viewed themselves as offering a service to retailers even more than to consumers. At this stage, consumer credit did not amount to a rationalisation of groceries' credit books. Indeed, the instalment credits were intended for financing small household investments such as refrigerators, television sets, etc. Moreover, traditional banks, which were more interested in financing industrial investments, moved away from consumer credit development.

In the 1960s, another form of consumer credit entered the credit market in France: the revolving account. This was a copy of North American initiatives, which were first created in the 1930s (Johnson, 1980), but which became fully established in the 1950s (Ohl, 1974) as part of the financial services offered by specific mass retail shops. In 1965, Galeries Lafayette (a famous department store in Paris committed to the democratisation of fashion clothes and goods) and Cetelem launched a revolving credit card, combining a credit service with a loyalty card. This credit card gave access to limited credit within a brand shop for amounts not exceeding one month of clients' salaries (*Les Affiches – moniteurs des soumissions*, 1969). Repayment conditions were quite flexible. This credit was developed with the aim of increasing shop sales and improving client loyalty. Purchases on credit indeed became easier, since the client needed only to open one credit account rather than on each individual occasion for purchasing goods on credit. It also allowed for the lowering of the minimum amount required to use credit, since the credit amount was no longer contractually linked to a specific good, as was the case for French instalment credit. Since these revolving credits aimed at increasing credit supply in shops, their goal was to satisfy both salesmen, seen as essential partners, and credit firms. Nevertheless, although development opportunities were identified, two phenomena limited its expansion: the tightening of credit supply in 1969 and the fact that the average amount of revolving credit debt remained low, meaning that the activity was considered a low profit margin business.

Towards the structuring of the market

Cetelem's activity evolved in the 1970s when the firm decided to focus its offer on existing clients who had adhered to its initial credit operation in shops. Three reasons justified this strategy. First, tests showed that the profitability of this kind of credit was higher. Indeed, existing clients were more likely to repay than unknown individuals selected by retailers, and the average amounts borrowed were higher (usually, credit for purchasing a car was offered to an existing client who had successfully repaid credit for financing a TV set).[4] Second, the fact that specific shops such as car retailers already had agreements with other credit firms led Cetelem to sell credit to their existing clients. It was almost impossible to convince car dealers to work with Cetelem, due to their existing agreements with credit companies. Last but not least, when credit companies were authorised to offer personal loans in 1972, Cetelem changed its strategy, as there was no longer any need for credit to be legally interdependent with goods and it was no longer necessary to work alongside specific retailers. This shift went beyond a change in the place where credit was obtained, and was more a shift in the philosophical conception of the activity: it was no longer a multiplication of single credit operations, but the maximisation of the profitability of each loyal client, who was encouraged to sign up to ever-larger amounts of credit.

Cetelem's success story is not only interesting in itself, but because the company was a leader whose activity model led the way in structuring the market. It defined the legitimate means of making profit: first, through credit operations in shops (instalment credits), and second, through new, higher levels of credit, such as personal loans, which were sold directly to former clients for a higher profit. After Cetelem, every credit firm wishing to enter the market had to position itself on the different axes Cetelem had set out as strategic: the means of contacting clients (shops, mail) and the type of credit the company would offer (instalment credit, revolving credit, personal loans). As for other markets, each actor adopted a position that was less strategically chosen than imposed by objective constraints (Bourdieu, 1997). For instance, in the 1980s new credit companies were unable to offer credit through merchant's shops or shop chains, as almost all shops already had credit company agreements, and had no choice but to develop their own activity through advertising. Similarly, smaller firms had to focus on revolving credit activities for two reasons: major companies considered them unprofitable, and they were unable to offer competitive pricing for larger credit amounts.

Nevertheless, unexpectedly in France, revolving credit turned out to be very profitable. It appealed to lower-class populations, who generated high profits for credit companies by using the credit money, not only to spread the payment of their purchases over time, but to bridge gaps, to "cover the end of the month", to the point where they became permanently indebted to revolving credit. Thus, Cetelem's leading business model was no longer the only highly profitable one. By the 1990s, the philosophy of the consumer credit market had been completely transformed (Ducourant, 2010).

The historical development of the activity as we have set it out does not evoke consumers' "needs", or credit firms' attempts to satisfy "demand", or cultural relationships to credit. Relationships between economic allies and state regulation have structured the market and the current state of the activity. We have equally highlighted the genesis of positions within the market. This offers insights that we will investigate in the second part of this paper: is there not only a link between credit company profiles and the credit they offer, but also the clients with whom they associate, and how can we explain such links? In the next section of this paper, we will look to discuss these connections, focusing on credit forms with a high proportion of lower-class household clients: revolving credit.

A hierarchical market

We have shown how the structuring of the market along two axes explains suppliers' positions. We will now turn to the question of how consumers choose specific suppliers, and how credit firms select their clients. We will offer insights into the "structural homologies" (Bourdieu, 1979) between clients' socio-economic status and credit characteristics. According to Bourdieu, structural homologies govern how supply and demand are matched, or, in other words, how people choose products that choose them.

Box 4.3 Who borrows what?

Does the consumer credit indebted population look like the French population? To answer the question, we figure out a metric of "social earmarking". Although this concept is borrowed from Viviana Zelizer, our use is much more basic (Zelizer, 1994). It intends to qualify each kind of consumer credit as far as the socio-economic level of its debtors is concerned.

"social earmarking" = (part of the debtors belonging to a socioeconomic level/part of the population belonging to a socioeconomic level) × 100.

The households' categories close to 100 per cent are as present among the debtors of a specific consumer credit as in the population. On the contrary, The households' categories who hardly reach 50 per cent mean that there are twice as few among the debtors than in the general population.

Table A Ratio of the social earmarking of consumer credits (%)

	Executives	Intermediary professions	Employees	Skilled workers	Unskilled
Revolving credit	51	118	146	136	141
Personal loan	105	116	104	122	106
Instalment credit	78	118	123	147	111
Consumer credit	97	117	110	122	109

Source: author's calculation; data from Patrimoine Survey (1998).

> The analysis of this metric reveals that some credits are more "socially marked" than others: revolving credit, and installment loans are low-incomers' credits, while personal loans are more neutral. Indeed, for instance, the weight of the unskilled workers among the revolving debtors represents 141 per cent of their weight among the French population. On the contrary, executives are under-represented among the revolving debtors: their weight represents 51 per cent of their weight in the French population.

First, we will analyse material from interviews with top credit company executives in order to examine the causes of the attraction of revolving credits for worker or employee populations. Second, we examine credit firms' selection processes.

The attraction of consumer credit companies' revolving accounts for low-income populations

According to the executives and top executives interviewed (n=31), there are three main reasons for the success of revolving credit and of credit companies among low-income populations: the treatment of lower-class clients by traditional banks, confidentiality practices, and the low level of repayment ability required.

The professionals interviewed consider that part of their firms' successes relate to the fact that traditional banks tend to treat low-income populations badly. This stems from French banks' bourgeois evaluations of clients, who have trouble with the differences in credit conditions banks and credit firms offer, and with the type of relationship imposed by banks in order to access credit.

> All right, we are expensive! That's true! But at the same time, we have, let's say, a social role, which is to offer access to credit that the banks refuse or look badly upon. We would never tell the client "I don't ever want to see you because your bank account is in the red".[5]
>
> (Deputy CEO of a consumer credit company, 2006)

According to this professional, banks' bad treatment of French lower-class people is a reason for their success.

> They are not the same people (those who subscribe to a personal loan and those who choose revolving credit), they are different. I mean, there is a relationship between the form and the content. People who go to traditional banks are people who dare to open the bank's door.
>
> (Financial Director of a consumer credit company, 2005)

In the prior quotation, it is no longer the bank's attitude that is emphasised, but the difference between two categories of consumers: people who dare to open the bank's door and people who don't.

Go and ask a bank for money, if you are a young lady, a student, go and ask and you'll see if a bank will give you money easily. Then, come and see us, it is much more likely that you'll get it. Of course, it will be a bit more expensive, since we take more risks, my clients, on the whole, have to pay for those who won't repay. There is, somewhere, a social role behind all that.

(Chief Executive Officer of a consumer credit company, 2005)

The recurrent reference to the credit firm playing a "social role" appears astonishing. This, of course, does not mean that they have developed a social supply rather than a commercial supply, but that they do not exclude the lower classes from credit and do not look down on them, unlike regular banks.

The second reason for their success lies in the confidentiality of the credit firms' practices:

You know, it's tricky when someone faces a temporary difficulty, in our revolving credits, we don't know everything, but we finance travel, gravestones, debts, furniture, a second hand car, car repairs (...) bankers are not adventurous about such things (...) you want my opinion? I GIVE the money to the clients, it's less traumatizing for them to ask us for money than bankers.

(Chief Executive Officer of a consumer credit company, 2005)

In interviews and in their own advertising, these professionals boast of the discretion, speed and impersonality of their decision-making in accepting or refusing credit. Some also highlight that documents such as salary slips are not required to justify household finances in order to obtain credit, and that no justification for the use of the money is required. They claim that these factors mean that banks cannot perfectly replace what they supply.

The third reason for success mentioned in interviews is linked to the clients' "profiles":

RESEARCHER: usually, in a market, matching is done through price. I have the feeling that this is not the case for the revolving credit market.

INTERVIEWEE: No it's not, because for this kind of clients, the perceived price is not the interest rate, but the level of monthly payment they are able to pay. I think this is specific to the money trade done with customers. Let's say for the "rabble", but not in a pejorative way! There shared point with the life insurance business. For some clients, it is not the payments or the fees that matter, but the ability to save small amounts each month. Professionals call this "saving ability". There is no market supply for ten to fifteen euros per month, except from firms which target low-income populations. Clients saving fifteen to thirty euros find it financially less interesting, because high fees are applied to them.

(Sales director of a consumer credit company, 2006)

The clients of revolving credit companies are thus described as more working class, and credit suppliers as the best match for them, as they take into account low-income households' saving capacities.

Our interviewees argued that banks were not the most appropriate credit agents for low-income households because the strategies and the social relations they imposed were a poor match. Credit firm customers were usually described as "lower class" and "working class". Such groups are over-represented among revolving credit clients. This seems not just to be the case because credit firms offer less restrictive revolving credit conditions, but also because clients would appreciate their impersonality, absence of moral/bourgeois values, the low saving ability requested, and the perceived real credit costs. These various factors explain and legitimise the success of French credit firms from the point of view of their top executives.

Having examined why modest households choose credit companies' revolving accounts over the conventional loans traditional banks offer, we will now discuss how credit companies select their clients. Indeed, the statement "clients chose the products which choose them" has never been truer than for the credit market, where credit firms directly select their clients using scored applications. We will then explain this second side of the homology: to what extent does the socioeconomic status of revolving account debtors stem from credit firms' decisions to offer less restrictive access conditions for revolving credit than other kinds of credit?

Credit application selectivity

As there is no Credit Bureau in France, credit companies have to develop their own scoring systems to select the credit applications that best suit their interests. These scoring systems have three functions: to standardise decision-making, to assess applicants' probability of defaulting on repayments, and to provide a steering tool to control the firms' margin ratios. We will discuss these functions and show how the score-based profitability controls that firms favour lead to less restrictive revolving credit access for households. Finally, we will show how at the market level, this strengthens the relationship between credit type and clients' socioeconomic status.

French companies historically created a streamlined means of selecting credit applicants with the aim of standardising decision processes. Indeed, in the 1950s, the instalment loans that were created for shop salesmen to offer required an objective selection process for assessing the creditworthiness of credit applications. Cetelem, for instance, developed a scoring formula allowing the most junior rank of salesperson to score their clients. It required only a pen, a questionnaire, and a calculation to make, the result of which could not exceed nine. The process was only professionalised years later with a scoring process that is defined below. This introduces the scoring system's second function: to grade credit applications:

> Long-term statistical analysis of a large number of clients, of the correlations between the course of the credit files (especially default payment probability

and client socioeconomic data) allows for client classification according to the potential risk they may pose. The statistical scoring technique thus assesses client quality using a set of mainly socio-economic characteristics. Its results are denominated in a score which classifies credit applications according to the default probability of the potential borrower.

(Question de responsabilité, Cetelem, June 2005)

Which variables influence payment behaviour statistically and thus the probability of a credit application being accepted? We were unable to access the scoring models because they are kept secret by firms. However, the executives we interviewed informed us that stability indicators account for payment behaviour statistically:

RESEARCHER: What are the most important variables?
INTERVIEWEE: All variables related to behavioural stability, such as job seniority, date of bank account creation, place of residence.
RESEARCHER: What about age?
INTERVIEWEE: You know, there are over one hundred variables in a score! (...) Family status, number of children, type of job held, the name of the bank where the client has a personal bank account...

(Financial Director of a consumer credit company, 2005)

The details the interviewee raises in the answer above helps to clarify how "stability" is understood. Socioeconomic status, too, is reflected in variables such as "type of job" and "name of bank".

Process standardisation and credit application classification do not suffice for explaining French credit companies' choices. We still need to understand how companies use their scoring software, where they set the cut-off line for accepting or rejecting a credit application, and what level of risk a company is prepared to accept:

> It is quite simple: for us, the risk corresponds to an adjustment variable related our targeted profitability level. As I told you, our price is constrained by the top. We have to cover commercial and management costs, and we also have to make some money! Once we have an idea of what level of profitability we need to achieve, we know how much risk we can take. This is why I was explaining to you that what really matters to monitor the mix margin and risk. This is the main point to understand. If you want to develop a credit business, you will not succeed by targeting the lowest risk level.

(CEO for France of a consumer credit company, 2006)

The above quotation reveals that risk level undertaken thus appears to be the firm's decision. The scoring tool is not a means to exclude potential "bad clients", but, in relation to the firm's decisions, to define what could potentially be bad client. The level of risk also depends on the type of credit, however.

INTERVIEWEE: You have to consider risk in relation to the pricing you get on each product [type of credit]. You simply cannot assess risk in the same way for a personal loan at a 4.5 to 5% rate for financing cars, a revolving credit sold at a 16% rate.

RESEARCHER: Do you mean then that access to revolving credit would be automatically less restrictive than a 5% car credit because the rate is higher?

INTERVIEWEE: Well, let's say, listen, that if the product's profitability allows you to take a higher level of risk, you can 'open up' access.

(CEO for France of a consumer credit company, 2006)

These professionals' explanations as to how profitability objectives have determined the development of consumer credit activity greatly help to show the purpose of the scoring system, in particular as regards firms' definitions of potentially bad/good clients. Thus revolving credit interest rates apparently allow firms to combine high risk with high profitability, allowing for less restrictive access to revolving credit. Low socioeconomic households therefore have easier access to revolving credit than other households. But another hidden consequence is that revolving credit's high cost puts off some higher socioeconomic households, restricting revolving credit even more to low socioeconomic households:

Of course there is a link between product and demand. Revolving credit differs from a personal loan, which attracts a different socioeconomic profile of client. People with high scores will choose cheaper money. By contrast, a household which accepts to borrow money at 18% must have a urgent need for cash which it cannot obtain at a lower cost elsewhere.

(Financial Director, 2005)

The interviews with top consumer credit firm executives discussed here highlight the other side of the structural homology between revolving credit and the low socioeconomic status of its clients. Because firms seek out high revolving credit profitability, low socioeconomic clients are highly represented. As high interest rates and high risk have been favoured, higher-risk households have their credit applications accepted and higher socioeconomic status clients have been de facto excluded. Although credit firms do not directly tailor credit prices to clients' default probabilities – each supply has a fixed price and firms decide whether to accept or reject credit applications – at the market level, fixing credit rate to individual client risk becomes self-perpetuating. Thus revolving credit has developed into an expensive credit supply for low-income populations.

In the following section, we will assess the structural homology that accounts for credit consumer market demand-supply matching, and its financial consequences for households.

The consequences of market hierarchy on low-income clients' borrowing conditions

How can we assess the extent to which household socioeconomic status determines borrowers' treatment? One can first examine credits' annual interest rates. The most obvious measure to assess is whether upper class households pay a lower interest rate than lower class households when taking out the same form of consumer credit. This does not, however, allow us to take into account the role of the genesis and the functioning of the market described above. To complete the picture, we must include two further indicators: first, the probability of subscribing to a specific type of credit to finance the same category of purchase. As revolving credit rates are higher for instalment credits, which in turn cost more than personal loans, we could highlight inequality of treatment if, for equivalent purchases, low-income households more frequently turn to the more expensive credit form than upper income populations. Second, we can measure the treatment of market clients in terms of the number of days required for repaying the same amount of money. Indeed, the final price of a credit depends not only on its interest rate, but also on the speed of repayment. We will combine three indicators in order to evaluate the different dimensions of consumer credit borrowing conditions.

We use statistical data from a national survey by the INSEE – Enquête Patrimoine – to measure French households' global indebtedness level. These data are unfortunately quite old as they cover the 1997–1998 period. This is, indeed, the only survey to ever have been carried out to comprehensively assess consumer credit debt in France. The Patrimoine Survey sample was randomly selected from the 1990 census and from a database of new housing residences. A total of 10,168 households replied to the survey, with a response rate of 80 per cent. The questions fell into two categories, which first related to households' capital assets, and second, to forms of household debt (credit type, credit firm, banks versus credit companies, and interest rate levels). We have applied responses given to the survey's second category of questions in the following analysis.

Interest rates

As stated earlier, all forms of credit in France are fixed in price, whereby credit companies or banks apply the same annual rate to clients for the same product. But at the market level, does this mean that indebted households of different socioeconomic statuses get the same average credit rate?[6] We will address this question by focusing on the annual rate of the two main consumer credit forms: revolving credit and the personal loan.

In 1997, the average declared personal loan annual interest rate in the process of being repaid amounted to 8.45 per cent (see Table 4.1). If we examine household socioeconomic categories in isolation, however, we find that this rate rises the further we go down the socioeconomic scale. For instance, skilled workers' personal loan rates were on average 1.3 per cent higher than for executives, such that skilled workers' personal loans cost 17 per cent more than executives' loans.

These figures show that revolving credit interest rates are always higher than personal loan rates, regardless of household socioeconomic status. Indeed, the average revolving credit rate is 14.71 per cent (see Table 4.1). When we compare the rates applied to the different socioeconomic categories, we can see that executives' revolving credit rates are the lowest, and 1.4 per cent lower than the average credit rate. Are these differences due to the fact that low socioeconomic households subscribe to credit companies' consumer credits, while upper socioeconomic households use bank loans?

The personal loan and revolving credit interest rates of banks are always lower than those of credit companies. In both cases, the average difference is about 1.5 per cent (see Table 4.2). Irrespective of borrowers' socioeconomic category, it is always cheaper to deal with a bank than a credit company.

These statistics highlight one feature of unequal market treatment: the credit rate applied to the poorest is higher than credit rate applied to the richest. They also highlight another interesting fact: credit companies are more expensive than banks. Such interest rates are the most obvious, but not the only indicators of unequal treatment.

What credits are chosen for which indebtedness reasons?

It is of interest to consider the type of credit that households of differing socioeconomic status choose when they decide to borrow money in order to finance the same form of purchase, given the differences in rates between personal loans

Table 4.1 Average annual interest rates according to the socioeconomic status of debtors

Socioeconomic status	Personal loan interest rate	Revolving credit interest rate
Executives	7.67	13.33
Intermediate Prof.	8.14	14.96
Employees	8.88	15.62
Skilled workers	8.97	14.19
Unskilled workers	8.5	14.59
Average	8.45	14.71

Source: Author's calculation; data from Patrimoine Survey (1998).

Table 4.2 Average annual interest rates according to type of lender

Supplier	Personal loan interest rate	Revolving credit interest rate
Consumer credit companies	9.88	12.92
Banks	8.42	15.4

Source: Author's calculation data from Patrimoine Survey (1998).

and revolving credit. If lower socioeconomic households use the most expensive form of consumer credit (revolving credit) more often than higher socioeconomic households to finance the same kind of purchase, this would highlight a second feature of unequal market treatment.

Data from the Patrimoine Survey highlight two different motives for purchase, which are financed by very different credit choices. These are "making ends meet at the end of the month" and covering extraordinary expenses (including tax and health costs).

Households that take on debt for "end of the month" expenditures show high levels of socioeconomic difference in their choices. Executives and intermediate professionals most frequently take out personal loans (62 per cent and 64 per cent respectively) while lower-income households choose revolving credit (between 57 per cent and 67 per cent depending on socioeconomic category). For "extraordinary expenses", personal loans are the most popular form of credit, irrespective of household socioeconomic category. Lower social classes use more revolving credit, amounting to over 40 per cent of debt for intermediate professionals, employees, and workers, as opposed to only 18 per cent of executive household debt.

An alternative means of measuring unequal treatment

A further dimension of credit pricing pertains to speed of repayment, as the longer the maturity, the higher the price finally paid. To assess whether socioeconomic status influences repayment speed, we created an indicator to estimate the number of days required to repay 1,000F of the principal (about €166). This measure does not take interest or real amount borrowed into account, but preserves the real monthly payment amount for credit declared in the Patrimoine Survey.

On average, 47.9 days were needed to repay 1,000F of the consumer credit debt principal (personal loans, revolving credits, instalment loans). We found differences between the different types of credit: 1,000F of revolving credit took 68 days, 64 days were needed for instalment loans, and 39 days for personal loan. As far as socioeconomic status is concerned, intermediate professionals and executives' speed of repayment was highest, requiring 41.6 and 47 days, while an unskilled worker needed 60 days.

Using the data collected by the survey, we were particularly struck by repayment terms for personal loans. Table 4.1 above indicated that personal loans were the least socioeconomically marked form of consumer credit, in as much as client households' socioeconomic statuses proportionally reflected those of the French population as a whole; but what about repayment rates? The lowest socioeconomic categories needed more time than the others to repay 1,000F. For example, workers' households needed 54 days, while intermediate professionals repaid within 37 days.

Thus for the same amount of money, repayment lengths are higher for the lower socioeconomic categories, and the interest generated is higher. Repayment

Table 4.3 Number of days needed to repay 1,000F of capital

Socioeconomic status	Number of days to repay a 1,000F personal loan	Number of days to repay a 1,000F instalment loan	Number of days to repay a 1,000F revolving credit loan
Executives	39.22	44.62	47.46
Intermediate Prof.	37.01	55.94	55.29
Employees	48.19	70.49	76.34
Skilled workers	47.57	70.18	69.76
Unskilled workers	53.96	70.95	81.63
Average	43.3	64	67.3

Source: Author's calculation; data from Patrimoine Survey (1998).

speed thus constitutes a further feature of the unequal treatment of consumers within the market.

This section has highlighted the consequences of the genesis and functioning of the French consumer credit market on borrowing conditions for indebted households. We have shown that even if the "exhibited price" is standardised and independent of the individual risk of each client, households access credit with borrowing conditions corresponding to their socioeconomic status, such that the market works against modest households.

Conclusion

In examining the genesis and the functioning of the French consumer credit market, we have shown that a market place of individuals free to choose their supply and firms free to determine their strategy is a fiction. Their strategies are more consequences of the structural constraints of the market and of firms' histories than deliberate decisions by firms evaluating profit opportunities and demand levels. Demand does not pre-exist the consumer credit market, and profit opportunities were scarcely foreseen.

We have also demonstrated how the matching of supply and demand is shaped by structural homologies. Structural homologies are a double-sided phenomenon: consumers choose products in the market place, which choose them as well. We have shown that when low socioeconomic populations in France access credit, they subscribe more frequently than others to expensive revolving credits offered by consumer credit companies. Meanwhile most credit firms, unlike banks, have no choice but to have weak standards when selecting clients. These two factors combine to reinforce unequal access to the consumer credit market against the background of banks' bad treatment of lower-class people, the desire of these people to access loans with confidentiality, and credit scoring's cut-off points.

We have highlighted three dimensions of such unequal access: interest rates are higher for workers and employee households, their repayment periods are longer, and they turn to the most expensive forms of credits: revolving credit. In the French consumer credit market as in many others, "the poor (still) pay more".

Notes

1 There are no Credit Bureaus in France. Each bank/credit company has to develop its own scoring software.
2 Banque de France, 2010.
3 The retailers mentioned are different from shopkeepers to which others' contributions to this volume refer. The latter are small grocery shops who accept late payments from their clients.
4 This practice is in fact similar to the method of "progressive lending", commonly found in the microfinance industry in developing countries.
5 Translations of interviews quotations are the author's.
6 The question implies that households of different socioeconomic status subscribe to different credit suppliers.

References

Bezbakh, P. (2006) *Inflation et désinflation*. Repères La découverte, Paris.

Bourdieu, P. (1979) *La distinction, critique sociale du jugement*. Éditions de Minuit, Paris.

Bourdieu, P. (1997) *Les structures sociales de l'économie*. Seuil Liber, Paris.

Banque de France (2010) *Barometer of over-indebtedness in juin 2010*, Paris.

Caplovitz, D. (1963) *The Poor Pay More*. The Free Press of Glence, New York.

Eber, N. (2000) "Sélection de clientèle et exclusion bancaire". *Revue d'économie financière*, Number 58.

Cetelem (2005) "Question de responsabilité", June 2005.

De Montlibert, C. (2006) "Les surendettés ou les déchus du monde économique". *Regards Sociologiques*, Number 32.

Ducourant, H. (2009) *Du crédit à la consommation à la consommation de crédits, autonomisation d'une activité économique*. Thèse de doctorat, Université Lille 1, 8 December 2009.

Ducourant, H. (2010) "Le crédit revolving, un succès populaire?". *Sociétés Contemporaines*, Numbers 74–76.

Garcia Parpet, M. F. (1986) "La construction sociale d'un marché parfait: le marché au cadran de Fontaines-en-Sologne". *Actes de la Recherche en Sciences sociales*, Number 65, November.

Garcia Parpet, M. F. (2007)"Mondialisation et transformation du monde viticole: processus viticole: processus de reclassement des vins du Languedoc-Roussillon", *Sociétés Contemporaines*, Number 68.

Johnson, R. W. (1980) "Credit in retailing: origins and trends", in R. W. Johnson *The Changing Universe of Retail Credit. Issues and developments in Third-Party Systems*. New York: New York University.

Laferté, G., M. Avanza, M. Fontaine, and E. Pénissat (2010) "Le crédit direct des commerçants aux consommateurs: persistance et dépassement dans le textile à Lens (1920–1970)". *Genèses*, Number 79.

Lazarus, J. (2007) "Les Pauvres et la consummation", *Vingtième siècle*, Number 91.

Lazarus, J. (2009) *L'épreuve de l'argent, une sociologie de la banque et de ses clients*. Thèse de doctorat de sociologie, EHESS, 29 June 2009.

Les affiches (1969) *Moniteurs des soumissions, journal d'information et de renseignements commerciaux juridiques administratifs, économiques et relatifs à la construction et au bois*, Number 39.

Ohl, J. (1974) "L'information et la protection du consommateur en matière de credit". *Avis et Rapport du Conseil économique et Social*, Number 5, Journal Officiel.

White, H. (1981) "Where do markets come from?" *American Journal of Sociology*, 87 (3): 517–547.

Zelizer, V. (1994) *The Social Meaning of Money: Pin Money, Paychecks, Poor Relief, and Other Currencies*. Basic Books, New Jersey.

5 Debt, credit and contractual synchrony in a South Indian market town[1]

Barbara Harriss-White

Introduction

This essay does not deal directly with over-indebtedness – the social relations of debt that actually pauperise – but instead with an aspect of financial vulnerability that enables accumulation for some while preventing accumulation by others. It has been little noticed in the existing literature on development and finance. This is the problem of unsynchronised payments in conditions where wealth is being created through systems of multiple transactions that require individuals to buy and sell commodities as well as their labour. A simplified example would be the deals required at each stage in a commodity chain for cotton, at its very simplest: production, transport, ginning, spinning, yarn transport, weaving, transport and wholesale, garment manufacturing with outsourcing and homeworking, more transport and wholesaling and finally retail sales. Payment periodicities that are asymmetrical, in particular having to pay for a purchase at faster speeds than one is repaid for a sale, can increase the burden of working capital requirements. When working capital is borrowed at interest, interest payments must enter the cost structure and reduce the profits of firms. Lack of synchrony in payment systems therefore has the capacity to pauperise.

This capacity to pauperise has policy implications. Over the last 35 years it has been regularly suggested that official development aid or formal sector bank funds should be routed through the informal business economy (Harriss-White 1994; Thorat, 2008). What have mattered to policy makers are three development problems: poverty, inequality in access to credit and lack of access per se – 40 per cent of Indian households are still 'unbanked' (Fouillet 2009). Banks could reach the unbanked if those who lend money informally to the unbanked and financially excluded were formalised as intermediaries for the banks.

Behind this suggestion, however, lies the assumption that the terms on which formal credit would be onwards lent would not exacerbate poverty. And an important characteristic of poverty in India is its relation to self-employment. While many poor households eke out livelihoods on wages, the commonest form of production in India is actually not wage labour but self-employment. The self-employed are not always among the poorest but the distribution of their incomes overlaps with that of wage workers (Lerche 2010; Harriss-White 2012).

Liberalisation has unleashed an epidemic of self-employment. Since 1990, the number of firms in India has increased, from 22 million to 38 million in 2005, 95 per cent of which are own account enterprises. Since 1990, economic census data shows that the average number of employees per firm has declined from 3 to 2.4 (Harriss-White 2013; Vidyarthee *et al.*, forthcoming). If liberalisation had created general wealth, firms would grow and start employing more labour. On aggregate at the all-India level, the story is the complete opposite.

The question of why self-employment has expanded during the period of the reforms is a puzzle involving the relations in which firms of 'micro-entrepreneurs' are embedded that allow only a few of them to be entrepreneurial enough to grow. Lack of access to bank credit – being 'unbanked' – does not mean lack of access to credit. The terms and conditions in which firms are locked into credit systems may be more important for their opportunities to accumulate than access to banks per se. Over-indebtedness and financial fragility are usually addressed in terms of inability of debtors to repay. But, as papers in this volume show, the firms of the poor juggle credit as well as debt – and in many directions. They may be *forced* to be creditors to powerful sellers. Debtors may repay but be locked into structures of costs and returns, where interest on working capital is one of the factors forcing a tiny firm to tick over in a state of 'simple reproduction' rather than to save and invest in the process of 'expanded reproduction', which characterises conventional models of capitalist accumulation.

This essay explores the theoretical and practical implications of lack of contractual synchrony in an informal economy of small town India, in which asymmetry in payments has been an enduring feature of market exchange. Our data pre-exists the contemporary period of reforms and continues into its early phases. They are not up to date. But to update them would require very time consuming and extensive, 'embedded' field research, which is not currently possible. Even without updating, our field material is relevant to the theme of over-indebtedness because it enables us to explore the phenomenon of lack of synchrony in payments and to show how it has persisted under conditions of economic dynamism and social change. It sheds light not only on the simultaneity of debt and credit among the mass of the Indian workforce but also on the question of the cockroach-like ubiquity of petty production as a feature of modern Indian capitalism, which expands by multiplication and not through accumulation.

The essay is structured as follows. We start by problematising the persistence of a vast contractual diversity in the rural–urban economy that has been noticed but greatly simplified in economic theory. We examine the physical, economic and social factors at play in price formation and the making of transactions. It then becomes apparent that the role in reducing profits and producing poverty of unsymmetrical lags in payment for purchases and sales of commodities in chains of transactions has escaped research altogether. Through two episodes of field research on the business economy of a small town in South India over a period of two decades of rapid economic and social change, we can focus on the institutions of business finance and the social character of the lagged payment systems that are normal practice in the commercial economy. From the heyday of the Green Revolution to the early reform period we find growing institutional intricacy and exclusive, segmented financial arrangements developing alongside considerable continuity in the major sources of commercial finance: formally rational banks, clan-finance and self-sufficiency. 'Weak' positions in contractual relations which force faster payment for purchases than repayment for sales accounted for two-thirds of cases in the random sample of the 1970s and characterised around half of the contractual norms in the set of top local firms we studied in the 1990s. At one and the same time, by requiring more working capital and interest payments than are needed for symmetrical payment systems, they can be, and are, pauperising; but we found that they also characterise the largest firms. These gain social prestige and economic control over production processes by advancing money and being able to bear slow payments. The fact of lack of synchrony in payments for commodities always requires additional information about other aspects of trade before it can be interpreted.

Contractual diversity in market exchange

The South Asian rural economy is characterised by persistent contractual diversity.[2] The state has not yet developed the capacity to enforce – or a material interest in enforcing – the framework of contractual law that it has created, under which contracts would be more homogeneous. There is also no evidence of institutional convergence with the deepening of market exchange: technologies and contractual forms co-exist and persist in a rich diversity. Even in the era of globalisation 'the market' is most accurately understood as bundles of contracts – formal and informal, implicit and explicit – embedded in the social structure and relations of capitalism. If we take labour contracts as an illustration, not only are they the result of physical capacity and 'human capital' in the form of education, they are also produced through what Bernstein (2009) and Lerche (2010) have called the emerging classes of labour. Non-market institutions of gender, kin, caste, ethnicity and religion affect the making of market contracts and can reduce negotiating space to zero.

In the theoretical literature, certain kinds of contract have been modelled as linking more than one 'market' – or being 'interlocked'. For instance, a single credit contract may lock labour obligations with land rental terms. Terms and conditions on water, land and money 'markets' may be fixed in a single contract, on money and commodity 'markets', or on land, labour, money and commodities.[3]

For analytical purposes, interlocked contracts are generally stylised[4] and their existence conditions theorised – or stylised contracts are paired and compared. They have generally been explained through two theoretical approaches. In new institutional economics, transactions on two markets are assumed to be voluntary and mutually beneficial; such a contractual form will internalise moral hazard, lower transactions costs and reduce the risk and uncertainty of counterfactual separate transactions.[5] In political economy, by contrast, interlocked contracts are not assumed to be voluntary or mutually beneficial – indeed they can be 'take it or leave it'. Bhaduri (1973) famously explained interlocked contracts as a 'class-efficient' way of extracting surplus. Whether such contracts can prevent technical change and growth in production is debated. Bhaduri theorises they act as an obstacle (1973); Rudra (1992) and Janakarajan (1986; 1996) claim that they don't have to. Which school of explanation is superior is a matter of the realism of their assumptions and their logic, and that in turn not only requires a priori reasoning but also *ex post* empirical testing. But neither of these two approaches to explanation examines constraints on freedom derived from social status and identity.

We know that the social relations of identity pervade actually existing contractual relations and must affect the evaluation of the relevance of theory. In two rural areas of West Bengal, Rogaly found that contextual relations of class and identity (notably age, gender, caste, locality and political allegiance) led to 13 contracts being *named*. In the region of Arni in Tiruvannamalai district, Janakarajan (1996) recorded another range of labels for labour contracts.[6] The labelling of contracts encapsulates a distinctive set of terms, conditions and social relations. We now know that a name may persist, while its role and significance can change.[7] Nevertheless the contract's 'label' sets limits to such 'internal' developments.

When it comes to towns however, and to mercantile transactions of money for commodities, it is remarkable that contracts are *not* named. This is due to there being fluidity in their (largely verbal) terms and conditions. Because of this fluidity, changed circumstances affecting the capacity to repay can lead to the renegotiation of a contract and non-compliance is rare. What traders call their 'strong ethic' may involve their 'strong-men' and can be reinterpreted in terms of power relations that underwrite the processes of accumulation (involving the secondary appropriation and the circulation of surplus through buying and selling) and social and economic differentiation through trade.

The argument here is concerned with the terms and conditions of the contracts that link commodities with money. It is based on sensitive empirical evidence about trade finance from Arni business surveys in 1973 and 1994. It explores the hypothesis that asymmetrical payments on informal contracts, that appear not to involve credit or loans while enabling the circulation of money, actually lock money and commodity markets in ways that aid accumulation by some and prevent it for many. An implicit null hypothesis – that contracts do none of this – underlies the following discussion.

Let us first consider a purely mercantile transaction.

The purchase and its price

Several factors over and above supply, demand and transaction costs affect the price of a commodity. Let us take the example of a basic food-grain – paddy-rice – to show the processes at work. The consignment size will affect the purchase price through the costs of bulking and transport costs to market. Larger consignments may also have greater heterogeneity in quality – and quality and variety also affect price. Weighing, testing for adulteration and quality (bad grain and moisture) will add to the costs of the transaction and be transmitted in the price. Price is also affected by deductions that compensate for interest foregone on advance loans to the selling party. It is rational not to charge interest on advance loans only if the returns to trading the total marketed surplus of the indebted party (via the non-contractual obligatory element in such a loan that is understood but never discussed by both parties – under which the indebted seller sells to the lenders quantities that are far in excess of what is needed for debt repayment) exceed what would have been got from charging open interest on the loan plus the returns from the purchase and sale of the repayment of the quantity loaned. Delayed transactions may also contain informal bets on future prices. In this case, the purchaser will wish to shed risk and will implicate the producer in the risk by reducing the element of price compensation for delay. All these factors may also be affected by the relative social status of the parties – though we know that acquired characteristics, such as reliability and competence, are replacing ascribed social status, or becoming an increasingly important attribute of status in market transactions. Last but not least, the price is affected by the lag in payment that is possible and also by the degree of compensation for that lag.

The sale and its price

Much the same arguments apply to a contract of sale. Meanwhile, between the moment of purchase and that of sale, stockholding or inventory incurs direct costs: those of rent, the costs of protecting and managing stock and the costs of deterioration or loss in storage. Interest on money locked up in stock piles up, and the opportunity to trade further and profit from differences between purchase and sales prices is foregone while goods are stored. All these components add to the cost of inventory. These, plus transport costs and the direct costs of the sales transaction – search, negotiation and enforcement – will be reflected in the price of the sale.

Unsynchronised payment

If the velocity of repayment on the sale is the same as the velocity of repayment on the purchase, then the implication for working capital requirements is that they have to cover the cost of stock plus the cost of the payment-repayment period. Working capital requirements are reduced if the first buyer can delay payment to the first seller and is repaid promptly, or if the first seller deposits their repayment with the first buyer. They are reduced further if the first buyer does not have to compensate the first seller for this, either through interest or through the price received by the first seller. Working capital requirements for the first buyer are increased if the second buyer can delay repayment by a longer period than the first buyer. They are increased further if the second buyer does not compensate for the delay either in interest or in price.

Synchronised regular transactions between trusted parties would minimise the need for working capital throughout the system of markets and transactions. Evidently, variations in working capital requirements have direct implications for debt, credit and credit risk. It is not only the entry requirements, conditions of supply and demand, the risk environment, and the technological requirements and social organisation of the industry that affect credit needs, but also payment asymmetries – the differences in the length of repayment periods for purchases and sales. As we explained in the introduction, these have been little studied. For decades the rural development finance literature has focussed on either the producer and/or the poor. The literature has recognised value chains, but mostly avoided the implications for finance and for returns of there being long chains of transactions.[8]

We will now see how these asymmetries relate to trade, debt and credit, using the South Indian market town of Arni for our case material. If, as Montek Singh Ahluwalia, the Secretary of the Planning Commision is reported to have said, anything before 2000 is pre-history, then so be it. Pre-history has never been anything but the cradle of modernity.

The social embeddedness of informal business finance

Long before the invention of 'value chains', anthropologists who studied Asian towns were observing what they called 'chains', 'hierarchies'and 'ladders' of credit.[9] They conceived the interlocking of money and commodity markets through payment asymmetries in terms of 'transactions' requiring 'loans', and we will first look at the social structure of such loans.

Clifford Geertz reasoned that since secure supplies require loans, traders have to be creditors but *wish* instead to be debtors. They have to lend widely to reduce the risk of the impact of default. But, even at high open or disguised interest, debtors are themselves secure under two conditions; first, if there are alternative sources of trade credit and second, if it is accepted that trade credit will never be fully repaid but juggled, rolled or rotated onwards. However, regardless of what traders would like, for traders generally to be debtors rather than creditors, as in Geertz's model, requires there to be an apex net donor of credit – which cannot be sustained in practice – as well as a competitive alternative for the debtor – which Geertz himself rules out, pointing to the social controls on default in systems of bazaar credit.

The three distinguishing features of business credit 'ladders' are not simply features of developing countries, but are found extensively under advanced capitalism too. First, they are socially structured and exclusive (Weber's 'pietistic loans'). Second, this exclusivity expresses a tension. On the one hand, dispensing with the need for collateral and reducing transactions costs make trade credit efficient. On the other hand, in marginalising those ascribed with social un-creditworthiness, it stabilises chains of debt and credit at the expense of barriers to entry that may be unjust. Third, final effective demand, in the form of the customer, is weakly organised. Customers tend to take the credit terms of retailers rather than sending undistorted price signals through the system of transactions.

Over and above considerations of risk, as a result of the variety of social relations of business, interest rates may exhibit a broad spectrum: from zero interest on loans between members of a family, clan or caste, through subsidised development credit of banks and the nuanced contracts of trade credit in which interest is interlocked with prices, to the openly extortionate interest of shady moneylenders and pawnbrokers. In urban-rural credit 'webs' each transaction fetches a higher interest as it moves outwards and approaches the rural producer/labourer. The apex lender who runs a wholesale business or a rice mill lends at lower interest than his agents and sub-agents, but receives guaranteed supplies in return.

Segmented business finance in Arni in the Green Revolution era

Arni is an agricultural market town in northern Tamil Nadu that has grown from a population of 30,000 in the early 1970s, when we first got to work there, to three times that now. Four decades of rural–urban economic biography is the subject of a book.[10] In this section of our essay we examine the synchrony of transactions in the dynamic era of the Green Revolution. Many institutions were involved in Arni's money markets. In 1973–4 the following facts were observed: (1) only a quarter of businesses had accounts with one or more of the four formal banks; (2) the stuff of trade involved credit relations with family and caste members; (3) petty firms participated in chit funds. Due to the risk of the manager absconding with the funds or subscribers who had received their full chit refusing to subscribe further, there was strong social control over these institutions; (4) pawnbrokers, jewellers and private moneylenders were regarded as degrading to borrow from; but were used by small businessmen for small urgent lump sums. Few pawnbrokers would lend to strangers, though they themselves were not averse to pawning backwards to banks. While bank interest on jewels was 12 per cent, pawnbrokers lend onwards at 18–24 per cent. Despite social opprobrium, the sector was easy to enter and increasingly crowded and its North Indian caste origins were being diluted. Caste affected access to pawnbroking and the terms and conditions of loans; (5) general traders and paddy wholesalers would lend to other traders at interest varying from 15–24 per cent for the former and 18–40 per cent for the latter, reflecting the economic security of the debtor; and (6) the largest informal loans could be got from 'private parties' on trust at the highest interest – 5 per cent per month, the point being that this was black money. Money markets were segmented and social control was exerted over the interest rates of each segment.[11]

The social structure of business finance in Arni in the Green Revolution era

Table 5.1 summarises the social structure of trade finance. A third of firms were self reliant and neither borrowed nor lent. Although some of these latter firms

Table 5.1 Social exclusivity in finance: sources of commercial finance

Caste	Type	Number of traders	% sample	Av annual turnover Rs '000
Chettiar	urban	11	12	159.8
Muslims	urban	8	9	142
Naidus	urban	6	6	264*
Tullu vellala	rurban	22	25	77
Agamudaiyan mudaliars				
Vanniar – gounders (Naickers)	rurban	11	12	121
Sengunthar mudaliars	rurban	4	4.4	55
misc	misc	11	12	108
Acharis/gold	urban	5	5.6	28
Service castes	misc	8	9	7.2
SCs	emergent	3	3.3	6.3

% traders reporting use of

Caste	1	2	3	4	5	6	7	8	9	10	11	12
Chett	72	–	9	–	–	–	18	–	9	36	–	64
Mus	68	12	–	–	12	12.5	–	–	–	25	–	50
Naid	16	–	–	–	16	16	16	–	–	33	–	33

	1	2	3	4	5	6	7	8	9	10	11	12	13
TVAM	57	14	—	—	—	—	5	23	—	14	27	—	33
Vann	45	9	—	9	18	9	9	9	9	9	27	9	56
Seng	75	25	—	—	—	—	—	—	—	—	—	—	25
misc	73	18	—	9	9	9	—	18	9	9	—	—	36
achar	60	20	—	—	—	—	—	—	—	—	20	—	40
Serv castes	100	14	—	14	14	—	—	43	28	—	—	—	28
SCs	—	—	—	—	66	—	—	33	—	66	—	—	—

Source: author's survey (1974).

Notes

*=warped by silk business.

Columns

1 to 4 = within family/within caste: 1 = investment funds without interest; 2 = working capital without interest; 3 = working funds without interest; 4 = consumption loans.

5 to 7 = other private sources.

5 = investment funds at interest; 6 = working capital without interest; 7 = working capital at interest; 8 = consumption credit.

9 to 11 = bank finance.

9 = investment funds at interest; 10 = working capital at interest; 12 = consumption credit.

13 = simultaneous lending and borrowing 'ladder credit'.

For *Caste* abbreviations in the lower table – see the upper one. The 29 castes in the 1973 sample have been classified in 10 groups. Large long-established urban trading castes include Chettiars, Muslims and Naidus (28 per cent of the sample); large, long established 'rurban' castes include Agamudaiyan Mudaliars, Senguntha Mudaliars and Naicker-Gounders – 40 per cent of the sample; Service castes (not necessarily plying their traditional trades) include Acharis, Potters, Barbers, Washermen and Cobblers – 9 per cent of the sample) Scheduled Castes are 4 per cent and miscellaneous 12 per cent. The caste-economy may be summarised as follows: dominant urban/rurban traders – 81 per cent; service castes 15 per cent, scheduled castes 4 per cent.

were not small, 'self reliance' was one way of expressing the lack of creditworthiness characterising petty firms. Among the business elite, *prestige* was attached to the kind of self-reliance that enables a trader to lend, while not borrowing. Of the majority that wasn't small or 'self reliant', within-caste funds were more important for long-term investment than funds from other castes. While the within-caste funds were vitally important for start-up capital for small firms, both were important for working capital. Within-caste loans were regarded as supportive of 'self-reliance', which for many traders was more desirable than being in a Geertzian state of debt. It is among the four biggest urban castes that trade loans were taken at no interest: the creditor benefited from regular transactions, and developed status in the form of merit and prestige equal to or exceeding the interest foregone – even if they could not actually be valued on a money metric. These were the business fractions that also borrowed from banks at interest – it was the big, 'progressive' firm rather than the progressive caste that could be observed developing. By contrast, the dominant rural castes and the service castes avoided banks and used family finance and private moneylenders. Scheduled Castes (SCs) or Dalits (the most oppressed castes) had started to move into the market as owners of firms (vessels, bricks and cycles). Unable to access any funds from their families and castes, discriminated against by others and proud of their self reliance, they borrowed when necessary from private moneylenders and occasionally from banks. As they put it to us, because they were excluded from many institutions of informal finance, they were being forced to be 'modern' and to make use of formal institutions whenever they could.

In Arni, instead of a uni-directional progress towards instrumentally-rational capitalism, we found three dimensions governing trade or business finance. These were: formally rational 'capitalist' in Weberian terms (using banks and informal lenders at interest for investment and working capital); 'clannish' (borrowing only from within the caste or family for investment, working capital and consumption credit) and 'self-reliant' (no borrowing for investment or working capital (and little rolling payments)).

Table 5.2 illustrates that 40 per cent of the sample was sited at one point or other on this triangle and the remainder were scattered within it.

Although the three polar categories show less variation within than between them, and although the largest firms are most engaged with formal capitalist institutions of credit, it is clear that the pattern of the Green revolution era did not imply a simple process. In a process of urban-industrial commodification and

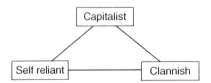

Figure 5.1 Dimensions governing trade or business finance.

Table 5.2 The disembedding of finance – 1973–4

	% of firms exhibiting polar characteristics of		
	capitalist	*clannish*	*self–reliant*
Urban castes	20	8	16
Rurban castes	17	11	35
Service castes	–	15	28
SCs	100	–	–
Average Firm size Rs'000	16	16.5	78
Average start date	1957	1957	1954

Source: author's survey (1974).

growth, the urban economy could not be shown to have been moving from the base to the apex of the triangle. Some very small firms – those of SCs – were using banks, as were small firms dealing in agricultural products.

Payment asymmetries in Arni in the Green Revolution era

The non-self-reliant businesses can be classified according to whether they buy and sell on credit, sell but do not buy on credit, buy but do not sell on credit, or neither (Table 5.3).

Firms rolling credit in both directions tended to be owned by urban castes, to be much larger firms, to deal in products of the agrarian economy and to be wholesale in scale. Self-sufficient firms dealing in spot transactions for cash tended to be rural castes, to have small gross outputs, to deal in goods of the industrial economy and to be retailers. Just as Geertz concluded, consumers were not well organised and lending to them was felt to be risky unless they were on government salaries. In between were groups with transitional economic charac-teristics. But in the 1970s, Arni's 'value chains' were shorter than in the twenty-first century. Of the most elaborate, silk, which involved transactions with yarn suppliers in Bangalore and markets in Chennai (then called Madras), half the firms did business on cash, only the largest firms were bound into relations of rolling credit on purchases and sales.

Of the firms delaying payment for both purchases and sales (or simultan-eously lending and borrowing from those with whom they transacted), a third had synchronised payment periods. But in two-thirds of commercial firms, traders reported they had to wait between 2 and 30 times as long to be repaid for their sales as they paid on their purchases and were forced to borrow funds from fourth parties.

Payment asymmetries in Arni in the early reform period

> Money is hard here.
>   (private lender, 1994)

Table 5.3 Credit relations of firms, 1973

Credit used for purchase/sale	% sample	% urban	Average annual output Rs '000	Average date of start
+/+	33	37	200	1956
−/+	20	33	70	1956
+/−	13	18	26	1957
−/−	34	13	31	1956

Credit used for purchase/sale	% firms traditional	% Firms modern	% Firms mfr	% Firms wh	% Firms ret	% clientele mainly urban	% clientele mainly rural
+/+	75	25	13	40	75	34	66
−/+	55	45	–	11	94	34	66
+/−	36	64	0	19	72	72	28
−/−	33	66	10	6	90	46	54

Source: author's survey (1974).

Notes
mfr = manufacturing; wh = wholesaling; ret = retailing.

In 1994 we were able to approach a group of 52 mercantile firms and discuss their finance. The set itself was not random but represented the town's largest firms plus those randomly selected in 'sensitive' sectors – notably private moneylending, pawnbroking and goldsmithing, scrap and re-cycling (a monopoly of Muslim traders) and sectors where Scheduled Caste traders work (fruit, vegetables, meat and cosmetics). These firms all generate profit from purchases and sales, and some also interleave productive activity with commerce. We asked whether there were regularities about payments and the question was meaningful to the owners of firms. We also asked whether contracts were given vernacular names, but the answer was negative. We then asked a new set of questions about payment arrangements. Some 52 firms were able to provide 59 sets of contractual norms for purchases and sales, since some firms worked in more than one commodity sector – see Table 5.4.

It is obvious that considerable diversity in the payment arrangements persists into the reform period.

Where the repayment velocity on sales is greater than that for purchases, the reference trader was earlier hypothesised to be in a 'strong' position. Where the reference trader had to pay back more quickly than he was repaid, we deduced that he was in a 'weak' position – because he required more working capital (at interest) than if repayment periodicities were synchronous. While the quantitative results are of no statistical significance because the set is not a random sample, they may be useful as a basis of further interpretation and research.

Only 12 per cent were in 'strong' positions – about the same proportion as in the 1970s. These firms are typically are paid in cash for their sales, while they may delay payment on their purchases by anything from two to over 30 days. While these included two of the biggest businesses (cloth and buses) the rest were all petty artisan crafts producing on advance payment (picture frames and gold) or Scheduled Caste petty traders in relations of economic clientelism (cosmetics and coconuts). A third reported making symmetrical payments – whether through advance payments (rare) in cash, or in long but symmetrical delays. It looks as though there was little change to the minor importance of synchrony. At 14 per cent of contracts each, symmetrical payment arrangements were bunched between spot contracts (involving all sorts of enterprises, including some of the most closely state-regulated commodities (e.g. alcohol and kerosene)) and contracts with long bi-directional delays of over 30 days (notably for rice and silk).

However, half the reported contractual norms involved the repayment velocity on sales being slower than payment on purchases – our hypothesised 'weak' position. Advances were given on purchases with delays of over 30 days on sales in 17 per cent of cases, while cash purchases had to contend with delays of 16–30 days in repayment on sales in a further third. Leaving moneylending and pawnbroking businesses aside, few were firms with obvious economic attributes of weakness – such as small size. Most were substantial enterprises by local standards, dealing in silk, agricultural inputs and products (groundnuts, bran and rice), provisions and scrap. In all these sectors, competition for supplies is crucial to accumulative success.

Table 5.4 Payment asymmetries – subset of 52 firms, 1994 (in % of total)

Sale	Purchase contract					
	Advance	Cash	2–15 days lag	16–30 days lag	>30 days lag	Number of contracts
advance	2	3				3
cash	3	14	2	3	6	17
2–15days lag	5	3	2	–	–	6
16–30 days lag	3	3	5	2	–	8
>30 days lag	17	7	2	3	14*	25
Number of contracts	18	18	6	5	12	59

Source: author's survey (1994).

Notes
N = 59 = 100%.
* Some lags were up to 90 days.
Except for Scheduled Caste firms, we have not yet classified firms by caste, by clientele and by the degree of urbanity and rurality of their business as we did for the 1970s.

Lagged payments could develop considerable complexity. In silk, one single case reported to us involved delays of 60 days for raw silk, 90–120 days for gold *zari* thread, 40 days for dyes and 30 days in payment for woven sarees, the latter with a 10 per cent compensation in price. Table 5.5, presenting the behaviour of a subset of 15 firms with the largest gross outputs, confirms that being a contractual creditor is more strongly associated with growth and size than being a debtor, and lends some support to the Geertzian hypothesis. But Table 5.6, which illustrates the institutions funding the biggest firms, reveals that the elite firms in the town certainly did not seek to be debtors. On the contrary, they developed and relied on their own funds and actively avoided debt if they could. In the end this self-reliant behaviour casts doubt on Geertz's hypothesis, at least as it applies to conditions in this town in the early reform period.

In the 1990s, about the same proportions of the 15 very largest local firms bought and sold goods with the same immediate (cash) and long (over 30-day) symmetries as in the larger set of 52 – 16 per cent and 13 per cent respectively. A smaller proportion of the top 15 (35 per cent as opposed to half of the set of 52) operated from apparently 'weak' operating positions. In 13 per cent of cases firms purchased on cash and were reimbursed for sales in over 13 days; while in 22 per cent of cases they gave advances on purchases with reimbursement on sales of over 30 days. We cannot avoid concluding from Tables 5.5 and 5.6 that – holding other things constant – the 'weak' position of self-sufficiency (Ss in Table 5.6) does indeed involve considerably more working capital than is the case for symmetrical or 'rapid-receiving' contracts. But the greater working capital requirement certainly does not constrain accumulation. Rather, the capacity to operate from the 'weak' position with more working capital than would be needed with symmetrical payments seems to signify business status, prestige and the capacity to be a 'net donor' of commercial credit. In this un-random set of firms, wherever contractual conditions are such that production can only take place on receipt of advance payments, we find the firms to which payments are advanced are most likely to be small. While we cannot infer process from a cross section in this case, a fruitful hypothesis for research, and one with far reaching ramifications given the growing importance of self-employment in India's informal economy, is that economic clientelism is a constraint on accumulation. It is the equivalent in the commodity economy of unfree or forced labour.

As well as having implications for working capital, contractual behaviour has implications for the taking of loans. Whereas in the 1970s we analysed contractual synchrony as being seamlessly intertwined with rolling credit relations, in 1994 we asked about trade loans separately and describe them separately here.

Financial institutions in the early contemporary period

Far from becoming more streamlined and/or dominated by state regulation, the financial architecture of Arni grew more complex with the passage of time. In the era of early liberalisation, the following trends were apparent: (1) the banks were widely reported by firms to be 'unavailable for us', i.e. unable to supply

Table 5.5 Contractual norms of fifteen firms with gross outputs exceeding Rs1 Crore, 1994

Sale	Purchase					
	Advance	Cash	2–15 days lag	16–30 days lag	>30 days lag	Number of contracts
advance	–	–	–	–	–	–
cash	7	13	–	13	7	6
2–15 days lag	–	7	–	–	–	1
16–30 days lag	8	–	1	–	–	1.5
>30 days lag	22	13	1	–	13	6.5
Number of contracts	4.5	5	0.5	2	3	15

Source: author's survey (1994)

Note
1 crore is Rs10million and the Rs $ exchange rate was about 33.3.

Table 5.6 Principal credit relations of fifteen firms with gross outputs exceeding Rs1 crore, 1994, (Rs cr)

Type	Gross output	Credit source
Silk	12	Ss
Cloth	7	Ss
Groundnut/paddy-rice	6.3	I
Cloth	4	Ss
Silk	3.6	Ss
Fertiliser/ paddy-rice	3	Ss
Rice Mill	3	Caste
Petrol	3	I
Rice Mill	1.6	Caste
Rice Mill	1.5	F
Buses	1.3	F
Lorries	1.3	I
Bran	1.1	I
Bakery	1.0	I
Thread/yarn	1.0	I

Source: author's survey (1994).

Notes
One crore is Rs10 million at a rate of about 33.3 to the US$ in 1994.
Ss = own funds/'self-sufficient'.
Caste = caste network.
I = informal finance.

loans openly for trade, or able only at excessive transactions costs compared with alternatives. Bank interest was 12–18 per cent; (2) family and caste remained vital sources of trade finance. In the case of Arni's Marwari pawnbroking elite, this meant a family *sangam* cum *bank*, which excluded non-Marwaris. But other smaller-scale family banking also took social exclusivity for granted; (3) unregulated chit funds had proliferated. Only two out of over 500, were thought to be registered. Conflicts of interest were likely to be at play, because the regulators themselves were alleged to be investing. Chits could amount to Rs1–2 lakhs over periods of 1–2 years; (4) pawnbroking had also expanded. The largest 5–6 firms were reckoned by a senior advocate to have up to Rs5 crores available.[12] For those forced to borrow, terms and conditions had deteriorated, while debt collecting agents of pawnbrokers (their 'strong men') had started to lend on their own account; (5) general traders continued to lend at much the same interest as in the 1970s, while paddy-rice wholesalers and agents were under threat of boycott and non-compliance in retaliation for much malpractice of their own; (6) from an estimated five or six shadowy 'private parties' mentioned with fear in the 1970s, the number of private lenders had trebled. The private financier had become a respectable profession eligible for entry to the Rotary Club or as an occupation for the next generation 'qualified' with MBAs. For urgent loans, interest could rise to 50 per cent ('30 per cent is rather low' mused one). An office-bearer of the Chamber of Commerce commented that private parties could 'bully local officials'. Certainly their growing armies of debt collectors could bully debtors; (7) temple trustees, officials, bank employees, teachers and lawyers also lent their savings into the system of money markets through finance companies. Only two of the estimated 160 of them were registered. Contracts took the form of informal promissory notes or verbal agreements, with interest of up to 42 per cent reported to us; and (8) moneylending and 'safe deposit' was also becoming a common element in the portfolios of silk and rice firms. Nonetheless, informal finance was working loose from commerce. Reputation remained the crucial collateral, and could be inherited. Much of this modest finance capitalism was black and its high interest encouraged investments with short-term returns.

Table 5.7 maps credit for business onto the concepts used for the credit analysis of the 1970s.

In the 1990s, formal credit was not necessarily being used by the biggest firms. It was accessed by firms dealing in highly regulated commodities, by agents of the corporate sector and – despite reports from north India of persistent exclusion of Dalits from formal bank credit[13] – by a few small firms run by Scheduled Caste traders. Informal credit institutions were twice as frequently used. Caste-based finance – 'clannish credit behaviour' – was still vital to some of the largest agro-commercial firms. The proportion of self-reliant firms looks to have remained roughly constant. At the two extremes, some of the largest firms valued their financial self-sufficiency and two kinds of small firms – the craft enterprises and most firms run by Scheduled Castes – were forced into self-sufficiency. While it was not surprising to find pawnbokers and professional moneylenders taking deposits, other firms also did this (in agro-trades and wine) and, irrespective of their licence, were effectively functioning as small, unregulated banks.

While we cannot make a rigorous comparison between the survey data for 1994 and that for the 1970s, it is clear that the nationally integrated urban economy[14] was still being governed by the three credit spheres identified in the 1970s and that there was no dramatic shift in their relative importance. Big firms in particular were not using formal banking institutions. That the era of early liberalisation was not associated with a movement of large firms towards using banks reinforces the evidence from research on labour relations, which shows that India's liberalisation is rooted in the informal economy. The assumption that instrumental rationality is associated exclusively with state-regulated institutions needs further investigation.

Table 5.7 Credit relations of a subset of firms – 1994 – (%)

Formal capitalist	Informal capitalist	Clannish	Self-sufficient	Lending out	Taking deposits
13	25	13	32	15	5

Source: author's survey (1994).

Conclusions

We hypothesised that asymmetrical payments on contracts that appear not to involve credit or loans actually lock money and commodity markets in ways that aid accumulation. We find that this is *not* disproved, but for reasons we did *not* expect. The most successful local firms lock money and commodities through contracts requiring them to bear risk and to finance net delays in payment. The least successful firms are those that cannot produce at all, except on money advances and/or prompt payments. The terms of economic clientelism associated with petty trade appear to constrain accumulation.

While they had to be net-creditors to ensure supplies, the most successful firms did not seek to be debtors, relying instead on their own funds and even 'holding deposits' for rural clients. Geertz's argument, that firms have to be creditors but seek to be debtors, did not hold for the commercial economy of the town of Arni in the 1990s. We conclude that by themselves, payment velocities and asymmetries are not solid indicators of accumulative power. Information on their implications for price formation – particularly the compensations in price that may be made for the (implied) interest on delayed payments – is essential in order to make sense of them.

We also conclude that debt relations and institutions mean different things for different kinds of business. For instance, for low castes the formalities of the bank are the default option since Dalits (the lowest Scheduled Castes) are excluded from other kinds of informal business finance; while for others, the use of banks is the result of dealing with heavily state-regulated items, where their accounts and money dealings have to be open to official inspection (e.g. medical drugs, kerosene and liquor). For another instance, self-reliance can either mean a lack of ascribed creditworthiness (in the case of low caste, small firms: 'fruit and veg' for example) or a matter of high prestige (for the upper castes in commerce and for big firms, both exemplified by silk businesses).

So we also conclude that the negotiation and regulation of payment asymmetries persist in expressing economic and social status, prestige and social exclusivity through a period of economic dynamism. During early phases of 'liberalisation', informal credit institutions proliferated. Trade credit was out of state control. There was no evidence of a movement towards the use of formal sector bank credit and every indication that family, caste and informal institutions remained powerful regulators of the business economy. These institutions may be efficient in terms of transactions costs but they are also social barriers, inequitable and differentiating. Hence, in explanations for such contractual behavior, the working of institutions of social identity must be incorporated alongside information and transactions costs, competitive conditions and features of industrial organisation.[15]

Although the evidence does not support a rigorous comparison, there also appeared to be no major change to the patterns of synchrony in payments, none to the value attached to financial self-reliance nor to the social relations associated with the more rapid receipt of funds in selling than in buying or with money advances on transactions within the town.[16] 'Modernity' is not a process of one-way change. Nor were consumers better organised with the passage of time. Consumer credit was still restricted to public sector employees. The hire purchase (on instalments) of consumer durables was still also restricted, since it was experienced as risky.[17]

Clearly, the extent to which economic and institutional change has undermined the arrangements reported here – which appear to have remained stable through the liberalisation of the 1980s and early 1990s – is a question demanding field research. This is a sensitive subject and not to be explored using the 'rapid' methods that are currently in vogue, let alone 'participatory' ones.

Finally, these results have implications for the policy question with which we began. While it has been suggested that official development aid or formal sector bank funds should be routed through the informal business economy in practice, many businesses have avoided banks; throughout the last four decades they have been put to such use through virement. For this engagement with the informal economy to become official policy, it would have to be accepted that some such lending would be highly risky. Much would be transacted at illegal interest rates; and all would be socially differentiating. Unless and until firms find it to their advantage to mediate all their transactions through banks on regulated terms and conditions, there is little possibility that such a routing of funds would do anything but reinforce the contractual relations that prevent accumulation by the petty producers and traders in the informal economy. This is precisely the class for which the Indian state has no coherent development project.[18]

Notes

1 I am grateful to IEDES, Paris-1, for the visiting fellowship in 2010 that enabled me to prepare and write this essay, to Dr M. V. Srinivasan, now of NCERT, New Delhi, who was my co-researcher in the field and to the editors for their perceptive responses to the draft.

2 See Rogaly (1996) for labour; Majid (1994) for land and Harriss-White (1996 a) for commodities.

3 Bhaduri (1973); Janakarajan (1993, 1996); Crow (2001).

4 This stylising may remove one of the most important feature of a contract – its internal variation.

5 Braverman and Stiglitz (1982); Bell and Srinivasan (1989).

6 *Mathu-aal* – cattle work exchange; *padiyal* – permanent labour with fixed pay; *kootali* – permanent labour with share payment subdivided between half permanent work – *arai* and full permanent work (including pledging female labour too – *muzhu*). *Dina-kooli* refers to the casual daily wage contract.

7 *Kootali* can now involve fixed pay. *Dinakooli* now more often means piece rate pay rather than daily wages.

8 The article by Long and Villarreal (1998) is an exception.

9 Geertz's Mujokur (1963), Fox's Tezibazaar (1969); Hazlehust's Ramnagar (1969) and Mines' Pallavaram (1972).

10 Harriss-White (ed.) (forthcoming).

11 Harriss (1981); Harriss and Harriss (1984).

12 A lakh is 100,000 while one crore is Rs10 million. The Rs to $ exchange rate in 1994 was 33.3.

13 Thorat and Newman (2007); Prakash (2010).
14 Basile, forthcoming.
15 Extremely well instanced in the case of chewing tobacco in Palladam (Harriss-White 1996b).
16 See Polzin, forthcoming and Harriss-White (2013) for changes in rural–urban relations involving money advances.
17 Polzin (forthcoming) shows that this has now changed and mobile fire purchase sales of a range of goods is now common in the surrounding villages.
18 Harriss-White (2012).

References

Basile, E. forthcoming 'Local-Global integration, diversification and informality: long term change in Arni during the late twentieth century', in B. Harriss-White (ed.) (forthcoming) *Middle India and its Dynamism: Four Decades of Rural-Urban Development in Tamil Nadu*, submitted to Palgrave.

Bell, C. and T. N. Srinivasan (1989) 'Interlinked transactions in rural markets: an empirical study of Andhra Pradesh, Bihar and Punjab', *Oxford Bulletin of Economics and Statistics*, 51(1): 73–83.

Bernstein, H. (2009) 'Agrarian questions from transition to globalization', in H. Akram-Lodhi and C. Kay (eds) *Peasants and Globalization: Political Economy, Rural Transformation and the Agrarian Question*, London: Routledge.

Bhaduri, A. (1973) 'A study in agricultural backwardness under semi-feudalism', *Economic Journal*, 83(1): 120–37.

Braverman, A and J. E. Stiglitz (1982) 'Share-cropping and the interlinking of agrarian markets', *American Economic Review*, 72(4): 695–755.

Crow, B. (2001) *Markets, Class and Social Change: Trading Networks and Poverty in Rural South Asia*, London: Palgrave.

Fouillet, C. (2009) 'La Construction economique, spatiale et politique de la microfinance en Inde', Doctoral Thesis, Universite Libre Bruxelles.

Fox, R. (1969) *From Zamindar to Ballot Box: Community Change in a North Indian Market Town*, Ithaca: Cornell University Press.

Geertz, C. (1963) *Peddlers and Princes: Social Development and Economic Change in Two Indonesian Towns*, Chicago: University Of Chicago Press.

Harriss, B. (1981) 'Money and commodities, monopoly and competition', in J. Howell (ed.) *Borrowers and Lenders: Financial Markets and Institutions in Developing Countries*, London: ODI, pp. 107–30.

Harriss, B. and J. Harriss (1984) 'A generative or parasitic urbanism? Some observations on the recent history of a South Indian market town, *Journal of Development Studies*, 20(3): 82–101.

Harriss-White, B. (1994) 'The question of traders' credit agency', in F. von Benda Beckmann and O. Hospes (eds) *Financial Landscapes Reconstructed*, Boulder: Westview Press, pp. 325–40.

Harriss-White, B. (1996a) 'Free market romanticism in an era of deregulation', *Oxford Development Studies*, 24(1): 27–46.

Harriss-White, B. (1996b) *A Political Economy of Agricultural Markets in South-India: Masters of the Countryside*, New Delhi: Sage Publications.

Harriss-White, B. (2012) 'Capitalism and the common man', *Agrarian South: Journal of Political Economy*, 1(2): 109–60.

Harriss-White, B. (2013) *Three Essays on Rice: Local Capitalism and the Foodgrains Economy in Northern Tamil Nadu, 1973–2010*, New Delhi: Three Essays Press.

Harriss-White, B. (ed.) (forthcoming) *Middle India and its Dynamism: Four Decades of Rural-Urban Development in Tamil Nadu*, submitted to Palgrave.

Harriss-White, B. and J. Heyer (eds) (2010) *The Political Economy of Development: Africa and South Asia Compared*, London: Routledge.

Harriss-White, B. and K. Vidyarthee with A. Prakash, E. Basile, A. Dixit and P. Joddar (forthcoming) *An Atlas of Dalit and Adivasi Participation in the Indian Economy*, New Delhi: Three Essays Press.

Hazlehurst, L. (1968) *Entrepreneurship and Merchant Castes in a Punjab City* Monograph number 1, Commonwealth Studies Centre, Duke University.

Janakarajan, S. (1986) 'Aspects of market interrelationships in a changing agrarian economy: a case study from Tamil Nadu', PhD Thesis, University of Madras.

Janakarajan, S. (1993) Triadic exchange relations: an illustration from South India', *Bulletin Institute of Development Studies*, 24(3): 75–82.

Janakarajan, S. (1996) 'Complexities of agrarian markets and agrarian relations: a study of villages in Northern Tamil Nadu', paper for the workshop on Adjustment and Development', MIDS Chennai.

Lerche, J. (2010) 'from "rural labour" to "classes of labour": class fragmentation caste and class struggle at the bottom of the indian labour hierarchy', in B. Harriss-White and J. Heyer (eds) *The Political Economy of Development: Africa and South Asia Compared*, London: Routledge.

Long, N. and M. Villarreal (1998) 'Small product, big issues', *Development and Change*, 29 (4): 725–50.

Majid, N. (1994) 'Contractual arrangements in Pakistani agriculture: A atudy of sharecropping in Sindh', DPhil Thesis, Oxford University.

Mines, M. (1972) *Muslim Merchants – the Economic Behaviour of an Indian Muslim Community*, Delhi: Shri Ram Centre.

Polzin, C. (forthcoming) 'Institutional Change in Informal Credit through the Rural–Urban Lens', in B. Harriss-White (ed.) (forthcoming) *Middle India and its Dynamism: Four Decades of Rural-Urban Development in Tamil Nadu*, submitted to Palgrave.

Prakash, A. (2010) 'Dalit entrepreneurs in middle India', in B. Harriss-White and J. Heyer (eds) *The Political Economy of Development: Africa and South Asia Compared*, London: Routledge.

Rogaly, B. (1996) 'Agricultural growth and the structure of labour hiring in rural West Bengal', *Journal of Peasant Studies*, 23(4): 141–60.

Rudra, A. (1992) *A Political Economy of Indian Agriculture*, Calcutta: K. P. Bagchi.

Thorat, S. and K. Newman (2007) 'Caste and economic discrimination: causes, consequences and remedies', *Economic and Political Weekly*, 13 October, pp. 4121–4.

Thorat, U. (2008) *Inclusive Growth: the Role of Banks in Emerging Economies*, Colombo: Central Bank of Sri Lanka.

Vidyarthee, K., P. Joddar and A. Desai (forthcoming) *An Atlas of Dalit and Adivasi Participation in the Indian Business Economy*, London: Three Essays Press.

6 The social meaning of over-indebtedness and creditworthiness in the context of poor rural South Indian households (Tamil Nadu)[1]

Isabelle Guérin, Marc Roesch,
G. Venkatasubramanian and K. S. Santosh Kumar

High levels of indebtedness amongst Indian rural households have long been a matter of concern. Official British field reports regularly express surprise and concern about high levels of debt in villages (Breman 2007; Cederlöf 1997; Hardiman 1996). Many Christian missions have also sought to encourage the poor to save and to get out of chronic debt (Cederlöf 1997). While "financial inclusion" policies (i.e. policies aiming at providing formal financial services to all) are at now central to the political agendas of Indian public policy makers (Garikipati 2008), private stakeholders such as NGOs and banks (Srinivasan 2009), and international organisations (World Bank 2007), this concern remains extremely pressing. Tragic cases of Indian cotton producers being condemned to despair, and sometimes suicide, over unmanageable debts are well known (Government of India 2007; Mohanty 2005). More recently, microfinance client over-indebtedness has also been highlighted. In various areas of Andhra Pradesh and Karnataka, it has been reported that thousands of clients have become trapped in vicious cycles of cross-debt from multiple microfinance institutions, which has led to worrying problems of extreme financial vulnerability and sometimes suicide (see Joseph in this volume).

This paper deals with other forms of over-indebtedness, examining the daily indebtedness of poor rural households in Tamil Nadu. In the villages examined, debt does not necessarily lead to the dramatic situations observed amongst cotton farmers or microfinance clients, but it can be nevertheless a source of impoverishment, pauperization and dependency. Census data indicates that Tamil Nadu is one of the states where household debt is the highest (NSSO 2003). Over the second half of the last century, debt sources have evolved and diversified. "Traditional" forms of rural debt based around extreme dependency between landlords and labour are fading away (Cederlöf 1997; Marius-Gnanou 1993), as also observed in other parts of India (Breman 1974; Breman *et al.* 2009). Labourers now have a wide range of borrowing options. Empirical studies in the early 1980s highlighted the dynamism and diversification of the rural financial landscape (Bouman 1989; Harriss 1981). In rural Tamil Nadu for instance, professional lending, which had historically been the preserve of specific castes, has opened up to other communities. Many local elites also used their cash surpluses to invest as loans (Harriss 1981). More recent studies underline that the ongoing diversification of Tamil Nadu's rural financial landscape is still going on (Ramachandran and Swaminathan 2005; Polzin 2009). Indian microfinance, having long been overshadowed by its Bangladeshi neighbour, has been growing exponentially since the 2000s. Tamil Nadu is, moreover, one of the states where microfinance has developed the most (Fouillet 2009). In March 2010, it was estimated that Tamil Nadu state had 12,641,706 clients (Sa-Dhan 2009), with a penetration rate ranging from 0 to 20 per cent (Fouillet 2009).

On the demand side, even if inequalities remain remarkably intractable (Harriss-White and Janakarajan 2004), the poorest and lowest castes are expressing a growing desire for social mobility. In Tamil Nadu, the increased importance of non-agricultural income and the implementation of wide set of social policy measures have clearly contributed to this (Harriss-White and Colatei 2004; Djurfeld *et al.* 2008; Vijayabaskar *et al.* 2004). Such desire for social mobility creates an increasing culture of consumerism, including in rural areas (Kapadia 2002). This is incited and perpetuated through massive advertising campaigns (largely through television), and facilitated by urban commuting and public welfare policies (such as bringing electricity to the countryside and the distribution of free televisions). Consumerism brings about genuine social competition between households and communities (Kapadia 2002). These social mobility aspirations serve to loosen and reconfigure ancient bonds of dependence, or at least alter expectations, bringing about the desire for a better position within existing local hierarchies (Djurfeldt *et al.* 2008; De Neve 2005; Heyer 2010; Gorringe 2010).[2]

It is in such a context of socioeconomic and political change that debt relationships should be analysed. Our hypothesis is that debt and over-indebtedness are both shaped by and constitutive of these changes. Consumerism creates norms, which many households are willing to follow without having the financial means to do so (the "paradox of aspiration" raised by Thorstein Veblen and also observed by Olsen and Morgan (2010) in Andhra Pradesh). Households are borrowing on a daily basis at slack financial times to make ends meet. They also borrow considerable amounts to marry their children, renovate their houses or invest in private education. Our data shows that debt servicing takes up around half of their monthly income on average. These figures are all the more worrying given the irregularity and uncertainty of incomes. Our observations have led us to investigate over-indebtedness as an issue in terms of the following questions: How should we analyse such trends? What is debt and what is over-indebtedness? Where is the line between the two, and who defines them? History and economic anthropology tell us that debt encompasses multiple meanings and a diversity of relationships. It is therefore likely that the term "over-indebtedness" will have multiple and possibly contested meanings.

This chapter applies a case study of four villages in the southern Arcot region of Tamil Nadu, combining descriptive statistics and qualitative analysis to present three main arguments.

First, if as in this chapter over-indebtedness is defined as a process of impoverishment through debt, then a large part of the rural poor can certainly be considered as over-indebted. Over-indebtedness is only transitory for some households, while for others it is chronic. What is clear, however, is that over-indebtedness as a concept has little meaning to the poor. Financial indicators are certainly useful (and will be used here) to quantify the cost of debt. To understand debt practices, motivations and rationales, however, it is necessary to examine how the poor perceive and experience debt. It also requires taking into account the diversity of debt meanings and debt relationships. Of those in extremely vulnerable financial situations, very few consider themselves as over-indebted. The contrast between exogenous categorisations and local subjectivities is striking. One could of course argue that the poor suffer from "false consciousness", in the sense that they are not even able to assess their own exploitation. Our explanation is different: we argue that the poor have their own "frameworks of calculations" (Villarreal 2009; this volume) and debt hierarchies (Shipton 2007). Such phenomena transcend questions of material or self-centred motivations and reflect issues of status, honour, power and individual and group identity. This is our second argument: individuals engage multiple criteria to establish debt hierarchies and to evaluate debt burdens. Though financial criteria certainly matter, the social meaning of debt is equally, or more valued. While some debts are dishonouring, others are not. This depends upon the social relation between the debtor and the creditor and their respective status. Caste, class, kin and gender relationships are instrumental here.

Our final argument is that households' strategies and practices towards debts are more motivated by maintaining creditworthiness than by paying off debts. Maintaining creditworthiness is both a matter of eligibility for loans in the future[3] and of self-dignity.

Data and context

This paper draws on data collected between 2005 and 2009 in four villages of the southern Arcot region of Tamil Nadu, located at the border of two districts (Cuddalore and Villipuram). They cover a continuous and relatively small area, varying between dry, rainfed tracts and the wet, irrigated areas, which are typical not only of Tamil Nadu, but also of much of southern and central India. In dry villages, agricultural opportunities are limited to one or possibly two types of crops, mostly paddy and ground nut. For about the past two decades, mainly male marginal farmers and landless labourers have been migrating to supplement their farm incomes. Some commute to nearby small towns, mainly working as manual or semi-skilled labourers in the construction or transport sectors. Others depart for a couple of months to Kerala to work in coconut plantations or local industries. A few households have opted for international migration. In irrigated villages, agriculture still remains a central occupation, both for landowners and landless labourers. Irrigated villages grow two or three crops and many producers are specialized in cash crops (sugarcane, paddy, cotton, ragi, flowers, mango trees, banana trees) and their cultivable lands are larger. Migration, mostly in the form of commuting to Chennai and Pondicherry, does exist, but it is much less widespread than in dry villages.

As elsewhere in Tamil Nadu and India, caste remains a fundamental feature of social, economic, ritualistic and political life. Local classifications of social hierarchy correspond roughly to administrative categories: at the bottom of the hierarchy one finds "ex-intouchables" (here mainly Paraiyars and a few Kattunayakkans), classified as Scheduled Castes; next come the "lowest-middle" castes (here mainly Vanniars and few Barbers), classified as Most Backward Castes, followed by "middle castes" (here mainly Mudaliars, Chettiars, Yadhavars, Agamudayars, Asaris and Padithars), classified as Backward Castes. Of "upper castes", those at the top of the hierarchy (here Reddiars, Naidus and few Jains classified as Forward Castes), many have left the village. They still own houses and part of their land (these usually on lease to lower castes), but have settled in towns and now invest in urban-based activities.

Our data combines descriptive statistics with qualitative analysis. As a first stage, qualitative tools (semi-structured interviews with men and women and key informants, group discussions and observation) were used to capture the diversity of borrowing practices and the way people talk about debt. As a second stage, mid 2006, a quantitative questionnaire was implemented on 344 households, with a stratified sample based on caste and level of irrigation (dry/irrigated). The survey focused on household socioeconomic characteristics and borrowing practices. This quantitative questionnaire aimed at providing a representative picture of household debt in the villages studied. As a third stage (2008–2009), we conducted a qualitative survey, which aimed at exploring in more detail the concept of over-indebtedness. The 20 per cent most indebted households were selected (totalling 68 households). This qualitative survey was based on semi-structured interviews and case studies, and served various purposes. One was to situate debt into a dynamic framework and to reconstruct households' experiences over time. Our aim was to examine the evolution of financial vulnerability over time and to assess its prospects of evolution, asking whether the households were trapped in a vicious cycle of rising debt, or if they were coming out of debt. People were asked to list the major events of their life (life cycle events, any livelihood changes, any migrations, etc.). For each event or noticeable change, they were asked to explain its mode of finance. Another purpose for the survey was to analyse attitudes and strategies toward debts, taking into account the diversity of debt relationships, both from a financial perspective (cost, repayment modalities, duration, etc.) and from a subjective perspective. This last step also involved interviews with lenders, who were asked about the loan terms, cost, duration, collateral requirements and sanctions for non-repayment, as well as how they evaluate the creditworthiness of customers and manage risks. Around 15 lenders with different profiles were interviewed.

Tables 6.1 and 6.2 list households' socioeconomic characteristics according to caste. We see that agriculture still follows caste hierarchy. Dalits are far less likely to own land (33.5 per cent against 69 and 71.5 per cent for lowest-middle

Table 6.1 Household characteristics (HH = 344)

	All	*Dalits*	*Lowest-middle castes*	*Middle-upper castes*
	n = 344	*n = 212*	*n = 104*	*n = 28*
Household size (no. of members)	4.71	4.66	4.66	5.17
Level of literacy (husband) (%)	55	59	43	68
% landowners	47	33.5	69	71.5
% concrete housing	29	26	27	61

Source: authors' survey.

castes and middle-upper castes respectively). Some Dalits are both farmers and agricultural workers, but very few can afford to be farmers only (3.3 per cent against 24 per cent for lowest-middle and 46.4 per cent for middle-upper castes respectively). However the level of Dalits' education is above average and though casual agricultural labour remains their primary occupation, they are over-represented in the category "employees, self-employed and pensions". Most often these are governmental jobs, most of which have been obtained through positive discrimination policies.

Over-indebtedness: what do the figures tell us?

In common with various monographs on different parts of India,[4] our survey highlights both the scale and frequency of debt. At the time of the survey, 91.3 per cent of the households were indebted. For those who were indebted, the average outstanding debt per household was INR30,500 (median 20,000), approximately one year's average household income. The amount of outstanding debt ranged from INR0 to 250,000. On average, monthly repayments were

Table 6.2 Livelihood profiles (HH = 344)

	All (%)	*Dalits (%)*	*Lowest-middle castes (%)*	*Middle-upper castes (%)*
	n = 344	*n = 212*	*n = 104*	*n = 28*
% casual worker agriculture only	38.7	45.3	31.7	14.3
% casual worker	7.9	8.0	7.7	7.1
% employee, self-employed, pension	14.8	18.9	7.7	10.7
% farmer-worker	23.3	21.2	27.9	21.4
% farmer	13.1	3.3	24.0	46.4
unknown	2.3	3.3	1.0	0.0
total	100.0	100.0	100.0	100.0

Source: authors' survey.

INR750 (median 390), amounting to around half of monthly incomes. Significant disparities in levels of indebtedness were also observed, which can be briefly summarized as follows.[5] Debt levels are higher amongst the middle-upper castes, landowners and those with a strong source of livelihood (for instance, producers are more indebted than labourers). As for the purposes for taking on debt, Table 6.3 shows how, in terms of debt size, the most significant reasons include economic investment (mainly in agriculture) and ceremonies. In terms of the number of loans, household expenses, economic investment and ceremonies are the most common purposes. Here too significant disparities emerge as regards debt purpose: low castes, landless households and labourers more often borrow to cover daily survival costs and ceremonies, while middle-upper castes, landowners and producers more often borrow for economic investment.

We will focus here on the results of second survey, which was conducted among the 20 per cent most indebted households.[6] The first notable result was that the same households' stated debt figures were substantially higher than with the first survey. A second interview made it possible to build trust and confidence, and to get more reliable estimates.[7] The average outstanding debt was INR96 791 (median 79,500), while average household income was INR21,600 (median 15,870), and the average monetary value of assets was INR69,885 (median 51,425). On average, household debt was 4.5 times higher than household income, and 1.4 times the monetary value of assets.

Three indebtedness scenarios were discerned using qualitative analysis and then confirmed by quantitative data:

- "Transitional over-indebtedness" (13 households, 19 per cent of sample): this category of household is highly indebted (INR36,868) in comparison to their annual income (INR25,945 on average), and spends significant levels of that income on debt repayment, without however becoming

Table 6.3 Debt purposes (HH=344)

	N	% loans	Average amount (INR)	% volume
Economic Investment	142	21.3	12,797	25.9
Ceremonies	150	16.5	13,366	20.9
Housing	65	7.1	16,416	11.1
Child education	91	10.0	11,157	10.6
Health expenses	113	12.4	8,079	9.5
Loan repayment	54	5.9	12,506	7.1
Household expenses	184	20.2	3,485	6.7
Cattle purchase	32	3.5	13,781	4.6
Land purchase	20	2.2	15,525	3.2
Durable consumer goods	26	2.9	7,165	1.9
Other	35	3.8	17,459	6.2
	912	100.0	10,515	100.0

Source: authors' survey.

overwhelmed by debt. Their debt repayment amounts on average to one-third of household income (INR485 per month). Debt servicing traps them at the level of poverty and prevents any form of wealth accrual. However these households use various strategies not only to stabilize their debt levels, but also to enable a significant reduction in the near future. These include expense reduction (withdrawing children from expensive private schools, postponing marriages or cutting general expenditure), migration and kin support (for instance, children being expected to repay debts contracted for their own marriages or education). A further strategy is maintaining good relationships with lenders, facilitating debt rescheduling without additional cost.

- "Pauperization" (26 households, 38 per cent of the sample): this category of household becomes pauperized by debt. In comparison to the previous category, outstanding debt is higher (INR73,027 on average) and yearly incomes lower (INR22,936 on average). Monthly debt repayment levels equal household income (INR1,872 on average per month). These households have already partly sold their assets, and have no prospect of improving their income. As a consequence their debt levels are gradually increasing, both for securing debt repayment and daily survival. The amount due is only theoretical, because in practice households are totally unable to meet payments. The debt is experienced mostly in terms of constant pressure and dependence on creditors. Escaping debt would be impossible in the near future: the households' main objectives are to maintain creditworthiness for as long as possible, which implies rotating debt and juggling between various lenders.

- The final stage is "extreme dependence" (29 households, 43 per cent of the sample). Not only is this household category's outstanding debt extremely high (INR144,959 on average), but its income very low (INR11,117 on average). The debt burden is such that it is impossible to repay. Most of these households depend on their close circle for daily survival. The cases we met received support from diverse sources, including close kin, a landowner, a priest and an NGO social worker. In some cases children are left in kin's care. There are also rather frequent conflicts with kin, which have probably contributed to their financial situation. They often become socially isolated, especially as regards ceremonies, being unable to make gifts or counter-gifts. Their dependence has considerable social and moral costs, especially in terms of self-dignity.

In terms of assets, we found no significant disparity of land ownership between the three categories. This was however the case for gold, which is very frequently pledged, lost and repurchased depending on cash flow. A total of 60 per cent of the households in the first category own gold (36 grams on average), as opposed to 50 and 34 per cent of the second and third categories (21 grams on average). Most of the third category's gold had been pledged at the time of survey.

Table 6.4 Over-indebtedness typology (HH=68)

	"Transitional over-indebtedness"			"Pauperization"			"Dependence"		
	Mean	Median	Disp.	Mean	Median	Disp.	Mean	Median	Disp.
Outstanding debt (INR)	36,868	15,000	50,414	73,027	57,050	54,690	144,959	125,000	88,524
Monthly income (INR)	2,162	1,225	1,904	1,911	1,590	914	926	692	734
Monthly repayments (INR)	485	359	442	1,872	1,591	1,459	4,391	3,155	3,392
Ratio debt/income	0.8	1.0	0.4	3.0	2.6	1.3	18.0	13.0	20.3
Interest rate	2.4	2.9	1.4	2.7	2.6	1.0	3.0	3.0	1.5

Source: authors' survey.

If we examine the main causes of over-indebtedness (see Table 6.5), the most frequent are ceremonies (42.7 per cent of households), housing and health (25 per cent and 23.5 per cent). These are followed by failed economic investments (17.7 per cent), most frequently obtained for agricultural purposes such as well digging or tractor purchase. Next come private education expenses (16.2 per cent), the most common of which are for private engineering schools, and teacher or hospital staff training. In a few cases chronic food insecurity, high interest rates, death, and legal problems come into play. Half of the households' over-indebtedness results from two or more factors. In half of cases, over-indebtedness also stems from income loss due to death, poor harvests, or health or alcohol problems that prevent a family member from working. Our data indicate that debt purposes are more frequently ceremony expenditure (especially marriages) among the "pauperization" and "dependency" household categories, while failed economic investment is more frequently a cause for the "transitional" category. Although all castes are present in each category, we observed that lowest-middle castes are over-represented, both in the second survey (focusing on the 20 per cent most indebted) and in the "dependency" category. They represented 30 per cent of the first sample, 47 per cent of the second sample, and 60 per cent of the "dependency" category. The small sample size does not allow for conclusions, however.

Of course, statistical data should be considered cautiously. Sources of income are diverse and irregular, and annual incomes are therefore rough estimates. One should also approach the monetary value of assets with caution, especially among the lowest castes, and for housing and land. Houses located in the *ceri* (part of the village reserved for the lowest castes) have a very poor market value. As far as land is concerned, many poor do not have the property titles and are therefore unable to sell or mortgage their land. Nonetheless, asset ownership strengthens borrowers' creditworthiness and his/her eligibility for loans. Debt figures are more reliable, as lenders and borrowers often enter lengthy negotiations, which they are easily able to recall. Borrowers have more trouble quantifying the amount of interest actually paid and the amount of capital outstanding.[8] In terms of timing and amounts, repayments are made on a highly erratic basis, and loans and interest durations are often renegotiated. Lenders regularly make concessions such that borrowers do not pay the full interest due. But such flexibility is repaid through other means, as we shall see in the next section. Keeping all the above limitations to the data in mind, we can still consider these as rough estimates of broad trends, especially as regards disparity between categories. Rather than the amounts as such, it is the differences between the categories that are meaningful, highlighting diversity of outcome.

The social meaning of debt

Not only should financial indicators be applied with caution, but individuals themselves have their own perceptions that differ radically from a pure financial analysis of debt. All the figures above are researchers' subjective constructions,

Table 6.5 Debt purposes (HH = 68)

	% households (All)	% households "Transitional"	% households "Pauperization"	% households "Dependency"
Ceremonies	42.7	21.4	44.0	51.7
Housing	25.0	21.4	28.0	24.1
Health	23.5	7.1	36.0	20.7
Economic Investment	17.7	28.6	20.0	10.3
Education	16.2	21.4	16.0	13.8
Food security	5.9	14.3	8.0	
Gifts	4.4	10.5	4.0	
Interest	8.8		8.0	13.8
Death	2.9			
Legal problems	2.9			6.9
Land	2.9	5.3	4.0	

Source: authors' survey.

Note
Total exceeds 100% because of multiple responses.

used to summarise the outstanding figures of each debt source. Most households are unable to spontaneously recall their total amount of outstanding debt. The fact they can barely remember their total debt is not necessarily because they are illiterate or ashamed to reveal the extent of their debt (which certainly takes place, but does not explain their difficulty summing up their debts). It is rather because they find little meaning in the concept of an amount of outstanding debt.

Anyone familiar with economic theory might find such observations rather surprising. Most economics textbooks state that money is a unit of calculation and a standardized means of payment. Thanks to this standardization, economic theory (and much of sociological theory) assumes that money is a means of individualization and an obliterator of hierarchies and statutory privileges. Monetary transactions, including debt, are expected to forge contractual relationships between individuals as equals. But ethnological and historical analysis of monetary and debt practices reveals that the impersonality and anonymity accorded to money is illusory (Bloch and Parry 1989; Bouman and Hospes 1994; Guérin *et al.* 2011; Guyer 1995; Lont and Hospes 2004; Morvant-Roux 2009; Servet 1984, 1996, 2006; Villarreal 2004, 2009; Zelizer 1994, 2005). Money and the practices stemming from it are above all a social construct. Money is embedded in pre-existing relations of rights and obligations, which it can influence but never destroy. As argued by Magdalena Villarreal (2004) in the case of rural Mexico, the calculation of value implicates complex webs of meanings and actions. She states that local processes of valuation often have more to do with identities and social relations such as gender, ethnicity and class than with monetary amounts. In the same vein, in a Kenyan context, Parker Shipton (2007) suggests that debt perceptions are shaped by and constitutive of social belonging. Far from being only economic transfers, monetary debts also entail obligations and entrustments: "what one borrows or lends helps define who one is" (Shipton 2007: 14). In other words, if we want to understand why the poor go into debt, to whom and how they experience each debt, the social meaning of debt is just as important as its monetary dimension. The social meaning of debt refers to the set of rights and obligations that link debtors and creditors, and their consequences in terms of social belonging, status and dignity.

In the Tamil language, the term "over-indebtedness" has no literal translation. Individuals use the term "drowned in debt", but very few consider themselves to be in this situation. It is instead the impossibility of taking on further debt that is considered a problem. Interviewees state that the worst situation is for those who no longer inspire trust and who have not kept their promises. When they are asked to talk about over-indebtedness, the borrowers rarely use the amount of debt as an indicator. It is more the *nature* of the debt and the nature of the *debt relationship* that determines whether debt is considered a burden or not.

We shall now look to classify the diversity of debt relationships. In the first instance, debts can be classified according to the profile of the lender. In the villages studied here, seven main categories of lenders can be distinguished. The most common forms are pawnbroking and "well-known people" (*terinjavanga*). At the time of the survey (see Table 6.6), 54.9 and 45.9 per cent of the

Table 6.6 Borrowing sources (N = 344)

	Amount (INR)			% HH using	% volume	Duration (nb days)		Price (monthly interest)[a]	
	Avg.	med.	max.			mean	median	mean	disp
Well-known people	17,013	10,000	200,000	45.9	41.2	690	601	3.73	1.23
Pawnbrokers	8,323	5,000	70,000	54.9	17.9	613	324	2.83	0.48
Shg	8,284	5,000	100,000	41.3	13.5	291	237	1.73	0.55
Ambulant lenders	1,548	1,000	12,000	30.8	2.0	246	235		
Family & friends	10,228	5,000	60,000	17.4	9.5	424	239	3.11	1.38
Banks	17,121	12,000	110,000	21.2	13.9	752	419	1.01	1.38
Shop credit	7,165	5,750	25,000	6.7	1.9				0.48
Total	10,515	9,000	200,000		99.98	520	241	2.7	1.28

Source: authors' survey.

Note

a Data for prices is missing for ambulant lenders and shops, as in many cases borrowers don't know the exact price.

households were using them, representing respectively 17.9 per cent and 41.20 per cent of the total debt volume. Moreover, 41.3 per cent of the households also held SHG loans (13.8 per cent of the total volume). Some 30.8 per cent of the households dealt with ambulant moneylenders (*Tandal* – which means "immediate"), but for very small amounts (1,557 INR on average, with these Tandal loans amounting to 2 per cent of the total volume of debt). Banks, relatives and friends are sources of loans for 21.2 and 17.4 per cent of the households respectively and amount to 13.9 and 9.5 per cent of the total volume. Few households (6.7 per cent) buy items on credit from shops.[9]

We shall now turn to the way the poor perceive debts and what their criteria are to assess the burden of debt.

First, the social meaning of debt clearly matters. Debt is a marker of social hierarchy in kinship groups, the neighborhood and community alike. People try to avoid debts degrading to their status, or at least try to pay back these debts first.

Second, the importance given to the social meaning of debt does not preclude financial reasoning, in the economic sense of the term. People look for low interest rates. They also search for flexible services, where repayment modalities and duration can be negotiated and adapted to their cash flow constraints. Moreover, they value other services that the lender is likely to provide (the "interlinked" transactions often described by economists).

Debt practices (going into debt and paying off debt) are the result of subtle calculations and trade-offs between financial and social criteria: in many cases, people deliberately prefer to pay high financial costs in order to maintain status. Unless high debt engenders certain forms of extreme dependence, it is not taken as a problem; but shameful debt is, as we shall see below. As we were often told, the problem is not debt, but to whom one becomes indebted. The social meaning of debt varies according to caste and class, kin and gender relationships.

Caste and class relationships

As observed in other villages in Tamil Nadu (Harriss-White and Colatei 2004; Ramachandran and Swaminathan 2005), debt is clearly a marker of social hierarchy between castes. This is acknowledged both by lenders and borrowers. Households' creditworthiness depends on their caste and conversely, debt practices shape social status. As stated above, the term "to be involved in debt" has pejorative moral connotations, implying surrender, dependence and even servility, which are low-caste attributes. Middle- and upper-caste members frame high debt among the lower castes as part of their "bad habits", stating that the group drinks alcohol, eats meat, does not monitor its wives and goes into debt.... This is not true, according to our figures: average outstanding debts rise along with caste hierarchy (Guérin *et al.* 2012b). It is, however, the case that financial markets are segmented along caste lines.

Borrowing from ambulant lenders is seen as the most degrading practice, reserved for low castes (and women). Ambulant lenders come to households' doorsteps, precluding any form of discretion. They do not request any collateral but use coercive enforcement methods. The lenders themselves state that low-caste individuals and women are more prepared to tolerate abusive language from them.

The sense of debt as something immoral also depends upon the hierarchical positions of the lender and the borrower. On the borrower's side, the norm is to contract loans from someone from an equal or higher caste. "They do not take water from us, do you think they would take money?" is something the low castes often said to us. On the creditor side, some upper castes refuse to lend to castes that are too low in the hierarchy in comparison to them, stating that it would be degrading for them to go and claim their due. To ask an upper caste whether he is indebted to a lower caste can be considered as an insult. As we were once told by a moneylender from the Jain caste (upper caste): "I cannot give money to them [low castes]. You see, I have my status, I cannot. How could I get my money back? I cannot go there, it is not compatible with my status." The testimony of Anja Pulli, who is a daily agricultural labourer and belongs to the Vanniar caste (lowest-middle caste) is also instructive:

> The value of debt is not a matter of amount; all depends upon from whom you borrow. Borrowing from them [lowest castes] is unthinkable. I would prefer not to organize my daughter's marriage than to borrow from them. Getting money from outside your caste degrades yourself, your own family but also your own caste.

As was discussed in the introduction, in Tamil Nadu traditional forms of patronage based on debt and extreme dependency are now fading away. On the one hand, the need for manual and permanent labour has considerably reduced with the development of capitalist forms of agriculture (Harriss-White 1996). Landowners are also increasingly likely to abandon agriculture to turn to urban activities. Moreover, landless labourers and marginal farmers have now increased access to non-agricultural labour (Djurfeldt *et al.* 2008; Harriss-White and Janakarajan 2004). A loosening of bonds of dependence has also been favoured by policy interventions based on affirmative action (Harriss-White and Janakarajan 2004; Heyer 2010) and in some areas by the growing political power of the low and middle castes (De Neve 2005; Harriss, J. 1999; Heyer 2010). Although it is likely that dependence bonds and hierarchy have always been contested, the poor now have a broader range of choices and opportunities to do so. Dependence as an issue weighs heavily on debt arbitrations and calculations. Individuals go far beyond the question of financial cost, measuring implications in terms of dependence and status.

As indicated above, debt to "well-known people" represents a large portion of total debt, both in terms of the number of loans and of volume. The relationships between borrowers and their lenders are meanwhile highly diverse.

Cost is a first way to compare different options: most "well-known people" charge from 3 to 4 per cent in interest monthly, which is considered a reasonable price, and around one-third charges 5 per cent or above.

Table 6.7 The cost of "well-known people" loans

Monthly interest rate	(%)
Below 3%	3.88
3 to 4%	65.95
5% and more	28.02
Unknown	2.16
Total	100.00

Source: authors' survey.

It would be misleading to compare the various options only on the basis of price, however. The use of the term "well-known people" presupposes the idea of mutual acquaintanceship ("I know him/her, he/she knows me"). There is then a broad spectrum of more or less contractual relations, embedded to various degrees in social and political relationships going far beyond a debt relationship.

First, there are professional lenders belonging to merchant castes specialized in moneylending (here, these are Mudaliar, Chettiar and Marwari). Their motives are purely commercial and they make no secret that theirs is a business. The terms of the transaction depend on the type of collateral: in the cases we saw, the cost is 4 to 5 per cent monthly in the absence of collateral; from 2 to 3 per cent with collateral (jewels, cultivatable land, tractors, bullock carts, etc.). A guarantor is needed at the beginning, after which repayment quality ensures the continuity of the relationship. Some such lenders specialize in pawnbroking (Chettiars and Marwaris). Over the last few decades in the area under study, some Vanniars have also come to specialize in pawnbroking (in the region Vanniars traditionally specialize in agriculture). They usually focus on smaller transactions and poorer (and low-caste) clients. Many of these lenders have sold land (particularly during the land reform period from 1969) and have used this capital for money lending. The amounts lent also vary according to the collateral, without which it is difficult to obtain more than INR30,000. With collateral, amounts of up to several hundred thousand rupees may be lent. Transactions are often undertaken differently depending on the borrower's caste. For those willing to lend to low castes, transactions can take place in the borrowers' village (by hiring a low-caste person as an intermediary and to collect repayments). "Low castes are untrustworthy and irresponsible", is a common view of lenders, "money burns their fingers". For this reason it is deemed safer to visit them on their doorsteps. In contrast, transactions with other castes usually take place in town, mainly as a matter of discretion. Strong networks within the village enable them to obtain information about potential borrowers (reputation, income flows, etc.) and to select accordingly. Though the relationship is contractual, borrowers refer to it as "well-known people" because a minimum of mutual acquaintanceship is required.

There are then diverse forms of debt that are embedded into wider relationships. In such cases, debt is used either as labour bondage (amongst big

landowners and mainly in irrigated areas) and/or for social and political purposes. While traditional bonded labour has almost disappeared, certain forms of
patronage still exist and the long-term relationship between landowners and their
labour or tenants is frequently linked to debt. The loan is a "privilege" granted to
faithful workers. Its financial conditions are quite favourable, with low costs
(0–3 per cent), flexible repayments and only rare full repayment of the principal.
Borrowers regularly pay back interest and from time to time part of the capital,
which allows them to reborrow. But money is just one aspect of the cost, with
the debt inscribed into a series of rights and obligations requiring multiple forms
of compensation. In contrast to the past, workers are not obligated to work exclusively for one owner and have freedom of movement. However, they are still
obliged to work first and foremost for the lender and to offer multiple services.
For men, these sometimes include irrigation, or numerous everyday services
such as running errands to the shops, and caring for children or elders. Women
have to make themselves available for domestic work when there are ceremonies, visitors, or when the master's wife is ill. Time costs can be considerable.
For landowners who still cultivate the land, lending money or leasing out land
serves the same purpose of bonding labour. Landowners clearly state that
because of the scarcity of labour in agriculture nowadays, the only way to ensure
the availability of labourers is to tie them with debt.

Lending money also serves social and political purposes. Many landowners
have shifted from agriculture to specialize in money lending (and possibly other
activities). They lend to their former circle of workers (who can also act as guarantors for other borrowers from their own castes, as above). They can also lend
to the workers, or former workers, of landowners of their caste. Interest rates
usually vary between 1 to 3 per cent and are negotiable. Some of these lenders
clearly state that they don't have workers any more but they still "give" money
to them and "help" them to maintain "self-respect". Some are highly involved in
politics and this is also a way for them to ensure a certain allegiance.

Lending money is not restricted to dominant castes and landowners. In the
four villages studied here, lenders were situated across all castes and classes
(defined here through the ownership of land and assets). Lending money is obviously used as tool for differentiation within social groups, between those with a
cash surplus to invest and those without. Differentiations arise on financial and
social grounds. Here too, money is frequently only one component of the price.

Such relationships have multiple costs, however, which include providing a
large range of free services, but also respect and deference. These social bonds
of dependence are publicly recognized at the time of public events such as ceremonies. Lenders are the first to be invited and are treated as guests of honour.
Debtors are meanwhile often expected to provide assistance with domestic tasks.
Others deliberately try to get rid of such bonds of dependence, even if it means
taking on very costly debts, financially speaking.

In other words, low castes and low classes (here, mainly casual labourers)
face a tricky choice between a certain relative form of protection that entails
moral and social dependency on the one hand, and a relative sense of freedom at

a high financial cost on the other. They struggle to make ends meet and have to meet survival expenses (health, food, etc.). They spend increasing amounts on social and symbolic investments such as marriage, education and housing. They also make choices that tend to entail high financial costs.

Kin relationships

Some of the most sensitive debts are kin debt. While family support is crucial for ceremonies and rituals, the role of kinship in everyday protection is, in fact, limited. Loans from neighbours and relatives represent about 17.4 per cent of the number of loans and 9.5 per cent of loan volume. To the question "Do you have relatives who can help you in case of a problem?", 54 per cent of the households in our first survey sample replied negatively. To the question "when you need money, whom do approach you first?", less than one-third (28 per cent) mentioned kin. Almost half (48 per cent) mention "well-known people".

Qualitative analysis clearly highlights that there are reservations and suspicions towards family support. Avoiding all requests is almost unthinkable. Indeed, permanent tensions play out based on kinship. Its role switches continuously between being a support and a burden, between solidarity and conflict. Conflicts are underpinned by secrecy of financial arrangements and misunderstandings about such opacity. These can concern whether loans have been left unpaid or badly repaid, misunderstandings about cash transfers (was it a gift or a loan? Is there an interest rate or not?), and loans used for "immoral" purposes, or diverted from the initial purpose, etc.

Honouring reciprocity in ceremonies has always been a source of permanent pressure. Many interviewees make clear that they prefer going into debt outside the family circle to meet their own needs. This is a matter of freedom, as kin support calls for constant justification. Some say they borrow from their kin only for "justified" reasons, which are mainly ceremony, housing and health costs. The obligation of reciprocity is also a burden. Not only should the debt be repaid, but the debtor should be able to lend in return when the creditor is in need. Borrowing is a potential source of conflict, shame and dependency upon kin (in the case of unbalanced exchanges), and sometimes exclusion. Borrowers are constantly seeking to limit these risks. The fear of dependency and shame because of debt relationships was constantly raised in discussions. Some chose handcuffs as an expression to highlight their fear of dependency.

Financial conflicts amongst kin perpetuate pre-existing competition amongst family members and lineages. In particular, tensions are often high between agnatic and uterine lineages. The maternal uncle's responsibility for his sisters (existing among most, if not all castes in the villages studied here) is often at odds with the needs and demands of his wife and children. The nature of financial arrangements and the conflicts they generate are also shaped by the status and rank of each party within the kin circle. The most sensitive debts are those that do not respect the rules of rights and obligations dictated by blood and alliances/bonds. For instance, borrowing money from the bride's kin is often a last resort, because it admits that the groom's family is unable to meet its responsibilities. Sometimes individuals may have no choice, but they will be prompt in repayments.

Gender relationships

Calculations and arbitrations between the financial and social costs of debt are also gendered. Data were collected at the household level and do not allow us to measure gender differences. From qualitative observation however, gender specificities are very clear. Men and women have their own financial circuits and money providers (as observed also by Harriss-White and Colatei (2004) in other villages of Tamil Nadu).

Some of these circuits are female-based and entail similar forms of exchange to those already described, namely reciprocity between close circles, market-based relationships with professional female moneylenders or hierarchical relationships with the wives of landowners, and also amongst kin.

When women have to borrow from male providers, they have to contend with the specific demand of preserving their "morality". Even if social norms are more "women-friendly" in Tamil Nadu than in other parts of India, especially the north (Agarwal 1994; Harriss-White 1990), there is still strong control over female bodies and women's sexuality. Even in low castes, where male control is less strict (Kapadia 1996), financial transactions easily become suspect. A woman who borrows from a man from outside the family is immediately accused of being an "easy women" or a prostitute. At the same time, sexual harassment, whether verbal or physical, is extremely common among male lenders when they lend to women. Thus women often face a trade-off between financial cost and the consequences for their own reputation as females. This trade-off is all the more complicated for single women.

To sum up our arguments, the financial indicators applied here demonstrate the role of debt as a factor in impoverishment. All 20 per cent of the most indebted households interviewed for the second survey are over-indebted, whether transiently, chronically, or condemned to extreme dependence. In many cases, however, the poor do not seek to pay off their debts (besides those which are the most dishonouring). Their main objective is rather to sustain or improve their creditworthiness.

Sustaining creditworthiness over paying off debts

Households' creditworthiness is above all a matter of trust, the term used locally when people refer to their ability to access credit. The fabric of trust covers many aspects that far exceed good credit history and repayment behaviour, and relates to every aspect of the borrowers' reputation. Creditworthiness is rarely assessed on the individual level, and often incorporates the reputation and morality of the whole family or even lineage (Harriss-White and Colatei 2004). Lenders often state that they take two levels into account. One relates to family and lineage, namely the family's history, its "ethical" background and "morality". The second level is individual, relating very broadly to the "quality" of a person. It is therefore perfectly rational that the poor attach an equal importance to their reputation.

Material matters do count too, of course, but their evaluation is highly subjective. Tangible assets include land, housing, jewellry, livestock, and income sources. As far as land is concerned, quality is as important as size, concerning matters of cultivatable land and access to irrigation, but also location. Land and housing in *ceries* (the area of the village to which the lowest castes are confined) have very poor market value. As far as income is concerned, not only does the number of household earners come into play, but also the frequency of their income and the household's ability to raise lump sums. In this respect, producer and migrant households have a clear advantage.

"Behaviour" also matters. As previously discussed, low castes are often seen as risky borrowers. Irrespective of caste, bad habits such as laziness, alcoholism and gambling are considered as indicators of poor repayment potential. As discussed above, respect and deference are also highly valued. Potential borrowers should equally show respect to their lenders and at times to their communities.

Last but not least, in many cases a guarantor is required in order to borrow from "well-known people", whatever the borrower's profile. The potential borrower's reputation within his/her own circle is therefore another fundamental criteria. Good faith is usually not enough, as lenders ensure that guarantors and borrowers have specific connections. Kinship, neighbourhood, labour and also SHG membership are taken into account.

Creditworthiness is not a given but demands constant maintenance, updating and strengthening one's reputation and relationships. Juggling is a fundamental component of this. Contracting debt in one place to repay it elsewhere is a constant practice. The poor often state that they "borrow and repay like they breathe" to convey the idea of this ongoing circulation of money. The English term "rotation" is also commonly used. The rotation of loans arises either out of genuine constraint or informed and calculated arbitrations. Juggling demands specific skills. More than juggling money, it involves juggling temporalities and social relationships (deciding whom should be paid and in what priority). Calculations include questions of cost (expensive debts should be repaid first), but also social considerations, both of which are closely interrelated, as juggling practices aim to maintain eligibility for future loans and to sustain the family's reputation.

When juggling is no longer possible, the household sinks into dependence (the third category mentioned earlier). Most have faced a succession of financial knocks, such that their assets (both tangible and intangible) gradually crumble. Households sell off their livestock, jewellery, sometimes their land, and exceptionally, their houses. Repayments start to take up an increasing proportion of their income. Their social network becomes exhausted. In other words, they gradually lose their creditworthiness, both financially and socially. Individuals state that it is worst when people know that you are struggling with debt. They start to avoid you and don't send you invitations any more because they are afraid to be solicited. The final stage is a stage of dependency and humiliation. This process is more or less violent and swift depending on the household's initial position, both in terms of assets and networks.

Conclusion

By its analysis of four villages in the South Arcot region of Tamil Nadu, the main purpose of this paper has been to examine the over-indebtedness of poor rural households. Far beyond the specificities of this particular case study, its analysis sheds light on theoretical debates regarding the nature of debt and over-indebtedness, and the role they play in broader socioeconomic and political processes.

Echoing a vast body of recent literature on poverty, we have found that the poor, regardless of gender, are far from motivated simply by the need to eat. Their daily lives are based around various strategies aiming at maintaining, protecting and sometimes increasing their sense of dignity. Both indebtedness and over-indebtedness are central to this process.

Rural poor households of course borrow because they need cash to meet certain specific needs. They naturally look for cheap costs, repayment modalities adapted to their cash flows and flexible conditions. However, debts are not just monetary flows for topping up irregular and low incomes, and for coping with unpredictable expenses. They are not just financial transactions defined in terms of amount loaned, repayment period or interest rates, but are first and foremost relationships between a debtor and a creditor. Debts are shaped by and constitutive of social relationships and social hierarchies, especially those related to caste, class, gender and kin. The social meaning of debt, which is defined here as the process by which debt sets debtors and creditors into local systems of hierarchies, is as important as its financial criteria. The social meaning of debt depends upon pre-existing relationships between debtors and creditors, and debt in turn strengthens, preserves and sometimes challenges pre-existing positions within local hierarchies. Depending on how debt is experienced and perceived, and on the nature of the relationship between debtor and creditor, and the set of rights and obligations that link debtors and creditors, debt may be a mark of respect, a source of honour and distinction, or conversely a source of humiliation, shame and sometimes social exclusion. Because of its social meaning, debt is also highly socially regulated, in the sense defined by Barbara Harriss-White (2003). According to their social membership and position within local hierarchies, and whether in relation to community or kin, men and women do not have access to the same lenders, and do not experience debt in the same way (Guérin *et al.* 2012b).

As a consequence, over-indebtedness as a definition cannot be restricted to processes of material impoverishment. Material pauperization through debt certainly does take place, and our figures highlight that debt repayments take up significant portions of households' incomes. But what also matter are the consequences of debt for social status: debts are valuated and ranked according to losses and gains of self-respect and dignity. "Bad" debts are rarely the most expensive, financially speaking, but those that tarnish the reputation of the family and jeopardize its future. Bad debts serve to reveal that a household is unable to maintain its position in the social hierarchy. The poor do undertake financial reasoning, but financial criteria are not a priority and debt behaviours stem from subtle arbitrations between financial costs and social status.

Our study also sheds light on the dialectic between micro and macro social processes. Debt and over-indebtedness among households and individuals within households are indicative of broader patterns of accumulation and distribution across a given society. In rural India, debt has long been a source of the impoverishment and exploitation of the labouring poor (Breman 2007; Hardiman 1996; Pouchepadass 1980). Our findings suggest that in the villages studied here, households' over-indebtedness highlights the contradictions of the urbanization and "modernization" of rural South India (Kapadia 2002; Olsen and Morgan 2010). Over-indebted households of course struggle to make ends meet and face material poverty. But some of them also have growing social aspirations, which are hardly compatible with income uncertainty and job precariousness. Social aspirations translate not only into expensive needs, but also into the willingness to engage in market debt relationships, which are also more costly financially than traditional relationships of dependency and patronage. In other words, those who are at the bottom of the hierarchy are faced with a Faustian choice, between on the one hand the financial price of the market, and on the other hand the social cost of dependency.

What could the role of microcredit be in this Faustian choice? Many of the families in our study have microcredit (41.3 per cent), but the amounts are rather low in proportion to their total debt (13.5 per cent on average). Household over-indebtedness is therefore in no way related to microcredit. Could microcredit then be a possible substitute for the debt ties discussed here, and help households to gradually get out of informal debt, as many microcredit advocates have claimed?[10] This looks unlikely for various reasons. First, as long as poor rural Indian households lack social protection and employment security – which unfortunately seems likely to continue for now – the sort of local financial arrangements discussed here have many comparative advantages. Second, households and individuals juggle with many various loan sources, each of which has its own economic, as well as social and moral, strengths and weaknesses. The multiple reasoning behind debt, as we have seen, is under constant tension and the site of subtle, complex reasoning and trade-offs. As a result, there is a plethora of complementary, and often incommensurable, non-substitutable financial practices (Guérin *et al.* 2012a). As a consequence, microcredit is not used as an alternative but as an additional source of liquidity, both to better manage time lags between revenues and expenditures and to better coordinate a variety of socio-financial relationships (Roesch and Héliès 2007; Guérin, under review).

Notes

1 Quantitative data were collected by Ophelie Héliès and S. Ponnarasu as part of an MPhil thesis (Héliès 2006). We sincerely thank them for their dedication and rigour. Qualitative interviews and statistical analysis were carried out under the RUME project (see www.rume-rural-microfinance.org) funded by the French National Agency for Research (ANR). We thank Marek Hudon, Barbara Harriss-White, Solène Morvant-Roux, David Picherit, Jonathan Pattenden and Magdalena Villarreal for their comments on an earlier version of the paper.
2 See also Picherit (2009a) for Andhra Pradesh.
3 As also shown by Solène Morvant-Roux in rural southern Mexico (Morvant-Roux 2006).
4 See, for example, Bouman (1989), Chandavarkar (1994), Collins *et al.* (2009), Drèze *et al.* (1997), Gooptu (2001: 54), Hardiman (1996), Harriss, B. (1981), Jones and Howard (1994), Mosse (2005), Pouchepadass (1980), Sriram and Parhi (2006).
5 Disparities between households are analysed in more detail in a further publication (Guérin *et al.* 2012b).
6 No other criteria were used for selection: we simply selected the 20 per cent most indebted.
7 Many people under-estimate their debt levels for various reasons, including shame, concern for confidentiality and fear of losing access to loans (for fear that the survey results might be disclosed to NGOs or governmental units). For further discussion of the challenges of collecting reliable data on debt, see Morvant-Roux (2006), and Collins *et al.* (2009).
8 In many cases, especially as regards pawnbrokers and well-known persons, monthly repayments include only the interest and the capital is paid at the end. Unpaid interest is added to the capital.
9 In order to limit the duration of interviews, the survey was limited to amounts exceeding INR500 and thus under-estimates the importance of relatives and friends.
10 The evolutionist scenario argument is found in various official reports in India (see for instance Government of India (2008); Nabard (2008) and beyond (see for instance the report *Finance for all* of the World Bank (2007)).

References

Agarwal, Bina (1994) *A field on One's Own: Gender and Land Rights in South Asia*, Cambridge: Cambridge University Press.

Bloch, Maurice and Parry, Jonathan (eds) (1989) *Money and the Morality of Exchange*, Cambridge: Cambridge University Press.

Bouman, F. J. A. and Hospes, O. (eds) (1994) *Financial Landscape Reconstructed: The Fine Art of Mapping Development*, Boulder, CO: Westview Press.

Breman, Jan (1974) *Patronage and Exploitation: Changing Agrarian Relations in South Gujarat, India*, Berkeley: University of California Press.

Breman, Jan, (2007) *Labour Bondage in West India, From Past to Present*, Oxford, Oxford University Press.

Breman, Jan, Guérin, Isabelle and Aseem, Prakash (eds) (2009) *India's Unfree Workforce of Bondage Old and New*, New Delhi: Oxford University Press.

Bouman, F. A. J. (1989) *Small, Short and Unsecured – Informal Rural Finance in India*, Delhi/Oxford/New York: Oxford University Press.

Cederlöf, Gunnel (1997) *Bonds Lost; Subordination, Conflict and Mobilisation in Rural South India* c.*1900–1970*, New Delhi: Manohar.

Chandavarkar, Rajnarayan (1994) *The Origins of Industrial Capitalism: Business Strategies and the Working Classes in Bombay, 1900–1940*, Cambridge: Cambridge University Press.

Collins, D., Morduch, J., Rutherford, S. and Ruthven, O. (2009) *Portfolios of the Poor: How the World's Poor Live on $2 a Day*, Princeton: Princeton University Press.

De Neve, Gert (2005) *The Everyday Politics of Labour: Working Lives in India's Informal Economy*, New Delhi: Esha Béteille Social Sciences Press.

Djurfeldt, Göran, Athreya, V., Jayakumar, N., Lindberg, S., Rajagopal, A. and Vidyasagar, R. (1008) "Agrarian change and social mobility in Tamil Nadu", *Economic and Political Weekly*, 43(45): 50–62.

Drèze, Jean, Lanjouw, Peter and Sharma, Naresh, "Credit in rural India: a case study", *Discussion Paper DEDPS/6*, London: The Suntory Centre/Suntory and Toyota International Centres for Economics and Related Disciplines/London School of Economics and Political Science/Hyderabad Institute of Public Enterprises.

Fouillet, Cyril (2009) "La construction spatiale de la microfinance en Inde", Doctoral Thesis, Université Libre de Bruxelles.

Garikipati, Supriya (2008) "The impact of lending to women on household vulnerability and women's empowerment: evidence from India", *World Development*, 36(12): 2620–2642.

Gooptu, Nandini (2001) *The Politics of the Urban Poor in Early Twentieth Century India*, Cambridge: Cambridge University Press.

Gorringe, Hugo (2010) "Shifting the 'grindstone of caste'? Decreasing dependency among Dalit labourers in Tamil Nadu", *in* Harriss-White and Heyer (eds), *The Political Economy of Development: Africa and South Asia Compared*, Routledge: London, pp. 248–267.

Government of India (2007) *Report of the Expert Group on Agriculture Indebtedness*, New Delhi: Banking Division/Department of Economic Affairs/Ministry of Finance/Government of India.

Government of India (2008) *Report of the Committee on Financial Inclusion*, NewDelhi: Government of India.

Guérin, Isabelle (under review) Juggling with debt, social ties and values.

Guérin, Isabelle, Roesch, Marc, Venkatasubramanian, G. and D'Espallier, Bert (2012a) "Credit from whom and for what? Diversity of borrowing sources and uses in rural South-India", *Journal of International Development*, (24): S122–S137.

Guérin, Isabelle, D'Espallier, B. and Venkatasubramanian, G. (2012b) "Debt in rural South India: fragmentation, social regulation and discrimination", *Journal of Development Studies*, DOI:10.1080/00220388.2012.720365 (early view).

Guérin, I., Morvant, S. and. Servet, J.-M. (2011) "Understanding the diversity and complexity of demand for microfinance services: lessons from informal finance", in Armendariz, B. and Labie, M. (eds) *Handbook of Microfinance*, London/Singapore: World Scientific Publishing, pp. 101–122.

Guyer, Jane (ed.) (1995) *Money Matters: Instability, Values and Social Payments in the Modern History of West African communities*, London/Portsmouth (NH): Currey/Heinemann.

Hardiman, David (1996) *Feeding the Baniya: Peasants and usurers in Western India*, New Delhi: Oxford University Press.

Harriss, Barbara (1981) *Transitional Trade and Rural Development*, Delhi: Vikas Publishing House.

Harriss, John (1999) "Comparing Political Regimes across Indian States", *Economic and Political Weekly*, 27 November.

Harriss-White, Barbara (1990) "The intrafamily distribution of hunger in South Asia", in Dreze, J. and Sen, A. (eds.) *The Political Economy of Hunger. Volume I: Entitlement and Well-being*. Oxford: Clarendon Press, pp. 351–424.

Harriss-White, Barbara (1996) *A Political Economy of Agricultural Markets in South-India: Masters of the Countryside*, New Delhi: Sage Publications.

Harriss-White, Barbara (2003) *India Working: Essays on Society and Economy*, Cambridge: Cambridge University Press.

Harriss-White, Barbara and Colatei, Diego (2004) "Rural credit and the collateral question", in Harriss-White, B. and Janakarajan, S. (eds) *Rural India facing the 21st century: Essays on Long Term Change and Recent Development Policy*, London: Anthem South Asian Studies.

Harriss-White, Barbara and Heyer, Judith (eds) (2010) *The Political Economy of Development: Africa and South Asia Compared*, Routledge: London.

Héliès, Ophélie (2006) "Du surendettement à son traitement: micro finance et macro enjeux: étude des processus de surendettement des ménages ruraux dans le Tamil Nadu, Inde, Mémoire d'ingénieur", Montpellier: Supagro.

Heyer, Judith (2010) "The marginalisation of Dalits in a modernising economy", *in* Harriss-White, B. and Heyer, J. (eds), *The Comparative Political Economy of Development Africa and South Asia*, Routledge: London, pp. 225–247.

Jones, J. and Howard, M. (1994) "A changing financial landscape in India: macro-level and micro-level perspectives, in Bouman, F. J. A. and Hopes, O. (eds) *Financial Landscape Reconstructed: The Fine Art of Mapping Development*, Boulder, CO: Westview Press, Chap 1, pp. 1–18.

Kapadia, Karin (1996) *Siva and Her Sisters. Gender, Caste and Class in Rural South India*, New Delhi: Oxford University Press.

Kapadia, Karin (2002) "Translocal modernities and transformations of gender and caste", in Kapadia, Karin (ed.) *The Volence of Development: The Politics of Identity, Gender and Social Inequalities in India*, New Delhi: Kali for Women, pp. 142–182.

Lont, H. and Hopes O. (eds) (2004) *Livelihood and Microfinance: Anthropological and Sociological Perspectives on Savings and Debt*, Delft: Eburon Academic Publishers.

Malamoud, Charles (ed.) (1988) *Lien de vie, nœud mortel. Les représentations de la dette en Chine, au Japon et dans le monde indien*, Paris: Editions EHESS.

Marius-Gnanou, Kamala (1993) "Socio-economic impact of the Green Revolution on Tamil rural society: the example of Pondicherry area", in *Pondy Papers in Social Sciences*, Pondicherry: Institut Français de Pondichéry, Number 11.

Mohanty, B. B. (2005) "'We are Like the Living Dead': Farmer Suicides in Maharashtra, Western India", *The Journal of Peasant Studies*, 32(2): 243–276.

Morvant-Roux, Solène (2006) "Processus d'appropriation des dispositifs de microfinance: un exemple en milieu rural mexicain", Thèse de doctorat en sciences économiques, Université Lumière Lyon 2.

Morvant-Roux, Solène (2009) "Accès au microcrédit et continuité des dynamiques d'endettement au Mexique: combiner anthropologie, économique et économétrie', *Revue Tiers Monde*, 197: 109–130.

Mosse David (2005) *Cultivating Development: An Ethnography of Aid Policy and Practice*, London and Ann Arbor (MI): Pluto Press.

NABARD (National Bank for Agriculture and Rural Development) (2008) *Report of the Committee on Financial Inclusion*, New Delhi: Nabard.

NSSO (2003) *Household Indebtedness in India as on 30.06.2002 All India Debt and Investment Survey* (AIDIS), National Sample Survey Organisation (NSSO) Fifty-Ninth Round, New Delhi: NSSO/Ministry of Statistics and Programme Implementation Government of India.

Olsen, Wendy K. and Morgan, James (2010) "Aspiration problems in Indian microainance: a case study exploration", *Journal of Developing Societies*, (26): 415–454.

Picherit, David (2009a) "'Workers, trust us!': labour middlemen and the rise of the lower castes in Andhra Pradesh', in Breman *et al. India's Unfree Workforce of Bondage Old and New*, New Delhi: Oxford University Press, op. cit. pp. 259–283.

Picherit, David (2009b) "Entre villages et chantiers: circulation des travailleurs, clientélisme et politisation des basses castes en Andhra Pradesh, Inde", Thèse de doctorat en ethnologie, Université Paris X Nanterre.

Polzin, Christine (2009) "Institutional change in Indian informal credit. An investigation through the lens of Arni and Vinayagapuram", Paper presented at the seminar "Market town, market society, informal economy", Wolfson College Contemporary South Asian Studies Programme, School of Interdisciplinary Area Studies, Oxford University, 8–9 June 2009.

Pouchepadass, Jacques (1980) "L'endettement paysan dans le Bihar colonial", in Malamoud, C. (ed.) *La dette*, Paris: Ecole des Hautes Etudes en Sciences sociales (coll. *Purusartha*, vol. 4), pp. 165–205.

Ramachandran, V. K. and Swaminathan, Madhura (2005) "Financial liberalization, rural credit and landless labour households: evidence from a Tamil Nadu village, 1977, 1985 and 1999", in Ramachandran, V. K. and Swaminathan, Madhura (eds) *Financial Liberalization and Rural Credit in India*, New Delhi: Tulika Books, pp. 157–177.

Roesch, Marc and Heliès, Ophélie (2007) "La microfinance: outil de gestion du risque ou de mise en danger par sur-endettement?", *Revue Autrepart* (44): 119–140.

Sa-Dhan (2009) *The Bharat Microfinance Report – Quick Data 2009*, NewDelhi: Sa-Dhan.

Servet, Jean-Michel (1984) *Nomismata. Etat et origines de la monnaie*, Lyon: Presses Universitaires de Lyon.

Servet, Jean-Michel (1996) "Community relations, individual, social and economics constraints in the savings and loans associations", African exain Cangiani (ed.) *The Milano Papers*, Montreal/London: Black Rose Books.

Servet, Jean-Michel (2006) *Banquiers aux pieds nus: La microfinance*, Paris: Odile Jacob.

Shipton, Parker (2007) *The Nature of Entrustment: Intimacy, Exchange and the Sacred in Africa*, New-Haven (CT) and London: Yale University Press.

Srinivasan, N. (2009) *Microfinance India: State of the Sector, Report 2008*, New Delhi: Sage Publications.

Sriram, M. S. and Parhi, Smita (2006) "Financial status of rural poor: a study in udaipur district", *Economic and Political Weekly*, 41(51): 5269–5275.

Vijayabaskar, M., Swaminathan, P., Anandhi, S. and Balagopal, G., "Human development in Tamil Nadu: examining linkages", *Economic and Political Weekly*, 39(8): 797–806.

Villarreal, Magdalena (2004) "Striving to make capital do 'economic things' for the impoverished: on the issue of capitalization in rural microenterprises", in Kontinen, T. (ed.) *Development Intervention: Actor and Activity Perspectives*, Helsinki: University of Helsinki, pp. 67–81.

Villarreal, Magdalena (2009) *Mujeres, finanzas sociales y violencia economica en zonas marginadas de Guadalajara*, Guadalajara (Mexico): Instituto Jalisciense de las Mujeres (IJM) and Instituto Municipal de las Mujeres en Guadalajara (IMMG.

World Bank (2007) *Finance for All? Policies and Pitfalls in Expanding Access. A World Bank Policy Research Report*, Washington, DC: World Bank.

Zelizer, Viviana (1994) *The Social Meaning of Money*, New York: Basic Books.

Zelizer, Viviana (2005) *The Purchase of Intimacy*, Princeton: Princeton University Press.

7 Protection and over-indebtedness in rural South India

The case of labour migrants of Andhra Pradesh

David Picherit

Emerging forms of credit and consumerism, as well as changing labour and social relationships are some of the contemporary transformations in rural India that low-caste manual labourers have to deal with on a daily basis. Restructuring of labour, development and consumption influenced by capitalism in India has put a lot of pressure upon the financial situation of the rural labouring classes. Indebtedness appears to be one of the most critical issues for the coming years. On a backdrop of social inequalities and structural poverty, manual labourers have been facing the gradual disappearance of local forms of patronage, unequal State scheme coverage, growing market-based forms of protection and the privatization of public goods (health, insurances, water, education, gas, etc.).

Often described as backward, rural India is nowadays the centre of attention for economic actors who consider it to be a market inhabited by entrepreneurs, innovators and consumers driven by an essentialist and cultural way of making business in the informal economy (*jugaad*). The success of microcredit in India has had a deep impact on the ways enterprises consider the poor: if they manage to save money, they can buy products. Multinational companies, such as Godrej, Danone or American International Group, design specific technological and social goods for the rural poor, which are sold through a variety of strategies and partnerships with banks, NGOs, State and international agencies in the sectors of insurance and health.[1] Other vital goods have been privatized, such as drinking water, which has become an unaffordable commodity in highly polluted areas.[2] The variety of State schemes aiming to guarantee 100 days work per year to the rural poor[3] or to deliver ration cards are, moreover, patchy in their coverage, and local political clientelist relations often determine who accesses them. While the shaping of labourers into consumers has entailed growing indebtedness for the consumption of basic goods, formal protections have remained scarce.

Given that consumption-indebtedness and labour protection are increasingly interrelated, this chapter will focus on the relations between debt and protection through a case study of debt-bonded labourers from a village of Mahabubnagar district in Andhra Pradesh and migrating to the construction industry in rural and urban areas. Neobondage in India is predicated upon a complex three-dimensional web, characterized by: (1) rising monetization of social relationships (and changing relationships to debt), caste and power relationships and an unequal hierarchical structure tailored to capitalism; and (2) economic exploitation and violence characterized by extra-economic forms of coercion (Breman 1996). By looking at how labourers negotiate debt, a relationship which roughly conveys the state of social, political and economical positions (Parry and Bloch 1989), I will explore how the blurred boundaries between indebtedness and over-indebtedness relate to the fluidity and segmentation of labour relations and forms of protections in rural India (Lerche 2010). As I will set out, the combination of capitalism and local forms of power has reconfigured in many ways the spatio-temporal dimensions of caste and class relations, through short-term, irregular and flexible social relations of labour, debt and protection. This process, which has been encouraged also by labourers looking to escape personalized, long-term and exploitative relations of debt-bondage, leads to – and is based on – employment insecurity, lack of support and renewed forms of dependence (Mosse 2002). Moreover, it detaches debt from social relations as a whole: debt has to be repaid whatever the violence of the methods of repayment.

This paper is based on 24 months of ethnographical fieldwork. During this period, I followed different groups of migrants – debt-bonded, daily-wage, task paid labourers – working in the rural and urban construction industry and shared their everyday lives in migration places and working sites. Along with them, I made regular back and forth trips to their village.[4] The local system of debt-bonded labour (*Palamur*) that was put into place in this district in the 1930s, although still in place today, has been deeply modified, due to the politicization and increasing affirmation of lower castes, new modes of recruitment of *maistri* (labour middlemen) and new forms of migration, but is also due to the reluctance of patrons to provide protection beyond the working season. However, the stronghold of the Reddys, the dominant caste of landowners in Telangana remains: they control land and labour, but also development resources they have managed to corner through their leading position in the different political parties, which they redistribute in unequal ways to followers.

The re-configuring of protection is key to understanding the boundaries between debt and over-indebtedness. Labourers' increasing refusal of personalized attachment and their quest for dignity, the transformation of migration and labour forms and changing relations of patronage and power have led to *multiple, temporary* protections, jobs and credits. Protection here is meant very broadly in acknowledgement of the blurred boundaries between State/market/patronage/NGO-based protections that labourers seek to access. Without considering those protections as equal, I am interested in the ways labourers *attempt to* secure their future livelihoods (a future which begins the following day) by mobilizing and alternating multiple types of social, political, religious and economic capitals such as the State, caste, family, NGOs, moneylenders, landowners and political parties. All of those protections imply varying degrees of domination, hierarchies, values and dependences for debt-bonded and daily-wage labourers, which often means deference and service, as well as humiliation and symbolic violence. As I will show, the changing temporality of social relations of labour and protection is key to understanding the rise of (over)-indebtedness: the intense circulation of labourers on multiple and short-term jobs, locally considered as a form of upward social mobility (compared to debt-bondage), allows improved access to multiple, small and short-term credits from numbers of people. However, the possibilities to negotiate repayment are limited, and to postpone those repayments remains dangerous.

The various debt-bonded labourers' positions in local power relationships, and their multiple ways to practice, conceive, resist, juggle, adapt and play with debt and social relationships will then be examined. This research is complementary to Viviana Zelizer's work (1979, 1994) on juggling money and social relationships. From intergenerational bonded labourers to others alternating between debt-bondage and daily-wage labour, many strive to manage structural insecurity (De Neve forthcoming; Guérin 2009; Heuzé 2009). In addition daily-wage labour relations does not mean free labour, but more often dependence-protection, job insecurity and livelihood precariousness (Picherit 2012). The transformation of personalized long-term ties into multiple, short-term and temporary dependencies expresses the contemporary tensions of relations of debt, protection and power, as well as the tactics, negotiations, and resistance that can be expressed upon the return to the village. The labour markets may offer job opportunities and upward social mobility for some people to get out of debt-bondage relations, experience daily-wage labour and acquire herds of animals. It certainly brings greater circulation between temporary jobs across various urban and rural spaces. This social mobility is nevertheless deeply unsecure and social trajectories can go down as well as up: the labour markets are highly fragmented along caste, religious and gender lines and the fluidity of labour relations mainly operates at the lowest segments of labour markets; fluidity shaped by the requirements of the construction industry: a labour force which can be adjusted on a daily/weekly/season basis.

By exploring the significance of debt in different social relations of labour, I would argue that over-indebtedness emerges when the moral, violent and physical obligation to repay a debt meets a lack of durable social and political protection-dependence and a decline in social and economic positions. It is this combination that transforms debt into over-indebtedness for people unable to gain access to capital in segmented credit markets. The first part of this article examines contemporary social and political changes at the village and district level. The second part explores the differentiated ways that debt-bonded labourers negotiate their debt relations on an everyday basis, and the third part looks at the changing meanings of debt in relation to the processes of social mobility.

Local transformations and debt relationships

Debt-bondage is an ideologically and politically sensitive issue for the Indian government. The definitions and appreciations of the scale of debt-bondage in India vary from 12 to 50 million (Lerche 2007). Duration, entrance and/or exit of the system of bondage are some of the criteria differentiating definitions given by the International Labour Organization, economists and anthropologists, who have discussed the relation of debt-bondage to capitalism. Classical economists deny that debt-bondage fits with capitalism, which is made of free labour (so-called bonded labourers have then freely chosen their situation) (Krishnaïah 1997). Marxists consider it as a survival or symbol of pre-capitalism (Ramach-andran 1990; Rao Mohan 1999), or as an exclusive form of coercion (Brass 1999), while postmodernist authors reflect on bondage as a Western construc-tion: debt-bondage is part of the local historical relationships of domination comprising exploitation and limited protection (Prakash 1990). Ethnographies of labour worlds more justly consider debt-bondage in India as a contemporary form of labour relation adapted to capitalism in various sectors of the economy (Breman 1996; De Neve 1999; Guérin *et al.* 2009, 2007; Picherit 2009; Breman *et al.* 2009; Shah 2006; Srivastava 2009). In addition, debt-bondage relations are part of a continuum of labour relations, beyond free/unfree labour dichotomies. As detailed by Lerche, the classes of labour (Lerche 2010) cover graded rela-tions to power, coercion, violence and poverty: this chapter aims to study how the economic, political and social positions among labouring classes express dif-ferent relations to indebtedness and protection, in order to bring insights about over-indebtedness.

In the district of Mahabubnagar, the *palamur*[5] system of debt-bondage is organized around a *contractor* who replies to government invitations to tender for the construction of canals, roads, dams and railways, etc. This contractor delegates the management of the labour force to several "*group maistri*" or *ped-damaistri* who depend upon several local *labour maistri* responsible for the recruitment of workers at the local level. Generally, the groups do not exceed 40 workers, both men and women (Olsen and Murthy 2000). Since the 1980s, the *maistri* share a similar background with the labourers: they are members of low castes (Gollas, Upparis – Backward Castes – and few Madigas – Dalits), which has a great impact on the logics of authority, social mobility and attach-ment of labourers. The *maistri* do not have the same assets and financial weight as the patrons and they cannot offer work in villages during the low season (Picherit 2009).

If *maistri* has often been characterized as an exploiter, one has to remember that his profit is minimal compared to that of the *peddamaistri*, often a politician: this system has been maintained due to the fact that most of the politicians in this area are involved in this business, whatever the political party. Rural leaders have secured their positions by capturing contracts for development and welfare programmes from the government and the construction industry. If Reddys have delegated the place of *maistri* to low-caste members, they have kept the position of *peddamaistri* and invested in machines, the two main profitable activities. Labourers can in no way rest upon a *maistri* to secure protection and they rather struggle to access development programmes cornered by political leaders and redistributed through unequal political patronage to followers.

Through the debt-bondage system, the workers are thus taken all over India for the construction of irrigation canals and dams. Since the 1980s, these migra-tions of debt-bonded labourers (from ex-untouchables, such as Madigas and, to a lesser extent, low-caste Gollas) have coexisted with the seasonal departures of workers to construction sites in Hyderabad and Mumbai for six to nine months a year, where they are employed as daily-wage labourers (this is particularly true for Gollas).[6]

These *Palamur* workers circulate between the cities and countryside and between debt-bonded and daily-wage positions in the construction industry. Furthermore, the debt-bonded labourers have gained some bargaining power by negotiating the possibility to change *maistri* and the amount of the advance. The current transformations are based on a swing between labourers' refusal of personalized attachment and a social and economic obligation to maintain links with local leaders, while the *maistri* are not keen or able to provide agricultural employment in the village during the rainy season.

The multiplication of forms of migration and work is integrated in a continuum graded along multiple and temporary degrees of dependency and helps to explain the strong diversity of profiles among bonded labourers. In this district, one of the most arid and poor of India, the streams of migration and forms of labour nowadays often overlap. This intense circulation of labour testifies to daily struggles for dignity, but also to the changing relationships of dependency, in which debt constitutes a crucial element of everyday inter-caste and interclass relationships.

First, debt-bonded and daily-wage labourers, as well as labour middlemen, can coexist in the same family. Second, a debt-bonded labourer works nine months for a *maistri*, and comes back to the village where he may work as an agricultural labourer and cultivate his own small plots of land (without access to water), while working as a daily-wager in the construction site when he visits his brother, employed as daily-wager in a nearby city. Third, from a diachronic standpoint, many daily wage labourers in urban city labour markets have worked previously as debt-bonded labourers, and while some managed to save money and buy goats, others are trapped again in the debt-bondage system. Unsecured salaries and positions, structural poverty and caste domination make social and economic positions highly vulnerable. Regularly changing *maistri* or going to urban areas to work as daily-wage labourers illustrates how relationships of personal attachment have transformed: dependence has become multiple and temporary.

This refusal of personal attachment, combined with local leaders' reluctance to bear the social and economic costs of patronage, drives those changes. The circulation of debts between moneylenders, *maistri*, landowners, self-help groups, shopkeepers and others constitutes a tactic which allows temporary and multiple protection as much as dependency. For many, the refusal is purely theoretical: whatever the changes, lots of continuities prevail. The caste-class relationships in the village are the basis of power and ex-untouchables are strongly discriminated against on the basis of their birth: they cannot enter the temple, share food with higher caste individuals, or even enter houses. They are not represented locally in political matters, while low-caste shepherds, such as Golla,[7] have managed to enter into politics through the regional party, the Telugu Desam Party, whose electorate is based on low-caste (though leading positions are held by Reddys, the local dominant caste) members. Transformations are deep, that is true, but the dominant caste of landowners maintains its central position in the organization of labour circulation, on debt and credit and on political affairs, while holding all resources driven by development (NGO, development programmes of the World Bank, DFID and other agencies).

The transformations of labour relationships have engendered two principal ways of limiting attachment: changing *maistri* and leaving the village seasonally as daily wage labourers. However, increasing loyalty to the *maistri* and landowner remains, for some labourers, a tactic to preserve security and protection.

Inter-generational debt and loyalty: reproduction of bondage

The systems of personalized attachment of agricultural labourers, like *baghela* or *jeethagadu*, and the inter-generational character and attachment to a particular *maistri*, have rarefied. At present in the village, only main landowners maintain a few agricultural workers who are bound on a yearly basis. They are particularly young, between ten and 15 years old, available 24 hours a day, given lodging – outside with the animals – and fed. The working day is around 17 hours. Clothing and health expenses are a priori the responsibility of the landowner. I have, however, never observed this: *jeethagadu* who are injured are asked to return to their homes and to take care of themselves.

For those labourers, leaving this relationship, however exploitative it may be, remains economically and socially out of scope. The labourers who used to be in this situation have become debt-bonded labourers in the construction industry, through a transfer of the debt from the landowner to the *maistri*. The amount of the debt is kept unknown, and no one really bothers. The *maistri* considers this labourer as property attached to him through patronage: "If I was not here to help him, what would happen to him? I provide work, shelter, food, life is like that for those people. They do not complain and are very loyal, not like others." This regular discourse is barely questioned by such labourers, all "ex-untouchables": the caste and class domination is deeply rooted and labourers maintain that they have no other option. Becoming daily-wage workers is beyond imagination.

This is what Swamy, a Madiga of about 30 years of age, expresses:

> My father died when I was just about so high [about 9 years old]. My mother continued to migrate with Maistri Ramullu from Kothapalle. I didn't work, I helped out, made tea and carried it. I started working later, had to eat. Each year the maistri gives my wife and me an amount of money, so we have to work; that is my life. My father had borrowed a lot. Both of my sons work with us now. The maistri has changed. It's Kondanna, Maistri Ramullu's eldest son.

This structural debt is reinforced by caste domination and ever-present patronage. At one extreme of the category of "bonded labourer", one is born with the debt contracted by one's father.

The amount of the debt is thus far from being relevant, as the relationship has not been translated into a financial terms. This point is important, as debt represents an attempt to put the cost of relationship into figures: financial debt does not appreciate necessarily within the overall situation between so-called creditors and debtors. In this sense, a small amount of debt could be more binding than a larger amount.

Even if the inter-generational character and attachment to a particular *maistri* has rarefied, maintaining privileged and long-term ties appears as an option for some workers in order to secure special status. This is the case of Golla Ballaïah, who constantly reinforces loyal ties with the *maistri*. He has become *gumpupam-pupedda* (trusted labourer in charge of the group when the *maistri* is away) under Mohan Reddy, the most important *maistri* of the village, whose family is among the most important landowners of the sub-district: Ballaïah finds regular agricultural work when he returns to the village. Their families have known each other from birth and are linked by a relationship of domination and an ongoing debt whose term is combined with a very uncertain future. It also sets the temporal dimension of the two protagonists' social relations.

On the one hand, the relationship is perpetuated as long as the debt is not settled. The creditor fixes the amount of reimbursement and the way in which the debt must be paid back: the amount of work to be done is determined by the *maistri* who is the only one, thanks to his mastery of the written language, to be able to guarantee the accuracy of his calculations.

On the other hand, this long-term dimension always establishes a more personal domination, a servitude, of which the compensation is affirmed daily through services rendered and markers of respect and loyalty. Trust appears in Swamy's words as a marker of their long-term relationship that each personally works to reproduce. Here, the length of the relationship engenders and renews trust and servitude.

Over-indebted from an economic point of view, the debt-bonded labourer has no possibility in this framework, and especially no intention of reimbursing his debt! Reinforcing this link and striving to demonstrate loyalty in the eyes of those who manipulate him in the short and long-term proves for Ballaïah to be a way to protect himself and to lessen risks.

Ballaïah is very much aware of the logic of leaving for Hyderabad as a daily-wage labourer or of changing *maistri*, and he is very clear about his own position. The inter-generational loyalty between his family and his *maistri*'s family allowed him to secure a situation that provides regular agricultural employment in the village during the rainy season, one aspect that the *maistri* cannot offer to any other bonded labourers. Ballaïah is one of the few in the village who has work throughout the year.

Dealing with debt and power relationships: changing *maistri* for dignity

The advance given by the *maistri* at the beginning of the season is increasingly becoming the core of the relationship (Guérin *et al.* 2009). Working and living conditions in migration are more or less equivalent and negotiating debt is the main issue during the time spent in the village.

After nine months of toil in stone quarries, on canals, dams, buildings or roads, for 12 hours a day, debt-bonded labourers return to the village: this means returning to the village hierarchies and returning and entering into power relations in order to contest, lessen or strengthen them. Returning to the village is the opportunity for two major but intermingled events: settling accounts with the *maistri* and negotiating a new advance; and finding an advance from a new *maistri*. This involves either a negotiation to obtain a greater advance or increase the circulation of debt; that is, negotiation, no longer with one *maistri*, but also with moneylenders and other *maistri*. This is also a way of demonstrating loyalty, multiplying temporary protection and forming or breaking alliances.

Changing *maistri* represents one of the main aspects through which labourers assert their dignity. The transformations of labour relationships, characterized by a decline of personalized attachments – through the combination of *maistri* and patrons' refusal to bear social and economic costs of protection and an increasing affirmation of low-caste labourers – allow labourers to change *maistri*, which means that the debt is taken by another *maistri*. The bargaining power of labourers is very low and changing *maistri* does not break with the bondage system: labourers "get by" within the system, working conditions being very similar no matter the *maistri*. It allows workers to affirm dignity and their relative autonomy among the search for the merest dependencies and protection. This brings about a lot of social play around negotiations, in which every player (*maistri* and labourers) is very much aware of the position and capacities of the other. Dignity is essential for labourers in everyday life, and the possibility to negotiate is frequently asserted as a gain against *maistri* and patrons. The latter know that once the advance is given, contestations are rare: labourers engage to follow the *maistri* and then wait until the end of the season to contest any conditions by changing *maistri*. Any resistance to the *maistri* is then smothered by this possibility and the *maistri* know that it is a tool for both the emancipation and discipline of the workers: conflict is postponed for later:

> "I won't work with him next season. I will go with Chandraïah. He (the present *maistri*) doesn't give anything, the labour camp is dirty and he shouts all the time. Chandraïah gives good advances and my brother-in-law has already worked with him, he knows him and will speak with him. If I contract a large amount, I will work it out with this *maistri*," explains Madiga Ramullu.

For Kushemma, speaking in front of a group of women, things are a bit different:

> They think that with a new *maistri*, things will be better. He smiles, he gives money, but then, what really changes? It's always the same. Working, eating, sleeping ... that's our life.

Kondanna's wife intervenes:

> Everyone chips in the village, we help each other when there are problems.
> For us, there is always a problem, the house, marrying off our first daughter,
> everyone wants money. What is one to do? The interest rate [*mitti*] is always
> the same, 3% a month. I have land, but there is no water, so we leave. We
> had a good *maistri* before, the new one isn't as good. I am looking for
> another. If he gives me an advance, that will do. We will settle the accounts
> at *dipāvali*.[8]

The goal of the *maistri*, and many of the labourers, is to never end a relationship.
Debt remains open as it circulates from *maistri* to *maistri*. The system generates
and preserves the labour force within the system: the debt is open and circulates
in the village, the centre of the organization of the circulation of labour and
power relations.

Many complex situations associate a strong will for emancipation with a
status of debt-bondage: the refusal of personalized dependency is confronted
with insurmountable poverty:

> "I go wherever I want," explains an angry Golla Daseratta. "I have worked
> hard everywhere, in Bombay, on the Narmada, in Goa, in Kanyakumari,[9] in
> Nagarjuna Sagar,[10] and he doesn't give me any advances. I have built canals,
> roads, dams! I don't need any *maistri*, I'll go to Hyderabad and will take
> care of my land. His food is disgusting, his camps are dirty. How am I sup-
> posed to pay him back? I have five daughters and three are to be married.
> I'll go to Hyderabad, I've already worked there. My daughters are with their
> useless husbands. They do not want to help me."

Two months after this narrative was collected in the village, Daseratta worked
with his wife and one of his five daughters in the north of Telangana for a new
labour middleman. One month later, however, Daseratta went to his two married
daughters' settled in a neighborhood of Hyderabad where daily-wage labourers
of his caste (Golla) migrated and found daily employment in construction. He
went back to the village, but faced the dominant members of his caste pressing
him to respect the contract. He returned to his *gumpu* (workgroup) in the north
of Telangana. Back by September for the festival of *vinayakacaviti*,[11] Daseratta
occasionally worked for a Reddy, landowner. At the same time, he negotiated a
departure for the new season under the orders of a new *maistri*: the former
having refused another monetary advance. He left again for nine months.

The migratory pattern is unchangingly and seasonally repeated year after
year. Daseratta, a debt-bonded labourer for the past 30 years, and fervent critic
of daily-wage labour, stated the following:

> Before the "Skylab",[12] I left with my wife for Karnataka with Suddakar
> Reddy, then with Indu Reddy; I worked with Govardhan Reddy on a canal

in Warangal, then with Mandadi in Anantapur, with Raja Reddy in Pocham-
pad, in Maharashtra on a dam, then in Pune, and on the great Kakatiya
canal. There, there were 3,000 labourers, almost all palamuru. Then, I left
for Chandrapur in Maharashtra.[13] I came and went four or five times after
sankrānti. I came and left near *dipāvali*.[14]

This narrative conveys several characteristic points of current transformations in
labour's social relations: an accrued circulation of labour in the rural and urban
zones and in agriculture and construction; an alternation between the debt-
bondage status of daily-waged labourer, of agricultural worker and even of landowner, but also frequent *maistri* changes; the possibility of expression, at certain
moments and in certain contexts, of the desire to escape from debt-bondage,
even the negotiation of these relations ("I go wherever I want, whenever I
want"). This is placed in parallel with a recurring statement of debt-bonded
labourers: "we go where the *maistri* tells us to go".

Daseratta was a goat-shepherd, debt-bonded labourer, *jitagadu*, daily-wage
labourer, agricultural worker, landowner and now, once again, a debt-bonded
labourer. When Daseratta and Govindamma left for the north of Telangana, their
youngest daughter, nine years old, was hired in a neighbouring town as a servant
in the village head's house: at his total disposal for 1,500 rupees per year. By
conceding his daughter in such a way, Daseratta was able to borrow 6,000 rupees
at 36 per cent annual interest[15] from his family.

Changing *maistri* represents one of the only possibilities for a couple to
escape personalized power, all while regularly playing on the use of kinship
terms with the new *maistri*. The pragmatism and the will to preserve a certain
dignity are striking. The wife's wish to work as a daily-wage labourer cannot
become reality, especially with five daughters to marry: it is necessary to leave
again, and it is above all the amount of the negotiated advance that will determine the choice of *maistri*.

Debt remains within the structured framework of the village, with its own temporalities based on religious festivals (which are also economic, *dipāvali* being the
time when accounts are settled with the *maistri*). These social plays, between the
search for dignity and dependency, are the stakes of the negotiations.

These labourers do not go out of this system of bondage. Indebtedness is fully
integrated into the power relationships that are constantly negotiated, resisted or
accepted.

Social ascension and decline: the path to over-indebtedness?

The boundaries between the different profiles are increasingly blurred. Some
labourers have been attached for generations; others have reinforced loyalties,
while others have tried to change *maistri* to preserve some dignity.

In addition, leaving the village seasonally as a daily-wage labourer represents
another option, which is far from signalling independence. Dependency
reappears in different manners in the workplace. First and foremost, the logics of

circulation are rooted in the village and its power relationships: to leave as a daily-wage labourer means securing the agreement of the *maistri* to partially clear the debt and to follow his own caste rules of recruitment (Picherit 2012). Success stories are rare in the everyday life of the village: social ascension is so unsecured that many go back to the *maistri*. The Gollas, who have opened a migration stream in a neighbourhood of Hyderabad, have had good success in terms of finances and prestige. However, the ones who benefit most from this stream are those who were already in good positions in the village before leaving as daily-wage migrants. For the debt-bonded Gollas who managed to leave as daily-wage labourers, they have no further financial security and in case of any health, housing or religious expenditure, they have no other option but to go and find a *maistri*: he is the only one to propose a large amount of money. Physical force is the remaining guarantee for those labourers.

It also happens that labourers willingly enter into debt-bondage in the hopes of obtaining a significant monetary advance. In this case, entrance into debt-bondage is due to pragmatic and family reasons. Negotiations are made, calculations established and one of the family's sons works to pay back debt for two to four years: a family can send a son to claim an advance at certain moments and reimburse it through labour, while his brothers may be agricultural or daily-wage labourers. Labour is thus guaranteed but, above all, subordination is relative: the *maistri* cannot abuse the labourer without risking the loss of the advanced money.

This servitude is most often due to necessity and survival. Extreme poverty, a failure in migration, the impossibility to pay back a loan, in other words any series of incidents, can weaken an individual's situation and lead them to migration under a *maistri*. This entrance into bondage, degrading in terms of social position and prestige, can be put into perspective by juggling with debt and a lesser subordination: *they get by*.

When I first met Chandraïah and Kushnamma, they owned a plot of several acres of land, a small herd of goats and two buffalos:

> That is my son. He studies in the nearby town in Inter 2nd. He is very good, he stays in a "hostel". He must study. Anita [their daughter] is at the school here. Over there are our goats, nineteen of them. We also have two buffalos … and four acres of land. There is no more water. We had three wells, the first lasted two years, the second three years, and the last, nothing. What can we do? A well costs a lot of money … 20,000 rupees maybe. I am a *kuuli* [daily-wage] and Chandraïah takes care of sheep and a little bit of the fields.
>
> Karimnagar, Rajahmundry, Srikakulam, Bombay, everywhere. For four years, we were with the same *maistri*. He passed away. We slept in tents for six months, two months in the village and then would go on migration. We didn't know how to get a loan.

They were nevertheless able to invest in a tube well first, then in successive herds: goat-herding is a caste trade and owning a herd is a true form of prestige. The accent on the children's education indicates a change of social position.

Kushnamma is worried about the current situation:

> We have spent 6,000 rupees for corn but the crop is sick and there will be no profit. Either we pay back or we lose everything. We have taken 40,000 rupees to buy some goats. One goat costs between 6,000 and 10,000 rupees depending on its size, shape and milk.... We pay 50 rupees a day each month for the care of the buffalos [...]. Then, we have 80,000 rupees loan on the house. The loans are private. We have two, 50% each.

The first loan of 40,000 rupees for the goats has been paid back. By "private", Kushnamma means a known and reputed person who only loans to recommended people offering some sort of guarantee:

> We went to see a well-known person [telisinimanisi],[16] my brother-in-law introduced us to him. Here, there is "3% mitti [3% interest rate]. We gave him bracelets and jewelry.
>
> This is very dangerous, they come at us, discuss in the village. They ask for which rice we buy, if our children go to school. If we don't give the money back, they will spread the word in the village and take everything. Those are the Reddy, they have all the money.

Another comes from the Government Bank of Kothakotta:

> That was for the well and the pump. That was seven years ago. We didn't have any money and the bank loaned us 40,000 rupees.

After discussion, the bank had in fact only loaned 28,000 rupees. The 12,000 remaining were determined by the regularity of the reimbursements. For this type of loan, the land is put up as collateral. If the bank spreads out the reimbursement installments, the "private", the *telisinimanisi*, sends thugs and does not hesitate to brutalize clients in order to get back the money.

A few months later, as soon as I returned to the village, the neighbour informed me that Chandraïah had passed away. The corn had been definitively lost and the son had stopped going to school. His mother harassed the NGO director for work: he used his network and the son became a "helper" on a worksite with a *maistri*.

This description outlines the shifting borders between forms of labour in a context of permanent insecurity: death, illness, work-related accidents and drought remind these Gollas of the precariousness of their situation. For this formerly debt-bonded family in the process of ascension, where the son and daughter's education was a crucial factor, sending the son on migration, as daily-wage or bonded labourer, is among the possibilities evoked by the mother after this death.

For this family, debt has become a burden. For years, they could manage to live on their own without depending fully on a *maistri* or high-caste landlord.

They had enjoyed upward social mobility, their social position in the village had changed, they had gained some respect among their caste-fellows, had shown everyone the investment they had made in education (their son being one of the few studying at this level). The land was used as a guarantee to project them in a near future and to get credit. The herd was displayed in the compound of the house in the late afternoon and Chandraïah had enjoyed the prestige of returning from the fields along with land and herd owners: an activity which, in the village, is the most prestigious position. Migrants' dreams are directed towards the village and the traditional activity of the Gollas, rearing goats, which is the most valued and promoted.

The death of the main breadwinner represents the beginning of the financial and social decline of the family: the vulnerability of this family, and others, is clearly shown through accident, risk and health problems, which can ruin the success gained from years of struggle. The loss of the harvest, partly due to the son's inability to tackle agricultural work (Indian school education strongly denigrates physical work and the father had not taught him agricultural tasks) and partly to different conflicts among kin fellows, represents an inability to reimburse the debt taken for the agricultural season. There is no safety net; long-term protection does not exist. The decline of the family is linked to the social obligation to reimburse the debt, in terms of family honour and prestige. For years, Chandraïah enjoyed his social mobility by limiting political and economic personalized relations. His pride, related to his past history of debt-bondage, was based on cutting dependence, a risky but successful tactic – until his death.

The social ascension initiated since they went out of debt-bondage is reversing. In order to repay the debt, the family's social position must change. The future expected by the son is highly compromised, education is stopped and he will have to work on a construction site as a debt-bonded labourer. The advance taken from the *maistri* is the only option to get a significant amount of cash: it will take at least four years of work to reimburse the advance.

Indebtedness, development and consumption

As briefly sketched in the introduction, the landscapes of protection have profoundly changed over the last 15 years. The State has failed to fulfill the promises to offer social security, universal access to health care or decent working conditions and rather encouraged the commodification of social goods. In the 1990s, the neoliberal policies of the Telugu Desam Party (TDP) in Andhra Pradesh, brought a huge number of development programmes targeted for specific categories of population (caste, age, gender...) that have been mostly operated through the leading political party. In the village, the microcredit program launched by an NGO in the 1990s has been delegated to a village committee to encourage village self-decisions. However, it then became controlled by one of the henchman of the head of the village, pushing clients to vote for the TDP. The TDP leader, who is also the hereditary traditional head of the village and the main landowner, has enjoyed a weak opposition for some time. However, the

TDP lost the State elections in 2004. If the head has maintained its power in the village, this defeat at State level has reactivated factions in the village between the Reddys: the Congress has gained enough weight to contest. This political competition has turned into struggles to control development resources from the government and has reduced labourers to followers, the only way to gain access to goods. To access the National Rural Employment Guarantee Act, one has to maintain good and loyal relationships with the head of the village and also with his henchman, who has been promoted as *maistri* by the former. Yet, local leaders have delegated *maistri* positions to Gollas and encouraged some to leave as daily-wage labourers to Hyderabad. Nevertheless, they have kept their control on migrants: the lack of sustainable resources from migration forces those labourers to re-enter into dependence when they come back to the village to access to any government scheme.

In this context, most state or NGO development programmes are embedded in local structures of economic and/or political accumulation operated by a variety of musclemen (Price and Ruud 2010), a trend that has also been observed in the neighbouring state of Karnataka (Joseph, this volume; Pattenden 2011). Those forms of protection are unreliable, temporary and subjected to caste affiliations to a political party: the participation to political activities is one of the requirements (self-help groups are key groups mobilized here and there) and debt-bonded labourers, away nine months per year, are the last to benefit from the redistribution. The Gollas are the ones who have benefited most from those labour and political transformations: the migration to Hyderabad and the political rise of the caste has ensured many of caste financial support, however fragile that support may be. They are, furthermore, now extremely exposed and targeted by companies as they are supposed to consume goods such as TVs and motorbikes, etc. This rising consumption does not escape local leaders, who invest in different forms of business: in 2011, due to his (violent) influence, the henchman of the TDP managed to sell 168 TV antennae for a private company that pays him through commission, despite the fact that there are only 20 TVs in this village of 2,000 people. Many Gollas have also accessed the housing scheme launched by the government and they have taken huge debts to finance the 30 per cent that is not paid by the scheme. Mobile phones are other goods that have made a decisive entry in the village. If Gollas have become increasingly indebted, they are the group that would not consider existing as debt-bonded labour anymore. The pride of their recent success makes them extremely exposed to over-indebtedness and all would be reluctant to use their labour force as an option to reimburse debt.

This examination of different debt relationships situates the complexities of power in rural India, while insisting on the limited agency of labourers in such extreme situations. The articulation between indebtedness, social change and decline of social position could refine what could be over-indebtedness in India. As I have shown, the concept of over-indebtedness could not be relevant for inter-generational bonded labourers and for most debt-bonded labourers. Those labourers do not intend to reimburse and few have expectations to go out of this relationship: if personal attachment and debt are contested by labourers, they can hardly move away from this relationship and its guarantee of employment. Despite the increasing monetization of the relationship, the debt is hardly conceived as something to be fully reimbursed and the inability to repay a debt is not a sufficient criterion for over-indebtedness.

This inability must be linked to a change into social relationships, stressing the obligation to reimburse. This is the second point. Over-indebtedness appears when the burden of the debt has to be reimbursed, when the possibilities of juggling between debts is over and when debt is associated with a decline of social position and prestige. Decline does not just amount to lost money, but a breakdown of future plans, social climbing, prospects and expectations. It means losing face after years of success and sometimes *garvam* (pride and arrogance) towards former co-workers. The segmentations within classes of labour coexists with multiple micro-hierarchies that are reinforced on an everyday basis by low-caste labourers eager to stress their upward social mobility by keeping others under themselves: returning to debt-bondage leads to huge loss of self-esteem.

Conclusion

The circulation of labour required by the construction industry has led to irregular, temporary and multiple dependences, recreating divisions and segmentations among labourers. The structural insecurity of labourers (Breman 1996, 2007) has allowed them to experience different jobs and to aspire for better conditions, but it has strongly hampered forms of solidarity. In addition, the circulation remains limited to the lowest segments of the construction industry: this is the main sector where Palamur labourers find jobs, and always at the lowest ladder of the industry.

Whatever the success, no one is free from the risk of setbacks. The slightest economic or family problem can bring to an end independence acquired over years of risk. The rejection of personalized attachment leads to the quest for a variety of forms of temporary protection, and access to local resources controlled by political parties and their henchmen. Submitting oneself to temporary dependency on *maistri*, moneylenders, and/or landowners, only provides limited protection. The crisis of patronage, market and State-sponsored forms of protection fosters over-indebtedness, which comes about abruptly when the inability to repay debt coincides with a lack of social and political capital, along with the moral, symbolic and physical obligations of repayment and a refusal of degrading positions. Despite monetization, debt-bonded labourers have little intention of repaying their debts. But the debts of daily-wage labourers are increasingly divorced from social relations and collected by "foreigners" (credit agents from NGOs and microfinance institutions), moneylenders and landowners keen to get their money back on time: they do not intend to create followers and are happy to use violent methods.

Such circulation of labour, fluidity of labour relations and improved access to multiple forms of credit is highly segmented along caste lines. Gollas have managed to alternate between debt-bondage, daily-wage employment and work as goat-keepers. A few have also invested (thanks to the advance of the *maistri*) successfully in a tube well and engaged in agriculture. Increasing numbers of Gollas have also started (small) money-lending businesses, bringing new, easier indebtedness prospects to their caste-fellows. The successful ones who are close to the major political party are increasingly talking about schemes in terms of rights. They are now targeted by the marketing industry and are eager to show off their success through consumer goods, but also aspire to better living conditions (Guérin *et al.* this volume).

By contrast, Madigas remain entirely unprotected, as advance sums from the *maistri* tend to be the only subject of negotiation: they remain nine months a year under the watch of the *maistri*. They still have virtually no access to any State scheme and are completely ignored by labour departments, NGOs, trade unions and social activists. The degree of exploitation is so great that the exploiters themselves are the only source of protection: they are the ones who "grant" a visit to a doctor in the most extreme cases, who "offer" one egg a weak, lend money for buying extra soap, alcohol and *beedies* (local cigarettes). This relationship with the *maistri* has become short term (negotiations take place every year) and labourers continue to try to access different forms of protection, notably the crumbs of the development schemes. The labourers' defiance of personalized attachment relationships should not be seen as unilateral resistance or victory, but as part of a more complex framework of transformations in social relations, where major landowners and *maistri* are not looking to maintain a large, regular labour force.

Debt circulation in villages between *maistris* and the labourers remains within the relational networks that shape the circulation of bonded and daily-wage labour. But this highlights the decline of protection beyond the labour domain (Servet and Saiag, this volume; Lerche 2010). The increasing rush for Indian rural markets by multinational enterprises and the privatization of protection through local-based insurance (life, health and so on), can only place a considerable further burden on families' budget(s).

Notes

1 In the State of Andhra Pradesh, the *aarogya sree* scheme is a private-public partnership providing (selected) free surgeries to the poor below the poverty line in private corporate hospitals: a huge part of the health budget of the State is transferred to the private healthcare industry against the reduction of the budgets of the primary health centres. In addition, this programme excludes labour migrants coming from other States to Andhra Pradesh.

2 In the district of Chittoor, Andhra Pradesh, "studies have revealed that the drinking and groundwater is polluted with high concentrations of uranium, 135 times more than the safe limit fixed by the World Health Organisation". Deccan Chronicle, 07/02/2013. See: www.deccanchronicle.com/120907/news-current-affairs/article/deadly-uranium-traces-found-chittoor-water.

3 This programme is the National Rural Employment Guarantee Scheme. One hundred days of work per year are provided to families below the poverty line. The

implementation greatly varies between villages, districts and States and it often happens that even main landowners get the benefits (without working). In the case study of this chapter, the scheme is hardly implemented.

4 Everyday observations, informal and formal discussions were the main tools used for this study.

5 Palamur is the former name of the district of Mahabubnagar (1929). Migrants are called, and call themselves, "Palamur" labourers.

6 Approximately 200,000 workers, one third of whom are bonded labourers (this is the proportion given by Olsen and Murthy, 2000), leave the district every year for nine months. The villages in which the fieldwork was carried out have between 50 and 70 per cent of the working-age population (15–45 years) on sites away from the village (seasonal variations). All migrant labourers are owners of plots of land – between one and five acres – but without access to water. The open wells are dry and water has been privatized: rice cultivation requires much water and the costly bore wells are only for the Reddys and the few Gollas.

7 "Golla" is the name of the caste in Andhra Pradesh whose traditional (and current) main activity is related to the rearing of goats. Classified by the Indian administration as a Backward Caste, they have enjoyed a significant social, economic and political ascension at the State and local level.

8 Religious festival in November: this is the time when accounts and advances renewed.

9 Place in southeast India.

10 Dam in Andhra Pradesh.

11 Hindu religious festival of *Ganesh*.

12 "skylab" is a famous time marker all over India, referring to the US space shuttle which crashed in 1979 (and the risk was high that it would crash on India (...and then on the village!).

13 Places are considered to be distant when they are between 300 and 1,000 kilometres from the village: this means different States, languages and food habits.

14 Religious Hindu festivals: these are important time markers in the organization of the circulation of labour.

15 The interest is commonly expressed as three rupees of interest for 100 rupees borrowed, without notice of the length of the credit. Here, it is 36 per cent of interest per year.

16 The prefix *telisi* means that they address a reputed person with whom they are already in a relationship. *Telisivikhyāti ou telisinivyakti* are two other expressions (less frequently used). The second one informs a kinship relationship, *viyyam* being the relation between the parents of the married couple.

References

Brass, T. (1999) "Towards a Definition of Bonded Labour', in Brass, T., *Towards a Comparative Political Economy of Unfree Labour: Case Studies and Debates*, London: Frank Cass, pp. 9–46.

Breman, J. (1996) *Footloose Labour: Working in India's Informal Economy*, Cambridge: Cambridge University Press.

Breman, J. (2007) *The Poverty Regime in Village India: Half a Century of Work and Life at the Bottom of the Rural Economy in South Gujarat*, New Delhi: Oxford University Press.

Breman, J, Guérin, I. and Prakash, A. (eds) (2009) *India's Unfree Workforce: Of Bondage Old and New*, New Delhi: Oxford University Press.

De Neve, G. (1999) "Asking for and Giving baki: Neo-bondage, or the Interplay of Bondage and Resistance in the Tamil Nadu Power-loom Industry", *Contributions to Indian Sociology*, 33(1–2): 379–406.

De Neve, G. (forthcoming) "From Field to Factory: Tracing Transformations in Bonded Labour in the Tiruppur Region, Tamil Nadu", *Economy and Society*.

Elyachar, J. (2002) "Empowerment Money: The World Bank, Non-Governmental Organizations, and the Value of Culture in Egypt", *Public Culture*, 14(3): 493–513.

Guérin, I., Bhukhut, A. and Parthasarthy, Venkatasubramanian (2007) "Labour in Brick Kilns: A Case Study in Chennai", *Economic and Politic Weekly*, 42(7): 599–606.

Guérin, I., Roesch M. and Venkatasubramanian, Kumar S. (this volume) "The Social Meaning of Over-indebtedness in the Context of Poor Rural Households in Tamil Nadu, South-India".

Guérin, I., Bhukhut, A., Marius-Gnanou, K. and Venkatasubramanian, G. **(Year?)** "Neobondage, Seasonal Migration and Job Brokers: Cane Cutters in Tamil Nadu", in Breman, J., Guérin, I. and Prakash, A. (eds) *India's Unfree Workorce: Of Bondage Old and New*. New Delhi: Oxford University Press, pp. 233–258.

Joseph N. (this volume) "Microfinance Repayment Crisis in a South Indian Town".

Heuzé, D. (2009) "Bondage in India: Representing the Past or the Present? The Case of the Dhanbad Coal Belt during the 1980s", in Breman, J., Guérin, I. and Prakash, A. (eds) *India's Unfree Workforce: Of Bondage Old and New*, New Delhi: Oxford University Press, pp. 147–169.

Krishnaïah, M. (1997) "Rural Migrant Labour Systems in Semi-Arid Areas: a Study in Two Villages in Andhra Pradesh", *Indian Journal of Labour Economics*, 40: 123–143.

Lerche, Jens (2007) "A Global Alliance Against Forced Labour? Unfree Labour, Neo-Liberal Globalization and the International Labour Organization", *Journal of Agrarian Change*, 7(4): 425–452.

Lerche, Jens (2010) "From Rural Labour to Classes of Labour. Class Fragmentation Caste and Class Struggle at the Bottom of the Indian Labour Hierarchy", in Harriss-White, B. and Heyer, J. (eds) *The Comparative Political Economy of Development: Africa and South Asia*, London: Routledge.

Mosse D., Gupta, S., Mehta, M., Shah, V., Rees, J. and KRIBP Project Team (2002) Brokered Livelihoods: Debt, Labour Migration and Development in Tribal Western India, *Journal of Development Studies*, 38(5): 59–88.

Olsen, Wendy K. and Murthy, Ramana R. V. (2000) "Contract Labour and Bondage in Andhra Pradesh (India)", *Journal of Social and Political Thought*, 1: (2).

Parry, Jonathan and Bloch, Maurice (1996) *Money and the Morality of Exchange*, New York: Cambridge University Press (reprinted 1989).

Pattenden, J. (2011) "Gatekeeping as Accumulation and Domination: Decentralisation and Class Relations in Rural South India", *Journal of Agrarian Change*, 11(2): 164–194.

Picherit, David (2009) "'Workers, trust us!': Labour middlemen and the rise of the lower castes in Andhra Pradesh", in Breman, J., Guérin, I. and Prakash, A. (eds) *India's Unfree Workforce: Of Bondage Old and New*, Delhi: Oxford University Press, pp. 259–283.

Picherit, David (2012) "Migrant Labourers Struggles between Village and Urban Migration Sites: Labour Standards, Rural Development and Politics in South India", *Global Labour Journal*, 3(1): 143–162.

Prakash, Gyan (1990) *Bonded Histories: Genealogies of Labor Servitude in Colonial India*, Cambridge: Cambridge University Press.

Price, P. and Ruud, A. E. (2010) *Power and Influence in India: Bosses, Lords and Captains*, New Delhi: Routledge.

Ramachandran, V. K. (1990) *Wage Labour and Unfreedom in Agriculture: An Indian Case Study*, Oxford: Clarendon Press, p. 321.

Rao, J. and Mohan, A. (1999) "Agrarian Power and Unfree Labour", in Byres, T. J., Kapadia, Karin and Lerche, Jens (eds) *Rural Labour Relations in India*, New Delhi: India Research Press, pp. 242–262.

Servet, J. M. and Saig, H. (this volume) "Household Over-Indebtedness in Contemporary Societies: A Macro-Perspective.

Shah, A. (2006) "The Labour of Love: Seasonal Migration from Jharkhand to the Brick Kilns of Other States in India", *Contributions to Indian Sociology*, 40(1): 91–118.

Srivastava, R. S. (2009) "Conceptualizing Continuity and Change in Emerging Forms of Labour Bondage in India", in Breman, J., Guérin, I. and Prakash, A. (eds) *India's Unfree Workforce: Of Bondage Old and New*, New Delhi: Oxford University Press.

Zelizer, Viviana A. (1979) *Morals and Markets: Development of Life Insurance in the United States*, New York: Columbia University Press.

Zelizer, Viviana A. (1994) *The Social Meaning of Money*, New York: Basic Books.

8 International migration and over-indebtedness in rural Mexico

Solène Morvant-Roux

Introduction

National and international migration dynamics across the world have been the topic of a great deal of research. Economic work in this area most commonly focuses on the consequences of migration, its "impact" on the wellbeing of migrant populations' places of origin (Orozco, 2002; Cohen, 2001). However, the question of reverse causality – for instance the links between poverty and/or vulnerability and migration dynamics – has been relatively neglected (Waddington and Sabates-Wheeler, 2003). Addressing these links can shed light on the dynamics ("push and pull" in economic literature) of voluntary migration, or forced migration undertaken as an act of last resort. Among the various sources of household vulnerability, this chapter aims to analyze the links between indebtedness and migration, and more specifically between the level of indebtedness and migration. As will be demonstrated, migration is most commonly associated with very high levels of indebtedness that can be termed as over-indebtedness. This concurs with observations made by David Mosse *et al.* (2002) regarding scheduled tribe populations in western India. Their findings reveal that relatively poor members of tribal groups are more likely to undertake long-term whole household migration to service high-interest debts acquired for subsistence purposes.[1]

After presenting the research context and methodology, the financial practices of populations will be considered. Research and close analysis of household financial strategies will be applied to debt as an institution (e.g., a set of permanently established rules constraining personal behavior, yet constructed through individual actions and in constant evolution).[2] This will reveal the existence of chains of indebtedness that have dual implications characterized on a group level by the social role of debt and on an individual level by the intense circulation of money through ongoing juggling practices between sources of income and credit (Guérin *et al.*, 2009). A critical assessment of the distinction between dynamic debt practice and over-indebtedness will then follow.

Indeed, whatever the context, an over-indebted individual (or household) can be defined as someone who is unable to repay contracted debt, in particular all or part of borrowed capital (Lazarus, 2009). This relatively universal definition encompasses very distinct realities. However, one key question remains. At what stage can one deem a household over-indebted?

Supported by an analytical framework considering debt as a social institution, our hypothesis is that local indebtedness plays out in terms of ongoing juggling practices between different sources of formal or informal credit, where income is highly irregular and there is a mismatch between income flow and the timing of ongoing or one-off expenditures. In contrast, over-indebtedness is reached when a household has to resort to a particular strategy over and above this "routine" in order to repay its debts. We shall see that if commuting is a normal part of this cash-flow management "routine", in a region where migration is recent and concerns only a small share of the population (in contrast to other regions of Oaxaca State such as Mixteca) migration to other Mexican states or to the United States of America results from a different sort of financial necessity. In these villages where migration dynamics are recent, without any previously established network for candidates to rely on, high cost and risk make international migration a particularly hard undertaking. This echoes many studies on the central role of social capital in migration. As Waddington and Sabates-Wheeler (2003: 14) highlight: "Migration may be too risky an option for poor communities lacking developed social networks with migration destinations." In line with this analysis, we will show that not all households can undertake such a strategy. Migration is resorted to only in a justifiable situation, which is rarely the mere draw of a higher salary. When indebtedness reaches a very high level, some households hence opt for this strategy rather than selling their land or livestock. The chapter will conclude with the effects of the financial crisis of 2007–2008 and its current manifestations on the migratory dynamics between Mexico and the United States.

Context and research methodology

Socio-geographical and economic characteristics of the observed/ studied villages

This qualitative study was conducted in the small village of San Balthazar, located in the Sierra Sur, a mountainous region in the state of Oaxaca. The inhabitants of this area are of the Zapotec[3] ethno-linguistic group and define themselves as such.

In the state of Oaxaca, more than 40 percent of the economically active population participate in primary sector activities, mainly in agriculture and livestock farming. Paradoxically, these activities barely represent more than 4 percent of

Table 8.1 Demographic data of the village studied

Village	Number of localities	Number of Inhabitants
San Baltazar Loxicha	7	2,873

Source: INEGI, XII Censo General de Población y Vivienda 2000, SIMBAD.

the state's GDP. In the Sierra Sur region, primary sector activities concern closer to 80 percent or even 85 percent of the economically active population (INEGI, 2000). Agricultural activity is predominant as it represents the main means of survival for households. The main crop is corn (or *milpa* when it is cultivated with the black bean called *frijol*) and is grown mostly for household consumption. The coffee crop, aimed for sale, is the second most important although it is not grown by all of the farmers. Some households live essentially on their production of corn and small-scale animal farming (chickens and turkeys). Monetary income can be derived from daily work for other farmers' fields or for employers in the construction sector. The majority of families own farm animals or participate in livestock farming. Apart from agricultural production, other opportunities available to complement monetary income indispensable for the survival of the household include small business, temporary farming work or salaried/unsalaried employment linked to construction.

The organization of peasant Indian villages in Mexico: community and religious responsibilities

The political-administrative organization of the regions composing the Mexican republic is founded on the municipal entity inherited since Independence in the nineteenth century. The municipality is governed at the level of each of the federation's states, through laws and State constitutions. It is, in a general manner, "invested with executive power and certain judicial competencies" (Dehouve, 2003: 5)[4] and normally governed by a municipal council elected for a three-year term through direct popular vote. At the heart of the municipality, the administrative hierarchy is as follows: the *Cabecera municipal* (county seat), *Agencia municipal* (villages recognized as municipal agencies), and finally, *rancherias* (sets of about a dozen houses).

The municipal authorities can ask for a sort of tax paid in kind to their citizens in the form of an unpaid participation in public works, known as *tequio*, forming the main part of the civil responsibility system adding to religious responsibility. The system of responsibility (*cargos*) makes up one of the main institutions of the village organization. Well studied by anthropologists, we will limit ourselves here to a short description of the system, which can be defined as:

> an obligatory rotation of hierarchical responsibilities between male members of the commune. The mode of designation of those responsible varies (cooptation, automatic designation, election and length of mandate) according to the responsibility, whether it be civil or religious.
>
> (Chamoux, 1987: 212)[5]

The indigenous community has been the object of several anthropological studies as it is assimilated to a resistance led on a dual front against the central state and, on an economic plane, against the penetration of the market economy. In this context, the system of responsibilities associated with a leveling of wealth would ensure the economic independence and political autonomy of the community. This is not to say that there is no socio-economic differentiation or inequalities among the households living in these villages, of course there are. A rich household can more easily escape the less prestigious responsibilities and is more likely to occupy the highest and most prestigious responsibilities.

Research methodology

Fieldwork carried out over a 15-month period provides the material used here to analyse the financial practices of indigenous Mexican families. During this fieldwork, different methodological tools were used repeatedly: immersion and exchanges in daily village life, narratives of practices englobing temporal and social dimensions, semi-directive interviews and finally a questionnaire-based investigation undertaken with the aid of investigators recruited and trained by the researcher.[6] This iterative approach not only enriched the quantitative collection carried out at the end of the fieldwork with recruited investigators trained by the researcher, but especially, it allowed us capture the gap between the data collected during in-depth interviews and those obtained through closed questionnaires (Morvant-Roux, 2006). Due to this gap, and in order to mobilize quality data, here, we shall only use data from 80 in-depth interviews carried out with a sample of households from different neighborhoods of San Baltazar Loxicha. Our field observations will also be used as additional support material.

Informal financial practices in the study context

In this rural context, characterized by rarity and irregularity of monetary income, indebtedness acquires a primordial economic function illustrated by the empirical data of Villarreal (2000), which unveils that the daily consumption of certain households is ensured, for half, by recourse to various forms of indebtedness. The object here is not to present an exhaustive inventory of the credit sources, we will only explain the main mechanisms and their modalities.

Credit sale (fiado)

Buying on credit is a common practice in the village shops (grocer's, pharmacy, etc.). It is a way for the shopkeeper to secure customer loyalty and to ensure the distribution and sale of merchandise. It gives the customer the necessary time to obtain liquid assets while being able to immediately acquire the food goods necessary for his/her family's daily consumption. However, the expression "se fia", indicating that the shopkeeper is inclined to give credit, is not used at random. The decision remains at the shopkeeper's discretion according to criteria that can be quite variable from one shopkeeper, and from one customer, to another. Therefore, the buyer's reputation as a good payer and the shopkeeper's trust can determine the decision of the latter.[7] This can also be linked to the shopkeeper's projects in terms of economic or other alliances (Chamoux, 1993). The practice of *fiado* is widespread in San Baltazar Loxicha, where more than 55 per cent of the people affirm having resorted to it. The conditions of *fiado* vary according to the individual and are mostly quite flexible. A high level of socio-economic interdependency seems to cause the adaptation to constraints that weigh upon the buyer's creditworthiness. The situation of two women that aws observed will help to illustrate this point:

> Mariana is a fifty year-old married woman. During a spontaneous conversation in front of Mariana's home, a travelling saleswoman appeared to sell her small plastic recipients. The price was about 3 pesos (US$0.30). At first, Mariana refused the offer, stating that she did not have enough cash. But she was still interested. So, she offered to come by some time later when she would have coffee that she could sell, which would give her enough cash to be able to buy the object. After a short hesitation, the saleswoman handed her the object, telling her to keep it and pay later when she got her coffee.

The strategy described above ensures the sale of the object and thus the distribution of the goods. For that, the salesperson had to adapt to the creditworthiness of the potential buyer and demonstrate great flexibility in the conditions of sale. The adaptation can go further and concern the conditions of payment. Thus, I asked the salesperson if she would accept payment in corn or coffee. She replied affirmatively stating that she could keep or sell the coffee (or corn). She concluded by saying: "everything is money!"[8]

However, sometimes firmness or strategy must be employed to obtain payment for goods without offending the customer:

> I (the investigator) spent many hours in one of the village pharmacies. This allowed me to observe the customers coming to buy medicine. One day, a woman came to buy some medicine for her sick child. When she went to pay for the transaction, the pharmacist offered her to pay what she already owed and then come back later to pay for the medicines that she wanted to buy that day.

Although this gesture seems accommodating; it was particularly interesting for the pharmacist because the borrowed amounts were not equivalent. The customer's arrears were 50 pesos (US$5) whereas the cost of the goods purchased the same day were 10 pesos (US$1). The pharmacist thus obtained the payment for the larger part of the debt in exchange for a new (but smaller) debt. By conserving the debt, the pharmacist conserves her clientele. This example translates the subtle interplay between the service rendered, which develops customer loyalty, and the recovery of the multitude of small debts.

Loans with or without interest within the neighborhood or the family

Two types of loans circulate within the close social circle (relatives and/or compadres):[9]

- small short-term no-interest loans allowing the borrower to face daily needs;
- larger loans with monthly interest rates beween 5–10 percent (this rate is comparable to the rates of professional moneylenders).

It is quite commonplace for neighbours and relatives (close relations or *compadres*) to provide services to one another. Notably to face daily needs, neighbors or relatives help each other with small short-term, no-interest loans. For these small loans, reciprocity is essential. Thus, beyond the reimbursement of the borrowed sum, the lender can "impose" a cash flow that the borrower must respect, otherwise they may not be able to depend on this lender in the future: "I know who I lend to and when I need, I will ask those people, we know each other."[10] (married woman, 32 years old).

Nevertheless, if the need for money exceeds the frame of the small loans, and it is known that a neighbor may have the required sum,[11] it is common to make a request before seeking a loan from someone in a wider, more distant, social network.

If this loan request exceeds a certain amount (superior to 500 pesos or US$50), borrowers enter an interest loan system. The monthly interest rates are often between 5 percent and 10 percent, which are more or less equivalent to those practiced by professional moneylenders. However, contrary to professional moneylenders, here, the form is less contractual as it requires no signature of any *pagaré* – promissory note on which the borrower recognizes and promises to honor his/her debt. Trust and sanction, the same implied for smaller loans, are at play here: "The loan source will dry up for him [the borrower who doesn't honor his debt]. He must go elsewhere." (Chamoux, 1993: 177).[12] Honoring one's debts is the only way to "keep the credit source open" (ibid.).[13] The loan period is one or two months, but, in reality, the implicit rule is that when a lender wishes to recover his money for a necessity, he will ask the borrower who then has a brief period to reimburse the amount: "I went to ask for it [the money], I need my money"[14] (married woman, 33 years old).

The conditions of this type of loan are not fixed, and may vary according to the individual but especially according to the need that motivated the request. For example, in the case of an emergency linked to an individual's health, it is generally not well looked upon if an interest rate is applied to the lent sum. Sometimes, the money is lent with interest only when the sum is destined for productive or economic activities. This moral marker of lent amounts can be illustrated by the practice of a woman who lends money to different people, family, neighbors, people living nearby. When asked if the people who owed her money at the time of the interview would reimburse her with interest, she replied: "No, because they didn't borrow the money for business, that is only when people do business [with borrowed money, emphasis added]"[15] (Married woman, 33 years old).

The circulation of money through small-scale loans for daily expenses or for larger amounts is intense. Cash-flow problems are often resolved thanks to exchanges of labor or food for agricultural work or construction work, or even the organization of festivals, notably for women.

However, if the requested amount proves to be more than what the close social circle can supply, or if it is the case of an emergency, the individual will then turn to a wider social network, resulting in more contractual relations.

Loans from professional moneylenders: turning to a more distant social network

The figure of the professional moneylender exists in the studied villages, but the difference with the interest loan described above is less at the level of the credit, which can be comparable to those practiced among relatives, than with the more contractual character and socially more distant relations. The *prestamista* (professional moneylender) represents a last resort. In other words, if a person has not found a solution in his/her network of immediate or distant social relations, only then will this alternative be sought. The amounts available at the professional moneylender's can also attain levels that are difficult to obtain within a close social circle. Indeed, the professional moneylender can lend 25,000 pesos (US$2,500). A written document (called *pagaré* or *vale*)[16] contractualizes the transaction; it is signed by the lender, the borrower and his guarantor. The interest rate can vary according to the people between 10 percent and 20 percent or sometimes even 25 percent per month.

Other forms

Other forms of informal collective organization were observed. In San Baltazar Loxicha, the village decided to recycle funds obtained from the sale of village pine trees. This amount was added to a public transfer, in the form of credit for the population. This fund reunites 505 associates[17] who obtained a loan in 1996 of between 300 pesos and 2,500 pesos each (US$30–$250), with a 2 percent monthly interest rate. As the sum was to be recovered rapidly, this fund should have increased with interest and constituted a new loan potential. However, the loans were only exceptionally reimbursed by the associates.[18] Finally, a micro-credit scheme has been implemented in the early 2000s. The microbank provides credit services as well as savings and remittances services. The question of the role played by microcredit with regards to over-indebtedness is not the scope of this chapter (see Hummel, Angulo Salazar and Johnson in this book).

Beyond characteristics such as amount, duration, interest rate, collateral requirement (etc.) it is necessary to understand the underlying economic, but especially, the social logics of indebtedness. The institution of debt in the context of research and the fine analysis of the financial strategies of the households stems from chains of indebtedness that have implications at a dual level. At the collective level, they characterize the social role of debt and ensure the economic reproduction of these local economies (Zanotelli, 2004).

At an individual level, the intense circulation of money illustrates the ongoing juggling practices between income sources and credit. The boundary between the dynamism of indebtedness and over-indebtedness practices must then be examined.

Debt as a social institution

In the Mexican villages studied, modalities and forms of debt are very diverse. Beyond the social dimension of debt, indebtedness within the social network is first used to meet unexpected expenses (health problems, deaths, etc.) or exceptional expenses (such as organizing a festive occasion, emigration, etc.). Second, it bridges a temporary shortfall of income in relation to expenses. All of these debt practices share the fact that the act of indebtedness is not limited to an immediate economic function. Rather, it reflects a historical construction of the conditions of economic and social reproduction within these villages (Zanotelli, 2004). We can highlight this through the observation of two major types of "coincidences" which illustrate financial practices observed in our study. First, these practices reveal a close relationship between two distinct facets of one and the same reality: savings and loans. The second "coincidence" refers to the fact that an individual can simultaneously occupy the role of *creditor* and *debtor*.

The coincidence of savings and loans

Money is constantly "lacking" in these contexts. Social obligations are numerous and the constant disparity between income and expenses makes indebtedness an inevitable way to face all financial needs. When asked how they save money, people often reply that they actually lend money to others. Lending is thus considered as a form of saving (see also Rutherford, 1999). In the indigenous communities of Mexico, all forms of wealth (not only coins and notes but also bricks, food products or cattle) may be loaned if the owner does not have an immediate need for them (Guérin et al., 2011; Morvant-Roux, 2009). Shipton (1995) has made the same observation in rural Gambia, where the slightest wealth, whether in cash or in kind, is loaned to conceal ownership and cement social bonds.

The logic of constant circulation of debt and credit is also illustrated by Francesco Zanotelli's interview of a local moneylender. When the researcher enquired about the risk of theft when lending substantial amounts of money, Don Graciano, a local moneylender, replied: "let them rob if they want to; all they'll find is letters [of credit, emphasis added], and they will be doing me a favour by recovering them." Don Graciano's reflection stresses the fact that he keeps no cash at home; the cash surplus available or even his savings have, in fact, been transformed into loans to other people.

One might object that lending to others constitutes one of the lucrative commercial activities of this person and therefore that it is natural that all her/his money be invested in this manner. Whilst this would be true, it should be noted that what Don Graciano described echoes practices observed among most of the people we met.

Besides savings made through the purchase of animals such as turkeys, chickens or cows, cash savings are not hoarded, but are most often lent to other people in need. The recurring argument is that money cannot be held onto if it is kept at home within a hand's reach, available for the slightest expense, which might not even be indispensable. Thus, when asked about monetary savings, many women stated that, having lent their savings to others, they kept nothing at home: "I have no money in the house; we've lent it" (San Baltazar Loxicha, woman, 25 years). In a type of coercion which allows one group of people to avoid spending their money (and to thus affirm their social distinction), and to provide a source of cash for the expenses of others, the rationale of the circulation of wealth underlying this practice applies to all forms of surplus – monetary or in kind – and whatever its origin.

Diversity of means used for the practice of "savings-loan"

The savings-loan, a loan in the form of commodities such as corn, allows cash-flow management (since it can be retrieved in times of real need) to be stored "virtually"[19] outside one's home. This strategy also takes the form of loans of bricks for constructing a house[20] or even loans of lime, etc. All "wealth," in whatever form, is liable to be the basis for loans if it is of no immediate use to the owner.[21] Animals are also lent, especially those playing a central role in the organization of social events related to the life cycle. The practice of loaning turkeys,[22] for example, is very widespread in the region where we conducted our research. Women play a central role in these practices:

Diversity of the origin of the surplus

The origin of the surplus does not appear to be an obstacle to this savings-loan practice. This strategy is also adopted by people originating from, but now residing outside, the community – especially those who have migrated to the United States. A portion of money received in the form of private transfers is in fact lent to the migrant's neighbors, relatives or immediate family, who take on the role of intermediary. In fact, this intermediary role is most often held by the migrant's mother. The rules for assigning the money received are drawn up with the migrant. Generally, a part of the sum supplements the income used by the mother of the family for various household expenses. Another portion is lent on a more or less long-term basis to people from the social network and serves as the savings of the migrant. The amounts lent through these transfers are high, and the interest rate is generally lower than that practiced elsewhere: between 3 percent and 5 percent per month (instead of 10 percent).

An analysis of local perceptions of usurious practices helps to better understand people's perceptions. Let us here return to Don Graciano and the analysis of his status as a professional moneylender as discussed by Zanotelli (2004). Prohibited by the Catholic Church from the Spanish conquest up to the nineteenth century, the interest loan is liable to convey a negative image of the person who exercises this activity within the Catholic population residing in the villages under study. However, such a negative image does not seem to be shared by most of the people I interviewed. The profit-making logic seems to be hidden behind the crucial nature of the service rendered. For Don Graciano, as for those who sought loans from him, his commercial activity is perceived as the rendering of a service and is so much the better appreciated if the person does not belong to Don Graciano's close social circle (neighborhood, godfather/godmother, kinship). But, in the case of those who belong to a more distant social network, a third person will most often play the role of go-between between the lender (professional or otherwise) and the potential borrower.

In conclusion to this section, when a person possesses cash that she/he will not use in the short to medium term, there is a pressure on her/him to lend it to others who do have an immediate need for it. Therefore, there is an intimate connection between savings and credit.

Thus, the *institution of debt* establishes a sort of "collective management" of individual surpluses of cash or of any "useful" goods. We have seen that this management is spontaneously achieved within close social circles, but financial flows may also affect more distant social relationships.

Creditor/debtor coincidence[23]

There is evidence of such a coincidence when looking at "chains of indebtedness,"[24] which characterize the populations' financial practices, regardless of their level of wealth.[25] In the light of our case study, Francesco Zanotelli's analysis (2004) seems to only partially uncover the reality of this phenomenon. In fact, Zanotelli stresses that a household uses various debt modalities at the same time. As one group of people enables another to cope with their repayments, networks of debts can be observed that shed light on the mode of reproduction of the local economy.[26] This strategy may, for instance, be schematically illustrated by the fact that person A borrows from B to reimburse C and D. Research by Villarreal's team also highlights such processes (Villareal, 2000: 70).

This may be further illustrated by the confidences of one woman interviewed during our study: "When in need, I borrow from a lady who has some [*money*, emphasis added], and I withdraw [that is to say, *borrow*, emphasis added] from another to reimburse the person who lent me the money" (Woman of 53 years, widow).

Zanotelli (2004) stresses that 25 percent of the households in his sample declared being in debt from three credit sources, 37.5 percent from two sources, and 25 percent from a single source. Our data confirms these results (see Table 8.2).

Table 8.2 Number of simultaneously active loans

	(%)
1 single active loan	65
2 active loans	24
3 active loans	10
More than three active loans	1

Source: Morvant-Roux (2006).

In the case of several simultaneously active loans, our data show that distinct categories of cash sources may be mobilized. We can divide the various sources of the loans into two major categories:

So-called *interpersonal, or private loans*: these cover financial practices established primarily between two individuals. This includes credit sale (*fiado*), loans with or without interest intervening within networks of neighborhood, kinship, godfather/godmother or even loans within an employment relationship.

So-called *collective or public loans*: these cover loans that cause several individuals to intervene in the form of an association or through the mediation of a group of borrowers. These include government loans, those which cover coffee producers or *tanda* participants (tontine or ROSCA), or even microfinance institutions, loans delivered by the Mexican credit union or by other banking institutions.

If we take into consideration the subsample of only those who have more than two simultaneously active loans, our empirical data show evidence that 64 percent approached at least two sources from distinct categories (private or collective as previously described).

In the context of the present study, Zanotelli's analysis falls short. It is therefore essential to go a step beyond the analytical framework he provides. The dual nature of the position each person occupies may be summarized as follows: person A seeks a loan from B to reimburse C while, at the same time, D is indebted to A. This chain does not imply any equivalence of the amounts however, which may be totally different. The lending capacity depends on the income sources but also the life cycle stage, number of children, etc.

Beyond the fact that households or individuals juggle several loans simultaneously, it is also common to find that an individual concomitantly occupies the role of "creditor" and "debtor." Collins et al. (2009) have shown evidence of such borrowing and lending practices in India, Bangladesh and South Africa (see also Shipton, 1995).

Our statistical data taken from a survey of 80 households highlights that each person simultaneously assumes the position of creditor and debtor. What emerges is that among the 65 percent of those who affirm having applied for one or more loans at interest over the period under consideration (the past 12 months), 45 percent (or 28 percent of the total sample) also lent money at interest to other people. As for no interest loans of small sums (category 2 of

Table 8.3), of the 61.3% who had applied for such a loan once or more in the period under consideration, 80 percent had also lent money in this form, which amounts to 49 percent of the sample.

Such dual positioning is observed among different categories of households – both wealthy and poor. In other words, differences in terms of wealth do not reflect one's position as debtor or creditor. Both types of households mix different types of debt practices for their daily life and therefore the debtor and creditor roles are not fixed in time.

These practices illustrate the important role of debt practices and their weight in the day-to-day economy of the village, while also reflecting the key role of "debt circulation" as a functional mechanism in the local economy.

Stephen Boucher's team (UC/Davis) conducted a survey in the same region in 2005 on 600 households' borrowing or lending practices in the preceding year. The data on borrowing strategies were collected with an amount restriction, e.g. only loans above US$50 were taken into account (ten days of wage for a daily agricultural laborer). Their data reveal that the majority of the loans were given to friends and relatives, but also, in most cases, no interest was charged:

- 90 percent of the loans were granted to friends (30 percent) and relatives (58 percent);
- average amount lent was US$100 (between 15–20 percent of daily wage for a daily agricultural laborer);
- loan term was either less than one month (40 percent) or without specified duration (30 percent);
- only 3 percent of the lenders required collateral;
- only 1.7 percent charged interest.

Another interesting result that confirms our own results deals with the fact that 12 percent of households had borrowed and lent money at the same period of time.

Our results concerning creditor/debtor identity have methodological implications with regards to indebtedness and over-indebtedness assessment. Data collection on debt practices and indebtedness usually takes into account the

Table 8.3 Offer and loan application within the social network

Type of loan	Total = 80 households (%)	
	Borrowing	Lending
1 Large sums, mostly with interest, medium term (2 months)	65	40
2 Small sums without interest, short term: neighbourhood, family	61.3	66.3
3 Credit sale/purchase: grocery store	88	–

Source: Morvant-Roux (2006).

outstanding debt level. We have shown that some households not only borrow money from different sources but also lend to others. In some cases we observed that a person needed money, but was constrained by the fact that the people to whom she/he had lent money had not yet repaid.

These lending practices and their timeframes need to be incorporated in the overall outstanding debt level assessment. According to our data, each household is at the center of multiple flows of money and wealth circulation within relatively large circles of relationships, which are but many intricate debt webs.

Both coincidences (savings and loans and creditors/debtors) described above constitute central features of the debt institution in the context studied. This has a dual economic and social function both at individual and collective levels (Guérin, 2000). It should be emphasized that debt circulation and its ongoing reproduction ensure the socio-economic functioning of the village. As a whole, therefore, indebtedness simultaneously represents a *double interdependence:* social and economic.

In previous work, we have shown that in this context of debt circulation, microcredit does not replace, but rather adds to these credit sources. It constitutes an additional opportunity to obtain cash and improve a client's creditworthiness, thus participating in juggling practices (Morvant-Roux, 2006 and also Guérin *et al.* in this volume).

Let us now address the issue of the link between indebtedness dynamics characterized by a kind of constant juggling between various credit sources, type of debts (relationships with the lender, timeframe, amounts, interest rates, etc.) and over-indebtedness.

It must be stressed that not all debts are equivalent. Some debt practices are driven by a logic of reciprocation and others by repayment (reciprocity versus repayment).[27] In the first category, there is an alternation and a kind of equilibrium between the "lender" and the "borrower." Debt does not remain on one side for a long time and therefore cannot be accumulated over an extended period. In the second category, however, equilibrium and alternation between the lender and the borrower no longer transcend debt practices. The timeframe is different and there is not necessarily alternation between the lender and the borrower (creditor/debtor). This category of debt makes the accumulation of debt possible and can thus lead to over-indebtedness. Nevertheless, it must be noted that the first category of debt, seen as an "aid" or "help", implying a balance within the social network, does generate some uncertainty as the borrower never exactly knows when he/she will be asked to reimburse the acquired loan.

Among the different modalities of indebtedness, debts within the close social circle of neighbors and/or immediate family are difficultly accumulated. Repayment is of course demanded, but if the debtor is not able to reimburse, he/she is exposed to a refusal at the time of any future solicitations. People call these debts "favors" (*favor*). The reimbursement of the sum does not bring a term to the debtor/creditor relationship because the person having solicited this aid commits to being solicited in turn. The debts contracted from the grocer can be placed in this category. The *favor* refers to small loans that provide assistance but do not subject the debtor to high reimbursement pressures. The debts contracted from a more distant social network, such as from professional moneylenders or more formal institutions, are more susceptible to be accumulated if they are not reimbursed and expose the debtor to over-indebtedness. These debts are qualified as *droga* (drug) and bear a negative connotation as they clearly refer to a badly considered, unmanageable situation. Indeed, the term *droga* suggests the possible accumulation of debt that could lead to some kind of over-indebtedness.

Over-indebtedness is difficult to identify and assess, given the irregularity of income and also the methodological challenges the researcher has to face to collect solid data on household income levels (borrowing and lending practices, etc.). When and at what level can a person be considered as over-indebted? What are the local indicators of over-indebtedness?

In the context studied, considering the part of indebtedness from informal sources (see above), over-indebtedness is not a judicial category as is the case in many so-called developed countries (Lazarus, op. cit.). Whatever the context, the over-indebted individual is nevertheless qualified by his/her incapacity to reimburse the contracted debt or debts and in particular all or part of the borrowed capital. However, this relatively universal definition conceals distinct realities. The crux consists in knowing at which moment the individual moves toward effective and explicit over-indebtedness. The answer cannot arise from ordinary evaluation either of incomes or of contracted debts. Our hypothesis is that the ongoing juggling practices between different sources of credit constitute the common local modalities of over-indebtedness in a context of intense irregularity of revenue and temporal gaps between this income and various common or exceptional expenses. However, over-indebtedness is perceptible as soon as the household implements a specific strategy, outside of this "routine" in order to reimburse their debts.

In the following section of this article, in light of national and international migratory dynamics, we shall attempt to show in what measure migration is brought about by a high level of indebtedness. Migration reveals an incapacity to obtain resources (revenue or credit from other sources) locally, which can indicate a situation of indebtedness. We will see that if migration is a possible way out for some, others cannot depend upon this opportunity to clear their debts.

Migration as a way to face over-indebtedness

In certain regions of Mexico, the migratory dynamic is significant (between 60 and 80 percent of working-age men) and has been structured over decades. This is not the case for the regions where we have carried out fieldwork. In the villages of the Sierra Sur in the state of Oaxaca, local commuting has allowed small-scale farmers to complement agricultural incomes for a long time. International migration only began at the end of the 1990s. In the 80 interviews carried out in the village of San Baltazar, Loxicha, local commuting is practiced by the majority of the households. The only individuals who do not turn to this practice are the rare producers of coffee with a yield higher than a ton. Punctual or local commuting, that is towards the state capital only a few hours away by bus, constitutes an accessible financial strategy for men (the women rarely or never leave the village). The salary is much higher (US$12 instead of 5 per day) and allows them to earn the liquidities to face certain expenses in just a few weeks: buying food goods, soap, school fees, etc. In general, this period does not exceed two to three months. However, strategies such as national migration and migration towards the United States (or even, in a certain respect, local long-term migration) are used to face much higher, and generally more exceptional, financial needs. Nearly one-fourth (25 percent) of interviewed households had experienced the migration of one or more family members, of which 50 percent had recently been to the United States (Table 8.4).

Among the reasons that incite households to opt for migration (as they appear in Table 8.5 below), reimbursement of debts was mentioned by 88 percent of the people. These debts were contracted mainly (66 percent) at different stages of the life cycle: a child's wedding, house building, studies or other social events[28] (majordomo). They also result from shocks experienced by the members of the household: sudden death, loss of animals, nomination by local authorities implying that the person named cannot take care of his land, etc. In our investigation, as well as the investigation carried out by the Mexican Association of the Credit Unions of the Social Sector (AMUCSS) in three poor regions[29] of Mexico, 60 percent of the households named to administrative or religious appointments affirmed that they were not able to economically prepare themselves for occasioned expenses.

This migration to "clear" debts seems to indicate that at a certain point the household can no longer confront the level of contracted debts. This was

Table 8.4 Type of migration among households with migrants

Migration	% of households with migration
Local (>2 months)	17
National	33
International (USA)	50

Source: Morvant-Roux (2006).

Table 8.5 Reason to migrate

Migration cause	(%)
Debts	88
Expenses linked to life cycle	66
Various expenses	14
Shock	20
Investment (project)	12

Source: Morvant-Roux (2006).

confirmed by the analysis of the debt amounts that caused a member of the household (the head of the household in most cases) to migrate (Table 8.6). The estimation of the average amount is well above the level of the debts of the sample taken at the moment of the study: US$2,150 vs. US$620 (Morvant-Roux, 2006). According to the vulnerability study carried out in 2010 by the Mexican Association of the Credit Unions of the Social Sector (AMUCSS), households owning a small plot of land (between 1 and 2 hectares) with agriculture as their main economic activity earn on average US$3,600 per year (AMUCSS, 2008). Our own estimations of this household sample are about US$2,000 per year.

These debts consist mainly of money borrowed from local professional or non-professional lenders (neighbors, etc.). The amounts and the loan period imply a payment with a monthly interest rate of about 10 percent to 25 percent.

Sometimes the situation of over-indebtedness is intensified by a shock on incomes:

> Fernando, coffee producer, had gone to work in the USA for four years. He left because he owed US$2,500 to another person in the village. The interest rate was 10% per month. He could not reimburse it as that year a hurricane had destroyed his coffee crop. He then decided to go to Los Angeles where someone he knew had offered to pay his passage at the border (US$1,200) that he could reimburse afterward with his salary. There, he would have to pay: (1) his expenses, (2) the expenses for the work in the coffee crop in his native village, (3) his debt, and (4) the expenses of his family who had stayed back. His salary was US$1,300 per month (equivalent to a year's salary in his native region). There, he did not learn English. He worked with Mexicans and 10 to 12 people lived in a little apartment for which they shared the rent, US$600. They shared food expenses.
>
> (Morvant-Roux, 2004: fieldnotes)

This situation seems to trigger over-indebtedness. Indeed, when juggling between different sources of credit or one's own monetary income becomes insufficient to repay one's debts, migration seems to be the only solution.

Sometimes, the level of indebtedness results from the sum of several loans contracted from distinct sources. This was the case for Eugenio, who had an administrative appointment that caused him to run into debt. He wished to clear

Table 8.6 Amount of debt before migration

	In US$
Debt amount	between 800 and 5,000
Average	2,150
Annual salary	1,200

Source: Morvant-Roux (2006).

his debts by migrating "I am in debt. I want to get out of it!"[30] The total amount of his debts was US$1,500 contracted from different sources:

- US$250 from a person in the village, at a 10 percent interest rate;
- US$800 from a local microfinance institution;
- US$450 from a local credit program, *crédito a la palabra*.

Illegal migration is nevertheless a risky initiative, and failure is common. This was the situation for a 43 year-old man who ran up a US$1,000 debt for animals, adding to US$1,700 to pay back borrowed money for a failed tentative attempt to settle in the United States. When successful, however, migration allows households to clear accumulated debts in the village.

Migration therefore represents a glimmer of hope of putting an end to the situation of over-indebtedness. However, it is not possible for everyone, for the following reasons:

1   the cost is high and engenders further debts ($1,200 US for the border passage).

   - Thus, Andres, a 38 year-old man having emigrated to the United States to clear a US$600 debt for his son's wedding had to run up an additional US$2,200 debt so that he and his son could pass the border. The first amounts received by his wife, Paula, between $150 and $900 a month, were used to pay back the coyote (people smuggler).

2   Migrants depend mainly on a social network already built up at the destination (Berthaud, 2009). It is difficult for families to rely on relatives settled at the destination to support their initiative because there is no established migratory network, as is the case in other regions of Mexico.

3   Migration is impossible for isolated individuals, notably widows:

A 44 year-old woman had become a widow several weeks before we met. Even though her financial situation was already quite serious, the death of her husband set off a critical situation of over-indebtedness. "I don't have any money ... my whole body's in debt!",[31] she said, summing up her situation. Indeed, after her husband's death, she borrowed US$800 with a 10% monthly interest rate in order to pay for the funeral. Also, she discovered that her husband had incurred many debts as he was an alcoholic. "I have many debts!",[32] she said.

To pay back these debts, she did not consider migration and wanted even less to run up more debts to clear the older ones. The strategies that she was considering at the time of our interview were the possible sale of her mule and continuing to work for others: domestic work (US$8 per month) and salaried agricultural work with her son (US$5 per day each). In other words, the situation of over-indebtedness seems relatively hopeless.

Conclusion

We have analyzed the links between migration (national and international) and over-indebtedness. In our view, migration constitutes a specific strategy adopted by households when the level of indebtedness is such that neither their usual income nor their social network can help them clear debts. Our field data reveal that these situations of over-indebtedness are essentially associated with life cycle event expenditures: weddings, house building, etc. Even though these events are globally possible to anticipate, the low levels and irregularity of income render the anticipation capacity inadequate. For non-monetary ceremonial expenses, mothers begin raising turkeys at the birth of their son. This is based on practices of loaning turkeys that the creditors will recover from each debtor just before the event (Morvant-Roux, 2006). For monetary expenses, it is not easy to save such large amounts of money and therefore the recourse to indebtedness becomes necessary. Although migration may be the only alternative to clear debts in cases of over-indebtedness, on the one hand it is not accessible to all, notably to women who are alone, and on the other hand, it does not always provide a solution.

However, contrary to other localities where migration produces perceptible effects in the local economy, the relatively marginal place of migration here does not lead to the enriching of the village and its inhabitants. Moreoever, if it allows individuals to cover social expenses, the flow of money that migration may generate provokes in return an escalation of social expenses rendering migration more and more unavoidable, so that men may accomplish their social and religious rites. This mechanism has been illustrated by Morvant-Roux and Berthaud (2011) in the neighboring state of Guerrero.

Globally, and contrary to other areas of the State of Oaxaca (Mixteca for example) in the Sierra Sur, the migratory dynamic has (until recently) allowed to palliate insufficient revenues or to confront exceptional expenses. It has not yet replaced other local economic activities. Families of migrants continue to ensure the sustainability of their agricultural production. Recent evolutions are, however, propitious for an intensification of migration as a source of main revenue for these rural economies. The main income-generating activity for the families living in this region, the coffee crop, is presently in crisis. Before the 1990s, coffee production provided a comfortable revenue source secured by IMECAFE (Mexican Institute of Coffee), which bought and resold the production and offered loans to farmers. Since the 1990s, the context has changed greatly: the tendency of lowering coffee prices after the liberalization of the sector and the liberalization of trade has led to a significant decrease in the producers' revenues (Berthaud, 2009).

For the great majority of the farmers, this crop no longer generates benefits. And yet, the local potential to diversify revenue sources has been reduced irrespective of national and international migratory dynamics. Thus, shifting from being a punctual phenomenon to confront the exceptional level of indebtedness, migration may tend to overcome the local activities, in particular agricultural activities. This is what has happened in other regions, notably in the Guerrero and in the Mixteca (Morvant-Roux and Berthaud, 2011). In parallel, many processes in place may accelerate this dynamic: intensified financialization and increased demand for goods produced outside and distributed in the localities. These aspirations to consume manufactured goods call for a certain level of creditworthiness that only migration may sustain at this stage.

Yet, as Jean-Michel Servet and Hadrien Saiag have analyzed in this volume, the crisis of 2007–2008 has affected the place of migration in these isolated rural areas and may impede these dynamics.

Migration is slowed because the options of integrating the local work market are less favorable but also because of the fact that the migrants settled in the United States, who are confronted with the lack of employment and over-indebtedness, are either obliged to come back or to rely on the financial support of their families in Mexico (see Villarreal in this volume).

Notes

1 See also Stoll (2010).
2 See Johnson (2009).
3 In the Sierra Sur and more specifically in the observed villages, the population is considered to be Indian, according to linguistic criteria. They belong to the Zapotec ethno-linguistic group. Although it is not the only group present in the state of Oaxaca (which has 18), it constitutes the largest ethno-linguistic group in this state, representing 65 percent of the indigenous population.
4 Original quotation: "investie du pouvoir exécutif et de certaines compétences judiciaires" (Dehouve, 2003: 5).
5 Original quotation:

> une rotation obligatoire de charges hiérarchisées entre les hommes membres de la commune. Selon les charges, civiles ou religieuses, le mode de désignation des titulaires varie (cooptation, désignation d'office, élcetion ainsi que la durée du mandat).
>
> (Chamoux, 1987: 212)

6 The sample of the quantitative study was 240 households.
7 The expression used for good payer is the following: "los que cumplen." The people who are trusted are called "los de confianza."
8 "¡todo es dinero!"
9 These relations, *compadres*, belong to the "ritual" and political family which includes godparents and close relations. These relations explicitly imply forms of punctual mutual aid.
10 "Sé con quien hago favor y cuando necesito voy a pedir a estas personas, somos conocidos."
11 Information circulates quickly in the neighborhood, social network. For example, it is possible to know when someone has recently received a large amount of money or if a couple, or an individual (who has no children) would be more likely to have cash assets. All the information related to the availability of cash assets is crucial. This information is mostly spread by women.
12 "la source de prêt se tarit pour lui [l'emprunteur qui n'honor pas sa dette]. Il doit alors s'adresser ailleurs" (Chamoux, 1993: 177).
13 "garder ouverte la source de crédit" (ibid.).

14 "Fui a pedirlo, ahora sí, necesito mi dinero."
15 "no, porque no quieren el dinero para el negocio, solamente cuando la gente hace negocio."
16 This document mentions the lent amount, the surnames and first names of the lender and the borrower, the interest rate and the negotiated terms, which are often negotiable.
17 Out of a total number of 461 households [INEGI, 2000], which does not signify total coverage. It is most likely that there may be two or three associates per household.
18 During our passage, the committee in charge of managing the funds was trying its hardest to make people pay at least the capital, because it seemed illusory to get back the integrality of the interest accumulated over the period (nearly ten years).
19 In the sense that the commodities consumed or goods used subsequently are not those that had been loaned.
20 This strategy was recounted to us by a woman who had purchased bricks when she had liquidity, but not enough money to carry out construction. She had, therefore, loaned these bricks in the hope of getting back the quantity loaned when she would be fully able to carry out the construction.
21 All the more so if the commodity in question is perishable and can, therefore, not be stored or kept for a long period.
22 The turkey occupies a central place in the ritual life of the localities where we conducted our surveys. Life cycle events such as marriage or the main festivals organized in the course of existence cannot take place without some turkeys being offered or sacrified; this can be seen as a question of prestige, but the health of the family or the fertility of the married couple also depends on the sacrifice of some turkeys. The women start preparing well in advance in order to ensure proper organization.
23 See Morvant-Roux (2006) and Collins *et al.* (2009).
24 "Cadenas de endeudamiento" (Zanotelli, 2004).
25 Of course, the quantity and frequency of financial ties would be higher.
26 His work is located in the villages of the Jalisco State, Mexico.
27 See Hénaff (2002) and Théret (2009).
28 It is interesting to note that "life's setbacks" are considered to be the main cause of over-indebtedness in France, for example (80 percent in reported cases). This figure is, however, contested by many actors and researchers who see in this a way for financial institutions to avoid any liability for their actions. In the context of the study at hand, life cycle events do not constitute sudden shocks for which households could not prepare.
29 Reference to study conducted in 2007–2008 in 1,000 households living in remote rural areas in the states of Guerrero, Puebla and Oaxaca.
30 "estoy endueudado ahorita, quiero salir fuera."
31 "No tengo nada dinero. Estoy endrogada del cuerpo."
32 "¡Tengo un montó de cuentas!"

References

AMUCSS (Asociación Mexicana de Uniones de Crédito del Sector Social A.C.). (2008) *Encuesta sobre la Vulnerabilidad de los Hogares Rurales* (EVHR).

Berthaud, A., (2009) "Quand la microfinance cible les migrants. Une analyse comparative des processus d'adaptation et d'appropriation autour d'un projet de microfinance dans deux communautés rurales du Mexique," *Mémoire de master professionnel*, Anthropologie and Métiers du Développement durable, Université d'Aix Marseille I.

Chamoux, M.-N. (1987) "La roue de l'infortune et le développement. Stratégies de mobilité sociale dans un village mexicain (1970–1980)," *Cahier des Sciences Humaines*, 23(2); 197–213.

Chamoux, M.-N. (1993) "Ruses du prêteur, ruses de l'emprunteur: les difficultés du crédit invisible", in Chamoux *et al.* (eds) (1993), pp. 167–188.

Chamoux, M.-N., Dehouve, D., Gouy-Gilbert, C. and Pépin Lehalleur, M. (eds) (1993) *Prêter et emprunter: pratiques de crédit au Mexique (XVIème–XXème Siècle)*, Paris: Editions de la Maison des Sciences de l'Homme.

Cohen, J. (2001) "Transnational Migration in Rural Oaxaca, Mexico: Dependency, Development, and the Household," *American Anthropologist*, 103(4): 954–967.

Collins, D., Morduch J., Rutherford, S. and Ruthven O. (2009) *Portfolios of the Poor: How the World's Poor Live on $2 a Day*, Princeton: Princeton University Press.

Dehouve, D. (2003) *La géopolitique des Indiens du Mexique, du local au global*, Paris: CNRS, p. 234.

Guérin, I. (2000) *Pratiques monétaires et financières des femmes en situation de précarité. Entre autonomie féminine et dépendance*, Doctoral thesis in economics, Lumière University Lyon 2, 627 pages.

Guérin, I., Morvant-Roux, S. and Servet, J.-M. (2011) "Understanding the Diversity and Complexity of Demand for Microfinance Services: Lessons from Informal Finance', in Armendariz, B. and Labie, M. (eds) *Handbook of Microfinance*, Washington: World Scientific Publishing, in press.

Guérin, I., Roesch, M. Venkatasubramanian, **(initial?)** and Héliès, O. (2009) "Microfinance, endettement et surendettement," *Revue Tiers Monde*, 197: 131–146.

Hénaff, M. (2002) *Le Prix de la vérité. Le don, l'argent, la philosophie*, Paris: Le Seuil.

INEGI (2000) *Censo General de Población y Vivienda*.

Johnson, S. (2009) "Institutions, Markets and Economic Development", in Deneulin, S. and Shahani, L. (eds) "An Introduction to the Human Development and Capability Approach", Earthscan, pp. 162–185, available online at: www.idrc.ca/openebooks/470–3/#page_185.

Lazarus, J. (2009) "L'épreuve du credit," *Sociétés contemporaines*, 76: 17–40.

Macaire, P. (2004) "Reconnaître les coutumes: le discours sur la loi face aux enjeux locaux," *Revista TRACE*, 46: 142.

Morvant-Roux, S. (2006) "Processus d'appropriation des dispositifs de microfinance: un exemple en milieu rural mexicain," Thèse de doctorat en sciences économiques, Université Lumière Lyon 2.

Morvant-Roux, S. (2009) "Accès au microcrédit et continuité des dynamiques d'endettement au Mexique: combiner anthropologie et économétrie," *Revue Tiers Monde*, 197: 109–130.

Morvant-Roux, S. and Berthaud, A. (2011) "Redistribution, protection et migration dans les villages indiens de l'Oaxaca et du Guerrero," *Finance et Bien Commun*, 2010/2–3(37–38).

Mosse, D., Gupta, S., Mehta, M., Shah, V., Rees, J. and the Kribp Project Team (2002) "Brokered Livelihoods: Debt, Labour Migration and Development in Tribal Western India," *Journal of Development Studies*, 38(5).

New York Times, "Money Trickles North as Mexicans Help Relatives", *New York Times*, 11/16/2009, Available online at: www.nytimes.com/2009/11/16/world/americas/16mexico.html?_r=3&hp.

Orozco, M. (2002) "Globalization and Migration: The Impact of Family Remittances in Latin America," *Latin American Politics and Society*, 44(2): 41–66.

Rutherford, S. (1999) *The Poor and Their Money*, Delhi: Oxford University Press.

Servet, J.-M. (1995) (ed.) *Épargne et liens sociaux. Études comparées d'informalités financières*, Paris: AEF/AUPELF-UREF, p. 309.

Shipton P. (1995) "How Gambians Save: Culture and Economic Strategy at an Ethnic Crossroad," in Guyer, J. I. (ed.) *Money Matters: Instability, Values and Social Payments in the Modern History of West-African Communities*, London/Portsmouth (NH): Currey/Heinemann, pp. 245–277.

Stoll, D. (2010) "From Wage Migration to Debt Migration? Easy Credit, Failure in El Norte, and Foreclosure in a Bubble Economy of the Western Guatemalan Highlands," *Latin American Perspectives*, 37: 123.

Théret, B. (2009) "Monnaie et dettes de vie," *L'Homme*, 2(190).

Villarreal, M. (2000) "Deudas, drogas, fiado y prestado en las tiendas de abarrotes rurales," *Desacatos*, 3: (69–88).

Villarreal, M. (2004) (coord.) *Antropología de la deuda, crédito, ahorro, fiado y prestado en las finanzas cotidianas*, México, DF: CIESAS, p. 388.

Waddington, H. and Sabates-Wheeler, R. (2003) *How Does Poverty Affect Migration Choice? A Review of Literature*, Working Paper T3, Sussex University, Brighton.

Zanotelli, F. (2004) "La circulación social de la deuda: códigos culturales y usura rural en Jalisco," in Villarreal, M. (coord.) (2004), pp. 77–108.

9 Multiplying debt and dependence

Gender strategies and the social risks of financial inclusion in Western Mexico[1]

Francesco Zanotelli

Introduction

A 2009 report by the Center for Financial Inclusion describes Mexico as "a country with both great need and great potential" to achieve full financial inclusivity by 2020. It moreover looks "to provide the analytic framework that will be drawn upon to bring Financial Inclusion 2020 to additional countries in 2010" (Ryne *et al.*, 2009: 1). The document bases its conviction on a number of conditions assumed to be already present in Mexico, including "exciting potential actions by service providers, facilitated by enabling government policies", which it views as having the potential to implement and monitor a model that could be exported more widely. The full financial inclusion the document calls for would entail "a state in which all people of working age have access to a full suite of quality financial services that includes payment services, savings, credit, and insurance" (ibid.: 4). The path it sets out for achieving this goal includes improved access to institutional credit through traditional credit institutions, or increasingly widespread commercial and social micro-finance institutions, and adequate government legislation. This view is widely supported by the main active experts in the sector (see Yunus, 2007; for a critical discussion see Hudon, 2009).

Those calling for the inclusion of the excluded are in effect defining and prescribing a solution for a problem which sees excluded people as being in a state of lack, deprived of a good (money) that should be guaranteed to them, as though they were empty spaces to be filled.

If we look at the realities of rural Mexico, which such documents discuss in the abstract, however, we can observe high levels of financial dynamism that call into question the criteria for inclusion and exclusion. There are indeed shortages of government credit,[2] and it is hard to access private finance from traditional credit institutes, which increasingly request material guarantees, especially in the current financial crisis. Other key forms of monetary circulation are taking place however, through the so-called channels of informal financing. For example, various private organizations offer a range of micro-credit to the population. The authors of the 2009 text, whose views are representative of the international debate on financial inclusion, are well aware of the conditions of "informal" credit and savings, but deliberately exclude them from their calculations of the level of access to the four financial services cited above (the "Financial Inclusion Scorecard").

If we want to address what is present rather than absent, as we will look to do in the following pages, we must first try to distinguish local criteria for assessing inclusion or exclusion from the existing typologies of credit. We must look to processes, the interconnectedness of social, political, ideological, historical, and economic conditioning, and how individuals interpret them and act in specific situations. Such processes, as we define them here, influence inclusion or exclusion from access to the monetary resources of others.

We will first draw on ethnographic data from rural Western Mexico to show that financial inclusion or exclusion is not simply a matter of whether or not there is technical access to monetary services,[3] but is a wider social condition enabled by group membership (i.e. kin groups, households, personal networks, communities), local models of human classification that label people through difference (i.e. social age, race, ethnicity, gender, nationhood, economic status) and a comprehensive sense of the person in a specific time-space configuration. From this perspective, financial inclusion can be approached as a culturally constructed process of social inclusion that facilitates and structures individual economic actions.

Our empirical discussion compares and contrasts two sets: intra-household monetary redistribution between parents, sons, husband, and wife; and the extra-household practice of sharing money through Rosca (Rotating Saving and Credit Associations). These groups are called *tanda* or *rifa* locally, mostly consist of women, and often include members of the same family (mothers and daughters, for example, often belong to the same Rosca).

Both sets are networks of social and economic dependence, but we will look to highlight their contrasting dynamics. Intra-household monetary redistribution as an economic exchange space reinforces gendered, generational hierarchies, while the Rosca system fosters a sense of mutual solidarity and cooperation among women.

We will not simply compare but also highlight the linkages between the two sets. The gendered hierarchy women experience within the household can allow us to understand why belonging to credit and savings associations is so marked by gender differences. Moreover, actors assign different meanings to money at different stages of its circulation (within or outside the household, in saving and credit groups). We should evaluate women's capacities and actions in the rigid hierarchy within which they live in terms of production and intra-household redistribution.

Our ethnographic case study suggests that women manage to find room for manoeuvre by multiplying and differentiating their means of indebtedness. Interestingly, the path to possible freedom from social dependence is not through the individually conceived autonomy of a liberal model of citizenship, but in the multiplication and differentiation of relations of dependency, by addressing requests for money and savings practices to various, diversified sources.

Greater attention must therefore be given to processes of multiplication of dependency through diversified financial sources. This will be methodologically central for wider research beyond the case of women, gendered monetary practices and the study of "informal" finance such as the Rosca. An important further focus for this research is the financial products of micro-finance institutions, which are rapidly rolling out throughout contemporary rural Mexico, raising the urgent issue of over-indebtedness.

Following on from this, it might then be possible to distinguish strategically diversified indebtedness that can address low liquidity and create new conditions for power negotiation, from impoverishment processes where the multiplication of financial commitments amounts to "over-indebtedness". The distinction between positive and negative indebtedness relations is difficult to quantify economically or in terms of interest rate. The "measure" lies rather in the quality of the dependence the relationship engenders.

From a methodological perspective, this chapter draws on both quantitative and qualitative data collected from 1996 to 2003 in two rural communities in the southern zone of the State of Jalisco in Western Mexico. These communities are very different in size: in 2000, the village of San Cristóbal Zapotitlán had a population of 1,900, while Zacoalco de Torres was the major town of a municipality of 26,000 inhabitants. Both communities have undergone similar historical processes, with strong regionalization during the colonial era and gradual centralization after independence (de la Peña, 1977; Roberts, 1980). Both have experienced similar socio-economic change resulting from integration into global markets, have tourist-oriented handicraft production, demographic internal mobility to the second largest metropolis in Mexico, Guadalajara, international emigration to the USA, and rising commercialization and agro-industrialization alongside neoliberal agrarian policies of public divestment. These shared factors allow us to discuss both ethnographic settings in this chapter without further contextualization.

We carried out two surveys through a structured questionnaire in San Cristóbal Zapotitlán (in 1996, from a sample of 48 households, and in 1998 with a team coordinated by Magdalena Villarreal, with 226 households, see Villarreal, 1998). The surveys looked to describe the community's social, demographic, and productive structure, giving particular attention to the sources and use of savings and credit. Data on the Rosca (Rotating Saving and Credit Associations) was taken from semi-structured interviews with participants. The case studies, which also concern the population of Zacoalco de Torres, come from ethnographic material from over approximately two years of fieldwork.[4]

The everyday economy of indebtedness

We will now briefly review the financial landscape (Bouman and Hospes, 1994) and the availability of credit access for the rural population. We would argue that the reproductive capacity of the population is strongly influenced by the availability of access to finance from others, in what Villarreal (2004b: 12–13) calls a "debt economy". The Mexican rural economy currently owes its repro-ducibility to income from unstable wage-earning work and increasingly precari-ous agricultural production for self-consumption, the remittances of emigrants to the USA, and the capacity to weave together social relations in order to juggle between times of real monetary production and consumption needs, through the investment of social and symbolic capital.

In our rural case studies, as in other Mexican examples discussed in this volume, the available financial landscape fundamentally consists of sale on credit (at small shops for daily consumption, weekly open air markets, from mobile vendors of furniture, jewellery, etc.); borrowing money from professional lenders charging differing rates of interest; small interest-free credit from kinship networks or neighbourhoods; bank agencies; credit and aid from State agencies for "development"; credit and savings cooperatives frequently organized by reli-gious figures; migrant remittances; and finally the *tanda*.

Data collected in 1998 from a census of nine rural localities in Western Mexico (see Villarreal, 1998) showed that indebtedness was widespread throughout the villages, particularly in terms of informal (or unofficial) sources of debt – around 35 per cent of family households – as opposed to official credits from banks, public institutions, NGO programmes – around 14 per cent of family households.

In 1996 I asked for the same data in a 48-household survey in San Cristóbal Zapotitlán. Of those interviewed, 56 per cent were indebted to an unofficial source, 15 per cent had official credits, and 10 per cent had both. Only 19 per cent said they were not indebted. Informal credit with high monthly interest rates of 7 to 20 per cent, and from 84 per cent to 240 per cent annually, operated by local *prestamistas* came second only to free credit from friends and neighbours. Almost all the residential groups stated that they were or had been involved in a *tanda*. In 1998, 45.9 per cent of the village households said they were used to asking for *fiado* (sale on credit).

The debt economy is all the more important if we bear in mind how different financial sources are linked up. Credit is often requested to pay off pre-existing debt from a different source. A debtor may beg to receive the first payoff of a *tanda* in the light of an interest payment deadline to a local usurer. In the 1996 survey, 25 per cent of households were indebted to three sources at once, 37.5 per cent to two, while just 23 per cent had only one source of debt. This furthers the "circulation of debt" within the community, and its reproduction assures the very functioning of the local economy (see also Morvant-Roux in this volume for similar findings).

Once the importance of the debt economy is recognized, it is important to consider what process may help strengthen or weaken the social relations sus-taining the various sources of indebtedness. Rather than limiting our observation to the social relations of saving and credit practices, we will also consider debt relations and connect them to the social relations of monetary production (i.e. wage labour) and redistribution (mainly within the household). Our methodo-logical concerns centre on the linkages between the different temporalities and subjects of monetary circulation and production, which micro-finance analysis often separates theoretically.[5] For this reason, we will also adopt a gendered approach to the analysis, because men and women's behaviour appears differentiated in the production, distribution, and circulation of monetary resources.

Gendered hierarchies of production and redistribution

We will now briefly contrast men and women's monetary production within rural settings and discuss redistribution within the household, highlighting how monetary points of control perpetuate the generational and gendered subordination of women. The earmarking of money by gender within households has been widely discussed in the literature,[6] but here we will contrast the links between intra-household monetary redistribution and extra-household monetary sharing within the *tanda*. We will show, for both sets, that money is subject to a gendered moral distinction, but also that there are contextual differences in men or women's control over money.

In contemporary Mexico, including its small rural villages, women labour intensively for monetary income. At the end of the 1990s in San Cristóbal Zapotitlán, almost the entire female population and many of its men worked producing handicraft figures and decorative flowers out of maize husks for the Tonalá international tourist market.[7] The two other main sources of employment were farm labour close to the village in fields managed by national and international agro-industries, exporting tomatoes, blackberries and chilli, and flexible work at electronic companies on the outskirts of Guadalajara. It was mainly women who were not yet married who had access to the labour market, however.[8] Marriage clearly leads to a change in status for women and this also affects their working life. They are no longer daughters but wives, and housewives rather than workers for a salary managed by their parents. For those who continue to work for a salary, as we will show, the money earned is set into a hierarchy where their husbands have a coercive role.

To support this argument, we will turn from the realm of production to redistribution within the household and between the couple "[...] because it is through redistribution that the dynamics of power come up, and we are able to observe the processes of negotiation of hierarchies" (Moore, 1992: 31). We will discuss the dynamics of redistribution for a married couple from Zacoalco de Torres whom we will call José (32 years old) and Maria (30 years old), and who have two young sons.[9] At the time of our study, they belonged to a poly-nuclear co-residential group, and lived in the same house as José's old father and mother, with their two as yet unmarried brothers.

At this stage in the developmental cycle, the two families in the poly-nuclear domestic group shared all the everyday aspects of their life: place of residence, food supply, a single fireplace, and the care of the vulnerable: the invalid mother and the young couple's sons. Money, however, was the exception. We measured the young couple's income and outgoings over a week in September 2003 and found that there were several daily exchanges within the household between the two families. The old father and the young husband took turns making joint payments for regular expenses such electricity for lighting or gas for the kitchen. Both family group members also took turns to cover costs including food, where tallies were not kept in what resembled a gift exchange practice. But unlike his brothers, who were not yet married and who gave all their earnings to their mother, José didn't contribute any money to the household budget. After getting married, he started to manage "his" money independently, although he had never left the parental house.

It is very different after marriage for women like Maria. After she moved, she stopped contributing to her original parental home's budget, like José. But the money she earned washing dresses or for traditional medicine treatments, and the money José gave her for everyday expenses, then fell under her husband's strict control. To understand this process, the model of Benería and Roldan (1987), produced during their urban fieldwork in Mexico City, is also highly valid for the rural setting we studied.

Benería and Roldan highlight five points of control that men exercise over their spouses through money management. The first concerns the information the husband shares about his earnings. On 21 September 2003, I asked Maria how much her husband earned. She responded as follows:

> I believe that his boss gave him 200 pesos.... Before he used to tell me how much he earned, but now, he forgets to tell me. Sometimes I ask how much he has earned and he replies 100 or 200, and then he will give me the rest ... but he doesn't tell me everything he earns.
>
> (Fieldwork notes, Zacoalco de Torres, September 2003)

The second point of control is the extent of the earnings that husbands choose to put aside for personal expenses, and how much they give to their wives. Maria says of her husband:

> [he] doesn't give me a fixed amount, because sometimes he earns more and sometimes less, and sometimes he does a bigger weekly shop and sometimes a smaller one, and in those cases he gives me less money. And sometimes he doesn't have any money to give me and sometimes he gives me a little bit.
>
> (Fieldwork notes, Zacoalco de Torres, September 2003)

The third point of control is how the husband supplies money to the fund managed by his wife. Maria's husband rarely gives her enough money to cover household expenses after getting his weekly salary. This restriction to Maria's purchasing power forces her to ask for money from her husband and to justify her request.

The fourth point is the nature of women's contribution to the common fund. In contrast to her husband, all the money Maria earns is put towards household expenses and costs related to the children.

The fifth and final point is the fact that the husband sometimes takes money out of the common fund during the week. Maria said that during the week, "he tells me to give him something for this or for that and I am left with less money. If I had more money I would buy more cloth to embroider and sell". In a separate interview the husband confirms: "I ask for it and she gives it to me. She gives me money from the money that I gave her."

The gender relationship that emerges is one of competition for monetary resources and the potential for ongoing conflict between husband and wife.[10] Household administration and women's choices to work outside the home or to start a business do not always cause conflict, however, and in some cases decisions are taken jointly (see Kreutzer, 2004 and Bastos, 2007: 117–18).

Benería and Roldán characterize gender identity in terms of specific behaviour, and argue that there is such a thing as "male money", and a shortage of "female money". We would argue that money can be gender-labelled where gendered dispute is at work, rather than in all circumstances. Before marriage, for instance, parents view the money that their children earn similarly, regardless of their children's gender, while after marriage the same money becomes gendered.

It is however undeniable that in contemporary Western Mexican rural society, the symbolic meanings and social patterns of gendered behaviour are available for use. Sometimes, and more frequently in conflict situations, these allow men to achieve a hegemonic position. Money management is one such tool to affirm gendered power. This "realm of calculability" (see Villarreal, 2009: 22, and her chapter in this volume) can help explain why when leaving the house and joining the financial association called *tanda*, there are differing behaviours and judgements based on gender.

Sharing debt and juggling with gender hierarchies: *the tanda*

One framing strategy for wives' actions and calculations, in the face of extreme dependency everyday at home, is to join a *tanda*. It is important to discuss this joint loans and savings tool for its strategic potential as a specific form of indebtedness in the context of different contrasting hierarchies.

A full explanation of *tandas* membership would highlight its complementarity between credit and saving, the availability of large lump sums and reliable payment schedules allowing to plan for expenses at specific dates, and the high level of social control and trustworthiness of members, which guarantees strong repayment performances.[11] Our focus here will be on why membership is female (see Table 9.1), and why men are often put off this financial institution.[12]

Given that missed payments can happen irrespective of gender, one could ask why men tend to view the *tanda* as a risky monetary mechanism, while women see it in a positive, pleasant light.

Women do not in fact find the economic dependency of a Rosca a heavy burden, even though this type of loan is particularly onerous compared to other financial options, given its lack of flexibility towards postponed payments or excuses for late payments. This form of credit probably helps women to multiply

Table 9.1 Characteristics of *Tandas* at work in San Cristóbal Zapotitlán during 1999

Organizer	Number of participants (sex ratio)	Number of turns and duration	Amount of money per turn	Total amount of money borrowed and received	Total amount circulated in tanda per year
Case A	31 (27f; 4m)	20 weeks	From 20 to 100	From 400 to 2,400	63,960
Case B	10 (unknown)	10 weeks	100	1,000	52,000
Case C	12 (unknown)	12 weeks	100	1,200	57,600
Case D	16 (14f; 2m)	10 weeks	50	500	24,000
Case E	10 (8f; 2m)	10 months	500	5,000	60,000
Case F	31 (29f; 2m)	25 weeks	From 50 to 300	From 1,250 to 7,500	130,000
Case G1	17 (15f; 2m)	20 weeks	From 20 to 40	From 400 to 800	20,800
Case G2	16 (12f; 4m)	20 weeks	From 50 to 100	From 1,000 to 2,000	52,000
Totals	143 (105f; 16m; 22 unknown)				460,360

Source: interviews with *Tanda* organizers, November 1999. The amounts are in Mexican pesos (10 pesos was roughly equal to €1 in 1999).

Notes
f=female; m=male.
Cases G1 and G2 were organized by the same person.

and diversify their sources of monetary dependence in the face of their social conditions, to pursue material goals while reducing their social and moral dependency at home.

In the case of Mexican *tanda*,[13] participants are mainly connected through social characteristics such as kinship links, or neighbourhood and friendship ties; the more long-lasting *tandas* are normally community-based, even if some are also promoted by groups of colleagues in educational institutions or factories. Given that *tanda* membership does not require any formal collateral, the institution relies on the relationship between individual participants and the organizer, in more of a dyadic than a collective model. If organizers do not know how to evaluate a person's trustworthiness, they tend not to immediately exclude individuals but to "test" them by making them last in the group for a pay-out. Potential sanctions in the form of exclusion from subsequent cycles are very effective, because news of such exclusion spreads quickly from the coordinator and the participant to the entire community.

Although *tanda* members join the group for economic reasons, they all compare this system favourably to other financial services, praising it for the cooperativeness, solidarity, and the affective elements typical of this form of indebtedness.

The terminology used for the Mexican Rosca also reveals other things. *Tanda*, which means "turn", is probably the most common, and refers to taking turns and cooperation between individuals. Another term is *cundina*, taken from the verb *cundir*, which means both to spread but also to increase and multiply; here, beyond reference to distribution, the idea of procreation is alluded to: a sum of money (the total amount) is impossible to obtain individually, but is created by a group by bringing together different units and shares of money. Another name for the Rosca is *rifa (rifar* means to draw lots for), which evokes the playfulness and the element of chance in how an individual's position is determined over the lifespan of a Rosca. But *rifa* in Spanish also means lottery, and in fact, when people get money from the Rosca, they speak of the sum they have received as if they have won a prize.

The language of the Mexican Rosca conveys a set of moral values such as cooperation, solidarity, sharing, and sociality. To indicate willingness for a person to join the group, the coordinator uses the term *invitar*, to invite to "my" *tanda*. The organizer once told me the words she usually uses in the first meeting:

> I say to the people: look, all together we are going to help each other. It is reciprocal help. It is neither mine nor yours. You come with the hope that you will receive soon and others come to save their money, but all with a same goal, we all have a same goal, what? To bring money together. Let's say, you have a need, you have the *rifa* and you satisfy your need, and you don't fall into debt in another place. So, I don't want to have a bad idea of you, I want that the 28 of each month you bring me the *rifa*, and if you don't want to bring it to me you keep it, and I come to your house to recollect it.
>
> (Interview with C., San Cristóbal Zapotitlán, 21 November 1996)

This speech setting out the rules of the institution also highlights the oral contract between its participants. The leader takes on the role of referee for a game that works thanks to shared values such as reciprocal help, cooperation, honour, and the authority participants assign to the leader.

Participants also raised the moral aspects of this economy in interview, stating that even though they sometimes felt tired of it they continued to take part owing to friendship or kinship ties with the organizer, and their wish not to hurt feelings (Table 9.2 gives an example of the social proximity and longevity of participating in a *tanda*). They also express gratitude to her for working to get them credit or forcing them to save for no real profit. Sometimes they show their gratitude by giving a small extra sum of money to the coordinator along with their regular contribution. But, as can be assumed in one case in San Cristóbal, and as Guérin highlights (2011: 573), the horizontal structure of a Rosca can have the potential to become hierarchical, with the organizer as a usurer and the participants becoming heavily indebted.

Men also sometimes join *tandas*, but usually only in an emergency and without staying for long. It also seems that *tandas* organized by men, or where many males participate, need a supply of constraint or control, as for example *tanda* organized in factories, where the *tanda* pay-out is made at the same time as the wage payment.

For a man, participating in or organizing a *tanda* in the village is an economic risk, but above all a social and moral risk that puts his honour, his face in the hands of others. The regularity and the circularity of the system, considered quite

Table 9.2 Social elements of a *tanda*, San Cristóbal Zapotitlán, 1996

Turn	Sex	Link with organizer	Longevity in the tanda
1	f	Friend	22 years
2	f	Daughter-in-law	19 years
3	f	Nephew	6 years
3	f	Daughter	2 years
4	f	Sister-in-law	3 years
5	f	Daughter-in-law of n°1	2 years
6	f	Sister of n°3	3 years
7	f	Nephew of n°1	1 year
8	f	Neighbour	5 years
9	f	Daughter-in-law	First time
10	f	Friend of n°1	5 years
11	m	Son	5 years
12	f	Neighbour	8 years
13	f	Neighbour	4 years
14	f	Daughter-in-law	4 years
15	f	Neighbour	2 years
16	f	Nephew of n°1	Unknown
17	f	Neighbour	Second time
18	f	Neighbour	First time

Source: interview with C. (organizer), 15 August 1996, San Cristóbal Zapotitlán.

restrictive, puts men at great risk of being unable to pay their turn, meaning that they prefer to stay out and to use diverse kinds of indebtedness – requesting money from friends, or a godfather, or their boss – if necessary to avoid or post-pone repayment, which the strict revolving, collective system doesn't allow.

For men, the moral code and self-representation as a man come into play by way of the need to defend one's own economic autonomy. It is clear that choos-ing a condition of debt and dependence through a rigid mechanism with limited space for bargaining and deferment deflects male identification.[14] As many organizers highlight, men do not appear on the lists of *tanda*, but often contribute through their wives' choice to participate. A deeper analysis, however, high-lights that women also participate in *tandas* in secret or with their husbands' dis-approval. Alicia also participated frequently in *tanda* and insisted that:

> [...] men are also very macho. Men go around saying "no, these (tandas) are women things, this isn't something for men" and instead it is, because they know well, it's just that they don't like to do this, they agree but they don't dare to do it. It's as if it seemed to them that it was only for women. It seems to them that they would be viewed badly if they did it. That's how they think.
>
> (Interview with A., San Cristóbal Zapotitlán, 14 December 1999)

Why, however, don't men simply avoid the system rather than, if asked, becom-ing annoyed about it? Tensions leading to quarrels between husbands and wives tend to arise through this indebtedness and savings system, because men often want to access the money that is outside the home and blocked in the revolving circuit.

It is clear that participation in *tanda* has set women free from one point of control over money. It helps them to plan long-term expenses and to control not just money, but also the expenses that will be made with that money. Women often use part of their salaries to pay into the *tanda*, which allows them to divert the money from home and the control of the husband. Using the *tanda* also gives the wife a moral weapon to persuade the husband to give her more money, and prevents the money from being wasted on alcohol with friends.[15]

Woman, in their condition of latent conflict with their husbands, thus gain room for manoeuvre through this specific modality of monetary circulation. Women can harness moral values that are shared by the entire community, such as the obliga-tion to return money, and willingness to cooperate with relatives, neighbours, friends, and fellow villagers. Men, as the head of the family, must prove their adherence. The added value of these associations is not, therefore, pure economic convenience compared to other modalities of saving for consumption, but women's chance to meet economically and, above all, socially challenging goals which may clash with the wishes of their husbands. The significance given to purchases made, and the means of obtaining the money for them, is how woman find a sense of ful-filment and increased pride. The following passage, taken from an interview with a (female) organizer of a *tanda*, illustrates this:

I like number one, because with number one I ... for example, this book-case that you see, it was my turn in my *rifa*, this sofa that you see, I get the *rifa* and I go to the shop and I buy it in cash. So the creditor doesn't come knocking at my door ... and it's better. I am owing it here to my own people. I like that when my husband comes back [from the USA] he will find something different, he won't find [the house] the same as when he left it.

(Interview with R., San Cristóbal Zapotitlán, 19 November 1999)

The temporary emancipation that the *tanda* gives the wife does not strike us as an early stage in the process of individualization from social links that modern-ization theory sets out. The wife emancipates herself from her husband by taking on other kinds of dependence through a form of financial association. Women find the space to assert their strategies through a form of socialization of private money.

Theoretical implications: multiplying sources of indebtedness as a strategy

Having examined the social hierarchy of gender and a specific practice that women use to address it, we can derive some more general inputs as to how people tend to meet their goals. We have observed that they try to free them-selves from certain kinds of dependence by multiplying and differentiating their sources of dependence rather than limiting it (see also Picherit in this volume, for a similar argument).

When observing the dynamics of indebtedness, it would thus be an error to reason in terms of the dependence-autonomy dichotomy and to view financial inclusion as a tool for liberation from the constraints of personal or community dependence in order to promote the assertion of subjectivity and individualism. The credits that the women we have seen so far actively pursue, temporarily free them from family constraints and moral judgments through other forms of dependence, and choosing whom to depend upon, rather than whether to depend upon someone or not.

These practices can be explained by how in rural Mexico, monetary depend-ence through indebtedness implicates wider class, gender, generational, ethnic, and religious categories that structure the hierarchical inclusion of the subject into a network of relations and wider society. Relations of indebtedness are situ-ated within a system of values shared by creditors and debtors regarding eco-nomic behaviour: they share such ideas as (1) openness to circulating money, even if it is private money, probably out of deep-rooted traditions of cooperation based on the religious, ritual and social organization of the community; (2) the right to ask for money, which does not entail the obligation to give, but implies an openness to lend, even if with added interest rates; and (3) the concurrence of saving and credit for circulation, not accumulation.[16] These sustain financial behaviour not just because local borrowers and debtors share the same set of values, but also because, as emphasized by Morvant (2006: 169–72, see also her chapter in this volume), they frequently experience each position in turn, linking up multiple sources of debt and reversing their positions from debtor to creditor and back again.

If we compare different sources such as the *tanda* and interest loans, we can reflect on the outcomes of the financial practices of rural settings, such as the concatenation of multiple sources of debt and regularly switching between the position of creditor and debtor. Both the *tanda* and credit with interest can be chosen as a way to circumvent the social burden of gender, or of religious and ethnic classification, but they do not have the same effects.

In order to stress this point I will apply Michel de Certeau's distinction between "strategies" and "tactics". In his original interpretation of the lessons of Bourdieu and Foucault on power, de Certeau proposes to define "strategy" as:

> The calculation (or manipulation) of power relationships where a subject or a subject of will or power is distinct from its environment. It requires a space that can be circumscribed as one's own and serve as the base for generating relations with exterior targets or threats [...]. A tactic is a calculated action based on an absence of individual space [...]. It does not allow to construct a global aim nor to distinguish the other as a visible, distinct and objectified totality, but requires insinuating oneself into the other's position.
> (de Certeau, 1990: 59–61, our translation)[17]

Following de Certeau's distinction, *tandas* participation can be viewed as a strategy because women create an autonomous space of control over money from which they can organize their future production and consumption, and set themselves relatively free from material and social dependence.[18] Credit with interest is closer to a tactic in that it plays for time, "allowing" people to manage material and social necessities, but without constructing the conditions for more lasting change (see Zanotelli, 2004 for a detailed analysis of this point).

The conclusions to follow will address the applicability of our discussion to the local social effects and risks of further sources of indebtedness such as micro-finance, and its implications for a qualitative definition of over-indebtedness.

Conclusions: questions for a qualitative definition of over-indebtedness

We must first and primarily take into account that – as we have seen for Western Mexico – local monetary markets are populated by individuals linked to each other by different modalities of debt, credit, and saving. Economic activities in this setting are founded on kinship ties, neighborhood solidarity, and community pressures. The idiom of debt rather than equivalence thus prevails in this financial market, and financial circuits with specific, constantly negotiated social norms determine access to money. It is first approached morally or socially, and only then economically. This reminds us that debt is not limited to an economic sphere of action: as a category, it originates in the organization of relationships between individuals in spheres of exchange that are difficult to reduce to a quantitative dimension.

From this standpoint, methodological topics for future research emerge to help address the question of financial inclusion and predicting the risks of over-indebtedness. Our ethnographic case study highlights the importance of looking to the moral dimension of indebtedness, and the social processes at work in financial relations. The same holds true for the social processes activated by the introduction of new, different sources of indebtedness and dependence such as micro-financial initiatives to local financial circuits. In contrast to the usual opinions of NGOs, which tend to consider their financial products as a positive substitute to informal over-indebtedness, recent research on the experiences of individuals with micro-credit (Morvant-Roux, 2006: 333–6; Villarreal, 2009: 161) has shown that development programmes are often received as a further opportunity to expand existing indebtedness, rather than restricting it. We must address the *linkages* between local and variously moral value-laden practices of indebtedness, and the micro-finance products that come into villages that maintain the pre-structured rules and principles discussed in this chapter. Which linkage practices might arise from this encounter? Might people incorporate micro-finance into their practices of multiplication of dependences, giving the micro-financial products the role of a strategy, or will micro-finance emerge simply as a tactic? Analysis of the social and moral linkages between the various financial practices, including micro-finance, will help to understand the local symbolic distinction between the normal dynamics of social and economic dependence and over-indebtedness.[19] The perception of micro-finance as a cause of over-indebtedness could be precisely due to a fracture between debtors and micro-credit agencies, to a shift of knowledge and lack of participation in structuring the system, a lack of shared categories of comprehension of the world, and a lack of shared paradigms between debtors and creditors (see Johnson in this volume for a similar argument). Following this position, true financial inclusion is not simply a matter of access to monetary resources, but calls for participation in the construction of schemes and a sharing of the values of the exchanges among all involved. In contrast, a valid definition of "over-indebtedness" has to consider the processes of over-dependence, wherein a mixture of socially organized domination, hierarchical classification of human beings, and a certain degree of acceptance of the subjugated to that condition, work together. From a moral perspective, over-indebtedness could be attributed to a single-direction flux of money, where debtors and creditors never swap places and do not share the same moral economies, which for (micro) financial institutions are based on repayment logic and for local financial systems are based on reciprocity.[20] In those cases, the moral burden of indebtedness can bring about abnormal levels of dependence.

A second and related point for defining over-indebtedness regards how debt leads to over-indebtedness, and the social and moral consequences of this for the individual. As with the Rosca, indebtedness to several sources can be viewed as a positive way to handle material and social needs. But what happens if people gradually lose the trust that allowed them to obtain loans in the past? Over-indebtedness can be seen as a step towards rupture and broken social networks; to exclusion and being drawn into other kinds of socialization that are more marked by violence, marginalization, and loss of property of the person; conditions that lie on the border between dependence and *alienation*. In this sense we can clarify the idea of over-indebtedness by exploring critical situations in the middle stage of a process that leads from a condition of normal dependence to alienation, where the path to the commoditization of the person (in different forms and degrees) is open. Despite positive responses to the experience of micro-finance, some ethnographic insights, such as that of Huq (2004) on the Grameen Bank in Bangladesh, have highlighted the great personal pressure that those who are affiliated to the "bank of the poor" experience if unable to repay their micro-debt. Such cases testify to the processes of over-indebtedness and over-dependence brought about by the growing presence of micro-finance in rural settings.

In April 2010 I was back in Mexico, visiting the little village of San Dionisio del Mar, an indigenous Huave (Ikojts) enclave in the Zapotec Istmus of Tehuantepec. During a talk with a woman about access to credit, she listed about six micro-finance institutions that have recently arrived in San Dionisio. Then, she sadly added:

> for this they are indebted, poor people, they take from one and from another, and they don't have a salary. Many people are indebted, some have lost their houses. Now they don't live in their houses. They have to start again, like when they were married. They don't know where to live.
>
> (Interview with F., San Dionisio del Mar, April 2010)

This comment highlights the need for great caution as to the social consequences of the drive for full financial inclusion.

Notes

1 I wish to thank the editors for their efforts in coordinating the volume and for their suggestions that have been extremely helpful in clarifying the arguments of this chapter.
2 Which, moreover, is only the outcome of recent historical developments whereby agricultural production has been dismissed from public financing programmes (Cruz Hernández, 1995).
3 A similar assumption has been recently stated by Guérin (2011: 582).
4 This chapter is based on quantitative data and ethnographic details previously discussed in a different framework of analysis in earlier publications (see Zanotelli, 2004, 2007, 2012).
5 One exception is the ethnography of Janet Carsten (1989), which has shown how money takes on different individual and social meanings as it passes through the realms of production, intra-household redistribution, community sharing through consumption and collective saving.

6 See, for example, Zelizer (1994). An innovative article by Olivia Harris (1981) probably first raised the question of the need for intra-household analysis of monetary flows. For a review of household definitions and gender dynamics of redistribution among co-residents see also McNetting *et al.* (1984), Cheal (1989), Wilk (1989), Gillian Hart (1992).

7 See Villarreal (2002: 437–51) and Zanotelli (2004: 81) for a description.

8 Comparing the quantitative data that emerged from the survey (Villarreal, 1998: 27) and the last available census by Inegi in 2001, we can trace a strict connection between average age at marriage (22 or 23 years old) and a shift for women from wage labour to domestic labour or in houses nearby.

9 I will use pseudonyms.

10 For similar examples in the Mexican urban context see Villarreal (2009: 143–4).

11 See Ardener (1964) for a classical description and a general definition of the main features of Rosca.

12 That is a widespread predominance in various settings worldwide. For a collection of ethnographic evidence see Ardener and Burman (1995). Johnson (2004) has offered an important model for the analysis of the gendered differential use of Rosca with ethnographic materials from Kenya. Guérin's recent review of gender and finance dedicates several pages to Rosca as one of the "women led financial circuits" (see Guérin, 2011: 569–73). In rural and urban Mexican contexts this has also been analysed respectively by Espinosa and Villarreal (1999: 243–6) and Villarreal (2009: 109–28).

13 See Vélez-Ibáñez (1983) and Zanotelli (2012) for a review of relevant literature, with particular reference to the Mexican context.

14 A similar attitude emerges between men of the town of Karatina in Central Kenya who prefer not to belong to Rosca groups because of negative feelings of depending on one another (Johnson, 2004: 1368). But in contrast to the Mexican case, in Kenya women accuse men of not feeling the shame women do; Mexican men avoid participating if they are unsure of their ability to pay precisely because of the risk of shame at public discovery of their fault.

15 For a similar interpretation see also Villarreal (2004b: 345–46).

16 Mexican *tanda* is an organized and institutionalized example of the conceptual unity between saving and borrowing, but other examples are easy to find, such as moneylenders and the reciprocity of money and work between neighbors or dwellers. Even a wedding gift is often seen as a way of saving, for example in the southern state of Oaxaca. In the Mexican context, evidence of this has come from different, unrelated investigations: see Zanotelli (2004: 99); Morvant-Roux (2006: 163–68); Villarreal (2009: 114).

17 Le calcul (ou la manipulation) des rapports de forces qui devient possible à partir de moment où un sujet de vouloir et de pouvoir est isolable. Elle postule un lieu susceptible d'être circonscrit comme un propre et d'être la base d'où gérer les relations avec une extériorité de cibles ou de menace. Tactic [is] "l'action calculée que détermine l'absence d'un propre. […] Elle n'a donc pas la possibilité de se donner un projet global ni de totaliser l'adversaire dans un espace distinct, visible et objectivable.

18 From a psychological perspective, they activate a process Bateson has called "deutero-learning". Vélez-Ibáñez (1983) applied this concept to describe the process of "trusting in trust" in the experience of Rosca participants.

19 The risk of an economic linkage between over-indebtedness and micro-finance has been denounced by Fouillet *et al.* (2007). See also the chapters of Hummel, Angulo Salazar and Joseph in this volume.

20 I take this distinction from Morvant-Roux (see her paper in this volume). The logic of reciprocity doesn't necessarily mean that there is no interest, as has been clarified by the analysis of balanced and negative reciprocity proposed by Marhsall Sahlins (2004: 194–8). An economy based on reciprocity is basically sustained in repetitive exchanges and in the construction and reproduction of social relationships.

References

Ardener, S. (1964) "The Comparative Study of Rotating Credit Associations", *Man*, 94: 202–8.

Ardener, S. and Burman, S. (eds) (1995) *"Money-Go-Rounds": the Importance of Rotating Savings and Credit Associations for Women*, Washington: Berg.

Bastos, S. (2007) "Familia, género y cultura. Algunas propuestas para la comprensión de la dinámica de poder en los hogares populares", in D. Robichaux (ed.) *Familia y diversidad en América Latina. Estudios de casos*, Buenos Aires: Clacso.

Benería, L. and Roldan, M. (1987) *The Crossroads of Class and Gender: Industrial Homework, Subcontracting and Household Dynamics in Mexico City*, Chicago: University of Chicago Press.

Bouman, F. J. A. and Hospes, O. (1994) *Financial Landscape Reconstructed. The Fine Art of Mapping Development*, Oxford: Westview Press.

Carsten, J. (1989) "Cooking Money: Gender and the Symbolic Transformation of Means of Exchange in a Malay Fishing Community', in J. Parry and M. Bloch (eds) *Money and the Morality of Exchange*, Cambridge: Cambridge University Press.

Cheal, D. (1989) "Strategies of Resource Management in Household Economies: Moral Economy or Political Economy?", in R. Wilk (ed.) *The Household Economy: Reconsidering the Domestic Mode of Production*, Boulder-London: Westview Press.

Cruz Hernández, I. (1995) "Transformaciones en el financiamiento rural mexicano durante el sexenio salinista: balance y tendencias (1988–1994)", *Cuadernos Agrarios*, 11–12: 95–120.

de Certeau, M. (1990) *L'invention du quotidien. I Arts de faire*, Paris: Gallimard.

de la Peña, G. (ed.) (1977) *Ensayos sobre el sur de Jalisco*, México: CISINAH.

Espinosa, R. A. and Villarreal, M. (1999) "Las mujeres, las 'malas rachas' y el endeudamiento: prácticas de compensación locales en el medio rural", in L. Vázquez García (ed.) *Género, sustentabilidad y cambio social en el México rural*, Toluca: UAES-Colegio de Posgraduados.

Fouillet, C., Guérin, I., Morvant-Roux, S., Roesch, M., and Servet, J.-M. (2007) "Le microcrédit au péril du néolibéralisme et de marchands d'illusions. Manifeste pour une inclusion financière socialement responsable", *Revue du Mauss*, 1(29): 329–50.

Guérin, I. (2011) "Do Women Need Specific Microfinance Services?", in B. Armendariz and M. Labie (eds) *Handbook of Microfinance*, London/Singapore: World Scientific Publishing.

Harris, O. (1981) "Households as Natural Units", in K. Young, C. Wolkowitz, and R. McCullah (eds) *Of Marriage and the Market: Women's Subordination in International Perspective*, London: CSE Books.

Hart, G. (1992) "Imagined Unities: Constructions of 'the Household' in Economic Theory", in S. Ortiz and S. Lees (eds) *Understanding Economic Process*, Lanham: University Press of America, 1992.

Hudon, M. (2009) "Should Access To Credit be a Right?', *Journal of Business Ethics*, 84: 17–28.

Huq, H. (2004) "Surviving in the World of Microdebt: A Case from Rural Bangladesh", in H. B. Lont and O. Hospes (eds) *Livelihood and Microfinance. Anthropological and Sociological Perspectives on Savings and Debt*, Delft: Eburon.

Inegi (Instituto Nacional de Estadística Geografía e Informática) (2001) *Estadísticas de Nupcialidad 2001*, México: Inegi, 2001.

Johnson, S. (2004) "Gender Norms and Financial Markets: Evidences from Kenya", *World Development*, 32(8): 1355–74.

Kreutzer, S. (2004) "'Una mujer con dinero es peligrosa'. Cuestiones de género en el manejo del dinero y la deuda a nivel familiar", in M. Villarreal (ed.) *Antropología de la deuda. Crédito, ahorro, fiado y prestado en las finanzas cotidianas*, México D.F.: Ciesas-Porrua-Cámara de Diputados.

McNetting, R., Wilk, R. R., and Arnould, E. J. (eds) (1984) *Households: Comparative and Historical Studies of the Domestic Group*, Berkeley: University of California Press.

Moore, H. L. (1992) "Households and Gender Relations: the Modelling of the Economy", in S. Ortiz and S. Lees (eds) *Understanding Economic Process*, Lanham: University Press of America.

Morvant-Roux, S. (2006) *Processus d'appropriation des dispositifs de microfinance: un exemple en milieu rural mexicain*, PhD thesis, Ecole Doctorale de Sciences Humaines et Sociales Université Lumière-Lyon 2, Lyon.

Roberts, B. (1980) "Estado y región en América Latina", *Relaciones. Estudios de Historia y Sociedad*, 1(4): 9–40.

Ryne, E., Gardeva, A., and Levai, D. (2009) *Mexico's Prospects for Full Financial Inclusion. A White Paper from the Financial Inclusion 2020 Project. Draft for Discussion*, Center for Financial Inclusion at Accion International, document available on line at www.centerforfinancialinclusion.org/publications-a-resources/browse-publications/300, accessed the 15 February 2011.

Sahlins, M. (2004) *Stone Age Economics*, London: Routledge.

Vélez-Ibáñez, C. G. (1983) *Bonds of Mutual Trust: The Cultural Systems of Rotating Credit Associations among Urban Mexicans and Chicanos*, New Brunswick: Rutgers University Press.

Villarreal, M. (ed.) (1998) *San Cristóbal Zapotitlán: Resultados Finales*, Guadalajara: Ciesas Occidente.

Villarreal, M. (2002) "Las mujeres del maíz: voces fragmentadas en el mercado global", in G. de la Peña and G. Vasquez León (eds) *La antropología sociocultural en el México del milenio. Búsquedas, encuentros y transiciones*, México D.F.: Ini-Conaculta-Fce.

Villarreal, M. (ed.) (2004a) *Antropología de la deuda. Crédito, ahorro, fiado y prestado en las finanzas cotidianas*, México D.F.: Ciesas-Porrua-Cámara de Diputados.

Villarreal, M. (2004b) "Divisas intangibles en las relaciones de ahorro y de endeudamiento: a manera de conclusión", in M. Villarreal (ed.), *Antropología de la deuda. Crédito, ahorro, fiado y prestado en las finanzas cotidianas*, México D.F.: Ciesas-Porrua-Cámara de Diputados.

Villarreal, M. (2009) *Mujeres, finanzas sociales y violencia económica*, Guadalajara: Instituto Jalisciense de la Mujer-Instituto Municipal de las Mujeres en Guadalajara.

Wilk, R. R. (1989) "Decision Making and Resource Flows within the Household: Beyond the Black Box', in R. R. Wilk (ed.) *The Household Economy. Reconsidering the Domestic Mode of Production*, Boulder-London: Westview Press.

Yunus, M. (2007) *Creating a World without Poverty: Social Businness and the Future of Capitalism*, NewYork: Public Affairs.

Zanotelli, F. (2004) "La circulación social de la deuda. Códigos culturales y usura rural en Jalisco", in M. Villarreal (ed.) *Antropología de la deuda. Crédito, ahorro, fiado y prestado en las finanzas cotidianas*, México D.F.: Ciesas-Porrua-Camara de Diputados, 2004.

Zanotelli, F. (2007) "Scegliere la dipendenza. Strategie di aiuto e di debito nel Messico Occidentale", in F. Viti (ed.) *Lavoro, dipendenza personale e rapporti familiari*, Modena: Il Fiorino.

Zanotelli, F. (2012) *Santo Dinero. Economie morali nel Messico contemporaneo*, Roma: CISU.

Zelizer, V. (1994) *The Social Meaning of Money: Pin Money, Paychecks, Poor Relief, and Other Currencies*, New York: Basic Books.

10 Does juggling mean struggling?

Insights into the financial practices of rural households in Madagascar

Betty Wampfler, Emmanuelle Bouquet and Eliane Ralison

Introduction

This chapter analyses 'financial juggling' practices among rural households in Lake Alaotra, Madagascar. A major rice-producing region located in the northern central plateau, Lake Alaotra is home to a diverse and competitive finance sector, where microfinance and agricultural finance coexist with a well-established informal sector. Drawing on several years of intensive fieldwork in the region, and more specifically on the analysis of 47 in-depth qualitative interviews conducted by the authors in September 2009, our examination of household financial practices reveals multiple configurations that may be qualified as financial juggling. Juggling here refers to the concurrent or successive use of various credit practices, formal or informal, by a given household. Households can juggle different formal financial institutions, different products within a financial institution and formal and informal credit.[1] This factual definition of juggling does not imply that juggling is equivalent to over-indebtedness, understood as a process of structural impoverishment from debt (Guérin, Morvant-Roux, Villarreal, this volume). Rather, our aim is to disentangle the situations and processes through which juggling can be a symptom of, or eventually lead to, over-indebtedness. To do so, we analyse juggling practices along with the socioeconomic context of the household, its position within a life cycle trajectory, and the rationales and representations that are put forward by the household members. Our results show that if juggling can reveal processes of over-indebtedness, it can also illustrate processes of creative adaptation to constraints on the local financial markets.

Many empirical studies deal with the diversity of formal and informal financial practices: credit, savings and insurance for poor and/or rural households (Adams and Vogel, 1986; Zeller and Sharma, 2000; Matin *et al.*, 2002; Bouquet and Cruz, 2002; Collins *et al.*, 2009; Guérin *et al.*, 2011). They analyse certain aspects (accumulation of loans, savings arrangements, linked transactions and their multifunctionality), highlight the diversity of needs (cash management, risk management, household and business investment), and the ways in which households are compelled to cope with an imperfect supply (which can lead to rationing or exclusion and poor quality of individual services).

Others focus on the linkages between the formal and informal financial sectors and question the assumption of substitutability, whereby the formal sector would gradually replace the informal sector. Work conducted in India (Bell, 1990; Roesch and Héliès, 2007; Guérin *et al.*, 2009) Mexico (Morvant-Roux, 2009), Kenya (Johnson, 2005), Peru (Guirkinger, 2008) and Madagascar (Droy, 1993; Zeller, 1994) highlight the way the two sectors coexist, or even – in South India and indigenous areas of Mexico – the way they leverage each other. Still others look more specifically at the logic that drives the choice to use a particular sector (Zeller, 1994; Johnson, 2005; Guirkinger, 2008; Guérin *et al.*, 2011). By highlighting how decision-making involves both monetary and non-monetary considerations, transaction costs and risk analysis, these studies demonstrate that households do not necessarily 'settle' for informal services as a second-best option, and that the embeddedness of economic decision-making in social relations pertains to both formal and informal finance.

More recently, several authors explicitly raise the issue of multiple sources of credit and debt: some to warn about risks associated with microfinance (Roesch and Héliès (2007 in India), others to put this risk into perspective by emphasizing households' financial management capacities (Collins *et al.* (2009) in India, Bangladesh and South Africa). This question is inherently empirical and requires case-by-case analysis to take into account the nature of supply and demand in specific contexts.

Our work is in line with these considerations and analyses juggling practices relative to credit in a defined context, using a specific framework. The context is characterized by a fairly dynamic economic fabric that associates agricultural and non-agricultural activities, as well as a diverse supply of formal rural finance relatively well adapted to local needs and constraints. The framework draws on the concepts of new institutional economics and economic sociology. The household is the unit of analysis and financial practices are explored from a livelihood approach. The framework also incorporates the changing nature of financial practices over the short term, by accounting for seasonality, and over the medium term, through descriptions of trajectories.

After presenting the study's methodology and context, we document the diversity of juggling practices, both in terms of type – juggling different formal financial institutions, products within a same financial institution, and between formal and informal finance – and in terms of purpose, by distinguishing three broad categories: juggling to access credit, juggling to pay off credit and juggling to get out of debt. Next, we discuss the concept of financial literacy and household vulnerability to demonstrate that over-indebtedness and juggling are not inextricably linked. Juggling can mean struggling and struggling can mean over-indebtedness in some specific situations that need to be empirically characterized. On the other hand, juggling can also be an elaborate, controlled and effective form of money management for households forced to deal with socioeconomic uncertainty and to make do with the limitations of one sector or the other, or individual financial products within the same sector.

Methodology

A conceptual framework combining new institutional economics and economic sociology

This study draws on the conceptual framework of new institutional economics and economic sociology. We define financial practices as contractual arrangements that occurr within a financial market fraught with market failures (information asymmetry, transaction costs and risk), with the resulting corollary of segmentation (between the formal and informal), rationing and transactions on adjacent markets (land and labour) (Stiglitz and Weiss, 1981; Bardhan, 1980, 1989; Johnson, 2005; Boucher and Guirkinger, 2007). To speak in terms of contractual arrangements allows us to analyse financial practices not as spot transactions but as a series of decisions and actions that unfold in different timeframes, and relate to different objects (and therefore pose potentially different problems): choice of provider, negotiation of terms, 'enforcement' of commitments (ex ante and/or ex post, through incentives and/or coercion). This does not mean that stakeholders are seen as agents driven exclusively by individual economic calculation nor that the arrangement itself is an isolated phenomenon removed from the market and non-market relationships that are the basis of households' livelihoods. On the contrary, the context of the contractual arrangement and the nature of social relations that bind individuals and households influence both what decisions are made (based on the desired outcome and perceptions of the range of possibilities and limitations) and how they are made (assigning monetary and non-monetary values, establishing priorities and hierarchies, analysing costs and benefits).

Context and social relations are not static: they are constructed and negotiated, and in turn shape the very course of interactions, whether they relate to contractual arrangements or other areas of social and economic life. For this reason, our analysis is in line with research in economic sociology that focuses on the principle of embeddedness (Granovetter, 1985; Johnson, 2005). By mobilizing the social dimension to explain market practices and economic outcomes, our analysis remains nevertheless grounded in the economic arena (Elster, 1989; Platteau, 1994a, 1994b; Barrett and Foster, 2007).

Our unit of analysis is the household, where strategies are formulated and implemented, and where the results on 'livelihoods', as defined by Ellis (1998, p. 4), are apparent: 'A livelihood encompasses income, both cash and in kind, as well as the social institutions (kin, family, compound, village and so on), gender relations, and property rights required to support and to sustain a given standard of living.' The household is not, however, taken as a 'black box'; it comprises individuals whose identity (men/women, parents/children), positioning, assets and rationales influence the rationales and practices of the household as a group.

A qualitative, contextualized approach combined with triangulation

The analysis draws on 47 in-depth qualitative interviews conducted by the authors in three villages of the Lake Alaotra region in 2009. The sample selection was done in a reasoned manner, based on a central criterion: the degree of the household's insertion in the formal financial system (bank or microfinance). The authors conducted semi-open interviews in order to characterize with precision the financial practices of households with regards to their productive activities and life cycle events, and to grasp the underlying economic and social rationales. Our understanding of short-term financial practices comes from a detailed description of an annual financial cycle; long-term practices were discerned based on a trajectory analysis of the activity and on asset accumulation since setting up the household. The interviews yielded systematic data on the households' demographics, their human and social capital, their assets, economic activities and income sources.

The three major financial institutions in the area – the cooperative networks CECAM and OTIV, and the commercial bank BOA (the reincarnation of the former state-owned agricultural development bank after privatization in 1999) also contributed to the study. Interviews conducted with senior managers shed light on juggling from the perspective of the formal financial sector. These institutions willingly shared their client list, thus facilitating the sampling process.

Finally, we leverage our in-depth knowledge of the economy and household financial practices in the Lake Alaotra region, acquired over several years through our own research and that of our students (Wampfler *et al.*, 2009; Bouquet *et al.*, 2007, 2009; Oustry, 2007; Zombre, 2010; Laigle, 2011).

Context

Lake Alaotra is a predominantly rural area with a strong economy and a relatively dense fabric of financial institutions. Located in the northern central plateau, the region is composed of vast plains surrounded by hills and plateaus of 1,100 m and 1,500 m. Large irrigation networks, developed during French colonization in the first half of the twentieth century, have enabled the development of 100,000 ha of rice fields. With an average annual production of around 300,000 tonnes of paddy, representing approximately 10 per cent of national production, Lake Aloatra is considered one of Madagascar's 'rice bowls'.

In irrigated areas, and to a lesser extent in arid zones, farming systems are increasingly diversified, with the development of market gardening in the off-season, and the integration of livestock: zebu cattle, pigs, poultry and dairy cows. High population density and relatively easy access to the market allow for a diversification of non-farming activities: petty trading, trading and processing of agricultural products, handicrafts, etc. The region's economy is thus relatively dynamic, bolstered by cash crops and non-agricultural activities, which translates into financial needs for productive activities.

The formal financial sector has its antecedents in state-owned agricultural finance institutions and has expanded considerably in the 2000s. The privatization of public banks led to the emergence of two commercial banks, BOA and BNI, which serve the three urban centres in the region. BOA also offers agricultural loans for large rice farmers with land guarantees. Two mutualist microfinance institutions, OTIV and CECAM, have branch networks in the region. Both offer agricultural loans (known locally as 'productive credit'), inventory credit ('village granary loans') and medium-term investment loans (called 'mutualist hire-purchase loans'). OTIV also offers a solidarity group loan for women. Development projects occasionally offer microcredit for productive purposes, or help households become members of OTIV or CECAM. Private rice processing companies offer input credit, reimbursed in rice.

The local supply of formal finance is quite singular compared to the type of microfinance found in some places in India and Mexico, for example (Joseph, Guérin *et al.*, Hummel and Angulo Salazar in this volume). Indeed, credit products are diverse and designed to meet different needs and constraints, including agricultural activities. Individual loans are more common than group lending; physical guarantees are used (albeit adapted to local assets: unofficial documents for land and houses, rice and animals); the amounts and conditions for disbursement and reimbursement account for seasonality; medium-term loans for investment are offered in addition to short-term loans; and there is no specific target population as opposed to the categories usually targeted by the microfinance industry, such as 'the poor', 'women', etc.

Informal credit is also very present, usually in one of the following forms:

- borrowing from family or relative, with or without interest, depending on the purpose of the loan and the circumstances of the people involved in the transaction. This type of credit generally involves small amounts for day-to-day living expenses; occasionally it may involve larger sums, in the event of health-related expenses, for example;
- *varo-maitso* (literally 'green rice'): This type of loan can be repaid in cash and/or in kind and corresponds to the sale of standing rice crops. When borrowing and repayment are in kind, the interest rate is expressed in terms of an overall reimbursement amount ('I borrow one *vata* – 14 kg – and I reimburse between two and three *vata*'), which corresponds to an interest rate of 100–200 per cent for a few months. When the loan is in cash, interest is expressed indirectly by the price of the *vata*, set by the lender at the time of the loan (generally between 2,000 and 3,000 MGA[2] per *vata*, i.e. two to three times less than the market price at harvest time, and thus roughly the same interest rate as in-kind loans). Traditionally used to finance agricultural expenses (namely transplanting rice), *varo-maitso* is also used to meet food needs during the lean season or, more rarely, to meet an unforeseen financial need (health problem, economic shock, etc.);
- cash advances provided by a rice trader (the 'boss') for 'sub-contractors' to buy rice from local farmers. While this practice is not a credit relationship strictly speaking (the sub-contractor is paid on commission), it is a common and implicit form of informal credit that entails 'working the money between the "boss's" two visits'. Generally, the sub-collector buys paddy, has it husked and sells it, thereby reconstituting the capital and pocketing the profit, before buying more paddy. Only profits from the last rotation go to the 'boss'. Depending on the boss's scale of operations, sums can be very high.

Table 10.1 Summary of formal and informal credit in the study area

	Formal	Informal
Interest rates	Between 3%–4% per month	Between 0%–40% per month (a)
		Sometimes implicit but usually not indexed over a period
Term	Between 6–36 months	From a few days to 6 months (or more, in case of rescheduling)
Rough amounts (in euros)		
Tens	X	X
Hundreds	X	X
Thousands	X	Exceptional cases (boss collector)
Purpose		
Agricultural	X	X
Productive non-farm activities	X	–
Investment	X	–
Health-Education	X	X
Social-Ceremonies (b)	–	–

Sources: interviews with households and local formal financial institutions.

Notes

a Authors' estimates according to terms and methods of calculation (the price of rice).

b Our surveys do not include cases of financing social or ceremonial needs (funeral rites, such as *famadihana*) with credit. Such cases exist, but in all those we encountered, financing came from the household's own resources or cash and/or in kind assistance from family members. This contrasts with the financing of health expenditures, which often involve the use of formal and informal credit.

We will focus here on rural households that are heterogeneous in terms of assets, productive activities and income. In our sample, households' annual incomes range between one million MGA (€400) and 24 million MGA (€11,200).[3] Regardless of their level of wealth, all households rely mostly on non-wage income, and develop to varying degrees both on-farm and off-farm activities. Depending on the household, this pluriactivity can be a defensive strategy (to ensure food security) or an offensive one (to develop activities, anticipate significant productive or domestic expenditures and accumulate assets). Pluriactivity is associated with self-financing strategies (use of rice stocks to finance other activities, diversification of activities and investments depending on foreseeable agricultural and non-agricultural expenses, etc.). We will not develop these self-financing strategies here, but will focus on how pluri-activity contributes to shape the demand for credit and creditworthiness (understood both as the ability to obtain and repay a loan).

Financial juggling

The section is organized around the three major types of practices that we use to define financial juggling: (1) juggling financial institutions; (2) juggling financial products of one institution; and (3) juggling formal and informal credit. Financial juggling, as defined here, is highly developed: of the 47 households studied, 33 have used a practice qualified as juggling during the year observed (2008–2009). This section aims to illustrate the wide variety of rationales behind juggling practices by relying on particularly illustrative case studies.[4] A given household may use a combination of practices (e.g. juggling financial institutions and products from the same institution) and therefore be illustrative of several of our sub-sections. To convey as faithfully as possible the systemic consistency of each case, we present each in full in order to illustrate several points of our analysis.

Juggling financial institutions

The level of development of the formal financial market in the Lake Alaotra region makes possible to juggle several financial institutions. For the most part, the literature tends to see this practice as 'bicycling' – taking a loan with B to repay one taken from A – and financial institutions fear it is a major source of household debt and delinquency (see also Angulo Salazar in this volume). Although our interviews confirm that the practice of 'bicycling' does exist, they also show that this perception is reductionist; the rationales behind juggling are multifold and, even though it involves risk taking, it is not inevitably a source of over-indebtedness.

Being a client of several financial institutions allows one to take advantage of a range of products that are complementary in terms of purpose (agricultural loans/investment, etc.), terms and conditions (e.g. Household 1, Household 2 and Household 3). Major rice producers have significant cash needs concentrated over short periods (preparation of fields, harvesting, etc.) and juggle institutions to circumvent loan ceilings and thereby access more credit. In the case of Household 3, the practice has helped double acreage in less than five years.

When households do 'bicycle' loans, it may be the result of a calculation designed to improve the household's cash management in light of pluriactivity and seasonal income and expenses (Household 4 and Household 1). We will see other examples in the following section juggling products from the same financial institution.

Household 1: Mr Anselme is an elected representative of OTIV and Mrs Béatrice is a member of CECAM and OTIV. Mrs Béatrice joined OTIV in 1999 to finance health costs. She took a loan of 100,000 MGA, which she struggled to repay by borrowing from her family. As a result, she borrowed only one more time from OTIV after that: a 300,000 MFG loan in 2001 to buy paddy that she then resold to a rice trader. Impressed by her acumen, the trader provided a cash advance of one million MGA to continue to buy rice. She used part of the money to repay her loan and tried to move the rest as quickly as possible by negotiating with other traders. She has been doing this since 2001. Because she had some repayment problems with OTIV (she speaks in terms of 'conflict'), she decided not to borrow anymore from the institution, opting instead to join CECAM. But her husband then decided to became a member of OTIV. Since then, they have been juggling the two sources of credit: she takes hire-purchase loans from CECAM for household purchases (furniture, TV, etc.) and her husband takes business and inventory loans from OTIV. Mrs Béatrice often makes payments to CECAM with her husband's loan from OTIV.

Household 2: Mrs Caroline is divorced and a member of OTIV since 2003 and CECAM since 2008. She started out with a 120,000 MGA group loan from OTIV to buy a zebu cow. Since 2005, she has taken an individual loan for rice production every year. In 2008 she joined CECAM to take a 400,000 MFG hire-purchase loan to acquire oxen.

Household 3: Mrs Dominique farmed 60 ha of rice fields in 2009. She finances the 42 million MGA in expenses by a bank loan of 25 million MGA from BOA, a productive loan of 12 million MGA from CECAM and savings from the previous year (five million MGA). Because the CECAM productive loan is limited to three million MGA, Dominique had her husband, daughter and son-in-law join the institution in order to obtain 12 million. CECAM is aware of this strategy and knows she has a loan from BOA, 'This is not a problem for anyone, I give all the necessary information and am loyal to both institutions, I am treasurer at my Church.' The director of BOA comes to see her at her home and she discusses with him the loan terms; this is how she was able to negotiate repayment in September when rice prices rise, rather than in August, when prices are still low.

Household 4: Emile is 40 years old, and has five children; four are schooled. His schooling expenses are high. He farms and drives a bush taxi. He has been a member of OTIV since 2006 and takes out an agricultural loan every year to finance his farming activities, the children's education and, occasionally, healthcare costs. He also takes advantage of OTIV's inventory credit. His wife became a member of CECAM in 2008 and uses inventory credit. He explains very clearly that they juggle the two MFIs to cope with their expenditure. He specifies that they take loans so that one can repay the next and so on. Access to both institutions also allows him to compare services. Having taken inventory credit with both, Emile believes that each MFI has strengths and weaknesses. In case of early repayment, OTIV allows borrowers to pay interest on the actual loan term while at CECAM, interest is payable on a fixed term non-negotiable. OTIV's interest rate (2.5 per cent) is lower than CECAM's (3 per cent). CECAM's guarantees are more stringent than OTIV's; CECAM requires members to pay shares proportional to the amount of credit requested, while OTIV only lends an amount proportional to one's savings. At the time of the interview, Emile was considering borrowing six million MGA between the two institutions in the near future, to build a house.

As the example of Household 4 shows, juggling institutions is sometimes part of a learning process, whereby households experiment with the financial market. Household 4's explicit comparison of the institutions shows that users have the capacity to understand the market, they are not passive 'market-takers'. It also reveals the multiple ways households makes decisions. In the case of Emile, it is the price that comes into play: the nominal/effective interest rate, as well as transaction costs (additional fees, guarantees and conditional savings). For Béatrice of Household 1, however, the quality of relationship with the financial institution takes precedence over price considerations, leading her to leave one institution for another, while still maintaining access to one she left behind through her spouse.

In some cases (Household 3), financial institutions are at least partially informed of their client's multiple membership and accept it after risk analysis. But, in general, such practices lack transparency, due to weak information systems and lack of information sharing between institutions. The position of financial institutions is ambivalent: juggling institutions is seen as a risk of household over-indebtedness and non-repayment, which must be reduced and thus justifies investment in improved information systems and credit bureaus. But juggling may be tacitly accepted, at least temporarily, when it comes to winning new customers from a competitor.

Juggling the credit products of one financial institution

Although still uncommon in other microfinance sectors, both institutions in the Lake Alaotra region offer a wide range of credit products: productive loans, inventory loans, working capital, education loans and investment loans. Diversification stems from a desire to meet households' diverse needs, especially in agriculture, but is also the result of competition. Products can officially be combined, sequentially or concurrently, on the basis of the borrower's situation. The product range thus creates many original opportunities for juggling.

First, there is the variation on 'bicycling', in which one credit product is used to repay another. This is often the case with inventory credit, used to repay a productive loan. Inventory credit can be a response to a cash shortage and, in some cases, belie an underlying debt problem, thus leading to impoverishment and greater vulnerability. Household 5 is a particularly dramatic example. In some cases, however, this practice works as a planned and controlled cash management strategy. The case of Household 6 shows that this form of juggling is seen in a positive light by the borrower, as a way to secure the productive loan and generate better profits by selling rice stocks six months after harvest, when prices are high. This positive perception is shared by financial institutions that encourage, even formalize this practice because it secures their productive loan portfolio.

Household 5: Francis farms 0.5 ha of rice fields, 0.25 ha of plateau and owns a plough. In 1999, due a family problem, he had to borrow 300,000 MGA from a local moneylender, repayable in kind, with 4 tonnes of paddy rice. Several bad years succeeded, and at the time of the interview, Francis had still not finished paying off his debt. He was paying between two and three sacks of rice (70 kg) a year, which did not satisfy the lender, who had threatened him repeatedly. He joined CECAM in 2006 to try to get rid of the moneylender. He took a productive loan in December for 300,000 MGA, pledging his own cow and his brother's. The loan helped finance work in the rice fields, and household consumption. Unfortunately, in April, a cyclone killed his cow and destroyed part of his harvest. He only harvested ten sacks of rice (700 kg); five were given to the moneylender, whose threats were intensifying. The other five bags were placed in a warehouse, as collateral for an inventory loan, to constitute a safety stock for the lean season and also to repay a portion of the productive loan. As this was not enough and he had nothing to support his family, he leased out half of his rice field (0.25 ha) for three years. This brought in 270,000 MGA, which he used to repay the productive loan and buy food. He kept 0.25 ha to feed his family, and negotiated an advance from his brother to buy seed. At the time of the interview (September), he was scheduled to repay the inventory loan in February. He was hoping to get a productive loan to repay the inventory loan, but since he had no more cows for collateral, was not very confident that CECAM would grant him the credit.

The year before, his wife had been contacted by a development project targeting women that offered training and credit for raising chickens. They joined the project and received a loan of 200,000 MGA from another financial institution to build a coop and buy chickens. At the time of the interview, the coop was in place, but an epidemic had killed all the chickens. He negotiated with the project to suspend the loan, but he was still slated to pay 250,000 MGA in November and did not know where he would find the money. Even by selling everything left in his possession, he would not be able to cover the reimbursement. Francis said that he was putting himself in the hands of God.

Household 6: After some hard years due to repeated health problems that sunk him into debt with informal lenders, Georges finally managed to develop farming activities and a grocery-bar, starting in 2005. In 2007, he joined OTIV to help grow his activities, and eliminate his dependence on informal credit. In December 2008, he took a productive loan of one million MGA, pledging his house and rice field as guarantees. Part of the loan was invested in rice production, another in the working capital of the grocery-bar. The rice harvest in late May 2009 yielded five tonnes, part of which was allocated for home consumption and the other part stocked under OTIV's inventory credit scheme (928,000 MGA). This allowed him to finance tuition in June and September (284,0000 MGA) for five children in private school. Between June and September, the family purchased rice on the market (when prices were low) for household consumption, so they could sell their stock for higher prices in September. The inventory credit also allowed Georges to repay part of his productive loan. OTIV is aware of this practice and encourages it; it appears in the client's file. Georges deems the arrangement suitable for both parties: he is able to access a productive loan that allows him to work, and knows he will be able to reimburse it with his inventory loan. And OTIV is sure the productive loan will be repaid.

Successive inventory loans to develop rice-trading activities[5] is another commonly observed juggling practice. Inventory credit, initially designed to facilitate access to credit for poor farmers lacking collateral other than their crops, and to improve their negotiating position on the local rice market, is then used to develop rice trading, an essentially speculative activity (Bouquet *et al.*, 2009). Our studies show that rice trading is not confined to affluent households, but is practiced by all income categories whenever they have some capital (Household 7).

Household 7: Huguette grows rice, tomatoes and beans on 1.5 ha, fattens two pigs a year and runs a small grocery store with stock she estimates at 500,000 MGA. She joined CECAM in 2006; before, she was afraid of financial institutions and credit. She changed her mind after seeing CECAM members grow quickly thanks to inventory credit. She took a productive loan, and then in 2008, took a small inventory loan against one tonne of rice from her own production and a little from rice purchased from others. She says she poorly managed her first inventory loan because she bought the rice too late, when prices had already increased. However, she believes that inventory credit is much better for her than productive loans, which require a guarantee. She plans to repay the inventory loan with the sale of a pig and income from her grocery store. Next year, she plans to take a much bigger inventory loan and start purchasing rice much earlier, when prices are low. She will finance the purchases by fattening two pigs to sell just before the rice harvest. She intends to use the money to buy a first stock, which she will store in the granary; she will then use the inventory loan to buy more rice and constitute a second stock. Thus, by using several successive loans, she plans to build up a much larger stock than in 2008. Her limit will be the size of her granary (five tonnes). In 2008, she was a novice in inventory credit. But she has learned a lot and is confident that she will manage to scale up her rice purchases next year thanks to inventory credit.

The case of Household 7 highlights the learning dimension that is at play in these financial practices. Experimenting with inventory credit has made households more aware of prices (the price of rice versus the price of credit) and has developed numeracy, a particularly important skill in rice trading. Without necessarily defining it quantitatively, most households involved in rice trading are aware of the spread between the purchase and sale price needed to cover the cost of credit and turn a profit. Our interviews also show cautious behaviour in certain households and the occasional securisation strategy to deal with price risk (Household 9).

The range of formal credit in the Lake Alaotra region makes it possible for clients to combine loans of different maturities. Households juggle different terms to finance, intensify and diversify activities (Household 8). Equipment loans, which are usually large and come to term at rice harvest time, are often reimbursed by inventory loans. Here again, juggling allows the household to hold on to its rice stock to sell it when prices are higher. Although all households are concerned, these strategies appear to be riskier for middle-income households (Household 9), a fortiori the poor.

Household 8: Isidore is over 60 years old. He owns 8 ha of rice fields, a husker, and he raises pigs (12 per year), geese and ducks. He and his wife have been members of CECAM since 2003. He uses productive loans and inventory credit every year. He took his first hire-purchase loan in 2004 to buy a motorcycle, by pledging his living room furniture; the second in 2006 for a roto-tiller and trailer, using the motorcycle and living room as a guarantee; and the third for 6.5 million MGA in 2008 to purchase the husker, guaranteed by the tiller and a plot of land. 'Without the hire-purchase loan, I would have never had the roto-tiller and trailer, let alone the husker.' He reimburses the hire-purchase loan in June with an inventory loan, which is reimbursed in December with rice sales during the lean season, together with income from the husker and the sale of pigs.

Household 9: Mr Joseph and his wife have 9 ha of rice that they cultivate only partially. They have 12 children, eight of whom are still dependent.

They grow rice, vegetables and flowers that the wife sells at the market. They have always self-financed rice production. They joined CECAM in 2007 because they needed a roto-tiller to plough faster and cultivate a larger portion of their land. They took a hire-purchase loan of 3.5 million MGA over three years. They reimburse the capital each June at harvest time, and pay interest quarterly. In 2008 and 2009, they took an inventory loan that allowed them to reimburse the June hire-purchase instalment; the interest was reimbursed with savings from the daily budget, placed in a savings account opened with CECAM. The reimbursement of the roto-tiller creates a lot of pressure on the family budget and they would like to pay it off quickly. To repay the inventory loan in 2008, they sold three tonnes in advance to a rice trader and kept just one tonne for the family. In 2009, they planned to do the same. In anticipation of rice price volatility (the year 2009 was unique due to political unrest), they also deposited in their CECAM account the money from the sale of an ox. If it turns out they do not need it to repay their loan instalments, they will use it to do work in the house.

Juggling formal and informal credit

Despite the variety of financial institutions in the Lake Alaotra region, informal credit is still practiced in its various forms: family borrowing, *varo-maitso* and cash advances from rice traders. The development of formal credit appears to have pushed back the practice of *varo-maitso*. But, as in other contexts (See Morvant-Roux and Zanotelli in this volume), many households with access to formal credit continue to use the informal sector. Again, the methods and uses vary.

Formal credit may be used as a substitution strategy, to bypass the informal sector, particularly *varo-maitso*, considered to be too expensive and the source of socio-economic alienation (Household 5, Household 6 and Household 10). But households' financial trajectories are far from linear and our interviews show interesting examples of formal financial users returning to informal credit. Being able to go back to the informal sector is useful if access to formal credit is suddenly cut off, due to a repayment problem or conflict (Household 10 and Household 11). It is also the result of learning, based on a comparison of product attributes, in which the formal sector does not necessarily come out on top. Simple and rapid procedures, proximity, privacy and the certainty of permanent access work to the advantage of informal providers and, in the eyes of borrowers, compensate for the higher interest rate (Household 11).

Household 10: Prior to 2005, Mr Léon and his wife relied on *varo-maitso* every year to pay the costs of planting. 'There is no guarantee, just a written contract, but it is not covered by the municipality.' In 2005, Mr Léon joined CECAM in order to stop working with *varo-maitso*. From 2005 to 2008, he took productive and inventory loans in succession, and was able to cease *varo-maitso*. In 2008, his granary was burglarized and CECAM held him responsible, forcing him to immediately pay off his inventory loan and to indemnify the other stockers. Mr Léon considered the decision unfair: since his granary had been approved by CECAM, he felt the institution should have shared the losses. Also, because he was compelled to pay immediately, he had no choice other than to sell a plot of rice field to meet his obligation. Therefore, he left the institution and was then forced to work again with *varo-maitso*. Shortly after that, his wife joined OTIV to take a productive loan, but at the time of the interview, they still did not have enough savings to borrow.

Household 11: Marie is divorced with six children. She farms a small plot, sells firewood and works as farm labourer and self-employed seamstress. She has been a member of OTIV since 2000. When she delivered her last child during the lean season in 2004, she had no money. She could not get a loan from OTIV because she already had one in progress. She borrowed 40,000 MGA from a moneylender, and reimbursed 80,000 MGA at harvest. In 2005, after a bad crop year, she did not manage to repay her productive loan of 100,000 MGA on time; she was two months late and OTIV imposed penalties. To repay, she had to borrow from her brother, and repay by working for him as a transplanter. Since then, she no longer wants to borrow from OTIV. For the small amounts she needs (less than 100,000 MGA), she prefers to use one of the three village moneylenders. It costs twice as much, but at least she doesn't have to make trips to get the money, there are no guarantees and she can count on the moneylenders' discretion.

Informal credit may be used to overcome limitations (Household 12) or short-comings (Household 13) of the formal credit supply. For example, because rice stocks cannot be recovered until the borrower has reimbursed the inventory loan in full, households lacking cash for reimbursement will request an advance from a rice trader, which is roughly the equivalent of a very short-term loan. In most cases, the advance is negotiated on the basis of a discounted price; the discount appears small to the household, but the implicit interest rate is actually extremely high. In the example of Household 12, it amounts to 2 per cent for a one- to two-day advance. The borrower nevertheless emphasizes the advantages of this arrangement, and the relationship of trust on which it relies.

Household 12: Mr Nicolas and his wife own 1 ha of rice field, three plots on a plateau and a vacant housing plot worth 500,000 MGA. They have managed to acquire agricultural and household assets over time. They grow rice, watercress and raise ducks. In November 2008, Nicolas' wife took a productive loan from CECAM for 600,000 MGA. She used part of the loan for rice production and part to buy a second-hand plough (350,000 MGA). In June 2009, she took an inventory loan of 810,000 MGA, of which she used 690,000 MGA to reimburse her productive loan. She used the rest of the inventory loan to buy 36 ducks. To repay the inventory loan, she will do as she does every year: ask the rice traders who know her well to give her a cash advance on her paddy so she can reimburse CECAM and access her stocked rice. They are villagers who trust her and do not require a written contract.

In a context marked by the seasonality of agricultural activities, a delay in the loan granting process can also lead households to use a bridging loan from the informal sector (Household 13). The timeliness of the loan process is indeed one of the first criteria clients/members use to evaluate the quality of a financial institution (Bouquet *et al.*, 2009).

> Household 13: Mr Oscar develops agricultural activities and a grocery store. In 2007, he needed capital to expand his store. He wanted to avoid the costly informal credit sources he had just managed to extricate himself from. Since he had assets that could serve as a guarantee, he turned to formal financial institutions. His brother and father-in-law had both borrowed from CECAM and both suffered delays in the granting process, which led to serious cash flow problems. His father-in-law was even forced to borrow from a moneylender as a result. Since OTIV granted loans in a timely manner, treated its members well and had the same interest rates as CECAM, he chose to join OTIV.

Finally, formal and informal credit can coexist in the financial strategies of households. This happens when informal credit is used for certain types of expenses, like household expenditure or during the lean period. Even members of formal institutions may choose to first turn to informal credit – emphasizing its proximity and flexibility – in the event of an unforeseen event. Health issues in particular are often partially addressed through a family loan that is often free (but not always), and comes with flexible repayment terms (Household 14). However, the family safety net may not be enough for major health expenses, in which case the moneylender serves as a lender of last resort (Household 15). The partitioning of formal and informal credit can also be observed among households who 'work the money' of their 'boss' rice trader (Household 1 and Household 16).

> Household 14: Paul and his wife own 1.5 ha of good rice paddy and 2 ha of bad paddy. To cope with their growing family and farm expenses (four dependent children, one at the university in Tana, one in a private school), they joined OTIV in 2007. Since then, they have taken a productive loan and education loan every year, which they have managed to pay thus far without too much difficulty. In 2008, their three-year-old son got sick and they had to find 60,000 MGA for the treatment. They thought of using the village moneylender, who practices *varo-maitso* at a rate of 10,000 MGA for 3 *vata*. But they ultimately secured a family loan that they repaid two months later, without interest, by selling early rice.

Household 15: Stéphanie is 43, a widow since 2002 and has three children (two still at home). She runs a small grocery store and rents land or share-crops when she can. In 2009, she started gardening on a small plot of rented land. Her eldest daughter, married, lent her money to pay the rent (40,000 MGA), and her eldest son left school to help with the farm work. She joined OTIV in 2000, aiming to expand activities and gradually build a house. From 2000 to 2005, she regularly took group loans from the village branch office. In 2005, the group disbanded following internal conflicts and OTIV asked the women to become individual members. By pledging her house (estimated at 350,000 MGA), she took her first individual productive loan of 350,000 MGA and invested it in farming activities and the store. But there was a drought and she could not pay off the loan. Because she had already reimbursed part of the loan, OTIV did not seize her house, but con-tinues to seek collection. In 2009, at the time of the interview, she still owed 100,000 MGA. Meanwhile, in 2008, she fell ill and was hospitalized. To pay the hospital, she needed 200,000 MGA; her parents and brother donated 100,000 MGA. For the remaining 100,000 MGA, she used *varo-maitso* in November 2008, to be repaid in cash (200,000 MGA) in June 2009. It was the first time she dealt with this moneylender; friends from the village put her in touch with him.

Household 16: Thomas is 60 years old, owns a small grocery store, trades rice and farms 1 ha of rice paddy and 0.5 ha of lowlands. In recent years, he started growing tomatoes through a sharecropping arrangement. Thomas is educated and worked for a rice company before losing his job during the recession of the 1980s. He continues to work for his former boss as a sub-contractor. He receives cash advances (e.g. three million MGA) to consti-tute a stock over a given number of days. But unofficially, he 'works the money' for his own trading activities. In 2006, he was the victim of a scam on a stock of rice bought with his cash advance: 12 tonnes of rice worth 600 MGA/kg were paid with counterfeit money. Thomas filed a complaint but it was futile. It was absolutely vital that Thomas repaid his boss, because of their long-standing relationship, and the economic opportunity the boss represented ('he is the source of my work'). To repay, he sold his furniture, motorcycle and bicycle and used the working capital from his grocery business and trade activities as well as the cash set aside to repay an OTIV loan.

He had been an active member of OTIV since 1999 and an elected member of the credit committee since 2002. Until 2005, he regularly com-bined productive and working capital loans. At the time of the fraud, he owed two million MGA on the OTIV loan. In 2009, he had only managed to reimburse 400,000 MGA. His relationship with OTIV deteriorated: he was dismissed from his position on the credit committee, complained of aggres-sive collection practices ('there is no privacy, many of them come all at once to intimidate and humiliate us'), and attempted unsuccessfully to renegotiate. At the time of the study, OTIV was threatening to auction off his remaining furniture, and recently informed Thomas that the case was going to court. He now owed 4 million MGA, with penalties.

The way households prioritize commitments in times of crises reveals the extent to which relationships and sanctions are embedded and hierarchized when households assess their possibilities and calculate their options. Thus, when Household 16 lost the capital entrusted by his 'boss', he chose to repay this informal debt first by allocating money dedicated to repayment of a formal loan: he preferred to incur sanctions from the formal sector (indeed very severe ones, with economic and social consequences) rather than lose access to this privileged bilateral relationship, the source of both credit and economic activity. The head of Household 15 did not call on her family to help pay back her formal debt, but obtained financial assistance for an equivalent amount when she was hospitalized. Conversely, Household 17 exhausted family resources to meet formal sector commitments – to provide a guarantee and to make on time repayment – thus initiating a precarious spiral that was ultimately compounded by a shortcoming of the financial institution (delayed payment) and an unforeseen external shock.

> Household 17: Ursula has been a member of CECAM since 2007. She took a 380,000 MGA productive loan in January 2008, pledging two ploughs, a sewing machine and a bicycle belonging to her brother. The credit was disbursed late, and she had repayment difficulties and appealed to her mother-in-law, who agreed to sell a plot of land to pay for the second instalment. In 2008, she needed credit, but as she was sure CECAM would not grant a new loan, she joined OTIV. She received a 400,000 MGA, 12-month loan from OTIV to develop a rice trading activity. She also agreed to transfer part of the money to her brother-in-law in exchange for letting her pledge his bicycle the year before. For this second loan, she pledged her parents' house. But instead of trading rice and lending some of the money to her brother-in-law, she used the loan to pay childbirth costs and court fees for her husband, tried for statutory rape. At the time of the study, Ursula had only repaid interest, using money from her brothers and sisters. With OTIV pressuring her for repayment of the principal, Ursula turned to her mother who agreed to rent a 1 ha rice field to repay the debt. Ursula also used *varo-maitso* to get through the lean period: 5 *vata* for 3,500 MGA/*vata*.

Discussion

Financial literacy

Our findings confirm those from other contexts (Collins *et al.*, 2009; Guérin *et al.*, 2011): rural households in Lake Alaotra, both rich and poor, have calculation and financial management capacities that are reflected in financial juggling.

Often quite sophisticated, juggling practices correspond to a variety of rationales and objectives. Juggling may be induced by an unexpected expense or a short-coming of the formal financial sector. But such practices also serve to anticipate cash needs and even underpin asset accumulation strategies, allowing house-holds to take advantage of the relatively dynamic economic context and diversified financial supply.

Households use both monetary and non-monetary criteria to make financial decisions. The price of credit, for example, expressed as an interest rate, but mainly understood in terms of the total cost of credit, is an obvious monetary element. The household practices observed in Lake Alaotra clearly demonstrate price sensitivity (for agricultural products and credit), particularly when it comes to rice trading and inventory credit. But other monetary criteria are involved, such as liquidity requirements needed to access a formal credit (in the form of compulsory savings, or shares indexed to credit uptakes), the time the money is tied up, the nature of collateral required and its value.

However non-monetary elements also come into play. When it is time to choose a service provider, households also think in terms of proximity, availability, discretion, long-term access and the risks involved in case of default. The quality of the relationship with the financial institution (or informal lender) – the level of confidentiality, the degree of respect or lack thereof (e.g. the possibility of violence in case of late repayment) – strongly influence household choices. And, when it is time to choose who to pay first in the case of multiple loans, the informal lender, with whom the relationship is often long-standing and perceived as more secure in the long term, may take precedence over the financial institution, even if it involves sanctions and cutting off access to cheaper credit.

Decision-making frameworks are not exclusively individual; they integrate to varying but often critical degrees, family and social relations. Ex ante, these relationships can be mobilized to expand access to informal credit (family members are usually the first to be contacted in time of need), but also to formal credit (to circumvent eligibility requirements, credit ceilings or constitute a guarantee). Ex post, the family can serve as a safety net when loan repayment is difficult. Repayment conditions vary from one family to the next; the arrangement may be a donation, or gift, or a contractual relationship whereby the debt is repaid in cash or labour.

Financial literacy skills are not static. They evolve through the learning processes that result from the households' economic activities, market interactions and decisions to use formal and informal financial products. Being able to combine credit products and compare financial institutions facilitates this learning.

Of course, financial calculations are not infallible. Imperfect information (on markets, financial products, etc.) can lead households to overestimate investment returns or underestimate price risk, thereby jeopardizing calculations. Expectations of just how much social and family networks will help out can also prove misguided. In addition to calculation capacities, unforeseen events and the degree of resilience of households also influence trajectories.

When does juggling mean struggling?

Juggling practices are observed in all categories of households and are not necessarily an indicator of vulnerability. There are, nonetheless, differences in the logics, constraints and effects of juggling practices, and our interviews reveal a clear split between reactive and proactive juggling.

When juggling is used to respond to an unforeseen event (health crisis, climate hazard, price volatility, etc.), it becomes a reactive strategy, marked by urgency and short-term, often risky, calculations. The outcome of this kind of reactive juggling will largely depend on the context, situation and trajectory of the household. The available assets, economic alternatives, social and professional networks mitigate the risk among affluent and median-income households. For low-income households, however, reactive juggling represents a significant risk that can increase vulnerability, and result in a spiral of over-indebtedness and impoverishment. Getting out of the poverty trap may take several years; this illustrates the temporal dimension of financial juggling.

But juggling can also be highly proactive: based on foresight, calculation, planning and savings, juggling practices can be used to pursue intensification, diversification and accumulation strategies. Here again, the temporal dimension of juggling stands out: short-term actions are part of medium- and long-term planning.

Reactive and proactive dimensions are often intertwined: households may manage ex-post a shock, and gradually rebuild a proactive strategy; or, conversely, a proactive strategy to accumulate may be compromised by an unexpected event, creating shock waves that households will attempt to mitigate. In our analysis, the proactive or reactive nature of juggling does not correlate with any particular personality trait (a tendency to plan ahead or to be passive); rather, it is reflective of the context and the household's position within a trajectory.

Although these two dimensions are observed in all household wealth categories, we can identify trends along economic divides. Among the wealthiest households, juggling practices are most often proactive, involve larger sums and are part of accumulation, intensification and diversification strategies. Among the poorest households, juggling practices are more frequently a reactive response, and imply greater risk. The difference is not so much in financial literacy as in structural inequalities and asymmetries in terms of household resilience.

Ultimately, in the Lake Alaotra region, microfinance reinforces households' juggling possibilities by broadening the range of options. These increased juggling options are not a synonym of over-indebtedness as such. Indeed, they can even facilitate trajectories towards greater empowerment, diversification and accumulation. However, they can also constitute a risk factor, particularly for poor households with fewer capacities to cope with external shocks. It is up to the financial sector and policy makers to find ways, based on a better understanding of local rationales, to contain this risk.

Notes

1 We can also talk in terms of juggling credit and savings, rice and cash (Bouquet *et al.* (2009)), identity of borrower and lender. Although these forms of juggling are mentioned herein, they will not be analysed as such.
2 1 euro=2,500 MGA.
3 This income range is confirmed by a recent study of rural households in Lake Alaotra (Bascou, 2010), which found average household income to be around five million MGA per year (€2,000), with very affluent rice farmers earning 45 million MGA per year (€18,000). A landless farm worker labouring 250 days per year earns about 500,000 MGA per year (€200).
4 Names have been changed for the sake of confidentiality.
5 This activity involves buying rice when the price is low – 250 to 300 MGA per kg – and selling it five or six months later during the lean season when prices reach 600 to 700 MGA per kg.

References

Adams, D. W. and Vogel, R. C. (1986) 'Rural Financial Markets in Low-Income Countries: Recent Controversies and Lessons', *World Development* 14(4): 477–487.

Bardhan, P. K. (1980) 'Interlocking Factor Markets and Agrarian Development: A Review of Issues', *Oxford Economic Papers* 32(1): 82–98.

Bardhan, P. K. (ed.) (1989) *The Economic Theory of Agrarian Institutions*, Oxford: Clarendon Press.

Barrett, C. B. and Foster, A. D. (2007) 'The Social Dimensions of Microeconomic Behavior in Low-Income Communities: Introduction to a Symposium', *Journal of Development Economics* 83(2): 253–255.

Bascou, P. D. (2010) 'Analyse du fonctionnement des exploitations de polyculture élevage et mise en place d'une démarche d'accompagnement des producteurs, Lac Alaotra, Madagascar', Master's thesis, Montpellier SupAgro-CIRAD.

Bell, C. (1990) 'Interactions between Institutional and Informal Credit Agencies in Rural India', *World Bank Econ Rev* 4(3): 297–327.

Boucher, S. and Guirkinger, C. (2007) 'Risk, Wealth, and Sectoral Choice in Rural Credit Markets', *American Journal of Agricultural Economics* 89(4): 991–1004.

Bouquet, E. and Cruz, I. (2002) *Construir un sistema financiero al servicio del desarrollo rural*, Mexico: Camara de diputados, Comision Desarrollo Rural.

Bouquet, E., Wampfler, B. and Ralison, E. (2007) 'Trajectoires de crédit et vulnérabilité des ménages ruraux: le cas des Cecam de Madagascar', *Autrepart* Numéro thématique 'Risque et Microfinance' (44): 157–172.

Bouquet E., Wampfler, B. and Ralison, E. (2009) 'Rice Inventory Credit in Madagascar: Diversity of Rural Household Strategies Around an Hybrid Financial and Marketing Service', Communication in: First European Research Conference in Microfinance, Bruxelles, 2–4 June.

Collins, D., Morduch, J., Rutherford, S. and Ruthven, O. (2009) *Portfolios of the Poor: How the World's Poor Live on $2 a Day*, Princeton: Princeton University Press.

Droy, I. (1993) 'L'usurier et le banquier: le crédit rural à Madagascar', in C. Blanc-Pamard *Dynamiques des systèmes agraires. Politiques agricoles et initiatives locales: adversaires ou partenaires?* Paris: ORSTOM: 291–311.

Ellis, F. (1998) 'Household Strategies and Rural Livelihood Diversification', *Journal of Development Studies* 35(1): 1–38.

Elster, J. (1989) 'Social Norms and Economic Theory', *Journal of Economic Perspectives* 3(4): 99–117.

Granovetter, M. (1985) 'Economic Action and Social Structure: The Problem of Embeddedness', *American Journal of Sociology* 91(3): 481–510.

Guérin, I., Morvant-Roux, S. and Servet, J.-M. (2011) 'Understanding the Diversity and Complexity of Demand for Microfinance Services: Lessons from Informal Finance', in B. Armendariz and M. Labie, *Microfinance Handbook* Washington, DC: World Scientific Publishing, pp. 101–122.

Guérin, I., Roesch, M., Héliès, O. and Venkatasubramanian, G. (2009) 'Microfinance, endettement et surendettement', *Tiers-Monde* (196): 131–146.

Guirkinger, C. (2008) 'Understanding the Coexistence of Formal and Informal Credit Markets in Piura, Peru', *World Development* 36(8): 1436–1452.

Johnson, S. (2005) 'Fragmentation and Embeddedness: An Alternative Approach to the Analysis of Rural Financial Markets', *Oxford Development Studies* 33(3&4): 357–375.

Laigle, N. (2011) 'Participation des services financiers aux stratégies de développement des activités des ménages ruraux: l'exemple du lac Alaotra à Madagascar' Master's thesis, Montpellier, Supagro Montpellier – CIRAD.

Matin, I., Hulme, D. and Rutherford, S. (2002) 'Finance for the Poor: From Microcredit to MicrofinancialServices', *Journal of International Development* (14): 273–294.

Morvant-Roux, S. (2009) 'Accès au microcrédit et continuité des dynamiques d'endettement au Mexique: combiner anthropologie économique et économétrie', *Tiers-Monde* (197): 109–130.

Oustry, M. (2007) 'Analyse des causes de non remboursement de credit au Lac Alaotra à Madagascar. Quelles implications pour les groupements de crédit de caution solidaire, les institutions financières et le projet BVLac', Master's thesis, Montpellier, Supagro Montpellier – CIRAD.

Platteau, J.-P. (1994a) 'Behind the Market Stage Where Real Societies Exist – Part I: The Role of Public and Private Order Institutions', *Journal of Development Studies* 30(3): 533–577.

Platteau, J.-P. (1994b) 'Behind the Market Stage Where Real Societies Exist – Part II: The Role of Moral Norms', *Journal of Development Studies* 30(4): 753–817.

Roesch, M. and Héliès, O. (2007) 'La microfinance, outil de gestion du risque ou de mise en danger par sur-endettement? Le cas de l'Inde du Sud', *Autrepart* (44): 119–140.

Stiglitz, J. E. and Weiss, A. (1981) 'Credit Rationing in Markets with Imperfect Information', *The American Economic Review* 71(3): 393–410.

Wampfler, B., Bouquet, E. and Ralison, E. (2009) 'Microfinance et investissement rural: l'expérience de crédit-bail du réseau Cecam de Madagascar', in *Exclusion et liens financiers – Rapport 2009 du centre Walras*. Paris, Economica: 255–276.

Zeller, M. (1994) 'Determinants of Credit Rationing: A Study of Informal Lenders and Formal Credit Groups in Madagascar', *World Development* 22(12): 1895–1907.

Zeller, M. and Sharma, M. (2000) 'Many Borrow, More Save, and all Insure: Implications for Food and Microfinance Policy', *Food Policy* 25: 143–167.

Zombre, U. (2010) 'Interactions entre marchés de la terre et marchés du crédit à Madagascar', Communication in: 4èmes journées de recherches en sciences sociales, Rennes, 8–10 December 8.

11 The social costs of microfinance and over-indebtedness for women

Lourdes Angulo Salazar

Introduction

The microfinance sector in Mexico is undergoing a number of changes, one of which is the modification of the laws that regulate it, which allow the operation of new entities and define organizational forms and operating parameters aimed at having more transparence, self-regulation, and reliability in these institutions.

The new regulations allow us to differentiate these entities. On the one hand, there are those that offer microfinance services of savings, loans, insurance, and remittance reception and payment, who observe the laws applicable and whose implications are supervised and regulated by Mexico's Secretary of the Treasury (Secretaría de Hacienda y Crédito Público, SHCP), the Banking and Stock Exchange Commission (Comisión Nacional Bancaria y de Valores, CNBV), and the National Savings and Financial Services Bank (Banco del Ahorro Nacional y de Servicios Financieros, BANSEFI). On the other hand, there are entities that offer microloans and, according to the source of their funds, are supervised by the CNBV and/or the National Commission for the Protection and Defense of Financial Service Users (CONDUSEF).

Ten years after the changes in the law, microfinance institutions in Mexico are still trying to deal with the adaptations and transformations required of them. They must belong to umbrella institutions with regional and national coverage, and prove to them and to the regulating bodies that they have management and bookkeeping processes to assess their credit portfolio, internal monitoring, and control bodies.

The difficulties and vicissitudes faced by the microfinance institutions generally increased with the financial and economic crisis in 2009, when their default rates went up. Among the institutions that were part of the study, Caja Popular Santa María de Guadalupe had an 18 percent default (CPSMG, 2009). Micro Banco de Oaxaca (MB) had a 12 percent default rate.[1] For both institutions, these rates are based on loans over 90 days overdue.

In this scenario, microfinance institutions have strengthened their credit risk management strategies and their handling of their overdue portfolio, which includes analysis of the indebtedness capability of their clients, backing up loans with all kinds of guarantees and applying peer pressure to clients and their co-signers or "debtors in solidarity" ("*deudor solidario*") in case of default in payment.

Microfinance institutions are also resorting more frequently to legal action and foreclosure against defaulters. Furthermore, as I will show later, stricter regulations have been enacted for the microfinance sector, leading to more frequent recourse to co-signers, whose obligations used to be a mere formality.

The aim of this chapter is to analyze the social implications of using such mechanisms both to prevent risks and to deal with the over-indebtedness of their clients. In order to do this, I analyze "money juggling," a widespread practice that contradicts the calculations of credit providers on what constitutes healthy financial management and a desirable use of loans. I suggest that although aggressive competition among credit providers, the absence of customer loyalty among borrowers or the lack of a "financial education" can help us to understand over-indebtedness, this happens when there is a conjunction of other factors, such as decisions based on incomplete information and the simultaneous occurrence of critical events, in circumstances that involve micro-loan providers and users of their services.

As I will show below, a poor woman who has developed a certain skill and has no trouble handling small-scale loans to earn a living by selling candles or food might not appreciate the consequences of large-scale indebtedness, since she is not familiar with the contractual terms and has not been duly informed.

I do not wish to insinuate that families or customers with debt problems are simply victims, although I have documented the tribulations that many of them undergo to pay back their loans, and the great lengths they go to meet their commitments. All the same, there are cases in which they deliberately suspend payments either because they figure that it is more profitable to invest in an operation that farther down the line will yield enough to pay off the debt and its financial costs, or because they have in their asset portfolio other resources that they can utilize once that supplier cuts off their credit.

The way people deal with indebtedness is related to the material and symbolic resources they have at their disposal, which are in turn delimited by their class, gender, and ethnic affiliation. A poor or indigenous woman might not find it so daunting to be short of the money needed to make timely payments to a micro-lender if she has the social relations, the information, or the knowledge that will eventually enable her to access new sources of liquidity to make up for the expected income and pay off her debts.

There are different ways in which trust and reciprocal support relationships are invoked between users and providers of microfinance services. Solidarity has different meanings and practices among people, and problems arise when these are extrapolated to the relationships of debt and commitments created between the client and her co-signer.

Evidence of this emerges when we analyze the workings of solidarity groups, which are often set up in the poorest communities because it is assumed that their lack of material assets is compensated for by an abundance of social assets. Aside from its classist and discriminatory bias, this principle overlooks the cultural codes and values that govern the practices of mutual aid in specific contexts and situations.

In the context mentioned above, the strategy of minimizing the risk of non-compliance through social collateral generates practices that differ from those expected. One of them is that users tend to limit their network of trust to their extended family, are reluctant to support those who are not members of it, find excuses to ignore requests from others, or accept to be co-signers only if they are given some monetary compensation in return. Thus, the use of these mechanisms leads to a paradox in which trying to activate and strengthen social links actually contributes to their degradation.

Insufficient attention has been paid to the social costs of over-indebtedness. In their eagerness to recover their money, micro-credit organizations exert pressure on their clients, either directly or through their co-signers. Women are stigmatized as slow in paying, and lose their membership in the group and the microfinance organization, and this makes them lose power and prestige within the family and the community. These are the issues this chapter deals with.

The social meanings of the moral obligation of reciprocal support are explored, as well as the connotations acquired by some financial practices depending on who engages in them and with what purposes, the assessment of risks, and the measures adopted to minimize them based on the information available and the analytical tools used to interpret it. For this purpose, I rely on the notion of frameworks of calculation and calculability processes proposed by Villarreal (2009; see also Villarreal, this volume), who suggests that these processes take place within certain frameworks of interpretation of the subjects and according to their specific position in identity categories of gender, ethnicity, and social class.

Methodology and context

The methodology used is a qualitative one, based on the ethnographic method and its tools, such as the observation of situations and participant observation, and open-ended and in-depth interviews with theme focus. The study was conducted in two regions in Mexico: the municipalities of El Grullo and Autlán in the state of Jalisco, and the district of Miahuatlán in the state of Oaxaca, in Mexico. Special attention was paid to a microfinance entity in each region: Caja Popular Santa Guadalupe (CPSMG) in the former, and Micro Banco Lismii in the latter.

Research work was conducted for three months in El Grullo and Autlán and for two and a half months in Miahuatlán; in the former, ethnographic work was centered in El Chante, a town with almost 2,000 inhabitants, which is part of the municipality of Autlán, 15 kilometers away from the capital city of the same name.

The interviews were conducted with women whose small businesses produce *tortillas*, bread and cakes, or who sell fruit or *tacos* in the town square, or toiletries and cosmetics door to door. Other women own grocery stores or work in the fields or in stores in Autlán.

Ethnographic work in Miahuatlán focused on women both in the city and in smaller towns in the same district. Although most of the interviews were with non-indigenous women, some indigenous women were also included. Their income generating activities are making and selling meals and tortillas, selling shoes and clothes, working as fishmongers, working in grocery stores, working in coffee production, paid housework, and clothes manufacture.

Zone of Autlán – El Grullo

The largest employment-generating activity in this area is sugarcane and the production of sugar in the Melchor Ocampo sugar mill. Another source of employment is the agave plantations, which usually employ men but some women are employed too. There are also some agricultural industries located 50 kilometers from El Grullo and Autlán. Fishing is carried out in three dams and several fish farms, as well as on the Ayuquila River. In El Chante, there are few stores that offer jobs: three grocery stores, an internet café, a beauty shop, two clothing stores, and a store that sells cell-phones and prepayment cards. There are also the employees at the government delegation, the teachers, a nurse, and a physician. Construction work is scarce locally. Most construction workers here go to work to Autlán, El Grullo, and more distant municipalities.

Nine formal financial entities in this region offer savings and/or credit services,[2] beside four bank offices. There are also three pawnshops.

Most of social base of CPSMG is in El Grullo, where around 55 percent of the 13,247 of its members live.[3] Its credit portfolio exceeded 445 million pesos,[4] with 336 million pesos in savings accounts. It has five more offices in the region, in the towns of Autlán, El Chante, Ayuquila, Ejutla, and Unión de Tula.

It offers savings accounts, investments, remittances and several modes of loans for productive activities, commerce, small industries, and services. It also offers loans for consumption or housing. During the period studied, and according to CPSMG's data, the main use of loans was for consumption (41 percent), followed by production (37 percent),[5] housing (19 percent), and purchasing medicines and hospital expenses (2.5 percent)[6] (CPSMG, 2009). The monthly interest rate ranges from 1.5 to 2 percent.

CPSMG only offers individual loans. The loan is estimated according to the member's savings and can be for three or even four times the amount saved, depending on the member's credit history. The *caja* uses the member's savings as collateral and, according to the amount borrowed, asks for one or two guarantors who are also member of the *caja*.

Miahuatlán

Located in the southwest of the state of Oaxaca, 42 percent of its population is Zapotec Indians. Indigenous and rural populations in this region depend mostly on the production of coffee, corn, and beans for their livelihood; they also produce *mezcal* and seasonal handicraft work. Families often raise livestock, especially goats and sheep. Emigration to the United States, very intense in other regions of Oaxaca, is less common in this region, although there is some internal migration on a seasonal basis to the agricultural fields of the states of Sinaloa, Baja California Sur, Baja California Norte, and Sonora.

In the town of Miahuatlán there are 17 entities[7] that provide regulated financial services.[8] There are also four bank offices, as well as five pawn shops and two wire transfer service companies.

The Micro Banco Liismi (MB) is part of the micro-bank network of the Mexican Association of Credit Unions (Asociación Mexicana de Uniones de Crédito – AMUCSS), with offices in the states of Puebla, Oaxaca, Michoacán, and Guerrero. Miahuatlán's office opened in 2000, and it now has 3,680 members. It offers savings accounts, insurance, wire transfer payments, and two types of loans: group loans, with an interest rate of 3.5 percent, and individual loans, with a 3 percent monthly interest rate. According to the manager, most loans in Miahuatlán are used for commerce (65 percent), followed by housing (35 to 40 percent), and consumption (5 to 10 percent).[9]

According to the manager, the 12 percent repayment default rate reported to the date of the study was attributed to a failure in obtaining accurate information regarding the indebtedness capability of members, a generalized reduction in consumption that had a negative effect on the members who applied for loans for commerce, and the fact that borrowers who owned more prosperous businesses preferred to reinvest the money they owed the micro-bank in the purchase of new goods for their business, which was more profitable, calculating that the profit they made would allow them to repay the debt and the interest on it.

The solidarity-based loan is given to groups, that function as a loan repayment guarantee. For that reason, groups of ten or more people are encouraged, and upon signing their application each member becomes a co-signer of the other members' loans, thus replacing an economic or material collateral. Each member is responsible for repaying his or her debt and makes the rest of the members do the same. If any member defaults, he or she is exposed to the peer pressure of the group, for, as long as the debt is not repaid, the group may not apply for new loans. Under extreme situations, the group will repay an individual debt.

As for individual loans, unlike other microfinance institutions, the micro-bank does not require its members to have a savings account when they are given a loan. A member joins the group as such with his or her loan application, and that is why the socio-economic assessment performed with every applicant is so important before a loan is authorized. The study also collects information on the co-signers. If the loan is between 3,000 and 15,000 pesos, the applicant is required to submit two co-signers; if the amount is higher than 15,000 pesos, some guarantee, such as an automobile invoice or a deed to a real estate property, is required.

In recent years solidarity-based groups have decreased due mainly to two reasons: (1) members prefer not to take the risk of non-compliance by other members because they have had unpleasant experiences, and (2) loan policies favor individual loans by offering higher amounts than those offered for group loans,[10] a practice that favors clients who own more social and patrimonial assets. The municipalities where there is greater use of individual loans are San Agustín, San Baltazar, and Ozototepec, with a majority of indigenous population.

Solidarity-based practices: theory versus reality

Programs of micro-credit and microfinance today have in common their use of various mechanisms, one of which, as has been mentioned, is the use of social collateral for group or individual loans. The first of them operates under the assumption that there is some kind of peer selection to find the most responsible borrowers. In both modes, microfinance institutions try to distribute the risks and costs derived from repayment default. From a financial viewpoint, working with group loans increases security for the organization because it reduces risk, particularly in urban environments where clients often move and there is therefore justified concern that they will take the money and run.

On the other hand, defenders of these programs emphasize the configuration of new social scenarios where non-tangible resources such as trust or collective solidarity emerge or are strengthened; however, it is worthwhile to raise the question of how the actors involved understand concepts such as solidarity, being a group, and trust, as well as what are the notions behind specific contents and practices.

Even in social groups like the indigenous towns of Oaxaca, where there are widely documented mutual support practices, when we enter the realm of micro-finance and social collateral, solidarity-based practices cannot be taken for granted, as can be seen in Yolanda's[11] comment

> someone dies and there we are, if your *compadre*[12] has a party, if you throw the *Guelaguetza*,[13] that solidarity is going to continue because it is part of the customs in Oaxaca. If you need a glass of water they will give it to you, they will invite you over for dinner, these people show solidarity, but only in those aspects.... When it's a loan, people don't trust anymore.[14]

The boundaries of reciprocity and solidarity among users of microfinance have already been documented by Shakya and Rankin (2008), who observed the contradiction underlying the solidarity-based group where members have to make sure that other members use loans properly, which reduces the space for solidarity and sometimes exacerbates inequality within the group. Similar conclusions were reached by Smets and Bähre (2004). Rahman (1999) analyzed the power relationships that appear within solidarity-based groups and between clients and officials of microfinance organizations.

In order to better understand the social dynamics in which the microfinance institutions take place, it helps to document the processes through which users turn to their social networks to have access to services. To do so, we must pay attention to the ways in which they weigh the commitments implied, the social arrangements they become involved in, the risks they anticipate, and the way they try to prevent them, especially in situations of over-indebtedness and in a scenario of economic crisis that has an impact on household incomes and their repayment capability.

And just like microfinance institutions put into practice different strategies to increase their levels of reliability and financial efficiency, their users try to find ways to get around certain restrictions and have access to credit.

Examples of the above are the practices that emerge when faced with growing difficulty in finding a co-signer. In both regions, willingness to co-sign is limited to family networks. If an applicant is not part of the family group or deemed unreliable, and overt refusal to become a co-signer may have a negative effect on relationships between neighbors, people make up pretexts to avoid giving their signature, or, once given, find excuses to withdraw it.

Another occurrence that has become common among micro-bank members in the south of Oaxaca is that applicants reward the support of their co-signers by paying the equivalent of a day's wages, because it is understood that they neglected their job to go with them to sign the contract. Some applicants at least cover their co-signer's travel to the microfinance institution office and offer a meal. Another arrangement is for the member to share the loan with the co-signer.

According to microfinance operators, these practices occur because "people believe that they are doing the other member a favor. We tell them 'it's not a favor that you are doing to the other person. It is an obligation. You are accepting to pay if she does not'".[15] In this respect, members attach a special meaning to being a co-signer, independent of what they are told by the micro-bank officials. By drawing on trust and reciprocity to ensure repayment of loans, the cultural meanings and the social and economic appreciations interwoven within those bonds are being overlooked. In the context of local meanings, being a co-signer is a favor and implies a greater burden of obligation, with reciprocity being expressed immediately. The money is a show of gratitude for help in securing the loan and a way to compensate the effort involved in interrupting domestic chores, taking time off from work, or making the trip from a distant place to the microfinance office.

The limits between "money juggling" and over-indebtedness

One of the strategies that people resort to in order to subsist is to "juggle" money,[16] and this becomes more visible when we study their financial practices. There is no shortage of examples of how people constantly make use of a combination of information on terms, interest, and amounts, develop skills that make funds more available to them, and somehow start gauging how far they can go into debt.

These mechanisms have been referred to by other authors as "debt recycling" (Rahman, 1999), "loan exchange" (Shakya and Rankin, 2008), "chains of indebtedness" or "debt circulation" (Zanotelli, 2004). In this study we identified as a very common practice, the recycling of debt using several credit sources.[17] The following cases illustrate this.

Rosa is a member of the two *cajas* in El Chante. She took a loan for 7,000 pesos from CPSMG. The branch manager (Pati) made a payment plan of 80 pesos a week, so Rosa would pay the loan in 36 months. Rosa applied for that loan to invest in her food stand business but she used most of it to pay another debt with the *Caja Solidaria* (CS) and kept the rest to pay the electricity and telephone bills. She uses debt to cover her everyday expenses because, according to her, her food stand is not profitable and she uses her income from it to pay only the minimum expenses at home.

Aída, another woman from El Chante, is a member of CSMG and CS. With her meager income, she has taken out several loans from the *cajas* and from the municipality of Autlán to buy a water reservoir and construction materials to make improvements on her house.

Aída administers the loans from one *caja* as the others approach their due date, but sometimes the payments due overlap with the need to buy gas and corn to make *tortillas,* or to feed the chickens that she will later butcher to sell. Sometimes she has had to give preference to these expenses, because she knows that her continued income depends on them. Of her troubles to make ends meet she says:

> I got a big loan (12,000 pesos, from CPSMG) that I did not finish paying because I bought a ton of corn for 3,000 pesos. I wanted to fill all my reservoirs to be on the safe side when the rains come. I do that every year. My brother told me that he would sell it to me at a good price, that he would bring it here packed and all that. I had to take that opportunity ... and that's why sometimes you don't have money to pay.... The payment was for almost 1,700. I had saved some money, and looking here and there I completed the payment.... This lady lent me 1,200 ... I got a loan for 500 and completed the 1,700.
>
> (Interview with Aída, April 28, 2009)

It is very important for Aída to be regarded as a respectable person, and one of the ways that she makes sure of this is, as she says, to pay her debts. She challenges the interviewer: "Go ask Pati Corona, who is in charge of the *Popular* (CPSMG), if I have ever failed to pay or been late in paying. Never, until now, as long as I have been a member!"

In the decisions and the calculations these women make, there is a combination of financial information (regarding normal or default interest rates and raw material costs in times of growth or shortage), the need for fresh money to momentarily relieve their household finances, reliance on their social networks, and a concern to preserve their good reputation (for more on this topic, see the chapter by Guerin *et al.*, in this volume). Further examples of this are the remarks made by Julia,[18] who is also a member of the two *cajas populares* in

El Chante. When she sometimes gets "deep in debt",[19] she borrows from the other *Caja* and covers her payments. If Julia owes money to both *cajas*, as happened recently when she had 6,000 pesos left to pay CPSMG, she knew she would have to pay them in three or four months. Knowing that in that time she would not be able to ask anyone to help her, she asked Raquel, her immediate superior at the delegation,[20] and she paid off her debt. Raquel, in turn, took this money from funds that she knew she would not have to account for in the following months. Thus, Julia was able to cover her debt with CPSMG; she applied for a new loan, and paid Raquel. "The thing," says Julia, "is to go around, and not to let anyone down."[21]

"Not to let anybody down," implies paying debts on time or making payments, explaining whatever trouble they are having, and negotiating new terms. This shows that the person is responsible for his or her debts and takes care of the debt relationship, and just as they ask neighbors for small loans, they also lend to others according to their financial capacity (see also Morvant-Roux, this volume). However, they are more cautious when asked to be co-signers for microfinance organizations. In these cases, their support is restricted to their families, and only in special cases to someone in town that they consider trustworthy.

The fact that clients borrow from one source of credit and then from another is a reality that microfinance organizations have to deal with every day. According to the data provided by Cooperativa SIFRA, 60 percent of their members also belong to of one of the larger *cajas* (CPSMG or Agustín de Iturbide or Cristóbal Colón), 25 percent are members of CS, and only for the remaining 15 percent is SIFRA their only option.

A variation of this debt recycling is the participation of a person who gets a new loan, which is then used to pay the debts of another member of the family. The source of credit may be the *caja* or the microfinance organization to which they already owe money, a new organization, or a local moneylender. As one of the CPSMG members describes it: "She borrows, owes, he borrows (her husband) to pay her debt, and that's how we go around."[22]

According to the directors of the microfinance institutions, this "going around" is a widespread practice nowadays, as a result of the excessive offer of credit and the members' lack of loyalty toward the organizations that have operated in the region for decades. According to the same source, if in the past it was difficult to live with a certain level of debt, in the context of the current economic crisis, the cases of indebtedness have multiplied. Faced with this situation, microfinance organizations are being more cautious when they analyze their members' capacity for indebtedness and are adopting more drastic measures to recover overdue loans; as Armando, manager of CPSMG El Grullo, explains:

> Yes, they lived in debt, they paid a loan and asked for another one, in a revolving fashion, and this is how they bought a piece of land to build their home, then they added a room, then another, the roof.... The problem is that they began to go into further debt with a *caja*, then they went with others....

Now there is terrible over-indebtedness going on and well, there have been cases in which they have been paying people to be co-signers … because the pressure forces them to cover the member's debt.

(Interview with Armando Curiel, April 29, 2009)

The inability to pay off overdue loans affects the member and the members of his or her social network because if a client fails to pay, the microfinance institution goes to his or her co-signer.

Demanding payment from the debtor through legal means or making the co-signers pay means (to the manager) that they "are distorting the relationship between the *caja* and its members." The distortions mentioned refer to the loss of that loyalty or the mutual distrust expressed between clients and organizations, and the wariness among the population when someone asks them to be a co-signer. In this sense, over-indebtedness involves not only the breach of a financial or monetary commitment between debtors and creditors, but also the reconfiguration of social relationships that were long based on trust and credibility. Thus the meanings assigned to the local categories of debt, guarantor and collateral – as Johnson discusses in this same volume – clash with what these terms mean for the microfinance institutions and the laws that govern them.

Crossing the line with "money juggling," and falling into a web of debt and being unable to get out, has to do with the excessive offer of services, the lack of loyalty toward the organizations and institutions, and also borrowing more than a person or a family can handle. But which are the processes through which that fragile equilibrium is broken and lead to the inability to pay the debts, and what role does each of the actors play in them? How is over-indebtedness perceived by clients and their peers, and by microfinance operators, and what sort of social responses do these situations bring about? I will try to answer these questions in the rest of this paper.

Over-indebtedness: different frameworks of calculability

Microfinance organizations base their reasoning, calculations, and processes on a definition of over-indebtedness centered on economic criteria, judging that these are situations where debt is greater than the client's income (ASPEC, 2009). Based on that, they usually handle levels of over-indebtedness according to partial or total non-compliance of payments, although there can be various levels of tolerance in the assessment of delay in payment.

In their work to deal with this problem, it becomes clear that their concern is based on this definition, which privileges arithmetic and the monetary aspect, and pushes aside whatever is in the way of their recovery goals: a long-term relationship with a client, or even the social bonds that exist within a group. According to Villarreal (2009: 135), we are dealing here with frameworks of calculability such as those "in which certain processes are enabled or disabled, with margins from which to make interpretations and the tools available to make them," where "identity differentiation acquires predominance," and within it "considerations of gender, ethnicity, generation, and social class."

Thus, the practices with which microfinance organizations face over-indebtedness from a position imbued with authority include: warning and educating their clients so they will not fall into non-compliance, not lending more than a certain amount of money, based on calculations of income/expenses of a person or a family, and the indebtedness margin recommended by experts on these topics. As Natalia, the manager of a microfinance organization in the south of Oaxaca explains, they base their work on:

> all the information that they [the clients] give us. For instance, a schoolteacher makes 9,500 pesos. That is his only source of income. He has two daughters in secondary school. He makes a list of his expenses, the most common in these cases: leisure, food, cell phone, payment of other debts, transportation, etc. Thus, his total expenses are deducted from his income, and from that net balance we calculate that 35 per cent is the payment capacity that person would have on a monthly basis, and based on that we establish the amount of the loan we can give him. Even if he applies for a 20,000 pesos loan, he will only be lent 10,000 because that is as much as he will be able to pay.

From this, we could deduce that one of the problems that requires an intervention is the fact that the members do not have the elements to determine their indebtedness capacity, that some economic rationale is absent from their management of their finances, that they are people who "mismanage"[23] their money, and that this is the reason why it is important to inculcate this financial education in members.

On the other hand, when we find out about the lives of clients who owe large amounts of money, we run into situations of great precariousness in which the financial decisions made have to do with the search of prosperity and wellbeing on the one hand, and, on the other hand, with investments in very high risk enterprises with which they sought to diversify their livelihood. As I will elaborate below, borrowing so their offspring may travel to the USA, pay a *coyote* (a guide who helps people cross the border illegally), and find a job there is a project that mixes aspirations for a better job and a higher social status, not only for the person leaving, but for the whole family. The same can be said of the improvements they make to their house. This enterprise combines the pursuit of a greater social valuation of the family and a reduction of its vulnerability. These are the kind of considerations that come into play in their decisions.

In contrast to what has been said about managers, program operators recognize that they have contributed to their clients' indebtedness, as remarked by Evaristo, who is in charge of an office of one of the microfinance organizations that operate in the Sierra Sur region of Oaxaca:

> in trying to help them we made them go into debt. We thought we were giving them support, but now with the courses we are taking we understand

that we did not do the right thing, because people applied for loans and we granted them without taking into account the fact that their only income is their wage as farm workers.[24]

In the region of the Loxichas he identifies a concentration of cases of over-indebtedness in two communities, and tells the story of how several of its members borrowed money so that their children could go to find work in the USA. However, when their children were unable to cross the border, they had to turn back and the parents were already in debt.

But reducing the loans to what the microfinance organization considers to be their indebtedness capacity does not solve the problem of indebtedness either, because once clients do not receive the expected loan, they go to another microfinance institution or moneylender who will lend them a little more.

And while one sector increases its market by inducing the indebtedness of its clients, others deploy measures to control delinquency. With this last purpose, one of the tasks that occupies most of the micro-banks' staff time is assessing their clients' financial strength.

Another major task is payment collection. From a few days before repayment is due, the staff conduct a preventive collection with every client. If the client fails to pay, he or she will receive numerous visits and his or her co-signers will be visited too, until the debt is repaid.

In the initial study, an aspect that is paid great attention to is the family links between the applicant and his or her co-signers. The more distant the link, the fewer objections will be raised by decision makers. The same criterion applies with a group.

All of the above, which from the point of view of a microfinance manual might look like a lesson to clients, is not exempt from complications if we take into account that the mutual help and commitment networks that operate under specific circumstances, are not activated in the same way in the financial and the economic spheres, and are frequently circumscribed to the network of kinship. Therefore, it is understandable that, when a group's interest is centered on obtaining a loan, it will be more likely to make sure that everyone pays than to help one other (when someone is in trouble) to repay a member's debt. For closer analysis, in the next section I will show some examples of women with large debts to the microfinance organizations. As I analyze them, I will show the ways in which the organizations encourage this indebtedness. In the case of the clients, decisions are, in many ways, made in a context of uncertainty and investment in high-risk projects that are supposed to allow them to obtain resources to overcome precarious life situations.

The economic and social costs of over-indebtedness

For a microfinance organization there are a number of costs if over-indebtedness rises too sharply. In the case of Mexican MF organizations in the process of being regulated, levels of repayment delays affect the appraisal given by the overseeing organization. If the microfinance organization does not obtain a good grade, it will not have access to certain governmental subsidies and support that, in turn, allows it to offer lower interest loans to its clients. The member-client ultimately bears the brunt of these high costs, because the microfinance organization must cover them with the differential between the active rate and the passive rate. The members must pay the normal interest rate, which is on average 3 percent a month, as well as the default interest, which ranges from 5 to 6 percent a month.

There is a moral and social cost to over-indebtedness that especially affects clients with a good credit history. One consequence is losing their membership. Once they have paid what they owe to the microfinance organization they are excluded, and their relationship with microfinance operators deteriorates. Trust is lost, not just because the members have not fulfilled their obligations, but also because they are often treated with disrespect by the officials who visit them.

Several testimonials by women members of a microfinance organization in the south of Oaxaca highlight this. One such woman is Luz María, who lives in Tamazulapa, south of Miahuatlán, and who shows concern about the threatening attitude of promoters. She and her husband owe money to several microfinance organizations and a private moneylender. She says that once, in order to pressure her, a manager told her that the collateral she had left at the microfinance office had been lost; she also told me that another representative had recently threatened to send her to prison, and that she had been abused by the employees in the branch office.

The financial and economic crisis in the USA. has had a negative effect on some people's practices and is the source of people's inability to pay in some cases. Some families have covered the loss of money remittances from the USA. with loans, as has Rosalba Silva from Miahuatlán, who was used to borrowing money from the micro-bank for her shoe sale business, but used most of her last loan to cover household costs.

There is also Luci, in El Chante, who borrowed 3,000 pesos from the *caja* so that her brother could give their mother the money that he sends her every month. In both cases, migrant workers had temporally cut off their remittances.

However, some cases are harder to handle because the amount owed is very large, because the migrant workers have not been able to find jobs, or because the money borrowed was used to finance an unsuccessful crossing of the border and all that the family had in the end was the debt.

An example of this is Celedonia, an indigenous woman who lives in Xitla, 20 kilometers from Miahuatlán. Although she is close to the region's largest urban center, Celedonia barely speaks Spanish, and reads and writes at a rudimentary level. She has the subordinate status and social disadvantages of indigenous Oaxacan women in general, which is the group with the highest level of illiteracy and the lowest level of schooling in the region (Reyes and Gijón, 2007). Indigenous women live their lives in the social isolation of the household. Cultural norms perpetrate gender inequalities, even in terms of sexuality and birth control (Becerril, 2004). According to official figures, only 46.4 percent of indigenous women of reproductive age use any kind of birth control method; this percentage is equal to the average national rate 25 years ago, and is 40 percent lower than the current rate among non-indigenous women.

This obliviousness of their rights and how to exercise them, together with their limited participation in the social and political life of their communities, is rooted in enduring gender ideologies that are part of the uses, customs and discourses that uphold ancestral traditions (Sierra, 2009).

Her limitations notwithstanding, this is the first time she has fallen behind and been late with her payments, and her debts grow as the days go by. She owes the microfinance organization 50,000 pesos, another 50,000 to Caja Popular Mexicana (CPM), and 64,000 to several local moneylenders, a disproportionate amount for a woman who scrapes a living from making clothes and small repairs to clothes for her neighbors. Her husband weaves baskets, with the help of their younger son, but the real sustenance of the family is the money their offspring send them from the United States. However, with that country's economy in crisis, they haven't been able to send her enough to pay the debt the family incurred to pay for their trip there.

At the CPM she borrowed so her two daughters could migrate, because the *coyote* charges 35,000 pesos for each person he gets into the United States. Then she got into debt with local moneylenders so her two sons and the wife of one of them could go. She borrowed 50,000 pesos from the microfinance organization, which she used to cover part of her debt to the local lenders, who charge an interest rate of 10 percent a month.

Her sons are unable to send her money because they have not found full-time employment. They only work for a few days, or a few hours a day, making barely enough to support themselves.

Both at the CPM and at the other microfinance organization, Celedonia left deeds as collateral. However, the pressure on her from their employees has been unrelenting. What annoys her most, she says, is that officials from the microfinance organization go to her house and yell at her, so that her neighbors cannot help but notice their constant visits. With so many of these visits – all from men – she feels ashamed because the workers who are repairing the street have been asking what those people want with her. She also says that the last time they came one of them – Herminio, the "short guy" – yelled at her: "Why do you lie to me? Why do you say you are good at paying when you're not?". "Yes," she says, remembering her response, "I lied to you but I am going to pay."[25]

Moreover, the last time Isidro went to her house, before the interview, he went alone and, without waiting for Celedonia to come to the door, he went straight to the kitchen, where she was. According to custom among indigenous people, this is not considered appropriate because it implies a personal contact with someone who is not related. He should have knocked hard on the front door and waited for Celedonia to come to the door. That incident made her feel uncomfortable and ashamed.

Situations of over-indebtedness and an analysis of what takes place in them allow us to appreciate the conflict between social and economic aims usually associated with microfinance programs. Microfinance organizations seek, by different means, to get the client-members to pay their debts, but they overlook the personal and family conflicts that these collection procedures generate, or disregard their effects in their effort to get their money back.

In my research in southern Oaxaca I documented another case in which the practices of the microfinance organization damaged interpersonal relationships among several members of the group and disempowered the debtor client-member, as a consequence of the pressure exerted to get her to pay.

Aristea is one of the founding members of the microfinance group. Before joining the group she received several loans, which she used to buy wax and other supplies to produce candles. Sometimes she needed money, and if she already had a credit she refinanced it. Thanks to her good compliance, she says, she would go to the *caja* and if she owed 2,000 pesos they lent her 5,000 more, which she would use to pay the 2,000 she owed and keep the remaining 3,000 for the supplies she needed.

The solidarity group got a loan of 15,000 pesos each. For the women it was a difficult experience and none of them was able to make their payments on time. The type of loan they were granted stated that the women would pay only the interest in monthly installments, and 100 percent (of the capital) on the date the loan was due. This sort of loan is the one usually managed in rural areas, given that farmers have a seasonal income, by which they sell their crops and then they schedule the payments. However, this is not possible for urban families that depend on trade or fixed monthly incomes.

From this group, it was Aristea who had the most problems in covering her debt to the microfinance organization. Before she was able to do it, she got into further debt with other credit providers. She went to the BASS microfinance organization, where they demanded she pay the debt of another client for whom she had been a co-signer. In order to pay that debt, she went to a moneylender who lent her 5,000 pesos. With that money and her own savings she paid off her debt at Elektra, where they lent her 7,500 more. She used this money to pay the 3,800 pesos that her co-signer owed BASS, and put the rest in her savings account so she could borrow 15,000 pesos. Finally, with this money, she paid the micro-bank. Added to the stress generated by the obstacles she had to overcome with the credit providers, Aristea was disappointed by her group's attitude in allying themselves with the staff of the micro-bank to exert pressure on her and her family. Her fellow group members, all of them women, explained in turn that it was their duty to demand that she pay or to take further coercive measures to this end. They decided, on the advice of the microfinance organization's staff, to speak with her husband and sons so they "would take matters into their own hands."

For Aristea, her fellow group members' alliance with the microfinance organization amounted to a restricted or denied reciprocity, besides the fact that involving her family would imply a loss of ground in the autonomy she had gained since, against her husband's opinion, she had decided to borrow money and therefore had to take responsibility for her debts. The group chose not to resort to Andrea's parents, although the threat of them doing so was another factor of stress.

These narratives contribute to a reflection on the convenience of taking into account the various dimensions where the exercise of the power existing in the relationships between clients and microfinance operators has implications, as well as the lack of appreciation of the social, political, and economic limitations faced by women in this kind of situation.

Finally, I would like to say a few words on what these cases teach us about over-indebtedness. The story told by Aristea reflects the way in which she dealt with her debts until the balance in her "juggling" was broken. Three elements played a key role in that lapse: (1), she got into debt for higher amounts that she had handled before. Furthermore, the conditions for the term of payment were not those she was used to: she was required to pay the full amount in one payment; (2), having obtained a housing loan at the micro-bank, she was not able to obtain the regular loan she applied for to work in her candle manufacture and sale business; that is, her income decreased because she had fewer raw materials; and (3), she had to cover unexpected medical expenses to take care of her mother, who lives with her.

All of this shows, following Guérin *et al.* (2010) in her study on financial vulnerability, the presence of two critical events (a reduced income and her mother's disease) and, on the other hand, an inadequate management of the credit terms by the microfinance organization regarding the amount of money lent and the term for payment.

As for Celedonia (and also following Guérin *et al.*, 2010) going into debt with several creditors to finance her children's journeys to the USA is indicative of an effort to widen her sources of livelihood, and in this respect migration to that country in search of employment is a very high-risk enterprise for the family. Not having obtained the jobs and the income expected, there is no flow of remittances as there had once been, and she has fallen into over-indebtedness. Celedonia owes 165,000 pesos to several microfinance organizations and local moneylenders.

Conclusions

Microfinance programs have economic and social impacts, the former pertaining to their offer of means to improve the livelihoods of the people, families, groups, and towns where they operate. Their social impact concerns the linkages, solidarity, and mutual support among users they foster. Their economic impact has received the most attention in research, while the social question has usually been taken for granted. In practice, trust and reciprocal solidarity have been taken as social commodities to be put to the service of financial goals and objectives, as we have highlighted in the practices and discourse of certain microfinance institutions. The financial and economic crisis has put microfinance organizations, and those using their services to deal with this environment, to the test, highlighting the problems and limitations of their strategies. Organizations have boosted their risk-control procedures, amongst others, by checking their clients' indebtedness capacities more thoroughly, gathering information on the ground, and screening both applicants and their co-signers in person. If possible, they access information from the credit bureau. Loan issuing organizations are boosting their loss prevention due to non-compliance with both mortgage collateral – which is more common in *cajas populares* – and social collateral. They are also resorting to strategies ranging from preventive collection prior to due dates, to putting peer pressure on clients and their co-signers if there are delays, and legal procedures if needs be. Such work so far appears to have been on the right track from a financial point of view, but socially, such practices are of dubious benefit. This chapter has highlighted these points by underlining the practices and social meanings inherent to how people come to own, take care of, or use certain resources as an exchangeable commodity in order to make a profit by their own calculations.

Microfinance organizations seem to be using the language of trust and mutual support relationships when they issue loans in a bid to ensure the money they are owed is paid back.

Just as trust and solidarity are assessed in those terms, users are also weighing up others more carefully, which has in turn affected the boundaries and circuits they operate within, changing the meaning of solidarity, kinship bonds, or neighborhood according to circumstances and the individual. Practices such as exchanging signatures for money highlights the difference made between help and favor, and the cultural meanings attached to them. Since being a co-signer is seen as a doing a favor, there is a greater reciprocal burden of obligation, which means the recipient shows gratitude by paying money in exchange for the help in securing the loan. Can such programs really generate social synergies? On the other hand, we should not rush to view them as negative, but should see them more as just another way people use to try and get around obstacles to credit and to creatively deal with everyday difficulties.

Another mechanism I have discussed is "money juggling," and when it leads to over-indebtedness. "Money juggling" goes against credit providers' ideas of what constitutes healthy finances; over-indebtedness is frequently seen as the outcome of careless spending and mismanagement due to a lack of a financial education or an excessive microfinance offer. From what I have discussed here, my conclusion is that over-indebtedness also stems from the policies and practices of microfinance organizations, in which clients make choices based on the limited information they have access to, when facing critical events in their families.

The social implications of over-indebtedness are the outcome of debt collection instrumentalizing and strengthening the organization of solidarity-based groups, which in turn put pressure on individual clients. This leads to women being stigmatized as slow in paying, losing their membership in the group and microfinance organization, and then losing power and prestige within the family and the community.

Although the micro-bank of Miahuatlán has done some very significant work with indigenous communities and has taken pains to employ local people to work with them, most of its employees are male and this is key to the cultural context and gender relationships in the families and communities they work with. A careful analysis of local perceptions of the procedures used, and their consequences for women, is needed.

The social costs appear to be higher for indigenous women than for non-indigenous women and the rest of the population, because indigenous women have fewer financial and non-financial resources. The disrespectful and discriminatory treatment of microfinance officers towards indebted indigenous women is part of a wider context of social and cultural devaluation that these women have historically endured. Microfinance institutions are unwittingly contributing to reproducing and reinforcing these conditions. Officials' hectic day-to-day duties prevent them from doing any more than reviewing loan placement and portfolio recovery statistics and coverage targets. Trying to combine such tasks with any kind of empowerment of the population would require them to reflect much more critically on the extent to which, and how, their actions serve to modify power relations between creditors and their families, groups, and communities, and among the microfinance institutions and their representatives themselves. In this regard, there is still a long way to go.

Notes

1 Natalia, regional manager of the MB, July 16, 2009.
2 Caja Popular Cristóbal Colón, Caja Solidaria, (CPSMG) and Caja Agustín de Iturbide; the Cooperativas SIFRA, an agency of Financiera Rural, Unidad Dispersora de Crédito, and farmer organizations dependent of the Partido Revolucionario Institucional like the Confederación Nacional Campesina (CNC) and the Confederación Nacional de Propietarios Rurales (CNPR), both formed by sugarcane workers.
3 Data obtained in 2007.
4 Between February and August 2009, the average exchange rate was 13.3 pesos for one dollar.
5 Loans to be used for commercial, agricultural, industry, and services activities.
6 These estimations are based on the 2009 report of the CSMG.
7 In the state of Oaxaca there are 350 credit organizations, whereas in the whole state of Jalisco there are 40 organizations.
8 CONOAX Familiar, Resplandor Internacional, Cooperativa ACREIMEX, SERFIOAX, Enlace Popular, Caja Popular del Sureste, Caja Popular Mexicana, SOFIPA, SEFILAT, Grupo Financiero BASS, CREBAINP, Desarrollo Empresarial Familiar, Sin Límites, COHIM, Banco Compartamos, MicroBanco Liis Mi, and The Unión de Crédito de la Coordinadora Estatal de Productores de Café (UCEPCO).
9 Natalia, regional manager of the micro-bank, July 16, 2009.
10 If it is a solidarity-based group loan, the top amount is 15,000 pesos, and if it is an individual one up to 50,000 pesos.
11 Manager of Unión de Crédito de la Coordinadora Estatal de Productores de Café de Oaxaca (UCEPCO).
12 *Compadre* relationships are established between the parents and the godfather and/or godmother of a child who is baptized, gets married, or even dies, in some indigenous communities. They create "bonds of indirect kinship through which a flow of goods and services is established among participants" (Gascón 2005: 192).
13 The *Guelaguetza* is a practice in indigenous towns in Oaxaca, which consists in mutual help based on a favor received, such as the help received to cover the funeral expenses of a family member; the beneficiary will pay that help back to each one of the people who provided it.

14 Interview with Yolanda Resendes, August 24, 2009.
15 Interview with Flor, August 20, 2009.
16 In the Mexican context, a more colloquial term to refer to these practices is to "ride" (*"jinetear"*) the money.
17 See also other papers in this volume (Hummel, Morvant-Roux, Villarreal, and Wampfler *et al.*).
18 Julia is a widow with three grown up children who lives in El Chante, Jalisco, and works as a janitor in the delegation's office, earning a meager wage (2,200 pesos a month). Unlike many of her neighbors, she at least has a steady job.
19 For her, "getting deep in debt" (*endrogarse*) means having to pay at the same time services, the telephone and the power bill, the *caja* payment, the loan's interest, the interest of the loan at the other *caja popular*, payment to her suppliers because she sells beauty products, and payment to the grocer who sells her groceries on credit. All told, it is almost 3,000 pesos more than she makes in her job.
20 The delegation is a local office that represents the powers of the municipal government. It performs several tasks, such as delivering information on several social programs, managing public construction, being responsible for cleaning the public spaces in town, granting permissions to throw parties in open spaces, and collecting fees for the water provided by the municipality.
21 Field diary with Julia, February 14, 2009.
22 Field diary, March 5, 2009.
23 "They drowned themselves through mismanagement," a manager of a microfinance organization in Oaxaca said about some clients with very large debts.
24 Field diary, July 17, 2009.
25 Celedonia García, July 18, 2009.

References

Alpízar Carlos A. and Claudio González-Vega (2006) *El sector de las microfinanzas en México.* USAID. Programa Finanzas Rurales, The Ohio State University. Available online at: www.microlinks.org/.../Mexico.InformeMicrofinanzas.pdf (accessed 2 November 2009).

ASPEC (2009) *Crédito y sobreendeudamiento de los consumidores en el Perú Investigación para el Grupo Andino de Consumidores,* available online at: www.consumidoresandinos.com/documentos/campanas/4/estudios/sobreendeudamientoperu.pdf (accessed 10 August 2010).

Ballescá, Mónica (2012) "La presencia del microcrédito en México. Una aproximación empírica desde la perspectiva de la pobreza", in Villarreal, Martínez Magdalena and Angulo Salazar, Lourdes (eds) *Las microfinanzas en los intersticios del desarrollo. Cálculos, normatividades y malabarismos,* Guadalajara: CIESAS-UPN-FOJAL, pp. 171–197.

Becerril, Albarrán Nahela (2004) "¿Microempresa familiar o familias en la microempresa social? El caso del Programa Mujeres en el Desarrollo Rural en Oaxaca", in Suárez, Blanca and Bonfil, Paloma *Entre el corazón y la necesidad. Microempresas familiares en el medio rural,* Serie PEMSA, GIMTRAP, México: DF, pp. 71–128.

Conde Bonfil, Carola (2001) *¿Depósitos o puerquitos? Las decisiones de ahorro en México,* El Colegio Mexiquense-La Colmena Millonaria, México.

Conde Bonfil, Carola (2005) *Instituciones e instrumentos de las microfinanzas en México. Definamos términos,* El Colegio Mexiquense, Zinacantepec.

Conde Bonfil, Carola (2008) "Potencial de las microfinanzas", in Gonzáles, Butrón, Arcelia, María, and Conde Bonfil, Carola (eds) *Finanzas populares y desarrollo local,*

Universidad Michoacana de San Nicolás de Hidalgo – Consejo Estatal de Ciencia y Tecnología – Centro Michoacano de Investigación y Formación "Vasco de Quiroga", Morelia, pp. 93–111.

CONDUSEF (2010) *Supervisión de las SOFOMES … ¿quién la hace?*, available online at: www.condusef.gob.mx/index.php/2010/1075-supervision-de-las-sofomes-iquien-la-hace (accessed 11 December 2010).

CPSMG (2009) *Convención Nacional 2009. Informe de actividades*, El Grullo: CPSMG.

Dash, Anup (2003) "Strategies for poverty alleviation in India: CYSD's holistic approach to empowerment through the self-help group model," *IDS Bulletin* 34 (4): 133–142.

Gascón, Jorge (2005) "Compadrazgo y cambio en el Altiplano peruano", *Revista Española de Antropología Americana* 35:191–206.

González, Adrián and González-Vega, Claudio (2003) *Sobreendeudamiento en las microfinanzas bolivianas, 1997–2001*, Rural Finance Program, The Ohio State University. USAID, available online at: www.portalmicrofinanzas.org/gm/document1.9.36019/Sobreendeudamiento%20en%20las%20micr.pdf (accessed 3 November 2009).

Guérin, Isabelle, Roesch, Marc, Kumar, Santosh, and Venkatasubramanian, Mariam Sangare (2010) *Microfinance and the Dynamics of Financial Vulnerability. Lessons from Rural South India*, RUME Working Paper, available online at: www.rume-rural-microfinance.org (accessed 10 July 2011).

INEGI (2010) *Censo de Población y Vivienda*, available online at: www.inegi.org.mx/est/contenidos/proyectos/ccpv/cpv2010/Default.aspx (accessed 3 November 2009).

Morduch, Jonathan (1999) "The Microfinance Promise", *Journal of Economic Literature* 37(4): 1569–1614.

ProDesarrollo (2009) *Benchmarking de las microfinanzas en México: Un informe del sector*, available online at: www.prodesarrollo.org/benchmarking (accessed 10 July 2011).

ProDesarrollo (2006) *Benchmarking de las microfinanzas en México:Desempeño y transparencia en una industria creciente*, available online at: www.portalmicrofinanzas.org/gm/document-1.9.36325/Benchmarking/microfinan.pdf (accessed 20 August 2010).

Raczynki, D. and Serrano, C. (2005) "Programa de superación de la pobreza y el capital social. Evidencias y aprendizajes de la experiencia en Chile", in Arriagada, Irma (ed.) *Aprender de la experiencia. El capital social en la superación de la pobreza*, CEPAL/Cooperazione Italiana, pp. 99–132.

Rahman, Aminur (1999) "Micro-credit initiatives for equitable and sustainable development: who pays?", *World Development* 27(1): 67–82.

Reyes Morales, G. Rafael and Alicia Sylvia Gijón Cruz (2005) Vulnerabilidad social de las mujeres y la población indígena en Oaxaca, 2005: restricciones y estrategias *Liminar. Estudios Sociales y Humanísticos*, V(2): 90–107.

Shakya, Yogendra B. and Rankin, Katharine N. (2008) "The politics of subversion in development practice: an exploration of microfinance in Nepal and Vietnam", *Journal of Development Studies* 44(8): 1214–1235.

Sierra, María Teresa (2009) "Las mujeres indígenas ante la justicia comunitaria Perspectivas desde la interculturalidad y los derechos", *Desacatos* 31: 73–88.

Smets Peer and Bähre, Erik (2004) "When coercion takes over: the limits of social capital in microfinance schemes", in Lont, H. and Hospes, O. (eds) *Livelihood and Microfinance. Anthropological and Sociological Perspective on Savings and Debt*, Delft: Eburon, pp. 215–259.

Villarreal, Magdalena (2009) *Mujeres, Finanzas sociales y violencia económica en zonas marginadas de Guadalajara*, Guadalajara: Instituto Jalisciense de la Mujeres – Instituto Municipal de las Mujeres.

Zanotelli, Francesco (2004) "La circulación social de la deuda: códigos culturales y usura rural en Jalisco", in Villareal, Magdalena (ed.) *Antropología de la deuda. Crédito, Ahorro, fiado y prestado en las finanzas cotidianas*, Cámara de Diputados LIX Legislatura, México, DF: CIESAS – Miguel Ángel Porrúa Grupo, pp. 77–111.

Zapata, Gabriela (2004) "Community Savings Funds: Providing Access to Basic Financial Services in Marginalized Rural Areas of Mexico", *Journal of Microfinance*, 4(2): 163–187.

12 The commercialization of microcredits and local consumerism

Examples of over-indebtedness from indigenous Mexico[1]

Agatha Hummel

Introduction

This chapter will discuss the credit mechanisms and the selected impacts of one microfinance programme on the socioeconomic life of the rural community of Sukurán in mid-west Mexico. It will particularly highlight the processes by which over-indebtedness arises within the framework of local socioeconomic relations. Although microfinance programmes were intended to improve the socioeconomic situation of disadvantaged people, factors such as the commercialization of microcredit services and growing consumerism in local communities have proved to be significant obstacles. Both of those factors have led to chains of indebtedness that have brought about over-indebtedness and social conflict. It is important, however, to stress that microcredit alone does not cause over-indebtedness, but is one of a set of contributing factors in the local and global context of microfinance practice.

We will illustrate the impact of commercialization through an analysis of the high hidden costs of microcredits and of which clients are not informed. MFIs have been aggressive in penetrating the market and in the psychological and marketing techniques they apply to their staff and clients. These practices highlight that in the ongoing tensions between the economic and social value of microfinance, economic value is currently predominating. We will study microcredit's impact on the community in terms of the interrelationship between the local household economic logic governing women's businesses and some forms of local credits on the one hand, and the market economy and microcredit on the other. The rise of local consumerism is also a continual concern in this paper. This rise both stems from the market economy penetrating the local community, partly through microfinance ventures, and also itself causes over-indebtedness. We will show how these trends feed into local credit practices such as credit juggling.

Our methodological approach is one of drawing on our ethnographic case study of socioeconomic relations and microfinance as a development programme in the indigenous community of Sukurán, where the author lived for a total of 11 months during five visits carried out between 2007 and 2012. The village lies in the mountainous region of Meseta[2] Purhépecha in mid-west Mexico, where around 4,000 inhabitants live in the village, and a few thousand natives of the village live in the United States as immigrants. We have restricted our study of microfinance programmes to one community, and two microfinance organizations were chosen for our study, on the basis of their active penetration of the local market at the beginning of our research.

Rather than taking a top-down theoretical definition of over-indebtedness, we will define it here in terms of our ethnographic study of a community as a situation where credit fails to improve a borrower's socioeconomic situation, and the debt accumulated cannot be amortized through credit relations in the community or local economic resources (see also Morvant-Roux in this volume). Moreover, over-indebtedness cannot simply be defined as an absence of repayments to a microfinance institution. The ethnographic evidence indicates that debt is often repaid through fresh debt, and that one individual can be indebted to several sources (Zanotelli 2004, see also the majority of the chapters in this volume). Borrowers may repay their loans to microcredit institutions, but can still be indebted in other ways.

The local economy in the indigenous village of Sukurán

Sukurán is a strongly indigenous community whose inhabitants all speak the Purhépecha language. The community is active in holding traditional fiestas and other social activities of an indigenous origin. A local system of traditional authority, where the males of the community democratically elect their village representatives, still operates, despite strong political party and state institutional influences.

Conapo,[3] the National Population Council in Mexico, has rated the whole population of the state of Michoacán's degree of marginalization as high, which is also the case of the village we studied (Conapo 2005, 2010).

The village inhabitants have various means of making a living and sources of income. The community self-manages its forests on the agreement of the authorities. Until recently, timber from the exploitation of the forests was still used to produce boxes for avocado transportation, which until recent years were the main economic resource of the village.[4] Avocado growing accounts for the largest share of the Mexican economy, but the rapid decline of forestry resources, and growing local ecological awareness, has meant that a considerable amount of timber for avocado boxes is now imported from other regions, or recycled from old avocado trees. The production of wooden boxes has rapidly declined recently, however, owing to changes in the international export regulations favouring plastic over wooden containers.

The community is close to a young volcano, whose first and most recent eruption was in the 1940s. Recent decades have seen the rapid development of tourism and related services and facilities such as hostels, bungalows, restaurants and guided horse tours to the volcano and the lava-covered ruins of the village. Tourism is the second most important economic activity in the village, but this too has recently been hit by the global crisis. International and national tourists come much less than before and their purchasing power has weakened. Consequently, sales of local handicrafts, a very important source of income for women, have dropped and families' subsistence has been threatened.

Other than these main income sources, farming – mostly of corn – continues, but the land is chiefly farmed for personal use. Cheap imported groceries have flooded the local market, which (alongside capitalist rural policies) has made small-scale farming unprofitable. Women mainly carry out textile handicrafts, sewing and weaving parts of the traditional indigenous clothing that is still worn by most women every day. Textiles produced in the village are sold both within and outside the community. In Sukurán women, men or whole families all run many different productive initiatives, including small basic grocery stores, construction material hardware stores, stationery stores with traditional clothes and materials, butchers shops and a shop selling cellular phones.

The local economy is still largely centred on the household, defined by Gudeman and Rivera as a small-holding outside the margin of profit (1994: 69). A household has two functions: to "maintain", "sustain", "support", or "keep" itself, and to 'augment' or 'increase' its base[5] (1994: 39–40). The household is thus an important institution of the village economy. Within and between households, the economy is not governed by profit but functions by "reciprocity" (Mauss 1979). In contrast, the capitalist economy is governed by "calculative reason" (Sahlins 1976) or "formal rationality" (Weber 1978), and the corporation is its basic institution. "The corporation possesses capital and tries to make a profit on it..." (Gudeman and Rivera 1994: 11).

This distinction is crucial to our analysis, given two phenomena our research has highlighted. MFIs adhere to and promote the profit motive within the community, while women's economic initiatives chiefly function within the household and consequently follow household or reciprocity logic. For example, most of the community grocery stores do not make a profit, but function within the household as a base; as do many handicraft initiatives. The village has grocery stores on every corner, which may not seem viable on account of there being too great a number of identical businesses nearby, but to apply formal economic logic would not be appropriate. These shops, which are mostly run by women, are also product stocks for household use. There is neither bookkeeping nor profit evaluation, as these initiatives do not exist for profit.

The local economy is not exclusively ruled by the logic of reciprocity, however. Given the long history of exchange with the external market, the economy in Sukurán is a mix of the logic of reciprocity and calculative reason logic. As Gudeman would say, the capitalist economy is cascading or colonizing the realm of mutuality (2008: 84, 117). By cascading, Gudeman means the process in which "market participants, through the search for profit, extend their reach to non commoditized things and services, such as forest preserves and domestic work..." (Gudeman 2008: 19). MFIs as market agents facilitate this process through the profit and consumerist logic they bring.

Local credit practices

Informal credit practices are as popular in Sukurán as in the whole of rural Mexico. People use these mechanisms to handle everyday economic shortages (Villarreal 2004: 12–13). Credits may strengthen or strain social relations, or damage them when there is unpaid debt. They also confer obligations that can be experienced as a burden.

Sukurán has many forms of credit with different social meanings, depending on the situational context.[6] It is most common to borrow from a family member with, mostly, no interest rates. Nevertheless, this type of family credit is strongly embedded in social relations, which can be seen as a form of non-monetary interest. Local moneylenders issue larger sums, and local social discourse or rumour closely monitors such debts. These credits are very expensive (with monthly interest rates of over 10 per cent) and people often try to avoid or pay them back as quickly as possible, even if this means taking out a loan from another source. A more neutral and diversified, yet less common, form of loaning, is to borrow from friends and neighbours (community members with whom an individual has closer social relations). This form of credit does not usually include an interest rate and its social meaning is constructed differently in each situation. Receiving credit from a neighbour usually results in closer spatially defined relations – it strengthens the community of neighbours in the same *barrio*[7] or block of houses. Credits between friends also strengthen social relations, unless the debts go unpaid, which may then damage social ties.

Another form of loan is local grocery store credit (*fiado*). By offering goods on credit, shopkeepers test their social relations, strengthening links or breaking them with non-payers. This form of credit also helps shopkeepers to maintain a client base (see also Morvant-Roux in this volume). *Tandas* (Roscas) are also a common practice among village women and an important form of group-based credit, discussed in this volume by Francesco Zanotelli and in Hummel (2008).

Women are the major mediators of credit relations, both on their own behalf and as representatives of their families. This, among other things, is due to the fact that men shy away from showing what can be experienced as weakness or inferiority in relation to other people. Women are almost exclusively the clients of microfinance organizations: MFIs promote credit for women, and credit relations are usually a woman's niche. Women are not the only administrators of the money they borrow, however, and men often spend or invest microcredits in productive enterprises.[8]

Microcredits are seen as a popular alternative to all these local credit forms, as they help to avoid the degree of social embeddedness that local credit entails. In other words, people believe that microcredits can allow them to become indebted without engendering local social ties.

Microfinance in the community

Microfinance products include microcredits, saving options, life insurance and social and economic education. The clients, who are mostly women, have little demand for the microfinance offer other than credit, only buying insurance or saving because MFI workers persuade them. Economic and social education carried out through weekly talks from some credit officers, and the practice of credit uptake and repayment, is incidental and not at the direct request of the clients.

Our observations and the statements of interviewees indicate that only 10 to 20 per cent of microloans are invested in women's productive ventures, for grocery stores, handicrafts or catering. These make at best very little profit, however, and the microdebts have to be repaid from various different sources of income. Many microloans are wholly or partially passed on to the husbands of the MFIs' clients, so they can count on their help with debt repayment.[9]

There are around six to eight working microfinance institutions in Sukurán. Some organizations have withdrawn due to the unmanageable non-repayment rates they have helped create, while a few have joined the market in the hope of meeting their particular goals (making a profit or helping the poor). At the end of 2010, Compartamos Banco had 139 clients in eight solidarity groups in the community and the number was growing after a drop in 2009 caused by the beginnings of the financial crisis. Some MFIs have up to 13 groups in Sucurán. We estimate that around 50 per cent[10] of the women aged from 15 to 49 in the village belong to a microcredit group.

This article particularly focuses on the policy and practice of one of the microfinance institutions: Compartamos Banco, which is an extreme case of the commercialization of microfinance. The market performance of Compartamos Banco is, moreover, largely responsible for setting the microfinance market standards in Mexico. Although higher amounts are not unusual, Compartamos mostly issues microcredits of 500 to 10,000 pesos (US$50 to 1,000), to women in solidarity groups of around 15 members for an average sum of 3,000 pesos per person. Loans are issued for 16 weeks with weekly payments, and the advertised monthly interest rates are 3.5 to 4.5 per cent, depending on the group's history and the number of members.

Policy and practice of microfinance

Aminur Rahman argues that "the emphasis on financial sustainability by the donors compels development agencies to change their ethics, or at least it creates an internal tension between 'compassion and capitalism...'" (Rahman 2001: 150). Some MFIs, especially those like Compartamos, have turned the sustainability principle into a regular profit venture. Any MFIs wanting to work in a non-profitable sustainable way are eliminated from the market by the more aggressive microfinance banks. Microfinance commercialization began in the late 1980s, when the Grameen Bank experience showed that the poor are bankable and "for-profit investment institutions and opportunistic individuals began to sense the huge profit-making possibilities in microfinance, resulting in a flood of commercial funding moving into the microfinance sector from the late 1990s onward" (Bateman 2011: 3).

Compartamos Banco was created in 1990 as a Mexican NGO. Its approach to the poor was based on the charitable philosophy of Mother Teresa of Calcutta. Fifteen years later in June 2006, Financiera Compartamos was finally given the legal status of a commercial bank at the Ministry of Finance and Public Credit of Mexico and changed its name to Banco Compartamos SA, Multiple Banking Institution (Houghton *et al.* 2008). Banco Compartamos is currently one of the most profitable banks in Mexico.

The high hidden costs of microcredits

Interest rates are a good example of how Compartamos commercializes its products. Its workers advertise credits with 3.5 to 4.5 per cent monthly interest rates. Almost all of our interviewees said this was lower than local moneylender interest rates of 10 to 15 per cent monthly. Only some of the village's micro-credit clients we interviewed in the village, such as doña Eva, highlighted that the difference between the money she gets as a loan, and what she has to pay, is extremely high:

> It is not fair. They say the interest rate is 4 per cent, but every week I have to pay interest based on all the money I have borrowed [...]. Additionally I have to give a 10 per cent deposit at the beginning (which is not deducted from the loan and also charged with an interest rate) and each meeting I have to make some additional payments: a fee for being late, a collection for the trip of the women from the group who will go to the city to deposit the weekly payment, savings...

Eva views all of these expenses as the cost of credit, not to mention the time invested in participating in meetings and enforcing that credit is paid back. One brother of a microcredit client in Sukurán put it as follows:

> Women can't find a way to cover their debts any more. These [MFIs]] are economic triangles. They put poor people at the bottom and two or three rich people at the top. It is practically a new kind of slavery because the women have to work for them.

The high costs of microcredits are also being reported in other parts of the world. Lamia Karim writes that villagers in Bangladesh are calling for more humane loan terms (2008: 24) and Sian Lazar writes of a social movement of microcredit clients in Bolivia fighting for lower interest rates (2004: 314). In 2008 there were demonstrations by borrowers in the region of the village we studied.

Chuck Waterfield meanwhile discusses the phenomenon of hidden credit costs (2008), explaining step-by-step how from 4 per cent of an advertised monthly interest rate, Compartamos reaches an annual 129 per cent interest rate. The discourse of the Compartamos employees is so persuasive however, that the majority of women are unaware of the real cost of credit and believe that microcredits are a lot cheaper than moneylenders. It is important to bear in mind that the credit costs are relative, and the opinion of the debtors is based on local knowledge influenced by the rhetoric of the organization, rather than numerical calculations.

The microfinance organization's discourse on interest rates is one method for marketing the product, and also proof that microfinance is a business that uses manipulation to gain clients and increase its sales. Beyond such non-transparent interest rate calculations, Compartamos interest rates are surprisingly high in comparison to the average MFI credit cost, given clients' low income levels, and its business appears to be highly profitable. Over recent years Compartamos has generated around 50 per cent ROE (return on equity) (Canal Hernando and de Ovando 2007: 53, see also Harper 2011: 50) compared to the 14.9 per cent average ROE of financially self-sufficient MFIs in Latin America (LAC Large FSS) (MicroBanking 2009: 59). Despite this high profitability, it has not lowered it interest rates. In 2006, the net income of the bank was $57 million. In 2007, several members of the Board of Directors and of its staff became multimillion-aires. Compartamos currently makes extremely high profits that end up in the hands of its counsellors, directors and external shareholders (Houghton *et al.* 2008, see also Bateman 2011: 6; Harper 2011: 50–51).

Psychological and marketing techniques

This organizational logic is reproduced throughout its internal relations, which are designed to facilitate meeting its institutional targets. Compartamos has a highly developed corporate structure and marketing techniques, including its interest rate calculation. The company has set up programmes to train and motivate staff, as its success largely depends on the commitment and efficiency of the employees who have to fight competitors on the market. Employees are under constant pressure to increase the number of clients and loan renewals. On top of a basic salary of about 5,000 pesos (US$500), which is less then three times the minimum wage,[11] Compartamos staff earn commissions for new customers and renewals of existing credits. The regional office consists of two units of credit officers, each headed by a supervisor. Units have to constantly compete for results, which is intended to motivate employees and boost their results, but such motivation is based on pressure and stress. Some employees even look for ways to force their customers to purchase additional services in order to get their commission.

The office is full of visual signs of the commercial profile of Compartamos. The walls are covered with tables of the rankings of employees and their weekly and monthly scores, while a map shows the numbers of groups in the region's villages and some blank zones available for exploration. Once a month at their weekly meeting, regional scores are compared to the national ones and winners are selected. There are also incentives for the individual goal of being top employee in the office, or of the company as a whole. The stories of past out-standing results by Compartamos microfinance credit officers are played in short video clips, compiled into files and reported in an internal newspaper called "ComparTips", for distribution several times a year to staff members.

Compartamos also organizes "office Fridays", when staff members do not work in the field but go to the office to do their administration for the week and compile and present reports for the units' coordinators, who process and send them to the company's general administration department. Every Friday there are meetings of units during which the credit officers share their problems and study difficult cases. There is a lot of pressure to resolve problems quickly, and if one credit officer is unable to handle a problem, the whole team is sent into the field to work it out. Once a month, there is a workshop where a specific topic is discussed. These topics include "Service", "Responsibility", "Teamwork" and "Profitability" and highlight the profit-focused profile of the organization.

Human and social topics are also discussed, such as "Passion", "Human Quality", "Temper" and "The person". These meetings are of a more psychological, or even therapeutic, nature. The main ideas in the workshops are summarized in short articles in "ComparTips". Once a month, a communal mass is held and followed by a barbecue, to integrate workers in a more private context. These activities are all designed by the central office to help create an integrated team and to promote general human values, first to be instilled in credit officers, and then to be applied to client relations. One such value is empowerment, which is not collective gender empowerment from the grassroots, but a kind that "refers to a process of delegating responsibilities and imparting autonomy to employees in an enterprise" (Palier 2005: 36). Microcredit thus promotes neoliberal and corporate empowerment, including for their clients who are expected to deal with their economic scarcity autonomously. As Lazar argues, MFIs create "empowered individuals, entrepreneurial, active citizens who will take responsibility for their own and their families' welfare, and who are prepared for the market rather than the state to provide for them" (Lazar 2004: 302).

Compartamos' sales techniques draw on deep knowledge of customer attitudes at each stage of the credit cycle. Credit officers receive a notebook called an *agenda*, which specifies the emotional states of customers at different stages of the credit cycle and recommends the best ways to handle customers depending on their mood. New products are recommended, to be offered at the beginning of the credit cycle when the women are still happy because they have ready cash. On the other hand, a renewal of a microcredit is offered at the end of the cycle when clients have difficulties paying it back and need to be motivated.

Compartamos has the highest capital out of all the MFIs and can afford to take greater economic risks, making it an undeniable leader on the microfinance market despite the critiques it has received from the more conventional microcredit sector. Other microfinance institutions in the community we studied are actors within those market relations and competitors with other MFIs. If Compartamos sets these standards through its dominating position, they have to adapt to the rules, which is why the credit officers of almost all MFIs in the village regularly use extreme methods to gain clients. They create groups out of haphazardly selected women in need of cash, some of whom have been rejected by other MFIs because of their previous poor credit history. They increase the number of groups in a community to the point that there are no more potential clients left in the village, while the search for new groups continues. This is mainly due to the hierarchical structure of the offices, whereby regional managers demand growing creditor numbers as targets because they have to prove their office's profitability to their bosses. Credit officers respond to this demand by finding more clients, regardless of their credit ability. This leads to strong pressure being exerted to enforce repayment from insolvent clients, who usually resort to local credit to cover their microdebts, resulting in microcredit over-saturation in the local market, and over-indebtedness.

Women meanwhile continue to take on microcredits for various reasons. First, they want cash for recent consumption needs the market has created. Second, local credits no longer suffice. Third, high credits (such as 3,000 pesos or US$300) are no longer available locally because credit relations have been harmed by unpaid debt.

Pressure exerted by microfinance agents and aggressive market penetration

Compartamos employees aggressively penetrate the market, increasing the number of credits and other products sales at all costs. They do not look for reliable clients, but sell their products to anyone potentially interested. Market competition then forces other MFIs to do the same. Although the bank's policy is for credits to be given to women with micro-businesses, or who are at least determined to establish one,[12] they usually do not verify in any detail the economic activity of the client and her capacity to get return on the investment. As discussed above, many women's businesses are part of the household economy. It is very difficult to assess the financial efficiency of local womens' businesses where only formal economic logic is applied. Credit officers usually make no effort to screen their clients, including assessing their real solvency. Credit officers are financially incentivized to show efficiency by finding new clients and they fail to check the creditability of borrowers. This leads to the over-indebtedness of non-profit making clients and credit officers then put them under pressure to repay. If a few groups in the community fail to pay, the whole Compartamos team from an office (credit officers and their coordinators) go to the community dressed in uniform, serious and firm in their speech and actions, and go directly to the debtors' houses. They use their strong, unified group image as credit officers, and the authority of the office manager heading their visit, to intimidate clients. They also take advantage of local disagreements with which they have become familiar during their fieldwork to exacerbate social conflicts and to put further pressure on debtors.

The following testimony, which recounts a very frequent occurrence, was told to us by a microcredit client as an example of credit enforcing, and illustrates MFIs' methods of pressure. Teodora had failed to pay various instalments, was not attending meetings and was never at home. The group committee said they could not do anything about the situation. The credit officer came on a different day to surprise Teodora at home, and convinced some of the group to go with her to look for the debtor. They went to Teodora's house but did not find her. They were told she could be at her mother's house, so they went there, but again she was not there. No one seemed to know where or why Teodora had disappeared. Meanwhile the majority of the debt enforcing committee left, too, returning to their activities and no longer wanting to participate in the search. The credit officer went back to Teodora's home and when her husband again said that she was absent, the officer entered the house uninvited and found Teodora hiding under the table.

These situations are common and are the consequences of the complex power relations and interplay of different interests that confront one another. Pressure may also be based on discourse. Individuals in the community are not used to facing open public pressure. Women are also afraid of debts being made public because of their relations with their husbands. The threat of an announcement on the local loudspeaker system persuades some debtors to repay their debts. Among other things, this is because there have been known cases of the violent punishment of wives who were hiding their credits from their husbands.

The above examples illustrate the power relations between credit officers with access to cash (who can give that cash to women in the community under certain conditions) and the clients who need cash and also have to comply with the rules of the MFIs in order to get credit. Clients are often treated like ignorant children who need to be educated. Group meetings often resemble primary school classes, where the teacher/credit officer explains the basic mechanisms of investment in a paternalistic style. Language is often a barrier, as credit officers do not speak Purhépecha and some women do not communicate in Spanish. In such situations they have to rely on their friends' translations and cannot fully participate in the meeting. Credit officers have the economic resources and knowledge of how to use them to "succeed", and are, as such, in a dominant position. Many women who use credits for not-for-profit investments lack this knowledge. This can be deemed exploitation because of the unequal power-knowledge relations, of which only the dominant party is taking advantage, and whereby the MFIs are profiting from the hard work of their clients.

Our observations, however, show that the women in the village are not the passive victims of dominance, even if they do not speak Spanish. The relation between the MFI staff and its clients is often an arena for negotiation. Women, for example, pretend that the solidarity group is coherent for the sake of getting credit, while credit officers in exchange turn a blind eye to the "unsustainability" of the borrowers' businesses.

The pressure that the commercialization of microcredits puts on clients, along with the frequent instalments, pushes them to increase their other loans in order to repay microcredits. This leads to a vicious circle of debt or debt recycling and, consequently, over-indebtedness, as we will illustrate.

In spite of its corporate strategy and aggressive marketing, Compartamos continues to promote a discourse of being a socially-focused development enterprise. Stories of individual success through microfinance are promoted among clients to display its social commitment. It also holds a contest for the best microfinance customer, the winner of which is presented as a role model.

Consumerism and getting indebted

Over-indebtedness in Sukurán is also down to growing local consumerism that originated in the cascading capitalist economy of the local market, partly as a result of microfinance. On the one hand, women do not invest the majority of microcredits in profit making enterprises because their productive initiatives are not-for-profit, on a household basis. Therefore they cannot generate sufficient cash to repay instalments and interests. On the other hand, a large share of microcredits is used for consumption.

In giving village women access to cash and encouraging their regular visits into town, microcredits have accelerated the latter's education in consumerism – the basic mechanism of the capitalist economy that also justifies the need for formal credit. Notwithstanding the fall in the economic standard of living caused by the economic crisis, as opposed to its rise in the 1990s, the villagers have been exposed to strong consumerist influences through contact with commercials and shop windows.

Microcredit clients have to travel to their nearby town to exchange the cheques they are issued from the credit officer for money, and then to pay instalments at the bank. They use this opportunity to shop in the city market and stores. Regular visits to town are also how they learn about urban lifestyles and consumption. The women thus develop the same consumerist patterns as those that are are popular in cities. They can buy products such as gas stoves, food processors, washing machines and fridges, which are still not very popular in Sukurán but are starting to appear in some households and to become social status symbols. Moreover, all of these utensils free up time, which can then be invested in further consumption.

The consumption patterns that microcredits have triggered can be seen in a comment by a taxi driver, who often drives women into town with cheques to exchange:

> The credit comes and they [women] immediately need a taxi to take them to the town, and they buy, they buy, they buy. And they say, take me there. And I say, but it will cost. It doesn't matter, they say, let's go!

One of the clients of both the MFIs we studied admitted:

> We buy things that we shouldn't buy. I am also like this. I buy what I shouldn't. I like something that I don't need and I buy it. Sometimes I buy clothes I do not need and then I just keep them and don't use them. We all buy things that we shouldn't buy. Sometimes I say to myself that I will not buy any more. But after a while, the temptation comes back and I buy. And immediately I regret it. Why have I bought it if I do not even use it?

The consumerist mechanisms that get women addicted to microcredits then enable them to consume. They state that they would be happy to quit constant borrowing and often promise to themselves that they will stop being a part of the solidarity group in the following credit cycle so as not to pay so much interest. However, when the microcredit credit officers start to announce new credit rounds, they quickly find excuses to join groups again.

Spreading consumerism is not part of microfinance public discourse. Nevertheless, bringing the village economy into the capitalist market through the escalation of consumption appears to be one of the informal goals of microfinance. As Katharine Rankin puts it, microcredits contribute "to the broader goals of deepening financial markets to areas that typically fall outside the purview of capitalist markets" (Rankin 2001: 28). This statement supports our findings that women contribute to the development of the global market economy through microfinance programmes, but that development does not necessarily contribute to the wellbeing of women.

In the village we studied, growing consumption was coming up against the limits of local economic capacities and recourses. The local economy was unable to adapt quickly enough to the level of consumption stimulated by increased contact with the external economy and spreading microcredits. When microfinance institutions started to operate in the village at the beginning of the twenty-first century, women could still juggle microcredits and local credits to maintain solvency. But this credit recycling soon instigated a vicious cycle of credit and over-indebtedness.

Over-indebtedness and the interrelation of different forms of credit

In Sukurán, all forms of credit are interrelated and people juggle them constantly. Loans from local moneylenders can be paid back through microcredits, family credits, etc. Microcredits can be used as capital for a moneylender to lend to other people with high interest rates, or can be paid with all kinds of locally available credit. Because local credits are interrelated, over-indebtedness is not just a problem between MFIs and their clients, but of generalized indebtedness and social conflict. How different forms of credit interrelate can best be illustrated through examples. In the event of the illness of a family member, or an accident leading to heavy expenses, a woman from Sukurán usually borrows from local moneylenders. But the burdens of social discourse (gossip and stigmatization), high interest rates, and short terms of payment encourage the debtor to look for a loan elsewhere and to be freed from commitment to the usurer as quickly as possible. Often the debtor takes out a microcredit, which is less burdened with social pressure than a family or usurer's loan, and which has slightly lower interest rates than usury.[13] However, before the credit is issued, she usually has to wait for a previous credit cycle to end. Sometimes she has to join a new solidarity group or even initiate such a group. Meanwhile, she just waits or borrows from her relatives or friends to pay the moneylender at least part of the debt. When she finally gets a microcredit she can pay off all or some of her debts and related interest rates. The problem then arises as to how to pay back the microcredit. The money, which has not been invested, is not profitable, and it is often necessary to turn to family members again. In some cases the solution looks to be a further microcredit, which eventually only increases the scale of the individual's debt relations and increases the interest rates she has to pay. In such a complex socioeconomic situation it is easy to lose control over one's debts when something unexpected happens, or when the total amount of interest is too high to be paid from the family income.

This credit juggling often leads to a vicious cycle (*círculo vicioso*) or chain (*cadena*) of debt. When the client pays off one debt with another credit, she usually ends up taking out further credit to cover the interests. The debts accumulate and she is unable to cover the expense of repayment from the family income.

The case of a Compartamos and OM client in Sukurán illustrates the mechanism of over-indebtedness through the vicious cycle of debt. Eva and her husband Tomás invested in an avocado plantation and fell victims to fraud. They lost the investment and were left with 10,000 pesos (US$1,000) debt and 10 per cent monthly interest rates to pay. This marked the beginning of several years' struggle for their economic and social recovery from over-indebtedness. She could not afford to pay the whole debt at once and had to pay 1,000 pesos in interest a month. For three months, Eva could not even pay the interest and took out another loan of 5,000 pesos with the same moneylender. She received only 2,000 in cash as the rest covered the debt from the unpaid interests. Instead of 10,000 Eva was now indebted for 5,000 pesos and had to pay 1,500 pesos in interest a month. To continue to pay the interest, she started to take out microcredit loans, until her debt level reached 50,000 pesos. Out of this 50,000, 40,000 peso was generated by the interest rates she had to pay to the various credit institutions.

Tomás left for the United States using a common strategy in situations of over-indebtedness, emigration (see also Morvant-Roux in this volume). He stayed there for two years, working hard and sending money to Eva. Remittances were used to pay off the old debt, the microcredit and, if they came at the right moment, regular expenses. If it had not been for the extra money from the husband's job (and if he had not been lucky enough to find a good job) the family would probably have become over-indebted. During our long conversations, Eva often complained about the high interest rates and the short time for repayment in microfinance. She had a rough idea of the fact that she was repaying double of what she had taken out as a loan. She admitted that she could cope without microcredits, but once she had started to take part in a few groups, it was difficult to quit. One debt was paying for another loan, and so on. Only when Tomás had returned with some additional savings (in addition to the remittances that he had been sending while working abroad), could Eva pay all her debts to the MFIs and free herself from the multiplied interest rates. A sizeable external cash boost was needed to escape the over-indebtedness.

This story ended relatively well. However, we came across situations where women who were indebted to four or five microfinance organizations had been pursued for many months and where some MFIs had finally had to cancel the debt, because there were no material goods they could threaten to confiscate (though this should not be an MFIs practice, according to their own formal rules). These women will not be accepted at the next credit cycle of the MFI to which they owe money until they pay it back, or in any of the microfinance organizations that are using the general debtors' database. Other MFIs in the village will probably also reject them as clients for several years until the memory of the case dies away and new organizations appear, ready to conquer the local market.

In other cases, credit officers try various methods to force their indebted clients to pay back credit. One of these is to make a client sell her goods informally to a credit officer at half price. The client can then pay, or rather is forced to pay, at least part of the debt from the money she gets from the credit officer. Credit officers then sell those products in the city at the regular price, thus gaining their commission.

The following example is a typical illustration of the complexity of over-indebtedness. Celestina had always been a very good microfinance client, but she started to take out credits from different organizations at the same time and lost control of her debts.[14] A couple of years ago, Celestina and a few other people created a group and solicited a tractor from an organization founded to help peasants. But half of the value of this tractor was to be paid for by the group. Celestina became indebted to Compartamos, among other sources, to cover her share and that of another group member who did not have money at the time, and was invited to join the group as a distant but trusted family member. At the same time, she solicited another subsidy that she was sure of getting. Meanwhile she spent her money as if she were not indebted. Unfortunately, the expected subsidy did not come and Celestina was left with a debt of around 200,000 pesos (US$20,000). At the time, her husband was working in the USA so she could count on some remittances. However, she was accused of adultery and stopped receiving the money from him for a couple of months, until they were reconciled.

Celestina could have left the tractor project, but as microcredits were available, she started to take on more credits (she was active in at least two MFI groups at the same time) and repaid them from loans from family and friends (one of her aunts even gave her the deeds to her house as a collateral for a credit for Celestina) and local moneylenders. She also resorted to tricks such as the one she used with the *tanda* group, to gather some significant amounts of money to pay her debts. To reassure her debtors, she gave away one small area of land she owned. The deal consisted in giving the land to the lender and asking him to pay for the missing amount in cash. However, she sold it to at least two persons at the same time. That caused not only a problem between herself and people she owed money to, but also between the different owners of the same land.

Celestina is now in conflict with many of the residents of Sukurán and in hiding from many people. It is almost impossible to find her at home. Her husband was recently deported from the United States because he was working illegally. The whole family is now trying to keep Celestina's debts secret because if her husband finds out about the amount of the debt it would probably lead to violence and serious conflict in the family. Celestina's aunt, who is trying to help her by lending her money and by accepting her in the Compartamos group in spite of her lack of solvency, says that Celestina is very stressed and sees no way out of her situation. However, she is not giving up and keeps up the endless cycle of borrowing and paying back. This process only seems to worsen her situation. Her aunt is also stressed because she is responsible for some group debts together with Celestina. The Compartamos group took a credit from the local money- lender to pay for the last payment, because they could not collect it from the members of the group. They were sure to pay it back immediately because the MFI always returns a 10 per cent deposit once the debt is paid. However, they could not free themselves from this debt because Celestina had taken another credit, and to do so she had pawned the document from the bank that allows the withdrawal of the group deposit from the Compartamos account.

Further details still could be cited here about Celestina's over-indebtedness problems. Every woman in Sukurán who knew her well told us a different story about Celestina's debts that, in many cases, also implicated the interviewee in question. Gloria, the OM staff member, who has known Celestina since the beginning of her credit history, concludes that Celestina's story is the best example of how MFI policy is negatively affecting the solvency of their clients:

> She was a very good client, she always paid on time, until she took too many credits and found herself unable to pay them with her regular income. We [the MFIs], through the aggressive microfinance campaign, have damaged her solvency.

On other occasions Gloria stated that she viewed MFIs as a bad influence for the majority of women in rural communities.

Accumulated indebtedness or credit juggling is a very common practice, which people successfully manage until the scale of credit expenses exceeds the regular family income potential and social capital of the indebted person (see also Angulo Salazar, Guérin *et al.* and Morvant-Roux in this volume). Constant indebtedness and the multiplication of parallel credits are not generally danger-ous for most of the village inhabitants in a stable economic climate. Being indebted is normal in the local socioeconomic context. Only once the amount and cost of the debt exceed the solvency capacity of an individual debtor or of her family, and her socioeconomic relations lead to serious conflicts, rejection or the exclusion of the indebted person, can indebtedness can be called over-indebtedness.

Low cash flows, irregular incomes, local economic instability and rising aspirations create a situation where microcredits are an additional burden.

Frequent repayments and high interest rates force clients to take out loans to pay their instalments. This leads to increased dependency not only on several different MFIs at once, but also on local informal credit sources (see also Rahman 2001: 150; Lazar 2004: 308). Rahman argues that the dynamics of microcredit cycles can lead to the emergence of new informal forms of credit: "The micro-lending and repayment regularity by grassroots borrowers may also encourage a new form of legitimate moneylender who entraps the most desperate of the poor in an upward spiral of debt." (Rahman 2001: 150). Karim agrees on this: "Contrary to the claims of the Grameen Bank and other NGOs that they have reduced traditional money lending through micro-credit NGOs, what we find instead is the reproduction of usury at multiple levels of society." (Karim 2008: 20). In Sukurán, local moneylenders are also prosperous, and microcredits have not weakened local usury. On the contrary, sometimes microcredits are even used to lend money to other people with higher interest rates. Rankin claims of micro-credits in Nepal that the "availability of credit often increases women's work burden and dependence on lending institutions [...] rather than generating enduring possibilities for autonomy and independence" (Rankin 2001: 32). Microcredits therefore seem to be disempowering, in spite of their empowerment mission.

The vicious cycle of credits connecting debtors to their extended families, neighbours and friends, means that unpaid individual local debts have not only begun to impact upon social relations, but also the economic stability of families. Some individuals take out credits to pay off someone else's debts or to compensate for unpaid loans issued to over-indebted relatives or friends. When microcredits lead to individual over-indebtedness, they also have an impact on the whole credit system and the social relations of the community.

Conclusion

Over-indebtedness is undoubtedly caused by numerous interrelated factors surrounding microcredit: (1) the widespread marketing and massive expansion of microfinance, and careless delivery of microcredit as a product to as many clients as possible, regardless of their credit solvency; (2) the use of credits for consumption, juggling several external credits and falling into a vicious cycle of debts and interest rates; and (3) rising consumerism. We argue that these are the main factors of over-indebtedness.

Ethnographic observation has shown that over-indebtedness is not just a matter of having taken out credit that has failed to improve individuals' economic situations. Microcredits often worsen families' objective socio-economic conditions.

Over-indebtedness should not just be viewed as oversized debt on the individual level. As one of the above examples shows, many people finally manage to overcome over-indebtedness by resorting to special measures such as emigration. But we should take into account that the whole community is involved in the sum of the uncontrolled number of microdebts and is implicated in the chain of credits, repayments and interest rates (see also Morvant-Roux in this volume).

Moreover, MFIs take advantage (with annual interest rates of over 100 per cent) of this externally injected cash flow into the community. Over-indebtedness affects the whole community via local socio-economic relations. Debt may be repaid to a microfinance organization, but further debts remain within local debt networks. An important further element of over-indebtedness is therefore collective indebtedness that destabilizes the local economy. Local over-indebtedness leads to social conflicts between creditors and debtors and their families.

Over the last ten years of microfinance in the village of Sukurán, its impact has been wide ranging. The programme has brought about some changes in gender and family relations, and for some beneficiaries it has led to significant changes in their lives, which shall be discussed in our further papers. As far as indebtedness is concerned, however, the impact of the microfinance ventures observed during our fieldwork was the opposite of the ideal model. The programme is not a tool for the poor to become economically independent, but instead makes them dependent on external institutions. It offers apparent freedom from the social embeddedness of credit, and low interest rates, but also uses solidarity groups and family ties to guarantee the payment of the debt, charging over 100 per cent in interest. The over-indebtedness it fosters leads to dependency on external financial institutions.

Notes

1 I would like to thank Gail Mummert Fulmer (PhD, professor at Colegio de Michoacán) and Aleksander Posern-Zieliński (PhD, professor at the University of Adam Mickiewicz in Poznań).
2 The term *meseta* as the proper noun in Meseta Purhépecha is sometimes replaced by the term *sierra*, both meaning mountains.
3 It is important to stress that the statistical data is highly relative as it is based on material indicators such as access to electricity, running water, sewage, salary level or even the percentage of dirt floor houses. These are clearly statistics taken from a materialist and developmentalist viewpoint. Wage labour may not, for example, be the sole source of a living for the family, and local housing standards may differ from urban ones.
4 Avocado, called green gold, is one of the most profitable products of the region.
5 The base is all the material stock that the family possesses: land, animals, house, etc.
6 The forms of credit to be found in Sukurán are similar to those described in Solène Morvant-Roux's chapter in this volume. However, the situations of their executions, typology and social interpretation may differ slightly from one locality to the other.
7 The *barrio* is a part of an indigenous community with its own patron saint and other ritual functions. Usually in the region, villages are divided into four *barrios*. This division has colonial origins.
8 For more information on the gender factor in credit and microcredit practices, see Villarreal (2004); Guérin (2011); D'Espallier *et al.* (2009); Espinosa *et al.* (1999); Rahman (2001); Karim (2008).
9 Women only partly using credit and passing some on to men, or acting only as mediators between the MFIs and the men in their families, is common in a variety of countries, but the cultural reasons vary. In Bangladesh, according to Lamia Karim, men use the microcredits given to their wives because, as they declare, their wives belong to them and so do the credits (Karim 2008: 15). But Goetz and Sen Gupta claim that access to credit may increase the woman's status as she becomes an important source of income in the household (1996: 53). See also Rahman (2001: 151).

10 I estimate this on the basis of the ratio between the number of microcredit groups – around 50 (in seven MFIs operating locally) – and the female population aged between 15 and 49 – around 1,600 – in the village (INEGI 2010).

11 The minimum monthly salary in Mexico is around 1,700 pesos.

12 From the point of view of Compartamos this rule protects the bank from insolvency in their clients and increases the chance of loan return. From the point of view of the clients it protects them from getting over-indebted.

13 At least in the discourse promoted by the MFIs. See the analysis of Compartamos interest rates above.

14 This opinion was expressed by one of the OM's staff member, a promoter who worked in different MFIs in Sukurán and knows well the majority of the clients.

References

Bateman, M. (2011) 'Introduction: Looking Beyond the Hype and Entrenched Myth', in M. Bateman (ed.) *Confronting Microfinance: Undermining Sustainable Development*, Sterling: Kumarian Press.

Canal Hernando, J. M. and de Ovando, F. (2007) "Reporte Anual que se presenta de acuerdo con las disposiciones de carácter general aplicables a las emisoras de valores y a otros participantes del mercado, por el ejercicio terminado el 31 de diciembre de 2007", available online at: www.colmenamilenaria.org.mx/uploads/media/Comercial-izacion_de_las_Microfinanzas_y_su_futuro.pdf (accessed 24 August 2011).

Conapo (2005) "Índice de marginación a nivel localidad", available online at: www.conapo.gob.mx/es/CONAPO/Indice_de_marginacion_a_nivel_localidad_2005 (Accessed 25 January 2013).

Conapo (2010) "Índice de marginación por entidad federativa y municipio", avaialble online at: www.conapo.gob.mx/es/CONAPO/Indices_de_Marginacion_2010_por_entidad_federativa_y_municipio (Accessed 25 January 2013).

D'Espallier, B., Guérin, I. and Mersland, R. (2009) "Women and Repayment in Micro-finance: A Global Analysis", *World Development*, 39(5): 758–772.

Epstein, K. and Smith, G. (2007) "Compartamos: from nonprofit to profit", *Businessweek*, December 30, available online at: www.businessweek.com/magazine/content/07_52/b4064045919628.htm (accessed 24 August 2011).

Espinosa, R. A. and Villarreal, M. (1999) "Las mujeres, las malas rachas y el endeudami-ento", in V. Vázquez (coord.) *Género, sustentabilidad y cambio social en el México rural*, México: Colegio de Postgraduados.

Goetz, A. M. and Sen Gupta, R. (1996) "Who Takes the Credit? Gender, Power, and Control Over Loan Use in Rural Credit Programs in Bangladesh", *World Development*, 24(1): 45–63.

Gudeman, S. (2008) *Economy's Tension: The Dialectics of Community and Market*, New York and Oxford: Berghahn Books.

Gudeman, S. and Rivera, A. (1994) *Conversations in Colombia: The Domestic Economy in Life and Text*, Cambridge: Cambridge University Press.

Guérin, I. (2011) "Do Women Need Specific Microfinance Services?", in B. Armendariz and M. Labie (eds) *Handbook of Microfinance*, London and Singapore: World Scient-ific Publishing.

Harper, M. (2011) "The Commercialization of Microfinance: Resolution or Extension of Poverty?", in M. Bateman (ed.) *Confronting Microfinance: Undermining Sustainable Development*, Sterling: Kumarian Press.

Houghton, M., Mordach, J., Porter, B. and Swanson, B. (2008) *La Comercialización de las Microfinanzas y su Futuro. La OPI de Compartamos. Debates y Aprendizajes*, México: MFI Solutions, LLC, USA and La Colmena Milenaria, A.C., available online at: www.cerise-microfinance.org/IMG/pdf/MBB_19_-_December_2009.pdf (Accessed 24 August 2011).

Hummel, A. (2008) "Local Economy and Different Forms of Credits in a Community of Purhépecha Indians in the State of Michoacán", Mexico, *Hemispheres. Studies on Cultures and Societies*, 23: 169–189.

INEGI (2010) "Censos y conteos de población y vivienda. Instituto Nacional de Estadística y Geografía, México, Michoacán de Ocampo, available online at: www3.inegi.org.mx/sistemas/iter/entidad_indicador.aspx?ev=5", (Accessed 15 December 2011).

Karim, L. (2008) "Demystifying Micro-Credit: The Grameen Bank, NGOs, and Neoliberalism in Bangladesh", *Cultural Dynamics*, 20(1): 5–29.

Lazar, S. (2004) "Education for Credit: Development as Citizenship Project in Bolivia", *Critique of Anthropology*, 24(3): 301–319.

Mauss, M. (1979) *Sociology and Psychology: Essays*, London: Routledge and Kegan Paul.

MicroBanking (2009) *MicroBanking Bulletin*, Mix Market, available online at: www.cerise-microfinance.org/IMG/pdf/MBB_19_-_December_2009.pdf (Accessed 24 August 2011).

Palier, J. (2005) "Defining the Concept of Empowerment through Experiences in India" in: I. Guérin, and J. Palier (eds) *Microfinance Challenges: Empowerment or Disempowerment of the Poor?* Pondicherry: Institut français de Pondichéry, available online at: www.rume-rural-microfinance.org/IMG/pdf_Microfinance_Challenges.pdf (Accessed 25 July 2012).

Rahman, A. (2001) *Women and Microcredit in Rural Bangladesh: Anthropological Study of the Rhetoric and Realities of Grameen Bank Lending*, Boulder: Westview Press.

Rankin, K. N. (2001) "Governing Development: Neoliberalism, Microcredit, and Rational Economic Woman", *Economy and Society*, 30(1): 18–37.

Sahlins, M. (1976) *Culture and Practical Reason*, Chicago: University of Chicago Press.

Villarreal, Magdalena (coord.) (2004) *Antropología de la deuda. Crédito, ahorro, fiado y prestado en las finanzas cotidianas*, México: CIESAS.

Weber, M. (1956) *Economy and society: An Outline of Interpretive Sociology*, G. Roth and C. Wittich (eds), Berkeley/ Los Angeles/ London: University of California Press, 2nd edn. 1978.

Zanotelli, F. (2004) "La circulación social de la deuda: códigos culturales y usura rural en Jalisco", in M. Villarreal (coord.) *Antropología de la deuda. Crédito, ahorro, fiado y prestado en las finanzas cotidianas*, México: CIESAS.

13 Mortgaging used sari-skirts, spear-heading resistance

Narratives from the microfinance repayment stand-off in a South Indian town, 2008–2010

Nithya Joseph

Microfinance institutions (MFIs) have been facing repayment crises in pockets of South India since 2006. This chapter presents and interprets one such crisis – in a town where MFI clients are largely reliant on the silk-reeling industry, controlled by religious leaders, for employment. From March 2009, clients refused to repay their microloans on the grounds that the aggressive pursuit of interests by institutions and individuals in the commercial microfinance sector had been responsible for increases in their financial vulnerability, leading to over-indebtedness. Narratives from a range of actors in the town are used here to understand the logic used to make this claim. Embedded in the context of daily relations of production, distribution, and reproduction in the town, these narratives reveal that microfinance did not exert an isolated pressure on financial vulnerability – and that financial vulnerability was not the only grounds on which over-indebtedness was claimed. Instead, they suggest that the manner in which the interests of the microfinance sector interacted with, and challenged, local interests and relations of power played a significant role in precipitating the crisis – which was as much about protesting unfair practices as it was about reacting to unmanageable debt. This case suggests that the project of deepening the gains from financial inclusion needs to take into consideration the dangers of under-regulated commercial microfinance, the existing regulation of local and global structures of accumulation by social institutions, and the complexity of the kind of debt relations that are analyzed here.

> The loudspeakers in all the mosques in Sitalaxmapalya, came on at midnight on the 28th of March 2009. Instead of the usual call to prayer, they broadcast messages announcing that dealings with all Kendras (MFIs) were forbidden henceforth and that anyone who continued to attend MFI repayment meetings or even to speak to MFI staff, would lose all ritual rites from the mosque, including last rights and burial rights, and would subsequently face banishment from Muslim residential areas.
>
> (MFI Borrowers, Focus Group March 2010)

MFI staff who lived outside the Muslim area, and hadn't heard the announcement, were shocked when local youth accosted them on their way to work, snatched their bags and set their account books on fire. If there had been signs that trouble was brewing in the town, the staff hadn't paid much attention to them. In any case they never imagined that they would lose control of the situation so completely, or that their lives were about to change so drastically after that day.

(MFI Field Staff, Focus Group March 2010)

The regional managers and executives of the seven MFIs operating in Sitalaxmapalya were surprised that this had happened in their star branch, but they were more prepared for what was to come. They were already locked in to negotiations with the Muslim leaders in two other silk producing towns in the state.

(MFI Area Manager, Interview April 2010)

Backcloth

In October of 2009, I read an article about a "revolt" against microfinance institutions (MFIs) in a town called Sitalaxmapalya[1] in the south Indian state of Karnataka. The author of this article described Muslim clerics in Sitalaxmapalya encouraging women to default on their loan repayments to microfinance institutions in order to protest against the exploitative lending behavior, of the numerous profit-oriented MFIs located in the town,[2] that were triggering over-indebtedness. The author compared the lending behavior of competitive profit-oriented MFIs in Sitalaxmapalya to that which caused the US sub-prime crisis, and suggested that the consequences in terms of over-indebtedness were also similar, despite the difference in the scale of lending. MFIs operating in the region responded to this article through their websites and blogs, arguing that the stand-off was a concatenation phenomenon caused by "money lenders, and businessmen who virtually employed the poor women as bonded labor" (Ghosh 2009), by shocks caused by downturns in local business, and by attempts of Muslim religious leaders to deny Muslim women access to credit based on Islamic financial laws and stipulations about gender (Akula 2009).

I'd been in Sitalaxmapalya in 2008, while the international financial crisis was brewing, and when the "bubble" the author of the article described would have been developing. I was, at the time, an intern with a non-governmental organization looking to provide health services to an MFI's borrowers. My internship began with a week-long stay in Sitalaxmapalya town, as induction in to the organization – and during this time I also doubled up as a translator for an anthropologist who was investigating solidarity amongst the members of MFI borrower groups. This time was one of complete immersion in Sitalaxmapalya microfinance. Sleeping in an MFI office, attending center repayment meetings that were scheduled early in the morning to allow staff contact with as many groups as possible before the women left to work, I spent afternoons interviewing in the town and in nearby villages for my anthropologist friend, and evenings holding informal focus groups with the staff when they returned to the office after an evening round of repayment meetings. I returned to Sitalax-mapalya repeatedly over the course of my internship – for field reports and audits – each time learning a little more about this colourful town nestled between large rocks and the tall green and white minarets of the local mosques. I became familiar with the busy main street that runs between the local bus stand and the railway station, and the many arterial roads leading to residential pockets occupied by either Muslims or Hindus.[3]

When I read about the repayment stand-off I was puzzled by the conviction with which different mechanisms for the production of the situation had been proposed, and how each was strongly refuted by various stakeholders in Sitalax-mapalya microfinance. In the grossly uneven distribution of financial access in India (Fouillet 2009) Sitalaxmapalya typifies a pocket where financial services for the urban poor have been concentrated. For this reason, understanding the events in the town contributes to an understanding of the consequences of the spatiality of national microfinance. The fact that four cases of revolt in Karna-taka all originated in Muslim communities in cities where the silk industry offered an important source of employment for poor women made it necessary to consider the ways in which the organization of the silk-reeling industry inter-acted with religious affiliation and with the growing influence of microfinance in the town. I was interested to understand the various competing theories for what happened in Sitalaxmapalya, how people's lives had been affected by the vast expansion in profit-oriented and competitive microfinance lending, and what effects it had on the local economy.

In the reports I read in 2009, I saw continuity with events and trends I had witnessed in 2008. I understood the prevalence of multiple borrowing in town from the genuine confusion my anthropologist friend encountered when she asked questions like, "how long did you know the other members in your group before you agreed to be co-guarantors?" Almost every respondent asked her which group she meant, and then went to explain that one MFI group consisted of her neighbors, while she was invited to join a second by her sister-in-law, whereas two others consisted of groups of her co-workers. I had heard MFI staff shouting at women – for being absent at meetings, for leaving their money with someone else, or for being in a rush to leave meetings – their response was that they needed to get to work or they would lose the day's wage. I had been told about the low pay and unpredictability of work in the silk-reeling industry that was one of the few sources of wage work for Sitalaxmapalya's poorest women. Reading how much lending amounts had risen, I had a sense of the speed with which the debt of borrowers, who hadn't been able to invest profitable enterprise and were making multiple loan repayments, could spiral out of control.

With respect to religion, I had encountered secularism in people's discourse and practice in Sitalaxmapalya, and yet had also witnessed the separation of the town's Muslims and Hindus in public venues and across the space of the large town. I had also witnessed interdependence, mingling, and exchanges between individuals from the two religious groups. For example, on the way to attend a function being hosted by a local MFI to celebrate its reaching 3,000 borrowers in the town, my anthropologist friend and I were stopped by an MFI borrower who invited us to chat with her in her *chai* shop, she talked about being the only Muslim in a borrowing group of ten women – and insisted that there was nothing remarkable about her position in that group. She pinched our hands in turn saying, "Muslim, Hindu, kya pharak padtha, beti? Koon, koon ek hi hai, na?" "Muslim, Hindu, what difference does it make, girls? Blood is all the same, isn't it?" Barely an hour later at the celebratory event I was surprised when, standing up, I noticed that the audience around me was divided neatly down the middle of the hall. One side of the aisle was black with the *burkhas* worn by Muslim women, while on the other there rippled a sea of colorful saris worn by Hindu women. Sitting in the audience, I had watched the women walk in to the hall but hadn't noticed the divide that was building up. I wondered what forces separated the two groups, what sense of identity did similarity of dress create, and what was the nature of any deeper sense of group identity that existed? Hearing of the repayment stand-off being described as a "Muslim revolt" a year later, I wondered what role, if any, religious beliefs and group identities had in producing the situation. Was it truly a religion-based revolt? If so how did it come about? Did religion influence vulnerability to over-indebtedness, or did it create a medium for resistance?

This essay has developed from a revisit to Sitalaxmapalya in 2010 (to the places I had encountered in 2008) to hear from various stakeholders their explanations of the causes and consequences of the repayment stand-off. I sought to understand how factors contributing to the repayment stand-off were analyzed, towards understanding how over-indebtedness was explained and evaluated in the context of the town. This led me to consider how the relationship between microfinance and other forms of credit were explained in terms of their varying financial costs, and also how the control exerted by social institutions over production in the town interacted with the changes in credit availability in the town created by the growth of MFIs. Accounts of the situation often included suggestions, and proposals for change, and I have also included these in this essay.

My conversations took me from the glass and wood-paneled office of the Chief Financial Officer of a Bangalore-based MFI, where I heard of how regional diversification minimized the financial impact of the crisis on the company's revenue, to the third floor MFI branch office in the Sitalaxmapalya market, where I met with field staff who were exhausted after spending their day going from door-to-door begging for repayments, and heard the branch manager despair that the whole year's collection had been less than the average amount due every day. I visited the fluorescent pink and yellow bungalow of a local religious leader, sipping the Coca-Cola bought by his wife. I spent time with twelve MFI borrowers, their families and their friends, returning repeatedly to a railway station *chai* shop and a tailoring unit, both funded by microloans, and to homes in the neighborhoods of *Rahmaniyanagar* and *Yarabinagar*. In addition I had spontaneous conversations in the market, waiting in the railway station and on the train to Bangalore. I spoke with men, as well as women, hearing their accounts as husbands, fathers, and brothers of borrowers, and as Muslim men in Sitalaxmapalya who were participants in the mosque meetings, concerned about the financial position of their religious group.

The narratives I gathered have needed integrating in order to construct the explanations for varying experiences of microfinance in the town and for the events that led to, ensued during, and persisted after the stand-off. Individuals explained the motivations for decisions concerning the revolt in terms of how they evaluated perceived changes in what Amartya Sen would term their capabilities (Sen 1999) and as individuals who are also members of multiple social institutions (Stewart 2004). I use the analysis of multiple situations described by these various actors to summarize the social relations of microfinance in Sitalaxmapalya and to integrate and synthesize their accounts of the relationship between the social and financial interactions involved in competitive profit-oriented MFI lending (amidst other credit sources) and the financial vulnerability of the town. The process of producing narrative accounts of microfinance allows this relationship to be framed by the commentary of local actors about the rules for financial behavior and social accountability in the town.

When policy that is being promoted as a tool for development comes under fire as microfinance has in Sitalaxmapalya, as in other isolated spaces over the last decade and more widely in recent times, it becomes essential to think of ways in which to understand and evaluate resistance. The analysis offered in the narratives from Sitalaxmapalya directs us to two suggestions about how this may be done: The narratives push us to ask whether the policy practices do not result in positive change; whether following Amartya Sen, they do not contribute to an expansion in people's abilities to live and function in ways they value; or whether the re-organization of resources proposed by a given policy is in conflict with interests of individuals or groups who have the power to challenge the policy in practice and, when access to resources is differentiated, whether it is interests that stand to lose from a policy that drive the resistance to it.

The narratives themselves suggest that what we must evaluate is the extent to which each of these two possibilities is true.

Theoretical considerations

The narratives direct us to explore and question the intentions of development policy, its means and mechanisms ("technologies"), and the methods by which to evaluate its outcomes. The intention of development policy can be presumed to be the production and distribution of a surplus (Harriss-White 2003a) controlled through a socially embedded process of negotiation of interests based on unequal power relations (Schaffer 1984). Accordingly, it becomes important to understand the organization of production and distribution in the town, which will be conditioned by the distribution of political and social power.

Harriss-White has shown how the local urban economy is stabilized by a matrix of institutions that are heavily regulated by non-state social institutions such as the structure of the workforce, social class, gender, caste, language and religion, in coordination with being regulated by the local State (see Harriss-White 2003a and 2003b).

Mushtaq Khan (2004) suggests that states (and their agencies) manipulate the set of interests governing capital accumulation – which can be conceived as "rents" – to further the process of economic transformation not only by incentivising productive investment (by allowing monopolies, and returns to innovation, risk-taking, learning, management, and disciplining that are in excess of putative counterfactual profits) but also by constraining, through fiscal transfers, the obstacles to their project. Responses to the latter include buying off and seeking to destroy powerful coalitions that lead to unproductive growth or opposition to the productive project, and compensating the project's victims.

In the social structure shaping accumulation in which *non*-state institutions dominate the informal economy, rents can be re-defined as the value resulting from the social and political institutions that interact to set the parameters for transactions. These rents are hard to quantify and value, granted the absence of a rent-free point of comparison. Yet, while only a minority of Khanian transfers can be precisely calculated, his notion of rents nonetheless provides a useful tool to frame the discussion developed later in this essay.

In my analysis of the narratives from Sitalaxmapalya I examine attempts to extract rents from the funds being offered at interest rates lower than those charged by other sources – by staff, clients, and local pawnbrokers. I then place rent-seeking in Sitalaxmapalya microfinance in the context of other rents that exist in the town, looking at organization and transfers based on religion, class, and language, amongst other institutions, and towards understanding the practical ways in which microfinance and local financial behavior interacted to reinforce inequalities.

The identification of rents in the context of the repayment stand-off will enable an attempt to address the implications of these forms and distributions of power in Sitalaxmapalya – though, due to the nature of the field evidence, the discussion is tentative. The Khanian approach can be used to extend the critiques of microfinance that see its ill effects as being entirely a consequence of commercialization of the sector. The richer theoretical frame it offers enables us to examine other ways of understanding factors affecting default; in particular those stemming from structural inequalities in the economies in which microfinance has been established (Guérin *et al.* 2012). Harriss-White (2009) uses Schaffer's approach to policy analysis to explain that policy is ultimately about political interest and makes the important connection with Khan's suggestion that effective development policy takes on the deliberate mediation of these interests. Harriss-White (2003a) suggests that it is important to understand that all policy generates its own resources and politics, including the politics of opposition.

Here I ask if the policy space that promotes commercial microfinance can be seen as a Khanian transfer which forms a part of state policy that intends to subsidize labor for capital (as Judith Heyer (2012) argues is the case in Tiruppur,

Tamil Nadu), by attempting to locate this transfer in the context of other relations, rents, and transfers which precede the existence of microfinance and which also challenge its functioning in Sitalaxmapalya.

Narratives of crisis

The first account I heard of events in Sitalaxmapalya told a linear story that is in many ways representative of the collective recording of the events of the repayment stand-off – emerging repeatedly in the first accounts offered by others in the town:

> Firstly, there were suicides and cases of women going to local lodges as prostitutes when they need money to pay back their loans. The Muslim Committee members heard about all this. At the same time, the silk industry was doing badly and they also started losing labor because they paid poorly, and so, women who had MFI loans chose not to go to work. Also, the factory owners insisted on people coming to work every day, even if they were very sick, because they said they had paid them an advance and if they didn't come one day that machine would be idle and they'd lose all that money. Even if you were sick and dying their men would be at your doorstep to drag you to work. Once the MFIs came in, people in situations like that, when they were so sick they couldn't stand, they would say, "Give me a week I'll take an MFI loan and pay back all your money. Hire someone else I'm not working for you." The owners didn't like that because it hurt their pride, they also felt they were losing control of their workers, and they'd have to retrain a new person, wait till they learned the work and all that would affect productivity. So they had something against the MFIs for a long time.
>
> Then a group of women headed by Lakshmi Sait signed a petition pleading with the Committee to protect them from MFIs that were harassing them to pay back their loans. In the petition, the women admitted that they had done wrong by taking loans they couldn't honour but they said that they were in a hopeless amount of debt and their situation was more dire because of the lending and collection practices of the MFIs. In view of the other developments – the suicides and prostitution and the labour problems – the Committee members were ready to support the women.
>
> (Rukiya, Interview 2010)

Further narration of events in Sitalaxmapalya revealed a more nuanced telling – about a series of events with a particular logic, but also with a peculiar set of contradictions. For instance, though the directive from the Muslim leaders resulted in all the Muslim borrowers in the city defaulting on their loans, it met with strong discursive and practical resistance from both male and female Muslims from different economic backgrounds, who organized a public protest to challenge the Muslim Committee members' decision. Though the Muslim leaders issued the directive, it wasn't only Muslims who stopped paying back their loans: a significant proportion of borrowers from other religions also joined the revolt. And the individual given credit for organizing hundreds of borrowers to sign a petition against the MFIs in Sitalaxmapalya, and for taking the complaint to the Muslim Committee was neither Muslim nor directly connected with the silk industry.

I first try to understand the claims that over-indebtedness and desperation were being caused by MFI lending, and then examine the narratives around the production of the situation, in terms of rents, including discussing the explanations for these contradictions.

MFI lending and over-indebtedness

Understanding the claims that over-indebtedness justified the repayment stand-off requires, first, the examination of the ways in which over-indebtedness was evaluated and explained by those who made the claims, and then the exploration of the reactions of other actors in the town to the analysis used to make these claims.

Examining actors' narratives, I found that the indicators of over-indebtedness used by residents of Sitalaxmapalya could be organized into two groups. The first encompasses *indicators of desperation*, and the second *indicators of resistance*. Indeed, the two may be linked: resistance might have come from very difficult financial situations triggering feelings of desperation, and might have built on knowledge of other borrowers' acts of desperation. The crucial difference is that acts of resistance emerge from some sense of possible agency to change a situation.

Desperation: The acts that can be seen as indicators of desperation include a few controversial but deeply disturbing incidents that are interpreted as extreme life-choice decisions, and other more widespread indicators of demand and need for money.

The extreme life-choice decisions described in narratives from Sitalaxmapalya include two cases of suicide and one accidental death that reportedly occurred when a borrower drowned while hiding from MFI staff and group members, by sitting in her water-storage drum, because she didn't have the money required to make the required payments (Ammi Jaan, Interview 2010). They include the case of one woman borrower selling her child to a group traveling through the town, described by a member of the local Muslim Committee (Interview 2010), among others, and cases of women going, "to lodges as prostitutes," because they felt that, "disrespecting themselves like that was better than being abused by the fifty other women in their center." They also include cases where families with outstanding loans from MFIs ran away from the town to start afresh somewhere else – reported both by borrowers (Ammi Jaan, Interview 2010) and by MFI field staff (MFI Field Staff, Focus Group 2011) who suddenly found borrower's homes abandoned and were never able to locate their residents again.

Local lenders claim that individuals' borrowings from sources of informal credit were much larger than MFI borrowings and that it was pressure from moneylenders that drove them to take extreme steps (Akula 2009; Ghosh 2009). Supporters of the repayment revolt argue that the pressure of multiple MFI loans, lent without scrutiny, the inflexibility of repayment times, and the forms of pressure being exerted by field staff collectively drove people to take their lives (Lakshmi Sait, Interview 2010).

The problem of the interaction of MFI credit and credit from other sources is an important one. The narratives showed that the discussion is less about which source of credit produced over-indebtedness than about how people feel each source complemented or conflicted with others to produce the situations that they experienced or witnessed. This will be discussed subsequently, while locating the social and economic role of microfinance lending in the context of other credit sources in Sitalaxmapalya.

Individuals explaining disappearances of others saw them either as necessary coping mechanisms in a system where lending norms were often exploitative, or as evidence of such deep financial irresponsibility that individuals disregard the consequences of borrowing and flee to escape accountability. Here, these acts are considered to be representative of desperation, because the costs of relocation – the financial costs of physically transporting a family and their assets, however limited, and the social costs of building new relationships, finding employment, establishing financial credibility – are so high in relative terms that they express a compulsion to migrate due to distress.[4]

The counterargument – that extreme acts of desperation are, unfortunately, sufficiently common that to attribute them to MFI lending is unfair – is made by some microfinance scholars (e.g., Harper 2011). To comment further would require access to the stories behind these extreme acts. This was not pursued in this research for both practical and ethical reasons. The interest here is in the ways in which the stories of these acts are told and retold across time and space, producing resistance against MFIs.

Two other, more widespread, symptoms of over-indebtedness were women's reported willingness, and indeed desperation, to sell items of daily use to repay micro-loans and their willingness to take loans from individual sources of informal credit at higher and higher rates. Lakshmi Sait, an entrepreneur, established moneylender, and microfinance center leader describes "people trying to sell everything they owned: from their old cooking pots and worn blankets, to their brassieres and old sari underskirts" to her, in order to put together the money needed to make their fortnightly loan repayment (Interview 2010). Numerous actors reported their, or other individuals', borrowing from established moneylenders, or from other women in the neighborhood who loaned out their MFI loan money at exorbitant rates, a trend that severely exacerbated the financial and social levels of indebtedness experienced by these borrowers (Interview 2010). Indeed the sale of items of daily use at very little profit, and the willingness to buy money at very high prices could form part of a useful indicator of over-indebtedness in particular contexts.

Resistance: Acts of resistance visible in the narratives offered by residents of Sitalaxmapalya broadly took the forms of defying lending rules established by the MFIs, and of moving local borrowers, local leaders, and local government to support their stand.

The reasons for these acts was often expressed in terms of having reached a threshold, with deeply indebted borrowers, other MFI clients, and religious leaders saying, we "couldn't take it any more" (Ammi Jaan; Lakshmi Sait; Rukiya, Interviews 2010). This sense of being pushed to a limit could have been because of their own inability to meet repayments, or because of the behavior of field staff towards them or towards other individuals in their groups who couldn't make their payments. Often it was a composite of all three factors.

Behavior of MFIs considered exploitative and unjust included the incomplete provision of information regarding the collective financial responsibility involved with MFI borrowing, and the collecting of commissions to set up or renew microfinance loans. One MFI borrower recounted:

> If one or two women didn't have the money to pay, they would insist that all of us sat at the meeting until they received the total amount. That meant nobody could go to work on time and sometimes they kept us for two or three hours so we would lose a day's wages. Many of us were members of several MFIs – so this started happening twice or thrice a week. People began to get angry with the staff and with the women who were not paying regularly.
>
> (Amira Bhanu, Interview 2010)

One MFI borrower who had also been previously employed by an MFI in the region explained:

> Once problems started the staff tried to maintain repayments by threatening women. One company started making all the women sit at a meeting until they somehow came up with the money and this was an effective technique because people had to go to work or send their children to school so ultimately someone would get desperate and pay the money for the person who didn't have her installment. Another company started sending staff to women's houses in the evening to remind them that they had to pay.
>
> One borrower felt she had to retaliate. She convinced people to sign the petition with the promise that if they signed they wouldn't have to pay back their loans. Some women had taken several fresh loans. It was tempting for them to have twenty or thirty thousand rupees in their hands without having to worry about paying them back. Others had taken these loans and spent them irresponsibly, without thinking, so it was convenient for them not to have to worry about paying back.
>
> (Rukiya, Interview 2010)

Through these narratives we see that borrowers explained these acts either as primarily being reactions to personal exploitation by MFIs, or as being in support of others who they feel were being exploited. In either case, they represented borrowers and residents of Sitalaxmapalya demanding a certain accountability and good behavior from MFIs. Indeed often these reactions were depicted as motivated by personal interest or as driven by personal outrage about MFI policy or staff behavior. Nonetheless, the stands taken were still seen to be serious, because implicit within these acts of resistance is the acceptance of losing access to MFI credit in the future.

The indicators of resistance suggest that measurement of resistance to micro-finance in terms of the proportion of people willing to resist and therefore to reject the credit offered by MFIs – and their explanations for this willingness – could also serve to define levels of debt that are "too high" either in terms of absolute financial cost or, as importantly, because they are believed to be exploitative and associated with unfair practices.

Credit in Sitalaxmapalya's structure of accumulation

The forms and sources of credit in Sitalaxmapalya, when the repayment stand-off began, included loans from rotating credit groups, borrowing from finance companies, *Badi-Khasu* or money for interest either from moneylenders or from friends and family, salary advances in the silk-reeling industry, zero-interest loans for the poorest from the Muslim Anjuman Committee, and *Mahila Sanga* or women's Self Help Group loans as well as MFI loans. The narratives revealed that, in addition to financial criteria such as the loan amount, pay-back period and interest rates, borrowers in Sitalaxmapalya evaluated credit sources and valued money according to a range of social parameters. These include the lenders' social affiliations, their interests and intentions in lending, the fairness of their lending policy, the opportunity cost to the lenders of loaning money, and an estimate of the total funds held by the lender. The interaction of these multiple economic, social, and micro-political criteria determined the ultimate value of the credit source and the extent to which rules for good behavior in terms of lending practices are followed.

Everyday borrowing: Everyone both bought and sold money in Sitalax-mapalya. Money that was borrowed was referred to as *Badi-ge Khasu*, literally "money for interest" and could have been from friends, family members, or local moneylenders. These transactions could have very different terms and different prices, in terms of interest rates and collateral but also social costs.

Other credit organizations: Rotating credit organizations offered credit amounts smaller than MFIs at lower money prices but higher social costs. Members were aware that the source of capital in these groups is the pooled resources of individual members and that the failure to pay the required amount meant losing an allotted share of funds in the current cycle and possible exclusion from credit groups in future. Finance companies offered credit that borrowers were required to pay back over shorter durations, but with greater flexibility, at interest rates that were more expensive then micro-loans.

Salary advances and the social organization of silk-reeling: The silk-reeling industry, called filiature locally, comprises of a cluster of family-managed units that are owned by Muslim capitalists, who also tend to occupy key positions on the Muslim Committee, and employ local wage labor. Like other such units in the state, they tend to employ a largely Scheduled Caste and Muslim labor force. Firm owners offer a sum as an advance to labor[5] at the beginning of the employment season – securing their labor for the season – and pay a low daily wage in addition. Low salaries, unpredictable work, and working conditions that put labor at a high risk of chronic respiratory disease and other industrial illnesses, make working in the silk-reeling units undesirable (Inbunathan 2008, Rukiya, Interview 2010). It's usually people from the poorest families who join filiature units when they are not able to meet basic needs or when a family crisis forces them to work because they need the money advance (Razaq, Interview 2010). If workers fall ill they tend to get caught in a vicious cycle when ill health lowers the number of days they can work and when heavy expenditure on health care increases their dependence on debt (Inbunathan 2008, Rukiya interview 2010).

Understanding the debt relations around the filiature industry is crucial in order to be able to understand the manner in which MFI operations took root in Sitalaxmapalya over the last decade, followed by the repayment stand-off. For laborers in the filiature units to be able to start their own micro-enterprise they require not only the capital for investment but also resources to free themselves from debt bondage. Where individuals are able to raise the funds for both, their ability to start up small-scale home units is further constrained by the relations that govern access to raw materials and to markets for silk thread.

The narratives reveal the ways in which the casual and vulnerable workforce of filiature firms is regulated, exploited, and, on occasion protected, by the owners of firms. However, before discussing them it is important first to explore the pattern of spread of organizations offering financial services to the poor to help understand the ways in which MFI operations interacted with, and altered patronage relations, leading up to the repayment crisis.

The entry and proliferation of MFIs

Organizations promoting the expansion of financial inclusion began working in Sitalaxmapalya in the 1980s. The central government-sponsored Urban Stree Shakti program entered Sitalaxmapalya in 1985, and began setting up Self Help Groups (SHGs) almost from its inception. Bank linkage of these SHGs, and lending to SHGs, began in the early 1990s (Regional Manager, Interview 2011) as part of the All India SHG Bank Linkage Project (SBLP). Initially these organizations offered Self-Help Group loans, which were disbursed from a corpus created through the pooled savings of Rs.20 a week from each of twenty members, in an order based on need and the principle of equal distribution. Between 1998 and 2004, Sitalaxmapalya witnessed the further growth of state-supported initiatives for women's self-employment administered through SHG movements. Several projects evolved under the ambit of the Karnataka Urban

Infrastructure Development Project (KUIDP), funded by an Asian Development Bank loan and the State government supported initiative. Urban Stree Shakti then expanded significantly under the umbrella of the micro-enterprise branch of central government-funded urban employment generation scheme, Swarna Jayanti Shahari Rozgar Yojana (SJSRY).

Around 2005, the profile of micro-lending in Sitalaxmapalya changed. The KUIDP and Stree Shakti projects came to an end because the NGOs implementing them wound up operations following the withdrawal of state support. These projects closed before the process of federating the SHGs into independently sustaining entities was complete, leading to a deterioration of some of the functioning groups (MFI Field Staff, Focus Group 2011). Simultaneously MF-NGOs began to set up operations in the city, employing the staff laid off from the KUIDP and Stree Shakti projects. Staff of a local MFI reproduced the discourse of profitability and sustainability prevalent in the international microfinance sector (Fernandez 2006): they explained that the failure of the SHGs to become self-sustaining within the stipulated period meant that a new mode of financial service provision was needed. These staff also pointed out that the SBLP suffered because of the pressures that competitive profit-oriented MFIs created in the market. The higher loan amounts offered by the MFIs made SHG-based lending schemes less popular amongst borrowers, and the higher salaries and more attractive perks made jobs with MFIs more attractive for staff.

Initially, with small lending amounts and strong financial incentives for repayments, micro-loans were disbursed and collected easily in Sitalaxmapalya. Significantly, with the interest to secure a large portfolio, making field staff lax about explaining and enforcing the preconditions of group solidarity (MFI Regional Manager, Interview 2010), as long as regular repayments remained the norm, microfinance loans represented an opportunity to borrow from outsiders, with significantly lower obligations – socially or in the workplace – to the lender. Maintaining an image of financial responsibility was important for future access to credit. The availability of larger loans upon repayment of initial loans gave individuals a strong incentive to make payments. Whereas other sources might have higher social and economic costs of borrowing and defined limits, given the rate at which the scale of MFI operations was increasing and the rate at which lending amounts were rising, borrowers felt that they were accessing an infinite source of money, limited only by their ability to make timely repayments. One MFI borrower recounted having heard a first-hand account from someone who had seen the account books of an MFI who reported that MFIs had "crores and crores of money" and made massive profits.

By 2008 at least seven MFIs were operating in Sitalaxmapalya, and each of these were large and regionally diverse institutions that were profit-oriented and attracted international investment. The amounts these institutions lent to each individual ranged from Rs.5,000 to Rs.30,000[6] and the interest rates ranged from 23–28 percent per annum – with a declining balance. The repayment of these loans occurred on either a weekly or a fortnightly basis, and the loan period was usually fifty weeks.

The large number of MFIs in Sitalaxmapalya can be seen as part of the trend in the industry to concentrate and cluster in order to make use of rents from the SHG movement and the existence of other MFIs. As more MFIs began to locate in the area, existing MFIs lost their monopoly control over segments of the market. The MFIs then changed their lending policies to offer higher incentives for people to borrow from them. A Regional Manager reported that the MFI he worked for started out by issuing loans of five thousand rupees in 2005, but "by the time of the crisis people were talking of figures like twenty and thirty thousand because each MFI was trying to offer more and attract more borrowers" (MFI Regional Manager, Interview 2010).

Increased individual loan size, and increases in the number of MFIs in Sitalaxmapalya pushed up the size of individual borrowing. Furthermore, field staff, who were offered financial incentives for forming a certain number of groups, started devising their own techniques to expand their market shares. Staff began to offer incentives for Center Leaders to form groups for them. Center Leaders in turn started "demanding vessels, or a sari between group members who wanted to be recommended for a loan sanction" and the pre-occupation with incentives made the enforcement of background checks lax (MFI Regional Manager, Interview 2010).

The crisis: desperation and resistance

Difficulties with debt servicing began to appear for many, and various, reasons –because families were lent money they had no way of repaying, because of shocks[7] in the silk-reeling industry, because MFI investment failed to be profitable, or because the time and energy costs of servicing multiple loans became very high – and MFI staff enforced the group guarantee clause. Borrowers who were making regular payments were suddenly faced with unexpected and serious increases in the cost of their loans because they had to pay the defaulters' shares in addition to making their own repayment. This rise in weekly repayments – translating to a sudden rise in the price of their micro-loans – created financial difficulties for borrowers and kindled resentment towards the field staff for insisting on enforcing a policy that they hadn't always been clear in explaining until then and for the inflexibility of their lending norms relative to other credit sources.

Once borrowers began experiencing problems with loan repayments, field staff devised innovative ways of disciplining borrowers and extracting payments,[8] thereby creating what Khan would call Monitoring rents that often drew from techniques used by local moneylenders and caused women to accuse them of being even worse than loan-sharks (Lakshmi Sait, Interview 2010).

Borrowers who had been faced with the difficulty of having to make inflexible MFI payments that offered no delays in desperate situations, cited this as a reason for choosing to eliminate MFI credit as a borrowing option, saying:

> With MFIs you have no option but to pay on time, there is no flexibility unlike with money lenders who are more than happy to let you take more

time and to collect interest for the delay. MFIs refuse to understand when people ask them to give them one more day or one more week.

The pressures of juggling multiple loans without a reliable source of income, and the threat of abuse from field staff and group members on borrowers' failures to make weekly payments, created a scenario where a large number of MFI borrowers needed small loans frequently and desperately (Mohammed Sahib; Interview 2010, Razaq; Interview 2010). These loans were taken from local moneylenders and from other borrowers who lent out low interest capital they acquired through MFI loans at very high rates. In the context of MFI lending in Sitalaxmapalya at levels heavily inflated by competition, these loans were the "micro-loans", and borrowers felt it was these loans that played a major role in reproducing the vulnerability created by competitive lending and their precarious conditions of work:

RAZAQ: No badavaru, indebted people, benefited from microfinance. The only people who became sreemantrigalu[9] because of microfinance were moneylenders. For them it was a source of cheap capital. They paid some women commissions to take loans and then lent the money out to other women who needed money urgently to pay back their MFI loans. And women themselves started lending out their MFI loans, and they made a lot of money, with so many other women being desperate for money to pay back their MFI loans.

(Interview 2010)

NAFEEDA: When you have money and someone needs it, you give it out for badi (interest) at the going rate. It's difficult to say what is microfinance money and what is business profits. So it's very difficult to say whether what they are doing is right or wrong.

(Interview 2010)

These accounts revealed not only that MFI credit existed alongside a range of other forms of local credit, but also that the funds the MFI offered were often transformed into informal credit. The difficulty of determining a fair rate of lending was not only a problem for MFIs, but also for Sitalaxmapalya's real *micro*-lenders who were lending to a desperate population. Though several individuals felt that these micro-loans played a very important role in exacerbating over-indebtedness amongst the most vulnerable, most were hesitant to take a stand about whether their behavior was right or wrong, seeing local lending at rates that borrowers are willing to pay as being a socially accepted and entirely inevitable practice.

MFIs on the other hand were seen as outsiders, with large amounts of money, clearly articulating the intention to "help the poor" and "aid development". Once difficulties began, their development intent became an obvious point for criticism and bargaining – when borrowers asked, "do they want to help us or exploit us?" – it was both a plea and a challenge.

This desperation, and this challenge, defined the framing of the petition that was taken to the dominant social complex of Muslim religious leaders and local capitalists. Though the revolt was enforced by the local leaders, using religion as a tool for control, the mobilization of the 200 or so women who spearheaded the resistance against the MFIs – taking the signed petition to the religious leaders – came about because of the position that a woman called Lakshmi Sait occupied. Lakshmi Sait is an Urdu-speaking Hindu woman who initially did domestic work for Muslim families and later became a successful businesswoman, well known as a local moneylender, with start-up capital from MFI loans and support from her family (Lakshmi Sait, Interview 2010). The nature of evidence makes it difficult to pinpoint her precise role in setting in motion the events leading to the stand-off; however, several accounts refer to the central role she played in organizing borrowers to protest, and to her connection with local leaders as her past employers. Her own account is consistent with this.

She explained the events that led her to mobilize women and religious leaders against the MFIs:

> Two women from my group ran away because they couldn't pay their loans. They were in my group in three MFIs and everyone started saying "You're the centre leader, you should pay their money." So I started paying Rs.300 a week for each of them. How much is that? 1,800 per week, on top of the 1,800 I had to pay myself to the six MFIs.
>
> I had no problem paying my share, and it was okay paying their share for a few weeks, but there was no way I could keep paying double for an indefinite amount of time. My husband also put his foot down and said that I should stop. So we tried to talk to the staff and asked them to help us out since people had run away and that wasn't our fault but they said, "You signed that you would pay and that was the reason we gave you the loans," and they continued to harass us to pay.
>
> At this time poorer people in the same situation came to me asking for loans, offering anything and everything they had as collateral. It upset me so much to see people desperate to sell their old pots and pans, their old sari-skirts. I just couldn't take it. I decided to get everyone to sign an arzee, a petition, and take it to the Muslim Committee.
>
> (Lakshmi Sait, Interview 2010)

Religion in the differentiated urban economy: Once Lakshmi had made up her mind to protest, she used the range of her social institutional affiliations to mobilize support for the revolt, just as she used them to establish groups of clients for MFIs and continues to use them to operate successfully both as food vendor and moneylender. Gender gave her access to spaces that the male Muslim Committee members would not have been able to enter. Language gave her access to the Muslim community, including its religious leaders, and religion gave her access to the Hindu community (Rukiya, Interview 2010). The support of Hindu women was important to the public profile of the resistance to the revolt, Muslim religious leaders were keen to assert that the stand-off was not a "Muslim revolt" despite the fact that, as we shall see later, they used religion to enforce control and despite its being reported in this way in the media. Lakshmi's narrative emphasizes the involvement of Hindus:

> They try to say that it was all Muslims but it wasn't. During the rally, I was right in front of the whole crowd with three others like me. There were three or four Muslims behind us and then three or four more Hindus behind them and then the whole crowd of Hindus and Muslims.
>
> (Lakshmi Sait, Interview 2010)

In their response to the petition, the Muslim Committee of Sitalaxmapalya organized a public meeting to discuss the ways in which they could prevent MFI lending in the area. They subsequently funded the rally that Lakshmi described.

Religious obligation was used to quell objections from Muslim men, by framing their support for the revolt as being necessary in order to fulfill their joint moral responsibility towards "our women" (Nafeeda, Interview 2010; Razaq, Interview 2010).

One young Muslim man, owner of a door-to-door clothes sales business, explained how he was concerned that the refusal to repay micro-loans would adversely affect his community, and how he was ultimately convinced by the religious-leader business-owner complex that protest against MFI action was required:

> I went myself to protest against the ban on repayments. Many of us gathered outside the Mosque one evening after the ban was announced. I felt that they were taking away from our credit-worthiness and spoiling the image of our people. I went straight to the headman and told him, "You are forcing us to lose our respect, now no one will lend us money anymore. How many weddings happened because of MFI loans?" I asked him, "Will you give us money to conduct our sisters' and our daughters' weddings? They challenged me, "Didn't marriages happen before MFIs came to Sitalaxmapalya? People will manage somehow, but we can't tolerate these outsiders exploiting our women, driving our women to commit suicide and forcing them into prostitution. Where is the respect in that? Where is your izzath, your pride?" Then I realized they were right, even though they may have been doing this for their own gains and even though they avoided making any concrete commitment to helping us. I kept quiet and went home.
>
> (Razaq, Interview 2010)

Other members of the Muslim community felt that self-interest governed the stand of the religious leaders, but they explained that they also felt that they were dependent on the Committee members for the protection they were able to offer them as a result of their economic and political power. They felt leaders could help with access to state resources, education, and employment, which discrimination against their religion otherwise denies them (Rukiya, Interview 2010).

They used their role as Muslim Committee members to discipline people who wouldn't have joined the protest, threatening to deny them access to "holy" services that they control, and threatening them with ostracization from the community and with consequences for their afterlife if they failed to cooperate with their instructions. As one Muslim woman recounted:

> They announced that they would take away our burial rites and wouldn't give us the holy cloth to cover our bodies when we died. If people continued to pay, they sent gundas to our houses and told us that we'd have to leave areas like Rahmaniya Nagar and Yarabi Nagar, if we didn't respect their directive.
>
> (Ammi Jaan, Interview 2010)

Women who came from families with successful businesses, or had skills that they could use for entrepreneurial activity and who were also free from debt-bondage, were more likely to report regret about the suspension of MFI services. However, their husbands still tended to abide by the Muslim Committee view that despite denying them useful credit, suspension of MFI lending was necessary, in order to protect the vulnerable women of the community.

Microfinance borrowers who felt they had benefited from the credit they received felt it was wrong for the religious leaders to deny them microfinance credit without offering an alternative or creating a solution to the structural inequalities that were, in the first place, causing the problems they claimed they were attempting to combat.

These borrowers recounted the response of leaders, on being challenged by them to offer them an alternative source of credit:

> When we went to the religious leaders and asked, "What do we do when we need money now, will you give us the loans we need?" They said, "Go to the bank or join the Mahila Sangas (Women's SHGs). We aren't telling you not to borrow money at all, just don't go to the MFIs."
>
> (Rukiya, Interview 2010)

In their analysis, these individuals suggested that the low loan amounts under the SHG-based schemes might have offered sufficient funds to supplement incomes and therefore worked to subsidize the labor force for capital. Meanwhile the higher loan amounts from the MFIs threatened the capitalist classes by raising the advances demanded by labor and by breaking its ties of bondage.

The religious-leader capitalist complex occupied a Janus-faced position – accepting, and even demanding, control over their employees as industrialists, and protecting the same people as part of their duties as religious leaders, or out of goodwill as their current or past employers. The religious leader I spoke to narrated the offer of a transfer from MFIs to call off the repayment stand-off, using it to emphasize his role as protector of the vulnerable:

I've been offered bribes from MFIs to get people to start paying back their loans. But I'd never take that money. To take it would be to drink the blood of the *badavaru*. What do I need the money for? Five-ten lakhs? I'm not in any shortage. No. I'd never take that money and commit such injustice to my people. My role is to protect them. No amount of money will tempt me.

The multiple ways in which religion was used – as a tool for control and to coerce groups of individuals in different ways – shows how religion contributes to the stability if not the rigidity of the local structure of accumulation in Sitalaxmapalya. It shows the ability of the capitalist class to call upon religion to resist and challenge changes in the patterns of rents proposed by MFI policy. It illustrates how multiple and interconnected affiliations bolstered the power of the religious-leader factory-owner complex and increased the vulnerability of the women who were either part of their workforce or were struggling in self-employment to stay out of waged work.

A member of the Muslim Committee argued that the problem with microfinance was that MFIs placed responsibility on women in situations where they didn't have the social authority to take on that responsibility. This view was supported by borrowers and by MFI staff. However, they also asserted that women who worked in the filiature factories were significantly more likely to report unmanageable levels of debt and were more likely to support the revolt. Being engaged in filiature work itself was often a result of poverty and of having an unemployed or unsupportive spouse, and the conditions of work – the terms of debt-based labour agreements, inconsistent work, and poor working conditions – added to the multiple interconnected deprivations faced by these women, whose vulnerability was central to the crisis (see Alkire 2008; Ariana and Naveed 2009).

By 2011, two years after the revolt, some women had gone back to borrowing from MFIs. Lending no longer happens in groups and in public spaces. Instead, money is delivered directly to group leaders who divide it amongst the group, and collect loan repayments.

Conclusions

The narratives from Sitalaxmapalya indicated that is important to examine both the initial boom in micro-lending and the subsequent crisis in terms of the contexts in which micro-lending existed in the town. Using the framework of rents offered by Khan along with the Social Structure of Accumulation (SSA) approach allowed us to map the interaction of micro-lending initiatives with local institutions that organize and regulate production and reproduction in the town. This enabled access to the nuanced and complex ways in which the organization of powers and interests in the town related to the forms of credit existing in the town and explained trends in the local micro-finance sector.

Employing Khanian and SSA analysis to navigate the narratives revealed the ways in which regionally powerful Muslim capitalists, in the filiature industry, used forms of control that included religion-based regulation to reinforce class hierarchies, reproducing the vulnerabilities of their largely lower- class female labor force. The industry employed residents of the town who lacked both the capital to set up their own businesses within the town and the ability to travel outside the town for work, for various reasons including their being mothers with small children who needed care or their being disallowed by religious rules to travel for work. The multiple interconnected vulnerabilities of the workforce made it possible for them to offer low wages, and irregular work, under poor working conditions – often maintaining complex patronage relationships with their employees who depended on them for seasonal credit – keeping their work-force indebted and obligated to them.

When micro-loans entered Sitalaxmapalya in the 1980s, in the form of Self-help Group lending, they occupied a space in an arena where a range of other forms of credit, including salary advances paid to employees in the filiature industry, already existed. Though the purpose of the SHG schemes was to promote employment-generating activity, actors from the town suggested that the restrictive size of the loans issued through Self-Help Groups, might have had less impact on empowering women who otherwise depended on irregular, unor-ganized, and generally scarce wage labor to establish entrepreneurial ventures. They could be seen as state transfers that served to subsidize labor for capital,[10] giving the filiature employees a small additional sum of money that allowed them to make ends meet.

The rapid spread of profit-oriented MFI operations in Sitalaxmapalya can be understood in terms of the different kinds of rents they were able to extract. MFIs extracted managerial and learning rents by employing staff who had been trained by organizations promoting SHG lending, and lent to a client base already informed about the functioning of group-based micro-loans. They extracted Schumpeterian rents in borrowing and investing large sums of money to be able to offer substantial loans to borrowers, and extracted conventional economic rents by lending at rates that were less expensive, financially and socially, than other forms of credit in Sitalaxmapalya.

That MFI lending both initiated and enhanced the income-generating ability of some households in Sitalaxmapalya cannot be contested. Several households used MFI loans to start, or expand, successful businesses using credit from MFI-loans.

Understanding the arrangements of credit sources and of power that preceded MFI lending allows us to understand that local capitalists felt threatened by the latter because they felt the inflow of cheaper, easily accessible credit weakened the control they had over their workforce (which they enforced through the dependence of their employees on the salary advance). Initially, dependence on salary advances and other forms of credit eased but, ultimately, MFI lending created significant difficulties for families who chose to use the less expensive, but larger, MFI loans for consumption smoothing activities, rather than take more expensive loans, and for those who borrowed but were unable to establish successful businesses. These families took loans from multiple MFIs hoping to be able to use new loans to service old ones, but they often found their debt spiraling out of control. Typically, it was the already vulnerable families, (who were often employees of the filiature industry because they lacked alternate employment) who struggled with their MFI loans. They had difficulty making repayments from their wages if they used the money for consumption smoothing activities. They also needed capital to repay debt to employers as well as to invest if they were looking to start their own business.

A Khanian and SSA-based analysis enabled us to see that the forces producing the repayment stand-off were complex. The stand-off did reflect serious difficulties of borrowers who were struggling with multiple loans for various reasons (as well as the resentment of borrowers who felt they were ill-treated by MFI staff, who used harsh tactics to maintain high repayment rates). However, it was the aligning of the interests of the local capital-religious leader complex with those of borrowers who felt that MFI lending had been unfair (on various grounds), that ensured that all Muslim borrowers in the town, including those who felt they benefited from MFI lending, participated in the stand-off. The reliance on local capital, which can often have interests conflicting with those of laborers, demonstrates that the dynamics producing the stand-off maintain strong continuities with the existing arrangements of power and points to the persisting vulnerability of a section of women in Sitalaxmapalya.

This preliminary discussion with stakeholders in Sitalaxmapalya suggests that a systematic study of national and state level politics, and the local structure of accumulation, is necessary in order to make a comprehensive assessment of the relationships between political interests and development policy process. Following Khan, the reordering of political interests must become the pre-occupation of the policy process. And building on Khan, this requires recognition of the importance of discursive participation and diverse forms of political mobilization that could facilitate the rearrangement of rents, redistributing powers and controls over the structure of accumulation in a more equitable manner.

Notes

1 The name of the town has been changed to protect the identity of people who contributed narratives to this account. Sitalaxmapalya is located 45 km outside Bangalore, the state capital. The population of Sitalaxmapalya is estimated to be approaching 100,000 extrapolated from the 2001 Census when the population was 80,000.

2 The State category of "financially excluded" applies to 80 percent of the families in the town, making 15,000 women eligible for MFI loans. Well over 22,500 loans had been issued by seven MFIs in Sitalaxmapalya when the standoff began (not including loans from the largest lender – including these would cause the figures to be much higher).

3 About 25 percent of the town's residents are Muslim. However, on average, Sitalaxmapalya's Muslim population is less financially well off than the Hindu population and so a larger proportion, over 60 percent of MFI borrowers, are Muslim.

4 Morvant-Roux offers more detailed analysis of relationships between migration and over-indebtedness in this volume.

5 The sums being offered in 2005, reportedly ranged between Rs.25,000 and Rs.30,000. This went up to the range of Rs.30, 000 to Rs.40,000 and in 2011 it has further increased to Rs.40,000 to Rs.50,000 (Interviews 2010–2011).

6 This, relative to self-reported household incomes that range from Rs.10,000 a year to a maximum of Rs.88,000 with a median income of Rs.40,080, according to IIM-B data (Kamath *et al.* 2010).

7 Following the liberalization of the market for silk, and increased quotas for imports of raw silk from China, the local market is constantly reacting to changes in the price of Chinese raw silk (Nambiar 2012).

8 Angulo Salazar, in this volume, writes of similar strategies being employed in Mexico.

9 Most people in Sitalaxmapalya were both borrowers and lenders; the term *Badavaru* was used repeatedly to describe people who depended on borrowed money to meet basic needs – while *Sreemantrigalu* referred to people who don't need to borrow to meet basic needs, but might borrow for investment representing a form of caste–class stratification observed amongst other groups of semi-urban Muslims (Harriss-White 2003b).

10 This is similar to what Heyer (2012) argues has been the intent of social policy in Tamil Nadu.

References

Alkire, S. (2008) *Using the Capabilities Approach: Prospective and Evaluative Analysis in The Capability Approach*. Cambridge: Cambridge University Press 2008.

Aiyar, S. (2009) "Anjumans deprive Muslim women of microcredit," *Economic Times*, November 8, 2010.

Akula, V. (2009) "Vikram's Response to WSJ," available online at: http://eulokesh.blog-spot.com/search?updated-min=2009–001T00%3A00%3A00–08%3A00andupdated-max=2010–01–01T00%3A00%3A00–08%3A00andmax-results=1, Accessed February 24, 2009.

Ariana, P. and Naveed, A. (2009) "Health," in Denuelin, S. and Shahani, L. (eds) *An Introduction to Human Development and Capability Approach*, London: Earthscan 2009.

Ariana, P. and Naveed, A. (2007) "Spread of the Self-Help Groups Banking Linkage Programme in India," Paper presented at the International Conference on Rural Finance Research: Moving Results. FAO headquarters, Rome, Italy, 19–21 March 2007.

Dichter, T and Harper, M. (2007) (eds) *What's Wrong With Microfinance*, Warwickshire: Practical Action Publishing.

Fernandez, A. (2006) "history and spread of the Self-help Affinity Group Movement in India," *Occasional Paper 3, 2006 of International Fund for Agricultural Development*, Rome.

Fouillet, C. (2009) "The economic, spatial and political construction of micro-finance – the case of India," PhD Thesis, Universite Libre de Bruxelles, Belgium.

Ghokale, K. (2009) "A global surge in tiny loans spurs credit bubble in a slum," *The Wall Street Journal*, August 13, 2009.

Ghosh, S. (2009) "Ujjivan's Response to the Wall Street Journal Article on Microfinance in Sitalaxmapalya," August 14, 2009, avaialable online at: www.ujjivan.com/news_WallStreetJournal_article_on_Microfinance_in_Sitalaxmapalya.htm (accessed February 22, 2101).

Guérin, I., D'Espallier, B. and Venkatasubramanian, G. (2012) "Debt in Rural South India: fragmentation, social regulation and discrimination," *Journal of Development Studies* (forthcoming).

Harper, M. (2011) "The Commercialization of Microfinance: Resolution or Extension of Poverty?", in Bateman, M. (ed.) *Confronting Microfinance: Undermining Sustainable Development*, Sterling: Kumarian Press.

Harriss-White, B. (2003a) "On understanding markets as social and political institutions in developing economies", in Chang, H.-J. (ed.) *Rethinking Development Economics*, London: Anthem Press.

Harriss-White, B. (2003b) *India Working: Essays on Economy and Society*, New Delhi: Foundation Books 2003.

Harriss-White, B. (2009) "Political architecture of India's Technology system for solar energy," *Economic and Political Weekly* XLIV(47): 49–60.

Heyer, J. (2012) "Labor Standards and social policy: a South Indian case study," *Global Labor Journal* 3(1): 91–117.

Inbanathan, A. (2008) "Social mobility in the context of occupational health: the case of silk reeling," in Kadekodi, G. K., Kanbur, R., and Rao, V. (eds) *Developments in Karnataka: Challenges of Governance, Equity and Empowerment*, New Delhi: Academic Foundation.

Kamath, R. (2010) "Ramnagaram financial diaries: cash patterns and repayments of microfinance borrowers," *Enterprise Development and Microfinance* 21(2): 101–117.

Khan, M. (2004) "State Failure in Developing Countries and Institutional Reform Strategies". Revised version of paper prepared for the Annual World Bank Conference on Development Economics—Europe 2003, IBRD/World Bank 2004.

Krishnaswamy, K. (2007) "Competition and multiple borrowing in the Indian Microfinance Sector," Institute for Financial Management and Research: Center for Microfinance, September 2007.

Nambiar, P. (2012) "The Chinese Silk Route," *The Times of India*, March 12th, 2012.

Nair, T. (2005) "The changing world of Indian microfinance," *Economic and Political Weekly*, April 2005.

Schaffer, B. (1984) "Towards Responsibility – public policy in theory and practice," in Clay, E. and Schaffer, B. (eds) *Room for Manoeuvre*, London: Heinemann.

Sen, A. (1999) "Democracy as a universal value," *Journal of Democracy* 10(3): 3–17.

Sen, A. (1999) *Development as Freedom*, Oxford: Oxford University Press.

Srinivasan, N. (2008*) Microfinance India: State of the Sector Report 2008*, New Delhi: Sage Publications 2008.

Stewart, F. (2004) "Groups and Capabilities," Paper prepared for the "Fourth Conference on the Capability Approach: Enhancing Human Security", University of Pavia, Italy, September 5–7, 2004.

Vanroose, A. (2007) "Is microfinance an ethical way to provide financial services to the poor?", *Economics and Ethics* (5).

Vanroose, A. (2008) "What macrofactors make micro-institutions reach out?", CEB Working Paper 08/036, October 2008.

14 Conclusion

Isabelle Guérin, Solène Morvant-Roux and
Magdalena Villarreal

Is microcredit part of the solution in overcoming poverty, or is it part of the problem? Do the poor have too much credit or not enough? Do they suffer from credit "rationing" or are they over-indebted? Is it access to credit that should be questioned or the way it is implemented?

Such are some of the questions the reader might hope to be addressed in the book's concluding chapter. However, at this stage, it should be clear that there are no simple answers to these questions.

We can see from history that perceptions of debt and credit have always been subject to a great deal of variation (Graeber 2011; Peebles 2010; Thérêt 2009; Shipton 2010: 41). On an individual level, taking on debt may be seen as a sin, as frivolous and irresponsible, or as the victimization, exploitation or domination of others. But it may also be seen as a tool for emancipation and self-accomplishment, an efficient way to develop a better future and a source of hope. At the group level, debt may be viewed as the most important form of oppression over dominated classes, and as reproducing inequalities and hierarchies. It may, however, also be seen as a powerful force for creating solidarity, affirming identities and a great stimulus for economic growth and social cohesion.

Obviously there are good and bad debts: those that release, liberate and enrich, and those that enslave, subjugate and impoverish. But how should we define good and bad debts? Who defines the criteria and why? Is a particular debt intrinsically good or bad, or can it be both? Are the criteria the same for everyone, or do they vary depending on the context, the social positioning of the debtors and the lenders or the periods of history?

Several lessons emerge from this collection of chapters, which may be of interest for policymakers, microfinance practitioners, their funders, and more generally, any person or institution interested in the microfinance industry.

The first lesson has to do with the concept of over-indebtedness. Who is over-indebted and who is not? How to measure and what, if anything, should we measure? As indicated in introduction of this volume, the line that separates "sound" indebtedness to over-indebtedness is extremely thin. Thus the need to not take it for granted but analyse it in its contexts.

Most of the literature on microfinance looks to assess the impact of microfinance on borrowers' wellbeing, or to deconstruct it as a new form of power and control over the poor (Fernando 2006; Rankin 2002). These two approaches are undoubtedly useful and necessary. The lived experience of microcredit *as debt*, fundamental as it is from a policy perspective, remains a relatively neglected area, however. Economic anthropology has shown that economics and finance are shaped by, and constitutive of, social relationships, moral values and culture. Economics and finance have no universal meanings, but a variety of meanings and formulations within particular cultures (Gudeman 2001; Hann and Hart 2011; Shipton 2007; Villarreal 2004). As argued by Shipton, while the impact of microcredit has drawn a lot of attention, something that few people have paid attention to is "people's perception and experience of financial borrowing and lending. Missing are social and cultural dimensions like kinship, ethnicity, ritual, religion and the deeper, broader entrustments and obligations into which they fit – or fail to fit" (Shipton 2007: xvii). Only scant literature examines how norms, institutions and values influence demand for, and use of, microcredit, all of which highlight the discrepancies between "foreign" and local categories. As is evident in various case studies in this volume, terms often considered universal such as "loan", "repayment", "interest rate", "solidarity groups" but also "debt" in fact take on a variety of meanings, which can lead to intractable misunderstandings.

The same goes for over-indebtedness. High financial costs and debt burdens are certainly an issue. The interest rates some microfinance institutions charge (not all) are simply exorbitant and do not serve any kind of social mission. The levels of debt that some households have to deal with in comparison to their income and assets are clearly highly problematic. Far beyond financial issues, as a number of case studies in this volume emphasize, debtors are also very sensitive to what can be labelled as *degrading debts*. Developers, policymakers and academics too often take an overly narrow vision of debt as something neutral that can be cancelled through reciprocation or repayment. Relationships between debtors and creditors are not just about money, goods or services, however, but entail emotions and feelings such as dignity, prestige and respectability, and also shame, humiliation, anxiety, anger, revenge or even friendship, gratitude and love. An example of a degrading debt would be a loan officer entering uninvited into the home of an indigenous family in rural Mexico, which is all the more degrading if the credit officer were a man and the debtor a woman (see Chapter 11). Another degrading debt would be a banker taking a suspicious view of the household expenses of a lower working-class family in France (Chapter 4). In India, it could be a debtor borrowing from someone from a lower caste in the local hierarchy (Chapters 5 and 6). In many contexts, it could be a male creditor sexually harassing a female debtor. It could also be a debt owed to a neighbour – including within so-called microcredit solidarity groups – who then spreads rumors (Chapters 6 and 9). Degrading debts can also be those that entail great dependence (Chapter 9), given that tolerance to dependence varies greatly depending on local social structures and individual aspirations (Chapters 6 and 7). A degrading debt may also be one that keeps growing and which cannot be reciprocated (Chapter 8). The perception and the meaning of degrading debts, as we can see, are *situated*; they are shaped by – and constitutive of – the social positioning of debtors and creditors in terms of gender, caste, ethnicity, class and location. They are neither fixed nor pre-determined, but the outcome of diverse structural mechanisms and specific contingencies, and thus they often vary across space (and time).

Other than the first chapter's discussion of over-indebtedness on a macro level, this volume looks at highly localized case studies from most continents (India and Bangladesh for Asia, Mexico and the United States for North America, Kenya and Madagascar for Africa, France for Europe). Experiences of over-indebtedness are probably as varied as the social, cultural and political contexts in which microfinance operates. Moral judgments of debt are far from universally the same. The frameworks within which they are calculated differ from one site to another and within diverse social strata and groupings. Debt can be considered a normal part of the human condition, as observed in Hindu societies (Malamoud 1988) or as something that should be avoided, as observed in rural communities in Maghreb (Bourdieu 1977). This has a direct impact on how people appropriate microcredit, and how they define and are exposed to over-indebtedness. For example, the microfinance crisis has been quite severe in Andhra Pradesh owing to aggressive microcredit marketing, the agrarian crisis (Taylor 2012; Servet 2011), and also perhaps to the very high propensity of local communities to get into debt. In rural Morocco, by contrast, lack of indebtedness is a matter of honour and there is a climate of reluctance to take on microcredit (Morvant-Roux *et al.* forthcoming).

A now commonly accepted definition of over-indebtedness in the microfinance sector is framed in terms of "sacrifice", inspired by the work of Jessica Schicks: "A microfinance customer is over-indebted if he is continuously struggling to meet repayment deadlines and repeatedly has to make unduly high sacrifices to meet his loan obligations" (Schicks forthcoming). The definition has clearly been formulated to help design appropriate customer protection measures. Its main strength is to be highly practical, allowing for a relatively easy quantification of over-indebted individuals or households. But this approach views repayment default to be the outcome of over-indebtedness, whereas we know from various contexts that repayment defaults may also be a deliberate choice (Chapter 3; see also Morvant-Roux *et al.*, forthcoming). "Strategic defaults" as the outcome of choice rather than incapacity deserve specific attention.

Moreover, to understand the *processes* and *consequences* of over-indebtedness, a broader, more dynamic approach is needed. This volume has adopted a definition of over-indebtedness as a process of impoverishment through debt, where impoverishment is taken in a very broad material, social, cultural and symbolic sense. A person becomes over-indebted if his/her debt significantly and continuously erodes his/her assets, standard of living and/or social network, status and reputation.

Some debts demand intolerable repayment sacrifices – over-indebtedness in the sense Schicks uses – but can ultimately allow the debtor to "get by" with a socially and/or materially improved position once the debt is paid. Given rising social aspirations, including among marginalized and vulnerable populations, and the efforts and sacrifices that some families are willing to make to improve their homes and pay for their children's education or marriages, this is probably not an unusual situation. In contrast, some debt situations may bring about impoverishment and the deterioration of living conditions simply because the person is unable to pay his/her debt. It is not the payment of the debt which is a source of sacrifice, but its non-payment, exposing debtors to the risk of seizure, expulsion, moral or physical harassment, social exclusion or extreme dependence.

Social impoverishment and material impoverishment do not always automatically follow on from one another. A debt leading to material impoverishment can still be accompanied by feelings of social mobility and integration. One example is that observed by Magdalena Villarreal with Mexican migrants in the United States who are highly indebted, but still maintain the hope of accomplishing the American dream of ownership. David Picherit also observes as much with migrant workers from low castes in Andhra Pradesh, as do Isabelle Guérin *et al.* with ex-untouchables in Tamil Nadu. In both cases, contractual debt, regardless of the cost, has the great advantage of reducing dependence on local patrons, even if this mitigation is probably incomplete and temporary.

While the social consequences of over-indebtedness, such as shame, humiliation and dependency are strongly highlighted by the various case studies of this volume, other impacts are also noted such as sexual abuse,[1] decapitalization and migration. In Mexico and southern India, migration is a means to deal with debts that neither existing incomes nor social networks can pay off (Chapters 7 and 8). We can reasonably assume that over-indebtedness sustains migration channels, which is probably true well beyond the two contexts studied here. We thus see that the political economy of debt extends further than that of local economies.

The second lesson has to do with financial inclusion policies and the role played by microfinance in the provision of financial services that "do not harm" their clients. Most present-day societies are, to different degrees, financialized. Therefore there is no doubt that the poor need financial services, whether to protect themselves against the hazards of everyday life, to invest or seize economic opportunities or to plan for the future. "Financial inclusion", however, is tricky. But, even though a significant number of microfinance promoters conceive their mission as poverty alleviation, good intentions do not necessarily ensure good outcomes.

An important lesson that comes out from this volume, however, is that microfinance alone is rarely the sole cause of household over-indebtedness. There are situations of impoverishment through debt in contexts where microcredit is absent. When microcredit contributes to households' over-indebtedness, most often it combines with other factors related to individual trajectories, structural inequalities and/or structural shocks. In Madagascar, for example, microfinance has been seen to boost the odds of expanding debt sources. For households, to have further juggling options is not necessarily a cause or a symptom of over-indebtedness, as it could facilitate diversification and accumulation. But it could be risky, particularly for poor households who are less able to cope with external shocks (Chapter 10). Microfinance could further households' over-indebtedness both due to mission drift and ignorance of local realities, with aggressive marketing (Chapter 12), excessive focus on certain areas and at times the same customers, opportunities to borrow from several MFIs at the same time (Chapters 11, 12 and 13), highly rigid repayment schedules which are poorly suited to household cash flows (Chapter 11) and local frameworks of calculation (Chapter 3). There has also been an erosion of local social networks due to various problems in so-called solidarity groups, and with the use of "guarantors" (Chapter 11). Several questions remain, however. At one level one can inquire into the effects on the "beneficiaries": a financial service is acceptable if at least it does not deteriorate the socioeconomic position of those who use it (income, assets, but also social networks, self-esteem, etc.). Another level has to do with broader structural effects. Should we promote market economies and market societies or should we instead try to back a "human economy", where the economy would be at the service of human beings, on an individual and a group level? The idea of human economy calls for the invention of new forms of solidarity and political engagement and renewed forms of exchange and relationships, the recognition that there is no unique path to development but a great variety of particular situations in all their institutional complexity, a holistic conception of everyone's needs and interests and the fact that what people want to maximize or optimize is never granted (Hart *et al.* 2011). It calls for different frameworks of calculation.

It is clear that the present-day microfinance landscape is mostly dominated by the logic of capital and market (Bédécarrats 2013; Fernando 2006; Bateman 2010; Servet 2006). Despite repeated pleas for innovation and adaptation – CGAP,[2] one of the leading institutions in the microfinance industry, has been talking innovation for years – the supply is still very standardized. A Malian peasant lady has a great chance to have access to the same services as her sister in a slum in Calcutta, though their needs are likely to be very different. Certainly, few institutions are able to innovate – an example is provided in this volume from Madagascar (Chapter 10) but unfortunately this is only a minority.

Rather than first approaching people with pre-formatted solutions, foreign agencies and microfinance promoters really wishing to help these people should first see how the latter already save, borrow and lend and then, if locally desired, find ways to help them to improve pre-existing practices (Armendariz and Labie 2011). Improved identification of demand is the first condition; it requires knowledge of local socioeconomic realities. The examples given in this volume provide evidence of the multiple motives and rationales underlying financial practices, and it appears that many microfinance promoters have not understood the diversity and complexity of their target clientele's motivations. Improved identification of demand also requires a more realistic vision of informal lending. Private moneylenders are too often disparaged as pariahs and caricatured as vermin. Examples given in this volume provide evidence of the very large diversity of informal lending practices – only some of them involve the "exploit-ative usurers" found in the literature or the media. And many of them, as exploit-ative as they might be, ensure a wide diversity of services, whether access to employment, land, governmental schemes, NGOs, religious spaces, etc. Without more fundamental structural changes, local intermediaries like these might be the least harmful resources the poor have access to. Microfinance alone won't change this.

An examination of pre-existing practices also entails looking at household indebtedness: are the people we target already highly indebted (as was the case for instance in many parts of southern India) and if so, does it really make sense to offer credit – given that credit is also debt? Far beyond households' financial positions, it also means looking at local economies and their absorption capacity. When debt starts to substitute income, as often seems to be the case, a massive injection of liquidity obviously raises issues. Several case studies in this book have shown how crucial it is to assess the absorptive capacity of local eco-nomies. How much external cash flow can a local economy take? This goes beyond the debate on "productive" (income generating) versus "un-productive" uses (consumption). It is related to the nature of local markets: Do we have emerging or saturated markets? Can we observe spillover effects (the activities created by microfinance leading to new ones and boosting local economies through trickle- down effects) or do we rather find saturation effects (the new businesses saturate local markets and therefore bring down the profitability of existing businesses) or displacement effects (one business is created but a nearby one closes)? If consumption financed by microcredit concerns goods that are produced locally with potential trickle-down and spillover effects (construction is a typical example), then "consumption", through rebound effects, may boost local economies and enrich local communities.

A CGAP note based on analysis of the current microcredit delinquency crisis has called for greater consumer protection and "good governance" (Chen *et al.*, 2010). We believe, however, that the problem is much deeper: the mission drifts discussed in this volume[3] illustrate the rising hegemony of a commercial and profit-oriented approach, which has reversed the initial priorities of micro-finance. We have shifted from a social project mobilizing financial instruments to financial institutions with (and, in some cases, claiming to have) a social mission. Not all institutions share this vision (Bédécarrats and Lapenu 2013), but commercial microfinance institutions have the most customers and handle the largest volumes. This profit-oriented approach has led to a frantic search for clients, the concentration of funds into small areas to minimize costs and considerable pressure on loan officers, who have profitability targets forced on them that, in turn, affect customers. This profit-oriented approach is also appar-ent in the intense competition between microfinance institutions. Rather than sharing markets and spaces and looking for unoccupied segments, they tend to target and accumulate in places that are already taken. They benefit from the learning effects of their predecessors, always with a view to reducing costs. This approach is also very clear among both public and private donors and investors, who focus their investments on a limited number of regions and microfinance institutions, where they have greater opportunities to advertise the benefits of their actions (Servet 2012).

Reality is, of course, complex and goes far beyond a Manichean opposition between "social" and "commercial" approaches. In some cases, non-profit statuses do not prevent massive private investments or bankruptcy. So-called "social" microfinance initiatives are unlikely to succeed in their mission where they are promoted or supported by populist and clientelist public policies or by local groups seizing microfinance to further expand their power. The evidence indicates that balancing social objectives and sustainability is a permanent challenge (D'Espallier *et al.* 2013; Lapenu 2002).

What seems clear, however, is that for-profit investments in MFIs often constrain them to position themselves in the most profitable segments of the market, to secure substantial profits and therefore to put strong pressure on loan officers at the expense of the analysis of clients' creditworthiness. Therefore the role of the "commercial" logic in over-indebtedness and at some point in repayment defaults should be subject to critical analysis. Finally, one might query the future of microfinance. The latest estimated figures of the Microcredit Summit Campaign show that the industry has recorded its first decline in client numbers (Reed 2013). In 2011, fewer of the world's poorest families gained access to microcredit and other financial services than had been seen in 2010 (195 million poor clients were served in December 2011, as opposed to 205 million a year earlier, of which 125 million were considered as the "poorest". This is in contrast to 138 million in 2010. This decline was due to the Indian crisis, when many MFIs shut down lending operations in Andhra Pradesh where the majority of their clients were based. Microfinance growth in Latin America has also been recorded to be in decline while in Africa (which has a very small share of microfinance), growth is increasing.

One may assume that in the coming years a number of investors and donors will withdraw, disappointed by meager results compared with the miracles announced a couple of years ago. But it is equally likely that the sector will take on new forms and attract new partners, as observed already in some countries. This includes, for instance, mobile banking, micro-savings, micro-insurance and microcredit for consumption.

To avoid excessive injections of cash compared to the absorption capacity of local economies, one option can be to incorporate savings with credit (Shipton 2010: 240). This has, for many years, been a common practice among locally organized savings and credit associations not linked to commercial MFIs. When resources lent are drawn upon local savings, borrowers do not get flooded with loans too large to repay. It is also observed that microcredit repayment crises have emerged in countries in which the industry was driven mostly by microcredit and where savings were very low (Chen *et al.* 2010). While the focus has long been on credit supply, current policies for financial inclusion are seeking to mobilize the savings of poor households. There is renewed interest in this long-standing topic today, in part due to disenchantment with microcredit and increasing focus on household vulnerability, saving services being supposed to allow for self-protection against the hazards of life, the anticipation of life cycle events, or investment. At the macro level, savings are supposed to contribute to the financing of the economy, but here too, we should pay attention to many possible ambiguous side effects of saving services. On the individual and household level, monetary savings can help stabilize household budgets, facilitate planning for life cycle events, or investments. But they could also undermine local practices of wealth storage (for instance precious metals and livestock). These practices are often seen as archaic and "traditional" but nevertheless have a social, cultural, symbolic and economic function that can be much greater than cash savings (Lont and Hospes 2004; Guérin *et al.* 2011). On the macro or meso level, saving is a growth factor only if used locally. When re-injected elsewhere – in favour of more attractive territories – its main impact is to weaken, rather than boost, local economies.

Micro-insurance for the poor to finance health, deaths, agriculture, etc., has also become a rallying cry over the past few years. Again it is an appealing tool on paper, and is supposed to improve households' capacity to cope with shocks and reduce their vulnerability. But its implementation conditions and its real economic, social, cultural and/or political effects are still very poorly understood. The principle of insurance – to cover a risk in advance that by definition will not occur with certainty – is poorly suited to local representation systems that tend to be based on reciprocity. Providing insurance services at an affordable cost for customers requires substantial subsidies, which public authorities and donors may not be willing to cover. For health insurance, the effectiveness of micro-insurance depends on quality of care, which is still very poor in many countries. Moreover, micro-insurance schemes are rarely implemented in partnership with employers, thus precluding cost sharing with capital and possibly legitimizing the informality of employment.[4]

Credit for consumption deserves specific attention as it is directly linked to our main tropic: households' over-indebtedness. There is today a wide consensus that a very large proportion of microcredit loans are in fact used for consumption, in the sense that their use does not generate direct income. Having long been considered taboo through the premise that the poor need only so-called "productive" credit so as to create income-generating activities, consumer microcredit for the poor as an idea is now not only accepted but celebrated. The book *Portfolios of the Poor* (Collins *et al.* 2009), for instance, which is a reference book for the microfinance industry and which indeed provides an excellent description of the complexity and subtlety of the poor financial practices, advocates that microfinance for consumption should be developed, arguing that this is an extraordinary opportunity to "open up the biggest single market one is likely to find among the poor" (Collins *et al.* 2009: 180).

Encouraging the poor to consume on credit obviously raises ethical and moral questions. Is it reasonable to encourage individuals or households who are already struggling for their daily survival to increase their consumption of commodities? At the same time, why should the poor not be allowed to consume?

Well beyond the microcredit industry, the consumption of the poor has become the new niche of capitalism.

C. K. Prahalad's late 1990s expression "the fortune at the bottom of the pyramid" has since become famous (Prahalad 2004). The idea is to convince multinationals, but also increasingly governments and NGOs, to focus on this new market niche. The first claim is that it is profitable. In 2004, Prahalad wrote that the poor have little money but that there are at least four billion of them and a daily market of $13 billion, which is significantly greater than the U.S. market alone. According to his estimates for different regions of the world, the poor have between 28 and 36 per cent of global purchasing power. His second claim is that the poor would be the first to benefit, thanks to trickle-down effects. The Bottom of the Pyramid Approach was launched online in early 1990, published by the *Harvard Business Review* in 1998, and then spread across the world (known worldwide as "BOP"), promising to revolutionize consumer markets and to invent new business models and marketing techniques for a massive yet poor clientele. The impressive success of mobile phones in the farthest corners of the planet shows its effectiveness. The BOP approach has inspired many multinationals that claim to promote "social business", but also governments, NGOs and multilateral and bilateral agencies who all seek to promote "inclusive markets."

The promoters of the BOP strategy have been criticized for their environmental recklessness and disregard of local economies, and they have recently developed a second version – BOP 2.0 (Simanis and Hart 2008). Blurring the boundaries between the already tenuous world of capital and development, BOP 2.0 proposes a model of consumption in "favour of the poor", as in the previous version, but now also "sustainable". The idea is to create real local economies and not to export models, to see the poor not just as consumers but "trading partners" and finally to focus on goods and services that are both suited to local contexts, and are socially useful and environmentally friendly. The use of participatory methods so favoured by the development industry has experienced a fresh boost with the goal of identifying local "needs", designing suitable goods and services, and then disseminating them through membership promotion.

Whitening cosmetic creams for women's empowerment, which were one of the emblematic examples of BOP 1.0, and which provoked the fury of Indian feminist movements, are no longer on the agenda. Innovation still focuses on specific distribution channels – for example with the creation of supermarkets adapted to the poor of southern countries – but also on modes of production and the invention of new products such as cosmetic creams, natural essences, generic anti-viral drugs for sleeping sickness, anti-malaria nets, purified water, chilled clay pots, improved stoves, sunlamps and nutritious food.

Targeting the poor implies very specific sales techniques, including selling in very small quantities, using "independent agents" and "multi-level" selling, such as the Tupperware model, which has been going strong over 60 years with success nobody would deny. Targeting the poor also means giving them the means to buy, i.e. to sell on credit. The development of the BOP consumer is therefore inseparable from the development of consumer credit. The poor of the South are a new niche market for many financial players, and the future of microfinance should be addressed within this wider context. New players include banks and financial institutions, whose offer has reached saturation point in middle-class markets: they are widening their clientele by building partnerships with the microfinance institutions they refinance. This is also the case for consumer credit companies, with the emergence of entities dedicated to the poor offering special services with specific technical marketing and sales methods, often inspired from informal techniques (home sales, coordination with migrant remittances, bonuses through highly valued items such as gold, etc.). Their numbers have exploded in recent years, particularly in Central and Latin America, but also in many parts of Asia and in some African countries. This is also the case for mass distribution, for which sales on credit are actively contributing to profit margins. The search for new market niches has led to the rise of unprecedented partnerships, combining retail outlets, NGOs and microfinance organizations. The principle of social business – the noble idea that a for-profit organization could pursue social purposes – has given renewed legitimacy to such partnerships. New information technologies – in particular smart cards and mobile phones – have facilitated the introduction of sophisticated financial services and costs to the most remote corners of the planet. "Green microfinance" is also on the agenda (Allet 2012). A growing number of financial institutions have dedicated a portion of their portfolio to environmentally friendly activities. Some are encouraging their customers to limit the environmental damage of their activities. Others are specializing in financing goods and services with low energy consumption and low emission of greenhouse gases which are supposedly compatible with the struggle against poverty, such as those mentioned above (renewable energy, improved stoves, solar lamps, refrigerators, etc.).

By promoting massive demand for durable consumer goods, consumer credit has contributed to the strong economic growth of industrialized countries of the twentieth century. To a certain extent, it has also played a role in social integration. But then it was coupled with active redistribution and social protection measures, and its cost was partially moderated by inflation. In the absence of such measures, consumer credit may instead cause or accelerate processes of impoverishment and rising inequalities, while maintaining the illusion of growth (or of non-recession). Very interestingly, the lessons of the global crisis of 2008, based largely on a regime of cheap credit, have in no way been learned. The system is probably less fragile because informal finance and migration (both much more prolific in the South) can partially absorb or hide the cost of debt.

Thanks to consumer credit, microcredit is experiencing a second wind and contributing to the constant renewal of capitalism. This raises the wrath of many anti-consumerist and anti-neoliberal lobbies. As an artifact of the unlimited commodification of public goods and the constant extension of the boundaries of individual responsibility, this capitalism with a "human face", in the words of Muhammad Yunus, would be no less than a forced march into the age of consumerism in the name of so-called needs created from scratch, or a new form of moralizing for the poor, now in charge not only of their own destiny but also of the preservation of our planet. These initiatives also attract a lot of support, probably because they offer reasons for hope, but also because consumption continues, probably more than ever, to be ambivalent. It is both liberating (who could complain about the fact that children can now do their homework with electric lighting instead of by candlelight) and alienating – what sorts of sacrifice will their parents have to endure to equip their home with solar lights (Guérin and Selim 2012).

While capital and commercial microfinance continues to expand, some initiatives can be found that seek to promote what can be qualified as "solidarity finance", which participates in the broader movement of the "human economy". Rather than reproducing the state-market nexus, these initiatives seek to liberate the poor and the marginalized from the oppression and unfairness of the market, the state, and the "community" by building relationships of solidarity based on equality, mutuality, cooperation and reciprocity.

Solidarity finance, rather than being imposed by top-down policies, often emerges from forms of collective self-organization initiated by different populations and/or organized groups in their respective localities or communities in order to enhance their capacity to manage their own economic resources. Within these new frameworks, economic practices are subordinated to social and human relations, reversing the classic logic of the market. Rather than using external, often foreign funds, they promote the mobilization of local investment. Rather than inserting local communities into global value chains, their main commitment is to create local networks by linking up producers, service providers and local consumers (de França Filho *et al.* 2013). Rather than encouraging the evasion of local resources, their main goal is to act as a stimulus for local development by relying on the multiplier effects of local spending (Servet 2006). Some of these initiatives are associated with alternative instruments to stimulate domestic consumption (i.e. local credit cards and local complementary currencies) that are recognized by local producers, traders and consumers and thus have the potential to boost the local economy (de França Filho *et al.* 2013). Rather than denying any form of politicization and claiming to be restricted to technical operations, some of these initiatives are rooted in political struggles, as for instance women's financial cooperatives engaged in unionism (Kabeer 2010). They believe that "development and struggle" are not contradictory, but should nurture each other. They also promote a renewed vision of political engagement, based on the lived experiences of local populations and not theories and doctrines imposed from above. Rather than strengthening pre-existing links of dependency between the "North" and the "South" through loans made in strong currencies that are expected to produce high returns, some of these initiatives also seek to create and sustain new forms of international solidarity, for instance by creating guarantee funds that make accountable use of local resources (Servet 2011: 140).

These solidarity finance initiatives often operate in the shadows of capitalist and commercial microfinance. They are much more realistic about their potential effects. They know that social and economic changes can occur only in the medium or long term. They therefore have many more difficulties in attracting the media and donors who are often obsessed by quick and clear "impacts". Their practical implementation is probably easier said than done. It is also likely that market forces or pressures from the State or donors through the promotion of "best practices" may oblige their promoters to make many compromises. Nevertheless, solidarity finance has the great merit of seeking to promote new forms of exchange, carried out within different frameworks of calculation, eliciting new social relations upon which to base economic and financial practices.

As stated at the beginning of this conclusion, debt and credit have always been a historical motor of both oppression and emancipation. Current forms of microfinance are a further illustration of this ambivalence. They can be a source of financial exploitation or solidarity. This is not simply a matter of goodwill. To make finance social and useful for the population it reaches demands a constant questioning of the expected and unexpected meaning of actions, and their effects on local societies. This volume is an effort in this direction.

Notes

1 This issue is addressed quickly by Guérin *et al.* in their chapter while it would deserve a full analysis. See for example the PhD thesis in progress by Nicolas Lainez (EHESS, France).
2 Consultative Group to Assist the Poor.
3 And also reported elsewhere and previously. See for instance Bateman (2010); Dichter and Harper (2007; Fernando (2006); Servet (2006).
4 For a critical analysis of micro-insurance in India, see for instance (Kannan and Breman 2013).

References

Allet, M. (2012) "Assessing the environmental performance of microfinance", *Cost Management* 26(2): 6–17.

Bateman, M. (2010) *Why Doesn't Microfinance Work? The Destructive Rise of Local Neoliberalism,* London: Zed Books.

Baumann, E., Bazin, L., Ould-Ahmed, P., Phelinas, P., Selim, M. and Sobel, R. (eds) (2008) *L'argent des anthropologues, la monnaie des économistes,* Paris: l'Harmattan.

Bédécarrats, F. (2013) *La microfinance entre utilité sociale et performances financières,* Paris: l'Harmattan (Collection Critique Internationale).

Bédécarrats, F. and Lapenu, C. (2013) "Assessing microfinance: striking a balance between social utility and financial performance", in Gueyie, J.-P., Manos, R. and Yaron, J. (eds), *Microfinance in Developing and Developed Countries: Issues, Policies and Performance Evaluation,* New York: Palgrave Macmillan, pp. 62–82.

Bourdieu, P. (1977) *Algérie 60: Structures économiques et structures temporelles,* Paris: Les éditions de Minuit.

Collins, D., Morduch, J., Rutherford, S. and Ruthven, O. (2009) *Portfolios of the Poor: How the World's Poor Live on $2 a Day,* Princeton: Princeton University Press.

Chen, G., Rasmussen, S. and Reille, X. (2010), "Growth and vulnerabilities in microfinance", *Focus Note* 61, *CGAP*.

D'Espallier, B., Marek, Hudon and Szafarz, A. (2013) "Unsubsidized microfinance institutions", Working Papers CEB 13–012, ULB – Universite Libre de Bruxelles.

Dichter, Th. and Harper, M. (2007) *What's Wrong with Microfinance?* London: Practical Action.

Fernando, J. (2006) *Microfinance: Perils and Prospects*, London: Routledge.

de França, Filho G. C, Scalfoni, Rigo, A. and Torres Silva, Júnior J. (2013) "Microcredit policies in Brazil: an analysis of community development banks", in Hillenkamp, I., Lapeyre, F. and Lemaitre, A. (eds) *Securing Livelihoods: Informal economy practices and institutions*, Oxford: Oxford University Press, forthcoming.

Graeber, D. (2011) *Debt: The First 5,000 Years*, New York: Melville House Publishing.

Gudeman, S. (2001) *The Anthropology of Economy: Community, Market, and Culture*, Oxford: Blackwell.

Guérin, I. and Selim, M. (eds) (2012) *À quoi et comment dépenser son argent. Hommes et Femmes face aux mutations globales de la consommation en Afrique, Asie, Amérique latine et Europe*, Paris: L'Harmattan.

Guérin, I., Morvant, S. and Servet, J.-M. (2011) "Understanding the diversity and complexity of demand for microfinance services: lessons from informal finance", in Armendariz, B. and Labie, M. (eds) *Handbook of Microfinance*, London/Singapore: World Scientific Publishing, pp. 101–122.

Guyer, J. (1995) (ed.) *Money Matters: Instability, Values and Social Payments in the Modern History of West African Communities*, London/Portsmouth (NH): Currey/Heinemann.

Hart, K., Laville, J.-L. and Cattani, D. (eds) (2011) *The Human Economy*, Cambridge: Polity Press.

Hann, C. and Hart, K. (2011) *Economic Anthropology*, Cambridge: Polity Press.

Hillenkamp, I., Lapeyre, F. and Lemaitrem, A. (eds) (2013) *Securing Livelihoods. Informal Economy Practices and Institutions*, Oxford: Oxford University Press.

Kabeer, N. (2010) *Gender and Social Protection Strategies in the Informal Economy*, London: Routledge.

Kannan, K. P. and Breman, J. (2013) *The Long Road to Social Security: Assessing the Implementation of Social Security Initiatives for the Working Poor in India*, New Dehli: Oxford University Press.

Lapenu, C. (2002) "La gouvernance en microfinance: grille d'analyse et perspectives de recherche", *Revue Tiers Monde* 172: 847–866.

Lont, H. and Hospes, O. (eds) (2004) *Livelihood and Microfinance: Anthropological and Sociological Perspectives on Savings and Debt*, Delft: Eburon Academic Publishers.

Malamoud, C. (ed.) (1988) *La dette*, Éditions de l'École des hautes études en sciences sociales (coll. *Purushartha*, vol. 4): Paris.

Maurer, B. (2006) "The anthropology of money," *Annual Review of Anthropology* 35:15–36.

Morvant-Roux, S., Guérin, I., Roesch, M. and Moisseron, J.-Y. (forthcoming) "Adding value to randomization with qualitative analysis: the case of microcredit in rural Morocco", *World Development*.

Peebles, G. (2010) "The anthropology of credit and debt", *Annual Review of Anthropology* 39: 225–240.

Prahakad, C. K. (2004) *The Fortune at the Bottom of the Pyramid: Eradicating Poverty Through Profits*, Wharton School Publishing.

Rankin, K. N. (2002) "Social capital, microfinance and the politics of development", *Feminist Economics* 8(1):1–24.

Reed, L. R. (2013) *Vulnerability: The State of the Microcredit Summit Campaign Report, 2013*, Washington: Microcredit Summit Campaign.

Servet, J.-M. (2006) *Banquiers aux pieds nus*, Paris: Odile Jacob.

Servet, J.-M. (2011) "Microcredit", in Hart, K., Laville, J.-L. and Cattani, D. (eds) *The Human Economy*, Cambridge: Polity Press, pp. 130–141.

Simanis, E. and Hart, S. (2008) *The Base of the Pyramid Protocol: Toward Next Generation BoP Strategy*, Center for Sustainable Enterprise.

Shipton, P. (2007) *The Nature of Entrustment: Intimacy, Exchange and the Sacred in Africa*, New-Haven, CT: Yale University Press.

Shipton, P. (2010) *Credit between Cultures: Farmers, Financiers and Misunderstandings in Africa*, New-Haven and London: Yale University Press.

Taylor, M. (2012) "The microfinance crisis in Andhra Pradesh, India: a window on rural distress", *Food First*, October 2012.

Thérêt, B. (2009) "Monnaie et dettes de vie", *L'homme* 90.

Villarreal, M. (2004) "Striving to make capital do 'economic things' for the impoverished: on the issue of capitalization in rural microenterprises", in Kontinen, T. (ed.) *Development Intervention: Actor and Activity Perspectives*, Center for Activity Theory and Developmental Work Research (CATDWR), Institute for Development Studies (IDS) and University of Helsinki: Helsinki, pp. 67–81.

Index

Page numbers in *italics* denote tables, those in **bold** denote figures.